THE GREEN BERETS IN THE LAND OF A MILLION ELEPHANTS

U.S. Army Special Warfare and the Secret War in Laos 1959–74

JOSEPH D. CELESKI

CASEMATE

Philadelphia & Oxford

AN AUSA BOOK

Published in the United States of America and Great Britain in 2019 by
CASEMATE PUBLISHERS
1950 Lawrence Road, Havertown, PA 19083, USA
and
The Old Music Hall, 106–108 Cowley Road, Oxford OX4 1JE, UK

Hardback Edition: ISBN 978-1-61200-665-9
Digital Edition: ISBN 978-1-61200-666-6 (epub)

A CIP record for this book is available from the British Library

Printed and bound in the United States of America

Typeset in India by Versatile PreMedia Services. www.versatilepremedia.com

For a complete list of Casemate titles, please contact:

CASEMATE PUBLISHERS (US)
Telephone (610) 853-9131
Fax (610) 853-9146
Email: casemate@casematepublishers.com
www.casematepublishers.com

CASEMATE PUBLISHERS (UK)
Telephone (01865) 241249
Email: casemate-uk@casematepublishers.co.uk
www.casematepublishers.co.uk

This book is dedicated to all the United States Army Special Operations veterans of the conflict in Laos who fought, served and sometimes lost their lives to prevent the communist takeover of the Royal Kingdom of Laos. It is also dedicated to those who fought alongside them in this struggle: the special operators of the Central Intelligence Agency, pilots of Air America, U.S. embassy personnel who served in Vientiane, the Laotian armed forces (both army and air force), the Thai volunteers, and the Hmong, Kha, and Lao Theung tribesmen and their families. Our thoughts go out to the families who have lost loved ones among the Lao veterans over the years and we thank them for their service.

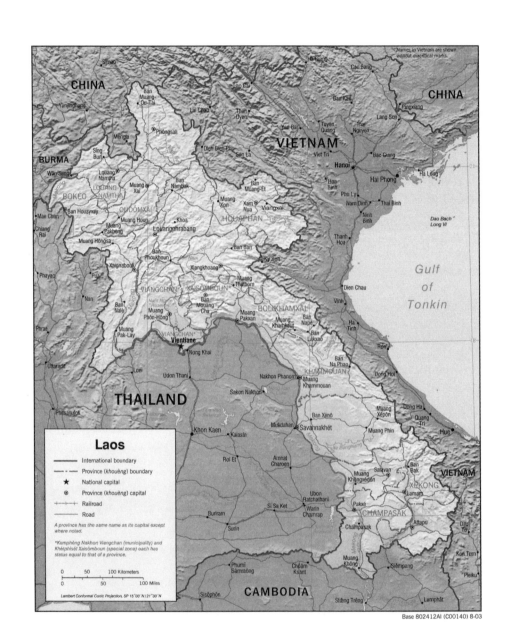

Names in Vietnam are shown
without diacritical marks.

CHINA

CHINA

Simao

Ban
Muang-
Ou-Tai

Ha Giang

Cao Bang

Yunjinghong

Lai Chau

Lao Cai

Ban Kan

Pingxiang

Mengla

Phôngsali

Dien Bien Phu

Thanh
Uyen

Yen Bai

Tuyen
Quang

Thai
Nguyen

Lang Son

VIETNAM

BURMA

Sing
Buri

Louang
Namtha

Muang
Xai

Sen La

Viet Tri

Hanoi

Bac Giang

Ha Long

Wan Seng

LOUANG
NAMTHA

Ban
Nambak

Ban
Muang-Et

Hoa
Binh

Hai Phong

Mae Chan

BOKEO

OUDOMXAI

Muang
Xon

Xam
Nua

Viangxai

Phu Ly

Nam Dinh

Thai Binh

Ban Housyxay

Muang Houn

Khoa

HOUA PHAN

Ninh
Binh

Dao Bach
Long VI

Chiang
Rai

Muang
Pakbeng

Louangphrabang

Thanh
Hoa

Gulf

Muang Hôngsa

Ban
Phoukhoun

Ban Ban

of

Phayao

Pua

Xaignabouli

VIANGCHAN

Xiangkhoang

Muang
Thathom

XAISOMBOUN

BOLIKHAMXAI

Ky Son

Dien Chau

Tonkin

Nan

Ban
Nalè

Nam Ngum
Reservoir

Muang
Phôn-Hông

Ban
Mouang
Cha

Muang
Pakxan

Muang
Khamkeut

Ban
Nape

Vinh

Phrae

Muang
Pak-Lay

VIANGCHAN*

Vientiane

Ban
Lakxao

Ha
Tinh

Ron

Uttaradit

Nong Khai

Ban
Na Phao

Loei

Udon Thani

Nakhon Phanom

KHAMMOUAN

Dong Hoi

Philsanulok

THAILAND

Sakon Nakhon

Muang
Khammouan

Khon Kaen

Kalasin

Ban Xénô

Muang
Xépôn

Dong Ha

Quang
Tri

Mukdahan

Savannakhét

Muang Phin

Hue

Roi Et

Amnat
Charoen

VIETNAM

Buriram

Si Sa Ket

Ubon
Ratchathani

Warin
Chamrap

Muang
Khôngxédôn

Salavan

Ban
Bak

Lamam

XÉKONG

Surin

Pakxé

Attapu

CHAMPASAK

Dao
Te

Champasak

Muang
Không

Siêmpang

Kon Tum

Phumi
Sâmraông

Chôâm
Ksant

Pleiku

Sisôphôn

CAMBODIA

Stœng Trêng

Lumphat

Laos

——— International boundary

– · – · – Province (khouèng) boundary

★ National capital

⊙ Province (khouèng) capital

+–+–+– Railroad

——— Road

*A province has the same name as its capital except
where noted.*

*Kamphéng Nakhon Viangchan (municipality) and
Khéiphisét Xaisômboun (special zone) each has
status equal to that of a province.*

0   50   100 Kilometers

0   50   100 Miles

Lambert Conformal Conic Projection, SP 15°00′N/21°30′N

Contents

Foreword

In retirement, I was intrigued to go back and restudy the glimpses of occasional mention of Army Special Forces and their role in the war inside Laos. Most of what was known by us were the activities of Operation *White Star*. Anything else about the role of Special Forces and their participation Laos was unknown (or rare). This book is about the pursuit of that knowledge.

Laos was called "The Land of a Million Elephants and the White Parasol." From 1954 to 1974, the U.S. government conducted operations in Laos to prevent the spread of communism and help defend the Royal Lao Government (RLG) against takeover by leftist coups and the alternative choice for the population: a communist government of the Pathet Lao (the Neo Lao Hak Sat—Lao Patriotic Front).

Additional American objectives were deterring incursions into Laos by the North Vietnamese Army (NVA) and prevent their use of the Ho Chi Minh Trail to infiltrate into South Vietnam. American policy objectives focused on keeping Laos a pro-Western democracy, and if not, at least neutral. The war was dictated by the competing interests of the three Lao factions: The Royalists (or Rightists), the Neutralists, and the Leftists (the Pathet Lao). The Leftists were ideologically aligned with the tenets of communism and were supported and supplied by North Vietnam, China, and the Soviet Union (and other communist-bloc countries).

President Eisenhower formed his decision to support Laos in light of the prevailing theory of the "Falling Dominos," in that if one Southeast Asian country fell to communism, so would the others. American operations were conducted by the Department of State, the Central Intelligence Agency, and selected organizations from the Department of Defense. These operations differed from the war next door in South Vietnam in that the authority to conduct the war and the exercise of command and control over various U.S. organizations was vested in the ambassadors assigned to the U.S. Embassy in Vientiane, Laos. Ambassadors Brown, Unger, Sullivan, Godley, and those who followed, each had full control over the military forces operating in Laos. One feature overwhelmingly shaped the American approach: the need to operate diplomatically and militarily within the Agreements and Protocols of Geneva, after the French departed from Indochina. The Agreement banned any intervention of foreign forces into Laos. American actions and policy (mostly conducted in a secret manner) would have to creatively maneuver around this restriction to provide monetary aid and military assistance to ensure Laos' security.

American secret operations were an orchestrated mixture of USAID, the Military Assistance program (MAP), "black" and covered operations, and a covert/clandestine program using tribal forces to confront the Pathet Lao. Based on their inherent capabilities, U.S. Army Special Forces (SF) became the "limited" and discrete choice for deployable land power in this struggle. A regionally aligned, global response force, with a low signature footprint, and with the capability to conduct guerrilla warfare or act as military trainers in a counterinsurgency environment, was just the fungible type of military unit American decision-makers found highly useful to confront communist, revolutionary movement expansion. Additionally, an attractive option for policy makers was deniability. The conditions of the war in Laos were almost tailor-made for the employment and use of the Army's Green Berets in what would become one of the first of the Special Operations community's "Long Wars." It would also begin the transformation of the force from utilization in small, limited tactical deployments to support the regional Commander-in-Chiefs, to one of large-scale operations of the force to support strategic, foreign policy objectives of the U.S. The 77th Special Forces Group (Airborne), later to become the 7th Special Forces Group, the 1st Special Forces Group (Airborne), and the 46th Special Forces Company (Independent) all operated or supported operations within Laos.

U.S. Army Special Forces operated under the doctrine of *Special Warfare*. Embodied within this doctrine were the three, interrelated disciplines for response to irregular warfare: counterinsurgency (COIN), Psychological Warfare, and Unconventional Warfare (UW—guerrilla warfare, subversion, and escape and evasion activities). Two Special Forces missions are key in a COIN environment: Foreign Internal Defense (FID—providing combat trainers and advisors) and UW (the training and employment of government or externally sponsored guerrillas).

There were four major uses of Army Special Operations Forces (ARSOF) during the war:

1. Operation *Hotfoot*, August 1959 to April 1961. This included the use of U.S. Army Green Berets and SOF communications and PSYOP personnel to train the Laotian Army via FTTs and MTTs (Field and Military Training Teams), all the while dressed in civilian clothes and with a cover story. *Hotfoot* teams became involved in some of their first combat operations during and after the Battle of Vientiane in December of 1960.

2. Operation *White Star*, April 1961 to October 1962. President Kennedy authorized the overt use of Green Beret teams from the 7th SF Group and the 1st SF Group to perform combat advisory duties with Laotian regular and irregular, guerrilla forces. The rate of combat involvement increased for Army SF. By the summer of 1962, over 400 Green Berets were operating in Laos. All American

forces in Laos (less the Embassy military staffs) were removed by October 1962 under the provisions of the new peace agreement in Geneva.

3. The 46th Special Forces Company (Independent) in Thailand began to advise and serve the war effort in Laos around 1966 (inside Laos, these operations consisted of only a few of their teams on a limited time basis) and trained Hmong guerrillas, Laotian infantry, and Thais using up to six covert camps throughout Thailand.

4. Project 404 SF Advisors – the Army Assistant Attachés (ARMAs). The SF ARMAs were assigned under Project 404 and operated throughout Laos between 1964 and 1974 to serve as field advisors to guerrillas and Royal Laotian Army forces (alongside other Army advisors), and with monitoring the implementation of the Military Assistance Program's delivery of combat equipment, arms and munitions to the Laotians. They also conducted information gathering activities in all five Military Regions of Laos.

Although not intended to cover the in-depth operations of SF units from South Vietnam, such as the MACV-SOG operations on the Ho Chi Minh Trail, the work necessarily included portions of those efforts as it related to Secret War in Laos. There were also other essential enablers as part of the story: the role of *Air America* to provide air support to the men on the ground and the supporting role of various aspects of Army Psychological Operations (PSYOP) teams.

The Laos veterans are some of the most interesting and fascinating operators within the SOF community. Many served first in the Korean War, then Laos, and went on to serve with distinction in the Vietnam War and other Cold War contingencies. They grew up in the era of the ideological struggle of the West versus communism; they believed in their mission and contribution to "Free the Oppressed" from totalitarian dictators and Marxist and Maoist inspired insurgencies. To a man, most desired a book which would put their individual and team efforts during the war into a larger perspective illustrating why Green Berets were in Laos and how their individual and unit contributions contributed to the wider campaign. Many only knew of their location and their job, but desired to understand the overall context. The running theme throughout most of their testimony was the "Ambassador ran the war; there was no doubt about that." It is a story of the SF Veterans "just doing my job" through innovation, adaptation, integration with indigenous cultures, and getting the job done under less than desirable conditions.

This book began its journey with the study of the essential keystone book which first peeled back the curtain of secrecy about the war in Laos and some of SF's role: Kenneth Conboy's (with James Morrison) *Shadow War: The CIA's Secret War in Laos*.[1] Other auto-biographical books written by a few of the veterans, although limited, were used to gain some context of operations on the ground. Many of the authors who wrote the earlier works on the Secret War in Laos lamented the fact that much of the material needed to complete their work was "shrouded in secrecy." Today, in most cases, much of the material has been declassified after thirty to fifty years of being compartmented (essentially beginning declassification around the 1990), and where not, was solved by having an appropriate security clearance. This was instrumental in perusing background material still classified in order to derive context to create an open-source, unclassified work.

The book is a product of exhaustive research, interviews, and travel over a four-year period. Every relevant government archive in the Washington DC area was used in its preparation, although material pertaining to Army Special Forces and their role in Laos was limited, surprisingly scarce, or not found at all. Following those efforts, use was made of other research assets from the military services, university libraries, military museums, and professional veteran associations. Of tremendous help were the command historian and his staff from U.S. Special Operations Command (USASOC) and the curator and staff of the U.S. Army John F. Kennedy Special Warfare Museum, both located at Fort Bragg, NC.

In cases where the search did not lead to any documents or archival material, it was necessary to rely on the veterans to obtain the only accounting of what could be uncovered for this missing gap in history. All the veterans of Laos worked to contact other veterans who served with them to ensure the details of their recollections. They then re-checked their documents (and searched to discover more) and placed their pictures in context to ensure the story was corroborated and was as accurate as possible.

It is one of the rarest and unknown stories about Army SF and its role with the interagency during conflict and provides lessons for today's special operations warriors operating in the irregular warfare environment. All mistakes are mine.

Joe Celeski
Buford, GA
October 2018

Acknowledgements

Many of the activities of the secret war in Laos still remain classified or are being lost as the veterans and participants of this war become lost to us. First and foremost, this publication would have not been possible without the help and assistance of the remaining Special Operations veterans who served in the kingdom. Just as capturing the exploits of the Greatest Generation from World War II, it is important to capture a war conducted in the cloak of secrecy and covert operations in a land far away, the secret war in Laos. Very little has been captured or written in detail of the experiences of these veterans, who unfortunately are passing away each year. This is their story and their work.

Various veterans' organizations provided great support throughout this project. These include Keith Stanley and Cliff Newman from the Special Forces Association, the Special Forces State Associations, Clyde Sincere from the Special Operations Association, Major General Richard Secord (USAF, Retired), the staff of the Air America Association, and the veterans of the various Hmong–American friendship associations (thanks to the help of Steve Schofield).

It is also important to recognize the patience and assistance from the staffs of museums and history archives that were prescient in collecting and storing a vast amount of archival material and pictures. The most revealing aspect of this search was the dearth of information and official reports of the exploits of special operators in Laos, lost or never recorded to history.

All quests for knowledge begin with the first step. This journey began with extremely helpful and patient support provided by Ms. Carrie Sullivan at the U.S. Army Center of Military History Archives Branch at Fort McNair. She provided some fruitful and interesting original documents from their archives which sparked my enthusiasm to tackle this subject and set the azimuth and desire to explore further.

Without a doubt, and known by many in the Special Forces community, is Ms. Roxanne Merritt, the horse-holder of much of Green Beret history at the Special Warfare Museum at Fort Bragg, NC. The documents, pictures, and artifacts on the period of the Laotian war were invaluable in getting the feel and impression of this conflict. Additionally, Ms. Merritt was extremely helpful in directing me toward many of the veterans of Laos and other enthusiasts and experts of the war in Laos, found throughout the U.S.A. and in Thailand. A special thanks goes also to the research assistant, Ms. Maria Forte, for her assistance with museum archival photography and the tour through the physical artifacts donated from veterans of Laos, stored in their warehouse at Fort Bragg, NC.

Dr. Charles Briscoe, the USASOC Headquarters command historian at Fort Bragg, NC, along with Mike Krivdo, Eugene Piasecki, and Troy Sacquety (command historians) were instrumental in providing personal guidance and direction on the thesis, layout, and design parameters for the work during their personal time as well as supplying key information on the history and capabilities of U.S. Army Special Forces during the 1950s and 1960s. I would also like to thank the IT and documents staff of the USASOC History Office, all who gave generous time to help and work on photos and documents.

I appreciate the hospitality and generous help of Mr. Paul A. Oelkrug, Coordinator for Special Collections, the Air America Archives, at the University of Texas, Dallas along with his research and archives staff: Dr. Thomas J. Allen, Ty Lovelady, and Ms. Patrizia Nava. All were patient and helpful during my search of the archives and perusal of photographs and maps to find the nexus of Air America in support of U.S. Army Special Forces operations in *Hotfoot* and *White Star* activities. They also generously allowed me to photograph various artifacts on display donated from Air America veterans.

The Vietnam Center and Archive at the Texas Tech University in Lubbock, Texas is a national treasure. Dr. Stephen F. Maxner (director), Dr. Kelly E. Crager (oral historian), and Ms. Sheon Montgomery (reference archivist) ensured my long drive to visit them was highly fruitful. My special appreciation to the opportunity provided me to visit the vast holdings in the archives and gain an appreciation of the works existing from veterans of Southeast Asian wars. Ms. Sheon Montgomery was of special assistance in maximizing my understanding of the virtual archive to find relevant materials for the research project.

In the Washington D. C. area, a special thanks to Ms. Tony L. Hiley, Museum Director for the CIA, Tom Ahern (historian), and Dr. Clayton D. Laurie (intelligence historian) for a very hospitable visit and their time and patience to hear out the project and assist with any documents about the working relationship between the Agency and U.S. Army Special Forces teams during the period of the war.

At the National Archives in Maryland, Martin Gedra and Stanley Fanaras worked hard before, during and after my visit to scrub a vast amount of Vietnam-era documents to find materials on the *White Star* period. This is also true of the librarians and archivists of the Library of Congress.

Of tremendous help was Steve Sherman and his assistance with the RADIX Press's *Who's Who in Hotfoot and White Star* and *Who's Who in the 46th Independent Special Forces Company* publications, along with help to contact the veterans of Laos and the 46th SF Company.

Paul Kulick was of special help in arranging for historical photographs of the Laotian period and photographic repair of donations from various veterans of the

Laos War. In many cases, damaged photographs over fifty years old were restored and provided back to contributors.

I would like to also thank the other librarians and staff of the libraries who assisted in the research effort. These include the Marshall Library at the National Defense University, the Air War College Library at Maxwell AFB, and the Library of the University of Minneapolis (Daniel Necas, the archivist and Ms. Jamie L. Hoehn, research assistant). The archivists and historians at the U.S. Army Center for Military History in Carlisle, PA, were especially patient and helpful.

Notably, it was the veterans of this war who contributed most to ensure a complete as possible story of this endeavor can be told. Where veterans were deceased, the wives, sons and daughters helpfully searched through their loved one's materials to ensure capture of their story. Archival materials, books, historical facts and figures provide the framework for military histories, but nothing can replace the actual experiences of those who participate and fight in war. This kind of resolution and context is only found by listening to the veterans themselves. In most cases with research on Laos, the veterans' recollections are the only existing accounts of what actually happened on the ground.

The stories and pictures in the work serve as the testimony of this time in their lives. However, some spent long hours and months during the project to ensure its completeness. Not all of the hundreds of veterans, historians, and archivists can be mentioned in this small space, but I must mention those who spent inordinate amounts of personal time and effort to see the completion of the project, month after month. A special thanks to Joe Bossi (now deceased), Scot Crerar (deceased), Bill and Ludwig Faistenhammer, Gene Gavigan, John T. Haralson, Tom Humphus, Michael Ingham, Frank Jaks, Khao Insixiengmay, Ray Millaway, John "Johnny" McCallum and the Gang of Four down near Orlando, Florida (including Steve Schofield), and additionally Ned Miller, Al Paddock, Gary Perkowski, John Roy, Bill Rouleau, Steve Sherman, Robert "Too Tall" Simmons, Clyde Sincere, Albert Slugocki, Vladimir Sobichevsky (deceased), George Stewart, John Sullivan, John Uhrig, and Billy Waugh. There were many others, who I hope understand my appreciation and receipt of mentoring throughout the project, even if space here precludes me from their mention.

A special thanks goes to my wife Judy Celeski, who was extremely patient and supportive through this project, and retired Colonel Vladimir Sobichevsky for their original artwork and illustrations. Vladimir is now gone, but his enthusiasm and dedication to the project were vastly appreciated, along with sharing his tour in Laos and over seventy photographs.

I would also like to thank my neighbor, Dave Verell, for his computer and IT skills to help with restoration of pictures, transferring slides to pictures, and extraction of stills from various (although few) films and video materials about the war in Laos.

Last but not least is acknowledgment of the professional job of the various editors and staff of Casemate Publishing to accept the work, correct the work, and to extend warm assistance and patience to help make the best possible story on this "Long War" engagement by army special operators. It is through their efforts and diligence that the quality of the final work was ensured.

Introduction: Army Special Warfare and the War in Laos

> "One may have noticed that although there is an abundance of literature on the unconventional derring-do of SOF, discussion of their strategic value is all but non-existent. That is a story much in need of telling, particularly since SOF assuredly will figure with increasing prominence in the strategic history of future warfare."
>
> COLIN GRAY, *ANOTHER BLOODY CENTURY*

One of the least known and understood applications of Special Operations Forces (SOF), post-World War II, was the use of U.S. Army Special Forces (Green Berets) to prevent the communist takeover of the Kingdom of Laos, or at least preserve its neutrality, during the years 1959 through 1974. It would be the first strategic challenge to the force since their creation in 1952. Could their use in Laos, independent from U.S. conventional forces, achieve U.S. foreign policy objectives for the Kingdom of Laos, converting their tactical application into strategic effect?

It was one of the first "Long Wars" for special operations, spanning a period of about thirteen years. It was also one of the first major applications of *special warfare* doctrine.

As described by Dr. Charles H. Briscoe in his article "The Good 'Ole' Days of Special Forces: Marginalized Before JFK," the leaders of U.S. Army Special Forces lacked strategic acumen for the threats of the Cold War and focused on fighting the last war (guerrilla warfare and partisan operations). This was reflected in the mismatch with prevalent doctrine and major warfighting methods seen as relevant in the 1950s. Conventional senior military leadership viewed Special Forces as non-contributors in any major conflict. States Briscoe, "To them, SF was ignoring the realities of modern war and the capability of Americans to survive 'behind the Iron Curtain.'"[1] In short, the problem before SF leadership was how to convert tactical actions into achieving strategic military and policy objectives, successfully. It was the war in Laos, and later Vietnam, which would provide the opportunity for Special Forces to begin to rectify and understand the proper strategic application of their unique form of military power.

It was a war shrouded in secrecy and kept out of view of the American public and one of the largest CIA paramilitary operations of the times. Covert operations in Laos and Thailand began with the activities of the Office of Strategic Services' (OSS) Detachment 404, responsible for the support of the Free Thai movement and efforts of clandestine operatives in Laos operating against Japanese occupation forces.

To fight in Laos was an adventure in a faraway, exotic land. Special Operations Forces (SOF) operators were intrigued by the whispers and cloak of secrecy in conversations about Laos. In some cases, news about the war in Laos was the impetus for recruiters to fill the community with volunteers hoping to deploy there. Many of the techniques formulated through trial and error during this war, and the ability to work in austere environments with native and tribal forces, informed future doctrine within the Army Special Forces community.

Laos was called "The Land of a Million Elephants and the White Parasol." It was a war involving three factions: the Royalists (or Rightists), the Neutralists, and the Leftists. In the first half of the war, the Royal Laotian forces deployed in conventional battalion formations to take on Pathet Lao communist insurgents, who were backed and supported first by the Viet Minh guerrillas, named later as the NVA (also called the PAVN—The People's Army of Vietnam). In the second half of the war this condition flipped: The Royal Laotian Government (RLG) now depended on its Hmong and Kha guerrillas to fight line battalion formations of the Pathet Lao and NVA, who became more conventional in their tactics.

With the fall of the French forces at Dien Bien Phu in 1954, the French Union of the three Indochina countries—Vietnam, Laos, Cambodia—evaporated. Under the Geneva Treaty stipulations, a residual French military training force was allowed to assist the Lao government in its self-defense. A military aid agreement was signed between the United States and the French government to support this effort. To further implement President Eisenhower's regional strategy to thwart communism in Southeast Asia, and prevent the "falling dominos" effect, the first ambassador to Laos—Ambassador Yost—was posted to the administrative capital of Vientiane, Additionally, the United States Operations Mission (USOM) began providing military aid and financial support to the new government in 1955. When Laotian security forces were found to be lacking in will, equipment, and tactics to thwart communist forces, America took steps to enter the war.

Veterans of the war remember vast, green-hued jungles and monsoon rains while conducting operations in the middle of nowhere; the Hmong guerrillas and Lao *tahans* (soldiers) were often shorter than the M1 rifles they were issued. Mountain ranges punctuated by towering karsts (vertical crags of eroded limestone), the fog, and the monsoon season posed challenges to supporting air, operating out of short airstrips and unimproved airfields called "Lima Sites." Crossing the Mekong was referred to as "crossing the fence." Humidity, insects, intestinal diseases, malaria and hepatitis put many a man in the hospital. Veterans remember the rice wine-drinking ritual, sipping through slender, communal straws. Water buffalo and glutinous white rice made up most meals.

Air America was the only air support initially for Green Berets on the ground. Bangkok was the R&R location of choice. Most veterans wore civilian clothes during their duties in order to continue the charade of no American military forces serving in Laos, per the Geneva agreements, and used the title "Mister" instead of their rank (if you even were told their real name). When in uniform, the popular jungle boonie hat became the vogue headgear (pinned up one side in the Australian style affixed with unit insignia). Many of the veterans of the war in Laos served with cover stories, such as being forest rangers, agricultural experts, or humanitarian aid employees. To work along with the CIA in covert and clandestine activities, U.S. military personnel were "sheep-dipped" and dropped from their service rolls for service in the ranks of the Agency.

USAID humanitarians bolstered the civic action programs (everyone heard or knew of "Pop" Buell) while CIA operatives and their controlled American sources (CAS), also known as "the customer," directed and supported clandestine ethnic tribal forces throughout the country.

In Laos they used *kip* for money and in Thailand they used *baht*. Per diem pay allowed for the purchase of tailored suits, gold bracelets and Rolex watches, and most wore some type of good-luck Buddha amulet. If one attended any kind of function in a village or town, a *bacci* (a welcoming ceremony) was held while Laotians and tribal villagers tied white strings around the guests' wrists. The *bonzes*, Buddhist priests, in yellow or orange saffron robes, were ever present. The local shaman was the spiritual counselor, medicine man, and soothsayer, and woe be to those who did not factor him into their operations and medical treatment to gain rapport and build relationships with their counterparts. French influence, French architecture, French military trainers, and French language were everywhere.

The Hmong guerrillas were fierce fighters, coming from warrior clans and tribes. The NVA was the most feared enemy in Laos, while the Pathet Lao were somewhere in the middle. The bulk of the FAR—Royal Lao Army Forces—were considered indolent, worthless, and permeated with corrupt leadership. Most of their units ran when confronted on the battlefield, or went to great lengths to not make contact with and avoid the enemy. Those who were well led fought bravely. For many of the Laos veterans this war was one of the most memorable and complex experiences in their life.

It was also the Ambassadors' War: Brown, Unger, Sullivan, Godley, and those who followed, each having full control over the military forces operating in Laos, often to the chagrin of the Joint Chiefs of Staff and the commanders of the Pacific Theater (PACOM) and MACV in South Vietnam (the Military Assistance Command–Vietnam). President Eisenhower's approach to the *limited war* doctrine of the 1950s was the provision of economic and military assistance to Thailand and

Laos to prevent the communist take-over of the two countries. U.S. aid and military assistance would ensure the two countries remained pro-democratic and pro-Western.

Into the Cold War

With the post-war disbandment of the OSS to make way for the creation of the CIA, many of those who worked in the OSS transferred into key positions of the military, the State Department, and the CIA and would shape the policies and decisions with respect to American involvement in the war in Laos. America had the talent, expertise, and the knowledge to pursue an effective military assistance program and a covert proxy war in Laos.

The Korean War redirected American attention from "containing" communism in Europe to focus on Southeast Asia. Fears of communist expansion into Indochina and the apparent realization of the "domino theory" of communist movements taking over Laos, Thailand, Cambodia and South Vietnam, dictated U.S. economic and military support to French military efforts and the defeat of the Viet Minh in Indochina. Asia hands understood military and economic support to Thailand would be imperative as the ultimate bulwark to stop the spread of communism in the region. General Donovan (OSS Director in World War II) would become the ambassador to Thailand in the Eisenhower administration. The newly created CIA, staffed with many of the Indochina hands from World War II, would become a key asset to confront the growing threat of communism in Laos and Thailand.

President Truman's NSC-48 was a policy to confront communism in Southeast Asia; its design was one of containment. It was also American policy to be the first to have a stake in the region, preventing any further spread of communist attempts to divide the world into "imperialist camps" and "people's democracies." There were stark lessons for ignoring this peril: the Chinese Communists' victory over the Chinese Nationalists, and the impact of the Korean War. The 1950s also saw an explosion of communist insurgencies in Burma, the Philippines, Laos, Vietnam, and Malaya.

Thailand would be considered the first "fence" to block the spread of communism. General Claire Chennault raised the specter of countries in the region "falling like dominoes" if America did not support the Chinese Nationalists against Mao Tse Tung. This soon became a battle cry in the Cold War, putting pressure on first Truman, then Eisenhower to do something about the menace. Eisenhower used the term in a policy speech: "You have a row of dominos set up, you knock over the first one, and what will happen to the last one is the certainty that it will go over very quickly." Military aid to Thailand began with the Mutual Defense Assistance Act, signed in 1949. In the words of the Pentagon, Thailand became "our unsinkable aircraft carrier."

With Thailand well prepared to battle communism, Eisenhower expanded his options in Southeast Asia to now view Laos also as a bulwark against the spread of communism. Given the geopolitical position and location of Laos, it would inevitably be the first "domino" to fall to communist expansion. Eisenhower warned his NSC staff, "We cannot let Laos fall to the Communists even if we have to fight, with our allies, or without them."[2]

By the mid-1950s, America would be on the path to American involvement in the war in Laos, soon followed by the introduction of military assistance and the deployment of military "technicians"—U.S. Army Special Forces—to begin the covert battle against the Pathet Lao and the NVA.

Conditions for the Creation of American *Special Warfare* Forces

The deficiencies created by President Eisenhower's "New Look" defense posture were the impetus for the Kennedy administration to expand military special operations and counterinsurgency capabilities. Under Eisenhower, defense strategy hinged on strong nuclear forces as a main deterrent; conventional forces would fight limited war contingencies. CIA paramilitary operations would be the tool in the toolkit for unconventional warfare skills required to tackle outbreaks of communist-inspired revolutionary warfare. There was only one catch: the cost of transitioning to nuclear forces became expensive, forcing the military services to cut budgets and end-strength in their conventional forces. Thus was born the strategy of limited wars (and low-intensity conflict doctrine): keep any military contingency effort small and prevent escalation to a nuclear incident.

Early lessons learned in the Cold War signaled that unconventional warfare and covert operations were more successful when a combination of CIA special operations and small, tailored military forces worked together. The Congo operation served notice as a good example. UN forces in and amongst themselves could not break the stalemate of the conflict (as assessed by military experts in the new Kennedy administration), but the CIA with military forces seemed to do well.

The Birth of a U.S. Special Warfare Capability: The Green Berets 1952–1962

After World War II, and with the onset of the Cold War, the great struggle of communism to reshape the world in its Marxist-Leninist versions of rule over society versus Western democratic rule reshaped the role for American special operations forces. Revolutionary war became the predominant form of conflict (with the exception of the Korean War, considered an outlier to major, general conflict). There was an abundance of lessons on the use of special operators in the application of counterinsurgency strategies to challenge insurgents, most notably the French and British lessons from the wars in Malaya, French Indochina, and Algeria.

By the early 1950s, the American military had become well attuned to counterinsurgency as the "way" of strategy to challenge subversion and insurgencies growing around the globe. To that end, the Department of Defense strengthened its ability to conduct counterinsurgency and psychological operations and created the 10th Special Forces Group (Airborne) and the Special Warfare Center at Fort Bragg, North Carolina. The newly formed Central Intelligence Agency (CIA), successor to the Office of Strategic Services (the OSS), had claimed the role in conducting paramilitary and covert operations through decrees from the National Security Council.

Creating a Special Operation Force

The first specifically organized Special Warfare force created post-World War II within the U.S. Army was the U.S. Army Special Forces, who soon earned the moniker of "Green Berets." In early 1952, the U.S. Army Psychological Warfare School was established at Fort Bragg and on June 20, 1952, the 10th Special Forces Group (Airborne) came into being, under the control of the 3rd Army, a U.S. Army Continental Command (USARC), whose patch the soldiers of the 10th SF Group (SFG–Airborne) wore until a Special Forces shoulder sleeve insignia patch was designed and adopted.[3]

The 10th Special Forces Group was soon designated for Europe, where it was expected this capability would be utilized behind the lines during a war with the Soviets. The 10th SFG moved to Bad Tölz, Germany in 1953, leaving half of their force as cadre to create the 77th Special Forces Group, September 6, 1953. With this additional SF Group, the 77th was soon designated as the worldwide contingency group. As commitments grew in Southeast Asia, the 1st Special Forces Group (Airborne) was activated on Okinawa, June 24, 1957. It would ultimately be the 77th—later designated as the 7th SFG on May 20, 1960—and the 1st SFG (Airborne) who would provide the Army SF military training teams to Laos.

In the 1950s a recruit into Special Forces was a volunteer, generally airborne qualified (or became qualified as soon as joining Special Forces), in good physical shape and with a general technical (GT) score higher than the average recruit. Many of the officers and NCOs attracted to Special Forces had been veterans of the OSS or had been in airborne units during World War II and Korea. Since airborne qualification was required, a large number of early Special Forces officers and NCOs came from the Army airborne divisions. Recruitment for Special Forces was accomplished by word-of-mouth, from army directives, briefings given at various army posts, and a well-known poster in the recruitment stations depicting a Green Beret soldier "on rappel." Special Forces-qualified personnel were awarded a "3" designator on their military occupational speciality (MOS). Unlike today, with the 18-series MOS, there was no military specialty code unique to Special Forces.

Mission

The mission of the U.S. Army Special Forces was to organize and train guerrilla or resistance forces for operations behind enemy lines. This also included subversion and sabotage, the establishment of auxiliary and underground networks, and a capability to set up and run escape-and-evasion networks. This type of land warfare is doctrinally called *unconventional warfare* (UW). In the early concept development of the force, special operations Colonels Volckmann and Bank working at the Pentagon were very diligent to ensure this "specialization" was distinctive only to Army Special Forces; they were not raiders, rangers, or psychological operations troops.

It was Brigadier General McClure's and Colonels Volckmann's and Bank's intent to pattern a Special Forces organization after the successful design used by the OSS in World War II. The Operational Group (OG, usually fewer than fifteen men) was the basic combat maneuver element assigned to support a guerrilla or resistance movement behind enemy lines, operating in an assigned unconventional warfare (UW) subsector. For a larger effort, two or more OGs could be combined and headed by a command element, the Area Sector Command. Multiple Area Sector Commands would require a higher headquarters for direction, support, and logistics. (One of the primary duties of a higher echelon headquarters in unconventional warfare is also to liaise and coordinate with senior leaders in the resistance movement, to include political figures.)

Thus, the Field C team would be the higher command, led by a lieutenant colonel, and with two additional officers and nine enlisted personnel. In what seemed like a confusing label, the "FC" was called a Special Forces Company. The FC could command and control three to five Field Bravo teams (the Area Sector Commands). There were three FC teams in a Special Forces group.

The Field Bravo team (FB) was headed by a major, with the same number of personnel as the FC. A Field Bravo team was designed to command and control two or more Special Forces teams. There were four to five FB teams in an FC.

The operators were organized as Field Alpha teams (FA). The role of the FAs was to advise and support guerrilla units with up to 1,500 irregulars. The original manning document for FAs proposed a fifteen-man team, with flexibility for fill. There could be four to ten FAs in the FB team. With downward adjustment of team strength based on the initial low fill of personnel, the typical FC had three FBs, four to six FAs in the FB, and roughly twelve SF personnel on the FAs (traditionally called the "A" team).[4] Additional FA members were augmentations from Civil Affairs, PSYOP, mechanics, and sometimes intelligence and engineer personnel. Teams were numbered consecutively, starting with FA-1, FA-2, and so forth until completing the number of all assigned teams in the Group. In some SF groups, this numbering system reached FA team 70.[5]

The distinctive green beret would not be officially adopted until President Kennedy's visit to Fort Bragg in 1961, where Brigadier General Yarborough, the Special Warfare commander, boldly wore his green beret during a military capabilities demonstration. Kennedy, very impressed, officially authorized the green beret as the unit's official headgear. Special Forces soldiers would thereafter be called the "Green Berets."[6]

Capabilities

The primary capability of the force to conduct guerrilla warfare resided at the SF A-team level. This gave an army theater commander the ability to conduct ground warfare in the enemy's rear area, through the use of proxy forces. Each A team could train up to one guerrilla-like battalion. As conversely, the A team could also operate in a counterinsurgency environment to train and advise indigenous security forces in counterguerrilla operations and in Internal Defense and Development tasks (IDAD, a country plan for an appropriate strategy in insurgency or stability operations). This was a force-multiplier capability, as an economy of force choice.

The team had the ability to train and fight with indigenous and irregular forces as light infantry, with the skills to also conduct psychological operations, civic action, and establish intelligence networks. One of the tasks for the team was to provide operational and strategic intelligence, along with targeting capability, for the theater commander.

The SF teams were trainers, instructors, and advisors, applying each role as needed. For combat operations, the SF team's job was to enhance the performance and capabilities of its assigned indigenous force. Various subjects were taught to achieve this objective: planning for operations, small unit tactics, field medical procedures, the running of air operations (resupply drop zones and landing zones), ability to call for artillery and close air support, and weapons effectiveness, to include the use of demolitions. Clandestine signaling and electronic radio communications procedures were also taught.

Teams also received additional training for the conduct of combat in a variety of remote and rugged terrain (mountain, swamps, jungle), and in extreme northern climes, applying winter warfare skills.

SF teams were capable of infiltrating via air (parachute and HALO operations, or helicopter insertion), land (to include mountaineering), or water (small boat unit operations and underwater demolition teams, UDT training).

With the policy decision to deploy military advisors and trainers to Laos by President Eisenhower, Army Special Forces were chosen to meet the call. Special Forces teams had some Southeast Asia experience when they earlier deployed to Thailand in the mid-1950s and training and advisory detachments were sent to South Vietnam in 1957. Small, adaptable, and physically fit, with an understanding of insurgency and guerrilla warfare, the men of the 77th SFG (A), and later the 1st SFG (A), deployed with the mission to live with and train indigenous forces and fight alongside them as necessary; this proved to be the deciding factor for their selection. The introduction and use of Army Special Forces in 1959 for duty in Laos would prove to be a very attractive option to the American ambassador in Vientiane.

Under President Kennedy, the U.S. foreign policy goal transitioned to ensuring Laos remained at least neutral, but not communist. As American commitment and effort in Southeast Asia switched to the war in Vietnam, Laos was viewed as a place to tie down front-line North Vietnamese Army (NVA) divisions and punish North Vietnam for their support to the communists in South Vietnam (with commensurate interdiction of the Ho Chi Minh Trail, the HCMT). Laos became a backwater war effort. When geopolitics dictated the real threat to the United States was a nuclear-armed Soviet Union, both South Vietnam and Laos were abandoned as the United States withdrew from the region and focused on supporting the NATO alliance in Europe.

The Bay of Pigs débâcle further put doubt in Kennedy's mind that large, paramilitary operations, on their own merit, were the key to success in counterrevolutionary warfare. One more key factor contributed to success or failure: the ability of a threatened and targeted government to "bear the burden" for the fight against subversion and insurgency. All of these factors shaped the thinking of appropriate U.S. counterinsurgency responses to the ever-widening brush wars erupting around the globe.[7]

In Kennedy's March 28, 1961 Special Message to Congress on the Defense Budget, he explained his policy shift:

> In the event of a major aggression that could not be repulsed by conventional forces, we must be prepared to take whatever action with whatever weapons are appropriate. But our objective now is to increase our ability to confine our response to non-nuclear weapons, and to lessen the incentive for any limited aggression by making clear what our response will accomplish. In most areas of the world, the main burden of local defense against overt attack, subversion, and guerrilla warfare must rest on local populations and forces. But given the great likelihood and seriousness of this threat, we must be prepared to make a substantial contribution in the form of strong, highly mobile forces trained in this type of warfare, some of which must be deployed in forward areas, with a substantial airlift and sealift capacity and prestocked overseas bases.[8]

A flurry of activity occurred within the National Security Council (NSC) to develop policy positions on U.S. capabilities to conduct counterguerrilla warfare, COIN, and paramilitary operations. Within the services, position papers were developed to identify Special Warfare units and capabilities. Kennedy, through National Security Action Memorandum 56, further issued instructions to each of the services to examine their ability to contribute to a counterinsurgency capability.[9]

The U.S. Army had the most robust capability, residing in its Special Forces Groups (even though not whole-heartedly supported by U.S. Army generals trying to preserve their ever-dwindling force structure). It was Kennedy's support and respect for the Green Berets which allowed for their rapid expansion. A regionally aligned, global response force, with the capability to conduct guerrilla warfare or act as military trainers in a counterinsurgency environment was just the fungible type of military unit Kennedy found highly useful to confront communist, revolutionary movement expansion. The war in Laos was tailormade for the use of Kennedy's Green Berets.

In any complex military contingency, using the right tool in the toolbox becomes important to the success of achieving the political objective. American unconventional warfare capabilities available for U.S. decision-makers for employment to Laos in the 1950s consisted of U.S. Army Special Forces, psychological operations forces, and proxy counterinsurgency airpower through the use of the CIA-propriety airline, Air America. Additionally, the Central Intelligence Agency employed covert operatives to conduct paramilitary operations to raise and train various tribal guerrilla forces.

Special Warfare

The term Special Warfare was defined in 1962 by the Joint Chiefs of Staff (JCS Pub 1, Chapter 1: 2 July 1962) as:

Counterinsurgency. Those military, paramilitary, political, economic, psychological, and civic actions taken by a government to defeat subversive insurgency.

Psychological Warfare. The planned use of propaganda and other psychological actions having the primary purpose of influencing the opinions, emotions, attitudes, and behavior of hostile foreign groups in such a way as to support the achievement of national objectives.

Unconventional Warfare. Includes the three interrelated fields of guerrilla warfare, evasion and escape, and subversion. Unconventional warfare operations are conducted within enemy or enemy-controlled territory by predominantly indigenous personnel, usually supported and directed in varying degrees by an external force.

Simply put, Special Warfare was defined as the contribution of United States' military forces to support the three categories of Special Warfare. The roles for Special Warfare units comprised the following:

- Leveraging existing host nation forces for combat (advisory assistance)
- Building host nation combat power, adapted to the circumstance and conditions (military assistance)
- Augment host nation with Special Warfare assets; integration of Special Warfare assets ("through, with, and by …")
- Covert and clandestine operations
- Support to guerrilla warfare
- Operations behind enemy lines (strike, intelligence-gathering, reconnaissance, infiltration and infiltration of Special Forces and clandestine units)

- Plus, other roles applicable to host nation forces in COIN

Much of Special Warfare is conducted on human terrain and in the human domain. The direct application of military power is replaced with the ability to leverage and influence others (force multipliers; economy of force) and to enhance and enable conventional force maneuver to achieve campaign military objectives. The effects achieved by the conduct of Special Warfare are generally exhaustive, erosive, and attritional (with the art of applying these simultaneously to create a fog and friction on the competitor). In this sense, Special Warfare is not based on large-formation maneuver as key to war. Special Operations Forces are not designed, nor rarely used, to participate in direct confrontations of strength with opposing military forces. The actions within Special Warfare (tasks, missions, and the conduct of special operations) are directed to operational and strategic objectives, vice tactical objectives.

Special Warfare includes a combination of both direct and indirect approaches to accomplish its objective—the term Special Warfare is the strategic "art" of this combination. In irregular warfare, Special Warfare is focused on the political–societal–psychological vulnerabilities of the competitor, not their military forces.

Force Utility

Force utility is described by strategist Colin S. Gray as a military's form of power to make a difference on the course and outcome of a conflict (and only if the operation is successful).[10]

According to General Rupert Smith, a nation's military force achieves higher utility when it understands its role in modern warfare is one of operating in a political–military environment.[11]

General Smith defines force utility as the ability to deliver results in proportion to one's capabilities. This necessitates the need to not only understand the strategic military imperatives of the conflict, but to also understand the political context, since wars of today are now "amongst the people." This will require military power which can be adaptive in its command and control, doctrine, tactics, techniques and procedures (TTPs) and can be scalable. Modern military force will be used in multinational environments, but not before understanding the geostrategic appreciation for the use of force.[12]

Military force is characterized by the physical components of military power—its means of destruction—along with its personnel, matériel, and logistics. If applied correctly (coercively), the force achieves an essence of *power* if it is successful in achieving the military aim and the political objective with relation to its opponent. Notes General Smith: "It follows that to apply force with utility implies an understanding of the context in which one is acting, a clear definition of the result to be achieved, and identification of the point or target to which the force is being applied—and, as important as all the others, an understanding of the nature of the force being applied."[13]

The role of military force, traditionally, is in defense of the country and to pursue (or protect) a nation's security interests. This role derives from the legal and moral power of the state to sanction the force's activities. Those forces outside of this legalistic determinant constitute "irregular" forces, which can also be a threat to a nation, so all competent military forces will have the capability to fight both regular and irregular conflicts.

Force Application (The Use of Force)

The application of force is based on a strategy that clearly articulates the aim of the endeavor and the political purpose for the exercise of military power. Force application requires gaining a relational advantage over an opponent (asymmetry) where the strengths of military power can have the greatest impact.[14]

General Rupert Smith offers the following checklist for proper application of force:

- The correct formation of the force for the situation at hand (sufficiency)
- Deployability
- Unity of purpose and command
- Sustainability
- Recoverability[15]

In short, General Rupert Smith's use of force (its correct application of *power*) is to influence an opponent, change an opponent's intentions or make him form a new one, establishment of favorable conditions, apply pressure at the right point, and win the clash of wills.[16]

Thus, some of the essential elements of military power include the capabilities needed to ameliorate or mitigate a situation, contain and control a domain or environment (impose order), deter or coerce, and if needed, destroy the opposing power.[17]

The use of force is sanctioned by the state to resolve disputes among states because there is no sovereign, higher power. This force is almost always military. In wartime, physical power is employed (the waging of war—a direct use of power) and in peacetime the threat of employing force is used as intimidation (an indirect form of power). Military force historically and predominantly is used more often in "peacetime" as an instrument of statecraft (a form of its utility). In this form, it is coercive for matters of diplomacy.[18]

Military force, exercised as a form of power, must be fungible, combining utility for both war and for statecraft. The basic essence of fungibility is that an action or substance can serve more than one purpose during its application.

From Tactical to Strategic Effect

To ensure tactical actions achieve strategic effects, and not just win the battle in front of one's self, the mission of the unit must be set in the context of how it achieves a strategic or a policy objective as the unit's purpose on the battlefield (and the outcomes are successful). Colin S. Gray calls this "The Challenge of Currency Conversion."[19]

It was inevitably up to the ambassadors in Laos, the State Department, and policymakers in Washington D. C. to employ Army Special Forces in Laos in a manner to achieve a strategic effect in support of diplomatic and foreign policy objectives.

The Secret War in Laos and Special Operations 1959–1974

A good example of a covert action, combining political action from the Department of State with paramilitary actions by U.S. intelligence, SOF, and other military agencies, was the conduct of the secret war in Laos. From 1959 to 1974, the U.S. government conducted operations in Laos and Thailand to prevent the spread of communism and defend the Royal Lao government against takeover by leftist coups and the alternate communist government of the Pathet Lao. These combined operations were conducted by the Department of State, CIA, and Department of Defense. U.S. SOF were key participants. The operations consisted of financial and economic material support from USAID, from aid provided by the Military Assistance Program (MAP), the use of Foreign Internal Defense (FID), and a covert/clandestine program using native forces to confront the communist Pathet Lao. All of these operations were commanded and controlled by the American ambassadors to Laos.

Phase I: U.S. Military Support to Laos—The Road to Involvement in the War

By 1959, the U.S. embassy became alarmed at the lack of proficiency of Lao forces, along with the lack of confidence in the French contingent to properly employ the weapons and equipment provided by the American military assistance program. An agreement was reached between the Lao government, the French, and the United States to allow U.S. Army Special Forces teams to serve alongside the French trainers and impart instruction on U.S.-supplied military equipment and weapons. In August of 1959, twelve Special Forces teams from the 77th Special Forces Group (Airborne) deployed to Laos and began serving in four of the Lao military training centers. Additionally, Lieutenant Colonel Arthur D. "Bull" Simons led the first Field Control (FC-3) team to command and control the effort from Vientiane. This secret operation was codenamed Operation *Hotfoot*. It was designed to provide training assistance in six-month, temporary duty (TDY) rotations. Special Forces trainers (often referred to as technicians) wore only civilian dress to provide the cover for the operation. (America, like other countries, was prohibited by the Geneva Agreement from deploying military forces into Laos.)

U.S. Special Forces Field Training Teams (FTTs)—twelve eight-man Operational Detachment Alpha (ODA) units—began deployment to Laos in August of 1959. In order to circumvent the Geneva restrictions, the Green Berets were placed on six-month temporary duty orders in order to not increase the number of American military personnel assigned to Laos (U.S. embassy staff were the exception).

During this same period, the CIA engineered the Lao elections of April 1960 with political action measures, ensuring the placement of a right-wing government supported by "their man" in the army—General Phoumi Nosavan. A setback to American political warfare (POLWAR) efforts occurred, however, in August 1960 when Captain Kong Le led his Special Forces-trained parachute battalion in a coup, advocating neutrality and removal of U.S. military assistance. Aid from America was cut off when Souvanna Phouma (the formerly ousted prime minister) was reinstated.

Lacking any financial backing from the United States, Souvanna approached the Soviet Union and the Pathet Lao to obtain additional external aid. The Soviets began military assistance to help the turncoat Captain Kong Le and the Pathet Lao forces, which soon retook the strategic Plaine des Jarres (PDJ) plateau in northeast Laos. Angry at the direction his country was headed, General Phoumi moved his forces to retake the capital and restore the right-wing government. The U.S. chose to back General Phoumi using embassy assets in the PEO (Programs Evaluation Office—an operating work-around due to the restriction preventing a Military Assistance and Advisory Group for Laos) and with CIA-sponsored Air America support and advisory efforts from Army Special Forces teams. With America reinforcing Phoumi's actions to replace the leftist government of Laos, and the USSR reinforcing Captain Kong Le and the Pathet Lao forces, the situation in Laos soon appeared to be an emerging superpower proxy war.

Phase II: Superpower Proxy War

The conduct of foreign policy with respect to Laos passed from Eisenhower to Kennedy; the Laos crisis became Kennedy's first foreign policy challenge in his new administration. He first considered military intervention. Task Force 116, comprised of U.S. forces in the region, was hastily formed by the Joint Chiefs of Staff and readied for action (to wit: military supplies to Thailand along with helicopters, the repositioning of three aircraft carriers, and forces put on alert in Japan and Okinawa). Choosing overt confrontation with the Soviet Union, however, was not desired. Kennedy had to consider other options to achieve his national security objectives. His first attempts were those of quiet diplomacy (Kennedy wanted to change Eisenhower's political objectives for Laos, from pro-Western, anti-communist, to neutrality). Kennedy's position was captured in an interagency telegram drafted by his Laos task force and subsequently sent out to key U.S. embassies and select allies in the region. The key paragraph is quoted from a longer message:

> We conceive of Laos as a neutral state, unaligned in her international relations but determined to preserve her national integrity. In order to exist in this special status, enjoy independence and territorial integrity, some temporary international machinery to guard this neutrality will have to be devised. Neutralized state would permit, except as provided by previous agreements, no foreign military bases, no foreign troops, and no military alliances. State of Austria may serve as precedent. An underlying assumption is that it is in the best interest of U.S. and USSR to avoid widespread hostilities in Laos.[20]

This approach, however, would be for naught as the communist Pathet Lao forces in Laos were gaining ground throughout the country and diplomatically Moscow, China, and North Vietnam had nothing to lose.

Not diplomacy, not war, but now a choice to conduct POLWAR. President Kennedy's next policy option was to consider a covert operation combined with a military UW campaign. This policy would be the new POLWAR option: extensive CIA paramilitary operation using tribal forces, along with SOF combat advisors, and supported by a Thailand-based and covert U.S. MAP.

In April of 1961, due to increased communist activity and violations of the ceasefire in Laos, President Kennedy took a series of initiatives to overtly "militarize" American efforts. As part of his overt diplomatic coercion, President Kennedy authorized the PEO to operate as a full MAAG. Special Forces trainers donned their military uniforms, carried their weapons, and began combat advisory operations with their Lao counterparts. The Special Forces training and advisory mission changed from Operation *Hotfoot* (originally twelve Special Forces teams) to Operation *White Star*.

Kennedy had his war in Laos. With this aggressive response from America, the Soviets agreed to stop their support to warring factions in the region rather than risk a confrontation with the United States. The CIA and Special Forces continued to support the Hmong and Royal Lao Government (RLG) efforts to fight against Viet Minh (NVA) and Pathet Lao on the PDJ. The main effort in Military Region II was supported by a move to establish a secret base at Long Tieng—also referred to as the "Alternate," or 20A (Lima Site 98)—just off the southwest corner of the Plaines des Jarres. The war continued its see-saw pace with Hmong offensives, followed by Pathet Lao and NVA counteroffensives, all driven by the monsoon season. Luckily, the superpower confrontation was averted.

By early 1962, Special Forces teams increased to forty-eight combat advisory teams for operations throughout Laos. The contingent of *White Star* teams was very successful in preventing any major communist gains. The Special Forces advisors of this effort left in October 1962, with the mission accomplished. The departure of SOF from Laos, however, did not last long. From 1964 onward, Special Forces advisors and Air Commandos would return to assist the ambassadors to achieve their goals in Laos.

Phase III: The "Ambassadors' War"

Ambassador William H. Sullivan replaced Ambassador Unger in November 1964 and sought full authority and direction for the war (including control of military forces), which was granted. Under his control, an increased covert effort began to succeed in Laos.[21]

To have access to air bases for maintenance and repair, the CIA established an operations center at Udorn Air Base, Thailand. It was named the 4802nd Joint Liaison Detachment (JLD).

The Department of State assisted efforts to reach *hearts and minds* through the USAID program. By 1965, USAID reported a $1.6 million budget for its Village Health Program alone, funding over 140 hospitals, serving 150,000 patients a month, and training 268 medics in the last fiscal year.[22]

Not comfortable with the U.S. ambassador running a war, the DOD began the covert Project 404 in 1966 to support the ambassador's efforts (augmentation of the military attaché offices in Vientiane), hopefully then having a hand in controlling U.S. military personnel serving in Laos. Special Forces officers and NCOs would serve as Project 404 military advisors in all of the military regions of Laos, from 1966 to 1974.[23]

The secret war in Laos was relegated to a side show due to efforts required to prioritize the war in Vietnam (but focus still remained on airstrikes along the Ho Chi Minh Trail). Outside Laos, Special Forces trainers from the 46th Special Forces Company (Independent) in Thailand continued their effort as trainers and advisors for Hmong, Lao, and Thai irregular and conventional units, operating out of six secret bases in Thailand.[24]

Phase IV: Ending the War

In October 1969, the U.S. Senate held hearings on the situation in Laos (during the Nixon administration). The secret war was exposed and went public. Even with this, Nixon continued the efforts in Laos. That fall, General Vang Pao (leader of the Hmong guerrillas, advised by CIA operatives and U.S. Army assistant attachés) attacked to retake the PDJ and confronted the 316th NVA Division. Vang Pao was supported by Air Force CAS and B-52 strikes. General Vang Pao's efforts at first appeared to be successful, but the NVA and Pathet Lao counterattacked in force and pushed him off the PDJ. The war reverted to one of maneuvers and attacks in a contest over the control of the PDJ. This lasted into the beginning of 1971, with neither side gaining clear advantage.

In February 1971, Operation Lam Son 719—a South Vietnamese Army cross-border offensive—was launched to attack NVA and Pathet Lao forces along Route 9, with its objective as Tchepone. The effects on civilians in this region from the severe level of U.S. bombing angered antiwar groups in the United States. As a result, Congress restricted funds for the war in Laos and Cambodia, along with restrictions on the further use of American military forces (Cooper–Church Amendment). Without air support, Hmong manpower was decimated.

On 22 September 1972, the Pathet Lao agreed to begin peace talks. On February 21, 1973, the Agreement on the Restoration of Peace and Reconciliation was signed in Vientiane, ending the Laotian civil war and establishing a provisional government. In June 1973, the United States signed the Peace Agreement in Paris to end the Vietnam War. With no policy option left, the United States withdrew its forces as the ceasefire operations began; Thai units also withdrew and the Hmongs were assimilated into the new security structure of the state (or fled as refugees).

In July 1975, the United States closed out its mission in Laos when the Pathet Lao drove out the moderates in the government. On 2 December 1975, the Laotian monarchy ended. The communist Lao People's Democratic Republic of Laos was formed.

For almost twenty years, the U.S. led a successful, interagency program (whole of government) of covert and clandestine operations, designed to prevent the communist takeover of the Laotian government. In this effort, America achieved its policy objectives, although the tragic outcome for the Hmong refugees continues to be a sore point for the veterans of the war. Special Warfare doctrine was vindicated as well as confirming the doctrinal relevance of SOF's strategic utility in the growing list of special operations core missions: Unconventional Warfare (UW), Foreign Internal Defense (FID), Psychological Operations (PSYOP, now Military Information Support Operations, MISO), and Civil Affairs (CA).

PART I

BACKGROUND

CHAPTER ONE

Fighting in the Land of a Million Elephants

"The Vietnamese plant rice, the Cambodians watch it grow, and the Lao listen to it grow."

COLONIAL FRENCH SAYING ON THE CULTURE OF THE LAO PEOPLE

The strategic success or failure of the use of force is dictated by many variables. A military strategy aligned with achieving policy objectives is highly important. Applying force in the correct way, and choosing the forces with the most utility, follows. However, there are other variables to take into consideration to ensure the maximum performance of military force. At the tactical level, this review is accomplished through a commander's estimate of the situation. At the operational and strategic level, the review is known as the conduct of a strategic appreciation.

In limited war, such as insurgency and counterinsurgency (COIN), the variables change. Key terrain may not be the holding of a major river crossing, but rather a village astride a mountain pass. Insurgencies and the conduct of COIN often take place in rugged, inaccessible terrain, precisely used to negate the strengths of the government forces. Depending on where the conflict might occur, a commander must take into account the effects of weather and seasonal patterns which can dictate the tempo and style of fighting in a larger way.

Human variables which dictate the style of fighting come to the forefront. Insurgency and COIN are fought on human terrain and in the minds and psyche of the populace. Legitimacy of the government in the eyes of the populace may be more strategically important than holding terrain. An understanding of culture, religion, and belief systems becomes just as important as knowing the enemy order of battle, and are often factors affecting the morale of friendly forces and the populace.

The geography of a country and its infrastructure, or lack thereof, must be studied with an eye to seeking advantage as to the tempo and place combat is offered. Men must train to operate in rugged terrain and military equipment may need retooling to operate in such environments.

All countries excel or suffer as a result of their geographical position on the map and from the historical events which impact their national existence. At the top of this pyramid is the relative nature of a country's economy, accessibility, national resources and the geostrategic pressures from its neighbors. Some adjacent countries, for instance, offer sanctuary to guerrillas.

Laos had all of these variables, much to the detriment of the ability to fight an effective war. An astute commander of either side would play to these strengths and weaknesses to jockey for advantage. The tangible and intangible variables dictated the art and style of fighting in this Southeast Asian country and how the militaries of the countries involved were utilized.

In ancient times the region of Laos was known as the Kingdom of Lang Xang (Land of a Million Elephants and the White Parasol). The kingdom was served ably by a succession of kings until around the mid-16th century when political power struggles and regional wars resulted in the division of Laos into three governing areas—effectually turning Laos into a backwater. In the latter half of the 1800s, the French, seeking colonial expansion and economic opportunities, arrived in the region and ultimately conquered Laos. The country was subsequently used as a buffer zone between British interests in Thailand and Burma against French holdings in Indochina. Through gunboat diplomacy, the French were able to reunify the three separated areas of Laos in the early 1900s.[1]

During World War II, the Japanese successfully conquered Laos and evicted the French. After the Japanese surrender in 1945, the Japanese assisted separatist movements to officially declare Laotian independence from France. To support this effort, Prince Phetsarath of the royal family formed an opposition movement to the reimposition of French control. Prince Phetsarath was helped by his two brothers: Prince Souvanna Phouma and Prince Souphanouvong.

However, the Western powers abetted France reclaiming Laos. This resulted in increased political opposition to the move and the resultant rise and formation of a resistance movement, the Lao Issara (Free Laos), the same movement supported by the OSS to resist the Japanese.

By September of 1946, the French once again controlled and dominated the country, forcing the three brothers into exile, taking with them their political philosophies to replace the French:

- Phetsarath dictated a military clash with the French
- Souvanna Phouma wanted to retake Laos with a legitimate political process
- Souphanouvong aligned with the communist Viet Minh

Souvanna Phouma eventually won over the debate and, through the political process, became the prime minister.

The Lead-up to War

There were three main causes for the secret war in Laos: (1) the disagreement of the three brothers on which style of government best suited the country, (2) communist expansion, and (3) superpower manipulation of the differing factions, to include sponsorship of proxy war inside the country.

In 1950, the French established Vietnam, Laos, and Cambodia as "associated" states within a French Union. As the communist threat grew within the French Union, the United States began military aid to the French to help stop its spread. The United States and France signed the Pentalateral Mutual Defense Assistance Act and by 1952 the United States was paying for one-third of the French war costs.

Frustrated at the continuing presence of the French in Laos, Souphanouvong convened a revolutionary congress on the Plaine des Jarres and formed a resistance government. The new congress formed for war and established their political arm, the Lao Patriotic Front, and an action arm, later to be named the Pathet Lao.

The Pathet Lao Communist Resistance Front (action arm) formed with the assistance of the Viet Minh to defeat the French and Royal Laotian Government's (RLG) allies. It was headed by The Resistance Committee of Eastern Laos with Prince Soupannavong accepted as its nominal leader. The first twenty-five-man guerrilla force was formed in January of 1949—recruits were from the hill tribes, including the Tai and Hmong.

In 1950, over 150 members of the movement met with Ho Chi Minh and the organization renamed themselves the Neo Lao Issara (Free Lao Front) with its armed wing incorporating the Pathet Lao. They adopted a Maoist people's revolutionary war strategy and began the first phase of the strategy, guerrilla warfare. The Viet Minh, as well as China and Russia, supplied and supported the Pathet Lao.[2]

In response, the French deployed one colonial battalion per province. With French training to raise a Lao military force, the first two 600-man battalions of the Royal Laotian Government—formed by the Mission Militaire Française (MMF)—were raised and employed as *bataillons d'infanterie laotienne* (BILs, the 1st and 2nd). In 1951, with the addition of two infantry battalions and one parachute battalion, the Laotian government's total military manpower was about five thousand. Owing to U.S. military aid, the number of battalions increased and were provided with American arms and equipment; moreover, additional counterinsurgency units were formed to expand the capabilities and number of government security forces. For example, the paramilitary forces known as Garde Nationale, consisting of 170-man companies of peasant militias, were formed. COIN light infantry battalions were also formed along with units known as Mixed Airborne Commando Groups (GCMAs).[3]

In 1953 four infantry divisions of the Viet Minh, along with the Pathet Lao led by Prince Souphanouvong, tried to capture Luang Prabang—a regional, historic governmental center and the home for the king—and were successful in seizing the

PDJ from the French/Laotian military forces. They were also successful in capturing the province of Sam Neua where they immediately established a rebel government. To assist in the fight to recapture this vital area, the CIA's Civil Air Transport (CAT) subsidiary asset assisted the French from May to June 1953 with C-119 paradrops. CAT was later to become "Air America."

In 1954 the Viet Minh defeated French forces at the battle of Dien Bien Phu, changing the security dynamic in the region. The Geneva conference of May 1954 split Vietnam into North and South, while Laos was declared independent and neutral. A ceasefire was implemented in Laos in August of 1954 to remove foreign troops and to demobilize and integrate Pathet Lao forces into the government's military forces.

The Geneva Conference and Agreement of 1954 spelled out the new security arrangement for the country of Laos. Two of the key provisions were:

- Prohibiting introduction into Laos of foreign or regular troops, or irregular troops, foreign paramilitaries, or foreign military personnel
- Prohibiting introduction into Laos of armaments, munitions, and war material, except for conventional items necessary for the Royal Government of Laos to defend itself

In response, U.S. policy objectives, which began during the Eisenhower administration, were to maintain a pro-United States country, secure freedom from communism, disrupt the flow of communist supplies, and adhere to the spirit of the Geneva accords. The U.S. strategy consisted of a political warfare covert operation (POLWAR), using clandestine interagency assets and unconventional warfare (UW) with special operations forces as needed, combined with the conduct of foreign internal defense (FID) and security assistance (SA) programs. President Eisenhower also acted to counteract subversive communist activities still ongoing throughout the region by increasing aid to Thailand and South Vietnam. The diplomatic response to the growing communist threat created a new security organization, the Southeast Asia Treaty Organization (SEATO).

With the many restrictions of the Geneva protocols to the Agreement, the priority of effort was focused on Thailand as the bulwark against aggression, starting with foreign aid programs, and then with military aid programs to follow. The U.S. military established a Military Advisory Assistance Group (MAAG Thailand).

Even with reduced foreign military assistance, the Royal Laotian Army—the Armée Nationale Laotienne (ANL) until 1959—was able to continue building in strength with up to 25,000 troops. Laotians, now weakened by the Geneva restrictions, sought a compromise to reduce the threat and worked out agreements with the Pathet Lao to form a coalition government. The Pathet Lao were also affected by the Geneva restrictions and could not win without North Vietnamese support. As a result, in

September of 1954 a leftist government was formed with hopes of attracting the Pathet Lao to lay down their arms and participate in the political process.

There was still a small loophole for the U.S. to operate, however; the provision of military aid could continue due to the allowance in the Geneva agreements, "except for conventional items necessary for the Royal Government of Laos to defend itself." Consequently, U.S. Ambassador Charles W. Yost, arrived in Laos to establish the U.S. Operations Mission (USOM) and started the process to provide "conventional" aid and military funding, along with continued French military support.

With the Geneva restrictions preventing additional foreign military forces operating in Laos, a program evaluations office (PEO) was established within the USAID section of the embassy instead of a MAAG-type organization, to work around the restrictions. Most of the PEO staff were retired military personnel who began to work through and with the French Military Mission (FMM). John Prados described the PEO:

> One special feature of the United States' operating mission in Laos was that military representation was not restricted to the attaché. There was a military advisory group in all but name, headed by a United States general officer. In deference to the Geneva Agreement, the advisory group was called a Programs Evaluation Office (PEO) and had the ostensible task of monitoring the effects of American Programs in the country. The PEO had its beginnings in December 1955, with the installation of a six-man staff at Vientiane. By early 1956, PEO was dispatching small teams of advisors to RLAF units, usually with Thai interpreters who translated English to Lao.[4]

After the national elections in 1958, the Pathet Lao gained enough political power to be included into the coalition government, alarming the United States, which subsequently halted U.S. economic aid to the new government as a sign of its displeasure. (This practice, known as coercive diplomacy, is a tool commonly used in political warfare.) A mini-coup by the Laotian Congress and other influential leaders ousted Prime Minister Souvanna and the Pathet Lao representatives, resulting in the formation of a new government which was anti-communist and pro-West. The Pathet Lao were enraged, and resumed their attacks on the government. Souphanouvong and the ringleaders of the revolt were jailed but later escaped to conduct a civil war and resume armed action.

In 1958 Brigadier General John A. Heintges provided the U.S. government a study and assessment on the security situation in Laos. His dire report resulted in an increased role for the PEO to add more military trainers and advisors to assist the Laotian government security forces. To circumvent the restrictions of the Geneva Agreement the Eastern Construction Company in Laos (ECCOIL) was formed as a front company to increase combat advisors. It was manned by ex-Filipino military personnel trained in COIN by the United States, as a result of Ed Lansdale's brilliant work to assist the Philippine government to contain the Hukbalahap insurgency. There were also uniformed officers of the U.S. Army, majors and lieutenant colonels, who served in each military region as advisors from the PEO.

The Geopolitical Situation

The geopolitical situation in Laos was framed by three regional competing interests, the first being the American position to prevent the spread of communism in Southeast Asia. The second major geopolitical interest was China's position to prevent foreign military forces and bases from being introduced into Laos. Although the Chinese never overtly intervened in Laotian affairs to any great extent, the threat of action by China dictated to some extent the level of American effort to assist Laos. What would be the trigger point to encourage a Chinese intervention?

The third competing interest was North Vietnamese attempts to conduct a war to reunify the two Vietnams, split as a result of the Geneva agreements. This required securing their flank in Laos and establishing a logistical route to support communist forces in South Vietnam—the Ho Chi Minh Trail. No country wants an enemy at their border. It was inevitable the North Vietnamese would use the Pathet Lao as their proxy to ensure Laos would not become pro-Western and impede their first strategic goal, the defeat of the French in Indochina, and later the defeat of the South Vietnamese government. The North Vietnamese held a long historical belief that most of Laos was really part of historical Vietnam, so in the long term it would need to be reincorporated back into the fold of a Vietnamese nation.

In addition, the overriding impact the Geneva Agreement had on the contending forces dictated the nature and style of the war in Laos. The United States always operated in Laos under the spirit and intent of the agreement, even though not being a signatory. Therefore, many of the military decisions made by the ambassadors in Laos were in the shadow of preventing potential opprobrium from the international community, always looking for violations of the Geneva neutrality posture and pressure to not widen the war, or introduce foreign military forces into the region. It was a naïve position and completely lacking in reality: the North Vietnamese basically ignored any restrictions to operations in Laos. So the war was fought with a geopolitical "wink and a nod" by all the contenders. Key to this approach was the need to operate overtly and keep public those things which complied with the Geneva Agreement (for example, the allowance for actions by the Royal Government to defend Laos); when needing to go beyond that, the war moved out of the public realm into the world of covertness, secrecy, and clandestine activities. It was labeled as "The Secret War" and the "Quiet War."

Position, Geography and Terrain, Transportation

Laos is about the size of Great Britain (or the state of Utah). Its northern half is comprised of rolling hill masses, limestone karsts, and triple-canopy jungle. In the northeast sits the Tran Ninh Plateau—the Plaine des Jarres (PDJ)—identified by its distinct features of rolling grasslands and woods. There are many tall, carved clay-stone jars spread throughout the plateau, which gives it its name. (The jars are believed to perhaps be burial urns from an ancient civilization.)

In the center is the Laotian panhandle, bordered on its eastern edge by the Annamite mountain chain (a physical barrier with Vietnam). The western edge of Laos holds the alluvial plains of the Mekong River and the border with Thailand. The base of Laos contains the Plateau des Bolovens, where many ex-French coffee plantations were situated. The pictorial image of a map of Laos is one of a large tree, or mushroom in shape, leaning to the left. It is also similar to Idaho, with its panhandle, if the image of Idaho is turned upside down.

Laos is a landlocked country dependent on the Mekong River as its major transit system to the south through Cambodia and on to the sea. There are few natural resources to sustain a robust economy. Like most of Southeast Asia, Laos is situated in terms of latitude and longitude in a tropical clime. It is primarily flat along the Mekong, a rice-growing basin, with the remainder of the country consisting of ever-increasing mountain ranges as one travels northeast, and east.

The Mekong River is the largest river system in Laos, flowing all the way from China, making up much of the western border of Laos, and down into Cambodia. In the central panhandle, the Xe Bang Fai was a contested river between government forces at Thakhek, Savannakhet, and Seno with the Pathet Lao and Neutralists in the Mahaxay region. In southern Laos, the Se Kong river flows from inside South Vietnam south through Attopeu and down into Cambodia. This river was also a part of the logistic trail of the Ho Chi Minh Trail network. (*Nam* is the Laotian word for river, used in northern Laos; *Xe* and *Se* are Laotian terms for rivers in southern Laos.)

Much of the mountainous regions and triple-canopy areas of Laos were inaccessible by government forces (lack of air and ground transport capability along with lack of roads). For most of the war, Pathet Lao and NVA forces dominated these regions. A commander could simply draw a crude line bisecting Laos from its north to its south and place government forces to the west of the line and Pathet Lao and NVA forces to the east, with two exceptions: the Plaine des Jarres plateau in the northwest, and the Plateau de Bolovens in the south. These two geographic terrain features would be contested by both sides. Where the few roads did exist, many crisscrossed both of these plateaus, a highly desirable feature for maneuverability and thus key terrain for control. The generally flat, rolling terrain, although open, allowed for the few places in Laos where motorized and armored operations could occur. Lines of operation ran along existing *route coloniales* (major roads), rivers (like the Xe Bang Fai in the panhandle), and river valleys (like Nam Bac). Other battles occurred on dominating terrain, generally mountaintops.

The remoteness and inaccessibility dictated by geography meant forces either moved on foot or on back of animals, or were restricted to vehicular traffic on the existing roads and tracks. The conduct of the war would require short takeoff and landing capability (STOL) aircraft and helicopters to overcome these barriers.

Where no roads existed in the jungle, or in hilly terrain, major trails and footpaths constituted the only means to rapidly move from one point to another. Unfortunately, hemmed in by the jungle, these spots became lucrative points to emplace ambushes.

In the hinterlands, transportation was limited to foot traffic or elephant, horse and ox cart where passage was wide enough.

The deficiency in roads impacted mobility for both Government forces and the Pathet Lao and NVA. There were no "mechanized" infantry battalions, armor being almost useless in the harsh terrain, with the exception of maneuver on the plateaus. The location of major military operations was predictable enough: along the existing major routes or valleys along major rivers. Operations also took more time than normal in order to plan for the infiltration and placement of forces, in phases. Key terrain during any battle became one of who could hold major intersections or dominating terrain to overlook the routes. Infantry forces were primarily footbound, after being dropped off by truck. One of the key solutions for Government forces to overcome this liability was the introduction of the helicopter, allowing for transport of major forces into an operational area. But even this advantage was limited by the amount of helicopters available and whenever the weather permitted.

The regional *bataillon parachutistes* served as the only effective rapid reaction force as they could be transported to the battle and inserted via C-47 airborne drops.

Transport of forces by fixed-wing aircraft also helped to overcome limited maneuver. Laos had improved airports at Luang Prabang, Vientiane, Savannakhet, and Pakse capable of handling aircraft up to the size of C-46, C-47, C-123, and in some cases C-130. When the CIA base at Long Tieng (Site 20A—the "Alternate") was built, the capability for large aircraft to use the airstrip was added, but was limited to daylight operations only. The major airstrips in these locations were hard-surface or PSP (perforated steel planking). Minor airstrips for cargo aircraft use were located in Nam Tha, Ban Houei Sai, Vang Vieng, Paksane, Attopeu, and the French military base at Seno.

Little communication infrastructure existed. Contact between villages and the major military cantonments was via long-range radio communications (HF, SSB), liaison aircraft flying into remote dirt airstrips, or ground messenger. There were no electrical lines outside of major cities, and access to electrical power was rare; power for many of the teams operating on the ground was via a generator.

The Lao People

In the 1950s there were an estimated two and a half to three million Laotians. About fifty percent were lowland dwellers of Tai extract, which were further divided into two branches: the Lao Loum (Chinese extract), and the Siamese (Tai). The Lao Loum were considered the ethnic Lao, populating the lowlands along the Mekong River and with cultural similarities to the Thai. They lived a sedentary culture, for the most part, and were wet-rice growers. This was a peaceful and non-confrontational ethnic group, which unfortunately would make up the bulk of the *tahans* (soldiers) of the Laotian Army.[5]

The Lao Thai prefer to live in upland, river valleys and were tribal in nature. For ethnic percentage counts they were grouped with the Lao Loum. They were agriculturalist who practiced *swidden* (slash and burn agriculture), mainly to grow rice, both wet and dry. They were distinguished by tribal colors, such as Black Thai, Red Thai, White Thai, and so forth, as worn and woven into their dress. The Lao Thai worked both for the Pathet Lao and for the Royal Government, mostly as village militia and Auto-Défense companies. They served as regional and local forces for the Pathet Lao.[6]

Society in the Lao Loum was dictated by one's place in a social hierarchy. Elites and established, aristocratic families held high places of government and society. Prominent family members were often the colonels and generals in the armed forces, often surrounded by other family members through a system of nepotism. This social structure prevented the growth of a professional and independent officer corps. It also created a cancerous elitism within the higher ranks of the officer corps. In some cases, the senior leadership in a military region resembled a form of warlordism fostering cronyism and corruption.

About thirty percent of the populace were Mon-Khmer living on mountain slopes (derisively called *khas*, or slaves), known as the Lao Theung. Most Lao Theung remained neutral during the war, but could be organized into 100-man defense forces if incentivized (money, weapons, food). In Operation *Pincushion*, the CIA, along with U.S. Army Special Forces teams, organized the Lao Thueng in the Bolovens Plateau area for operations against the Pathet Lao from 1961 through 1962. These types of guerrilla forces were employed again during the late 1960s.

The next largest minority population in Laos was the northern Lao Sung hill tribes (Sino-Tibetan extract) consisting of the Hmong (Meo) and Mien tribes who were considered a warrior class and made up about twenty percent of the population (of that, about eight percent were Hmong). The Hmong preferred to live in high altitudes. It was the Hmong in the north organized in Special Guerrilla Units, and then later in regiments under the *groupe mobile* system (GMs), who predominantly fought against NVA and Pathet Lao in the Plaine des Jarres region (Operation *Momentum*). The Hmong also used a color system to distinguish tribal affiliations—Red Hmong, Black Hmong, White Hmong, and the Striped Hmong being the four largest groupings.[7]

Chinese and Vietnamese ethnic groups made up the rest of the population. The two major languages in Laos were French and Lao. The Lao language is an extract of the Thai language and is very similar. For this reason, Special Forces teams were provided Thai interpreters to facilitate their mission. The interpreters were often from Thai intelligence forces, Thai Special Forces, and Thai police forces. (There were also numerous dialects among the hill tribes.)

The ethnic groupings lived separated from each other, causing a distrust between one another. The lowland Lao considered the highland Lao as social inferiors. This separation contributed to the weakening in national fervor to participate in the war: nationalism and patriotism did not exist to a high degree.

The Monsoon and other Weather Effects

Laos experiences two annual monsoon cycles. The first arrives from the southwest and drops its rain (and winds) beginning roughly in May and ending sometime in November. The second is a "dry" monsoon which lasts from November to May, the northeast monsoon. This monsoon bypasses Laos with its rains but it does bring cooler temperatures to the country, lasting into February. From February to May, temperatures rise to bring the hot and humid weather known throughout the region.

The "wet" and "dry" monsoons would dictate the timing of major operations in the Laotian war. During the wet period, operations requiring the movement of vehicles and troops were hampered by the muddy conditions of roads and trails. Ammunition became wet and unusable and uniforms and equipment were affected by mold and deterioration. In some cases, depending on the location, the training of Laotian forces ceased due to extremely heavy rains.

Clouds, mist and fog formed by the monsoon dictated the success or lack of airpower. With cloud cover, the Pathet Lao and NVA could conduct operations without fear of strafing and bombing from USAF and Royal Laotian Government (RLG) aircraft.

Government and Politics

The Kingdom of Laos was a constitutional monarchy and a form of parliamentary government which inherited an administrative and bureaucratic system from the French. It was a governing system run by elites and powerful families who viewed their time in government as a means to better themselves, their families, and their clans at the expense of the Laotian citizen. By its very design it fostered self-serving politicians without a sense of patriotism and nationalism required to address the internal security threat of the Pathet Lao. Like other facets of Laotian culture, society and geography, Laotian politics were characterized by regionalism, favoritism and nepotism. Corruption was an inevitable byproduct of the system. This lack of unity hampered efforts to mobilize and put the nation on a war footing, dooming the creation of a viable internal defense and development plan (IDAD) as a response to the insurgency. Bernard Fall noted during his time in Laos the effects of this "balkanization":

> What really counts in Laotian life is what happens to one's own clan in one's own valley. What happens elsewhere might just as well happen on the moon for all that it matters in the values of the local villagers. If the Laotian appears self-centered and un-interested in world events, it is certainly not of his own choosing; his country made him that way. Thus, "patriotism" in Laos is at best a furious regionalism.[8]

The king ruled Laos from the royal capital at Luang Prabang. The political, civil, and administrative government of Laos resided in Vientiane.

The country was divided into twelve provinces for governance. By the early 1960s, four new provinces were added, for a total of sixteen. The lowest polity in Laotian governance was the village, the *ban*. *Bans* were headed by an elder or a village chief. The village chief was called the *Náy Bān* or the *Phô Bān* (*Náy* or *Nai* means elder in the Laotian language).

This system led to immediate loyalties to the region, family, clan and tribe heading the various levels of government, all looking out for their self–interests. Any effective attempt at governance required forming coalitions from various political parties or neighboring clans and tribes. Government in Laos "evolved" into three political factions: Rightists, Leftists, and Neutralists which would plague attempts to create any unity. Politics played a role in the selection of senior military officers, with their choice based on loyalties and political leanings. In many cases, lowlanders mistrusted highlanders, southerners mistrusted northerners, and so on. This factionalism and regionalism would often hamper attempts to move forces from one province to assist in another province during major battles.

Lack of government services from Vientiane and the overtaxing of clans and tribes in remote regions, combined with the corruption inherent in this system of governance, gave the Pathet Lao plenty of grievances to harp on in the psychological operations and indoctrination techniques used with villagers.

The lack of forethought and investment at the central planning level and the hoarding of supplies, arms, and ammunition by "regional" military commanders doomed attempts to prepare for large-scale offensives on the part of the government and created an inefficient logistical system. These were the very factors of why the PEO planned to introduce American trainers and advisors into the mix in 1959. In addition, much of the U.S. support to the Royal Lao Army and the Royal Lao Air Force was predicated on how the winds blew in Laotian politics. In accordance with U.S. foreign policy, military aid flowed to those who were non-communist, anti-communist, and against neutrality.

To support Laos during the war, the American ambassadors used the tool of USAID and the Military Assistance Program dollars to turn off or turn on the spigot, based on the direction of Laotian politics; money and aid, and training and assistance would only happen if the Royal Laotian Government prevented the Pathet Lao from gaining entry into a coalition government.

Religion and Belief Systems

For Laotians, a belief in Buddhism on the part of lowland Lao and the worship of spirits and animism on the part of mountain tribes were factors in their combat performance.

Laotian troops were often described as serene, lazy and non-caring, and often relying on fate to determine the outcome of things rather than take matters into their own hands. The illiteracy rate was high: common Laotians scorned education as something for the elites. Buddha would dictate their lot in life, not a piece of paper from a school degree. Commanders often lacked concern for the future welfare of their troops, preferring to live in the "now."

At the level of the soldier, Laotian units were extremely hesitant to kill other human beings, and often left the fate of battles in the hands of Buddha. (Running away often solved the dilemma.) Tom Humphus, a *White Star* veteran with Laotian troops in the Mahaxay region, 1961–62, recalled: "The Lao are reluctant to go on offense—they don't like to kill people. However, the Lao can fire some mortars. They will bring scorn on you. I asked them once, 'Hey, how do you fire mortars so effectively if you do not want to kill anything?' They replied, 'Because it is up to Buddha. We only put the round in the mortar, but where it goes and what it does after that is not us, it is in the hands of Buddha.'"[9]

The Buddhist religion was administered by *bonzes*—Buddhist monks—and was community-centered around the religious edifice, the *wat* (pagoda). Buddhism was practiced by the lowland Lao. The belief in karma manifested as a lack of concern for long-term effects on life or a worry about what the future could bring. The bulk of the Royal Armed Forces were Buddhists, as was its leadership. It was extremely difficult to impart strategic planning within the high command and develop an effective counterinsurgency response which might take years to prove fruitful (based on this sense of fatalism).

Many of the Buddhist soldiers wore a Buddha amulet to ward off enemy fire. Amulets were also hung on barbed-wire around defensive positions to ward off evil intentions from the enemy and to provide protection. American advisors took note of this practice and incorporated this belief system into training and tactics, to their benefit. They also often wore an amulet themselves, as a show of solidarity. Colonel (Retired) Vladimir Sobichevsky explained:

> They wore Buddhas around their neck. It's kind of interesting, and I found out that that they believed that the Buddha around their neck would deflect a round shot at them. I guess it was comical, because they would test the Buddha. They would put this little Buddha on a tree stump and shoot at it. If they would miss, they were happy. *Jopa la lai! Jopa la Lai!* If they hit it and shattered it, they were also happy because they discovered that it was a bad Buddha. *Bo choap! Bo choap! Bo choap Buddha!*[10]

The Spirit World

In the tribal world, and in the world of other non-Buddhists living in the mountains of Laos, spirit worship was practiced. There was also some animism practice and ancestor cult-worship. The spirit world was dominated by *phi* (various spirits). *Phi* could be found in the body (thirty-two guardian spirits known as *khwăn*) which regulated the body to keep it in balance. There were also earth spirits, found in the trees, rocks, forests, streams, and other inanimate objects. Tribal villages normally each had a spirit house for the *phi* to reside (small replica houses built on a pole). Within individual homes, *phi* served as house and family guardians.

Steve Schofield was assigned to the 1SFG on Okinawa after he completed training group at Smoke Bomb Hill, Fort Bragg, North Carolina. From Okinawa, he went on temporary duty (TDY) to SOG as a replacement for a medic who was wounded and evacuated. After he returned to Okinawa, he was recruited by USAID, serving five and a half years as the USAID Public Health Advisor for Military Region II in Laos (working with Edgar "Pop" Buell). His primary responsibility was to manage the village health program, but he also had a classified mission to train and equip the Hmong Special Guerrilla Unit's medics and to perform search and rescue (SAR) for downed U.S. and Allied air crews. He remembers the aspects of *phi* and spirit worship during his tour in Laos:

> Hmong often feared the bad Phi that lived in certain rivers or mountains. It was said the Hmong would stand and fight to the death before they would cross a river. (It could also be that I never knew a Hmong who could swim!) Phou Bia, the highest mountain in Laos, was said to be inhabited by the bad Phi. When treating villagers in remote area, I would often ask the local Shaman to work with me so as we could combine our treatments. The Buddha amulet: They were triangular or square medallions with a thong or metal necklace, and with a picture of Buddha in the middle. The rim and Buddha were often gold or silver. They could also be made of stone, ivory, or jade. It had to be given to you, along with the strings of friendship tied around your wrist.[11]

The understanding and implementation of *phi* worship was conducted by the shaman and *phi* masters, known as the *măw*. Shamans performed ceremonies by covering their heads in black cloth and then bouncing up and down, in order to make a connection with the spirit world for consultations.

The knowledge of the *phi* and ancestor worship was important to the daily life of the Special Forces advisor. If ranges and landing zones needed creating, it was important to consult the locals and conduct a ceremony to please the *phi* of chopped down trees and cleared rocks and bushes.

Staff Sergeant Robert G. "Bob" Willis served on Captain Nagorski's FTT, training Kha Guerrilla Unit K-8, near Saravane in 1962. Pleasing the *phi* became essential one day to their mission: "One day, Lieutenant Colonel 'Bull' Simons flew in via a STOL aircraft. We had a very roughly built airfield. Obstructing the airfield was a 'spirit tree' the Laotians did not want us to remove. After Lieutenant Colonel Simons' pilot almost crashed making the landing, he had me send a message back to headquarters to airdrop some *kip* so we could have a ceremony, kill some buffalo and eat it, and demo the tree! He took off with no problem!"[12]

Respect for various traditions concerning the *phi* was important in building relationships with tribal elders. Shaman healing was often performed in conjunction with modern medical procedures conducted by Special Forces medics.

The French Military Training Mission

Even though France granted independence to Laos and allowed it to form a new government within the French Union, the French desired to militarily protect its investment in Laos and moved to form and develop the Royal Lao Army—primarily as a security hedge against the Viet Minh and the Pathet Lao. The Royal Lao Army (called the National Lao Army—the NLA—by the Laotians but titled in French as the Armée Nationale de Laos) would remain under the command and control of the French in order to ensure that its organization, doctrine and training conformed to the French Union Army's military standards. The French forces in Laos were called the Forces Terrestres du Laos and commanded by a French colonel.

In 1950 the government of France sent forty officers and sixty NCOs to Vientiane to begin their advisory and training duties under the name of the Mission Militaire Française Pres le Gouvernement Royal Laos—MMF/GRL. (A separate set of advisors and trainers was sent shortly thereafter to perform the function of training the military police—the Gendarmerie Royale.)[13]

The MMF/GRL reported to French forces in Hanoi, not the Laotian minister of defense. Training of Laotian soldiers was conducted in the French language by the soldiers of the MMF/GRL and French military doctrine was thoroughly incorporated into all instruction. The training consisted of basic soldier skills, technical training in such things as vehicle operations and maintenance. Officer and NCO schools were established. Select members of the RLA, with high motivation and education would be chosen by merit and sent to advanced military leadership, staff, and technical courses in France. In time, these types of schools would be established inside Laos with a wider array of technical courses added (communications, medical skills, and other subjects). In 1952 training courses were added for the fledgling Royal Laotian Air Force and the Laotian Navy's River Flotilla.[14]

A hallmark of this evolutionary period for the RLA was the mistreatment, animosity, and downright contempt the French displayed toward the Laotians. The French military training mission appeared reluctant to conduct more than basic skills training and never trained the Laotian army how to plan and conduct higher-level military operations, reserving this role for themselves. There certainly was no introduction of the tactics and techniques required by the Lao security forces to confront the Pathet Lao through a proper counterinsurgency campaign. Lao military leaders and units were not given the skills training required to perform this function.

By 1954, with the defeat of the French at Dien Bien Phu, the leadership of the RLA began the transition from French control to Laotian control, incorporating the old French Union Army forces remaining inside Laos into the RLA, with a subsequent end-strength of about 17,000 soldiers. Even with this new autonomy, the RLA could not divest themselves of French military manuals, staff papers in French, and French training techniques, all due to lack of funding and the difficulty in translating French military terms into the Laotian language.[15]

The PEO was established in light of the adherence to the restrictions of the 1954 Geneva Agreement which did not allow for the United States to place a military assistance advisory group (MAAG) in Laos. Under the USOM (the embassy's United States Operations Mission), U.S. military equipment and funding had been channeled through French forces in Hanoi. With the French high command gone from Vietnam, and the Laotian army now running itself, the U.S. required a direct conduit (the PEO) to provide arms and equipment to the RLG. In this arrangement, however, the French MMG/GRL still maintained authority over Laotian army training matters.

Soon, the small PEO staff (mostly retired military servicemen operating in civilian clothes) began to deploy in small teams out to the military regions in order to monitor the disbursement and care of equipment from the U.S. Military Assistance Program. How the equipment was to be used and incorporated, however, remained under French control.

As American aid and influence increased, French influence waned. French equipment and arms were no longer coming to Laos. Adapting to this situation, in 1960 the French Military Mission was changed to become the Mission Militaire Française d'Instruction Pres le Gouvernement Royal du Laos (MMFI/GRL). Cooperation with U.S. trainers ended in February of 1961 when the agreement lapsed.[16]

A reduced French contingent would remain in Laos until the Communist takeover of Laos in 1975.

The Enemy Threat: The Pathet Lao (Land of the Lao)

The internal security threat in Laos emanated from the Pathet Lao, a communist movement which used both subversion and "armed struggle" with its military forces to contest the Royal Laotian Government throughout the country. Ho Chi Minh should rightly be considered as the grandfather, architect, and mentor of this revolutionary movement, beginning with his creation of the Indochinese Communist Party (ICP) in 1930.

At its best, the Pathet Lao could be viewed as a nationalist, independence organization dedicated to uniting the various factions in Laos to free it from the yokes of imperialism. The Pathet Lao campaigned on the notion of loyalty to the Kingdom of Laos, social justice, and respect for ethnic and religious factions throughout the country. On several occasions the Pathet Lao announced their willingness to participate in a coalition government. At its worst, which proved to be the case upon its negotiated political victory in 1975, it was exactly what communist movements in the Cold War transpired to be—a totalitarian movement, a proxy and surrogate for the North Vietnamese, and a ruling power infused with the ideology of Maoist and Marxist-Leninist principles.

The goals of the Pathet Lao resistance front were unification of the Lao people, social reform (vis-à-vis a communist model), and expulsion of imperialists (the French and later the United States). The movement claimed to be neutralist, but relied on the Viet Minh, and later North Vietnam for its external support.

Organization

The People's Party of Laos (Phak Pasason Lao) provided the direction for all political and military operations of the Pathet Lao. The Pathet Lao armed forces (the Lao People's Liberation Army—LPLA) were subordinate to this body. Pathet Lao Supreme Headquarters was located in Sam Neua, where an abundance of caves among the limestone karsts provided concealment and protection from air bombardment and artillery fires. Phomvihan Kaysone (a resistance fighter since the 1940s) was the overall commander and principal leader at the central headquarters. Khamtay Siphandone was the commander-in-chief of LPLA; General Phomma was the commander of regional forces in south Laos.[17]

The LPLA was organized in a tiered structure. The regulars of its armed force were formed into line battalions along with supporting structure for communications, logistics, medical, and transport. The battalions were organized into line companies, platoons and squads. Although the exact structure of the battalions was not known, one can surmise the battalions included units for reconnaissance and heavy weapons platoons among its companies. Regular line battalions were the best equipped and most proficient of the Pathet Lao fighting forces. Regular line battalions were augmented by independent companies, called *ekalat*, which reinforced the regulars and the NVA when large operations occurred in their region.[18]

In 1969, RLG and U.S. intelligence agencies estimated the strength of the Pathet Lao regulars at 110 battalions deployed across Laos. This would have given the Pathet Lao an effective fighting strength of 28,270 fighters and 16,400 command and support troops, for a total of 44,670 men.[19]

The second tier of the LPLA consisted of regional forces (district/canton). Regional forces fought at the district level. In some respects, these forces were more agile and adept than the regulars due to familiarity of their area of operations and ties to the supporting civilian populace for information, food, lodging and medical care. The composition of these forces may have ranged from between twenty and eighty men in each unit. Exact estimates of their total number were never ascertained by intelligence sources.

The final tier level of fighters was the village militia. These were basically home guard-type forces, probably not very well equipped and clothed in local garb, similar to Viet Cong guerrillas in South Vietnam. Village level forces were headed by a canton military leader, with supervision over a cluster of villages. They operated at the squad level, and if large enough, platoon level, with perhaps eight to ten men and women in a village unit. Again, it was impossible for the government to ascertain the total number of these forces; nor was it possible to estimate the numbers of populace who acted as auxiliaries to support the Pathet Lao as part-time guides, scouts, lookouts, preparation of booby traps, and other supporting tasks. The population also served as a means of financial and logistics support. The Pathet Lao levied taxes on villagers for both money and for food, mainly rice quotas, to feed the troops.

As are all guerrilla movements, the Pathet Lao was lightly armed at first, with a variety of World War-II arms, much of it captured from the French and the Lao territorial forces. As North Vietnam increased their support, the Pathet Lao became equipped with heavier communist-bloc weaponry.

The Enemy Threat: The North Vietnamese Army (PAVN)

After the 1954 Geneva Accords the Viet Minh became the People's Army of Viet Nam (PAVN) but were generally referred to as the North Vietnamese Army (NVA). Strategically, the leaders of North Vietnam did not desire to conquer and occupy Laos nor was there any desire to establish a North Vietnamese-run government in Vientiane. North Vietnamese leaders may have feared a larger intervention by U.S. forces and knew they could face international condemnation if the NVA moved to take major Laotian cities along the Mekong valley (violations of the Geneva agreements). This task would fall to the Pathet Lao and the Laotian communists, who were directed, controlled and supported as proxy agents and surrogates for the North Vietnamese.

The North Vietnamese Army was employed in Laos to conduct three strategic endeavors. The first was to maintain border security between Laos and both South and North Vietnam. The second strategic effort was to support the Pathet Lao in their fight against the RLG. The NVA ensured gains made by the Pathet Lao were not lost during the government's counteroffensives. The NVA worked hard to ensure a buffer area remained in communist control, allowing full advantage for their forces to cross from North Vietnam into Laos unhindered and to provide a base area for the Pathet Lao. In time, the NVA would take the primary role in this endeavor, using the Pathet Lao in a supporting effort. The third strategic task, and considered the primary goal, was to establish logistic lines of control in what would become the Ho Chi Minh Trail.

The defeat of the South Vietnamese was paramount in the communist strategy for victory. This would require a long-term effort for building and protecting the trail as an infiltration pipeline for equipment, arms and soldiers into South Vietnam, as well as serve as a cross-border sanctuary to Viet Cong and NVA forces. From the Ho Chi Minh Trail's initial creation to the end of the Laotian war in the mid-1970s, NVA forces operated almost with impunity from any the attempt of the RLG to interfere with this operation.

NVA offenses tended to follow the monsoonal wet and dry periods. The dry period in Laos, roughly from the fall to late spring, was more advantageous to NVA movement when roads were good, troops and equipment did not suffer the debilitating effects of rain, and attacking forces could maneuver and conduct fires with good visibility.

To assist the Pathet Lao the NVA established a training and advisory command headquarters on the Laotian border, *Doan* 100 (Group 100), after the Geneva agreements. This 300-man unit was commanded by Colonel Chu Huy Man. A hundred of their cadre were assigned as political advisors to the LPLA.[20]

In this early period, the NVA did not directly interfere in the Pathet Lao efforts; rather, they maintained a posture to prepare for a political victory by the Pathet Lao in a coalition government. However, the NVA was prepared to militarily support the Pathet Lao if ever the RLG capitulated from communist military offensives.

In 1959, with the collapse of the Laotian efforts to form a coalition government, the NVA began integrating their forces among the Pathet Lao. To command and control this increased effort, *Doan* 100 was replaced with *Doan* 959, which was now forward-headquartered in Sam Neua Province. In July of that year, North Vietnam provided arms and equipment to the LPLA and Pathet Lao for their attacks on FAR outposts in the two northern provinces.

NVA troops were respected in their fighting ability by both RLG and Pathet Lao forces. The Pathet Lao military arm—the LPLA—considered the NVA to be "well trained, unusually well disciplined, militarily competent, and possessed of high morale."[21]

It was at this same time Hanoi understood the need to expand its war into South Vietnam. This would require securing the Laotian panhandle region in order to build an infiltration trail into South Vietnam—the Ho Chi Minh Trail. NVA operations began on the trail in 1959. Throughout the war, the NVA command would establish additional *Doans* for specific functions: tactical areas of responsibility, logistics, and other functions.

The *Doans* reported to two major NVA commands directing the war in Laos: the Northwest Military Region located at Son La in North Vietnam, responsible for the six northern provinces of Laos, and the Fourth Military Region Command in Vinh, responsible for the six central and southern provinces of Laos.[22] In 1960, the NVA established a series of border defense battalions. These units were under the command of provincial military commands with the mission to operate into Laos for up to fifty kilometers. Their primary role was to ensure RLG forces did not operate in this fifty-kilometer zone, thus ensuring a security buffer and flank protection of NVA and Pathet Lao forces. The border defense battalions were manned by 500–600 NVA. As time went on, the border defense battalions would assume main force battalion missions against RLG forces.[23]

In time, the NVA began to operate in a more aggressive manner by employing divisional-level units in northern Laos.

The NVA Organization

There were three categories of NVA: military advisors, "volunteers," and main force, mobile units. Early in the war, the advisors and volunteers wore Pathet Lao military clothing in order to blend in, but by the late 1960s this pretense was dropped and NVA forces wore regular NVA clothing.

The NVA worked to remain separate from the Pathet Lao and the local population. The NVA kept their activities low key and concealed in order to ensure the Pathet Lao appeared as the defenders of the people. Although the NVA supported Pathet Lao offensives, rarely did any members of the USSF *Hotfoot* and *White Star* teams confront NVA soldiers. This would change in the mid-1960s when Project 404 SOF personnel experienced attacks on RLG forces they were advising on the Plaine des Jarres by the NVA. During the battle of Moung Soui, Project 404 personnel were hastily evacuated when RLG forces came under attack from NVA units of the 335th, 174th, and the 924th independent battalions.

The NVA was a predominantly infantry force, organized by divisions, brigades, regiments and battalions. These units were backed up with regional battalions and volunteer battalions.

In 1968, NVA forces in Laos were estimated at 40,000 troops; by 1970 this had grown to an estimated 67,000 troops, with 25,000 of those employed on operations to support the HCM Trail.[24]

During the period 1970 through 1971, the NVA conducted division-sized attacks on the Plaine des Jarres, brigade-sized operations in central Laos, and division-sized attacks in southern Laos in the Bolovens Plateau region. NVA operations in 1972 and 1973 were conducted in light of the ongoing Paris peace talks and consisted of jockeying for advantageous positions before a ceasefire was forced on them.

Government Forces: The Forces Armée Royales (FAR)

In July of 1959 the Laotian army was spread across five military regions and operated at the battalion level. First called the Armée Nationale Laotienne (ANL), they were newly designated as the Forces Armée Laotienne (FAL). In September of 1961, they would assume the title of Forces Armée Royales (FAR), which would last until their disbandment.

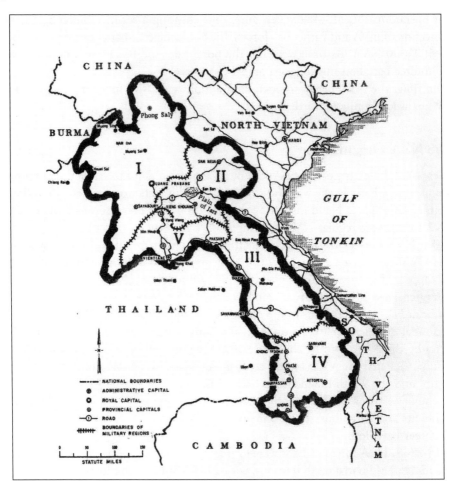

Map of Laotian military regions sourced from DARPA report "Suitability and Effectiveness of Weapons and Equipment Used in U.S.-Supported Operations with the Royal Laos Army (U)." Research Analysis Corporation, Staff Paper RAC-SP-1 (SEA), September 1962.

The military region commanders reported to the ministry of defense in Vientiane. A military regional commander exclusively controlled forces within his military region and had no responsibility for combat operations outside his territory. The *bataillon parachutistes* performed this out of sector role, as mobile reserves.

Laotian army forces consisted of three elements: the 25,000 infantry and paratroopers in their line battalions (BI—*bataillon infanterie* and BP—*bataillon parachutistes*), about 40,000 in the volunteer battalions (BV—*bataillon volontaires*) and the home defense and village defense forces (ADC—the Auto-Défense de Choc, also called the Maquis).

The allotment to regional commanders for ground forces was one battalion of BI and one battalion of BV for each province within their military district. In 1959, there were twelve provinces in Laos. In some cases, the military region commander also had the use of a separate regional battalion (*bataillon regionale*—BR). The amount of ADC units varied based on assets to recruit, train, and equip local defense forces.

The senior commander of each military region employed his forces around major towns, with a mix of outposts (no doubt influenced by the French hedgehog system and the forts and camps within each region, left over from the French territorial and French Union forces tactical deployments against the Viet Minh). Outposts and remote camps were reinforced with the *bataillon volontaires* units and ADC forces. *Bataillon volontaires* were responsible for the training of ADC forces in their military region.

If well led, adequately trained, and cared for, Laotian infantry battalions gave a good account of themselves against enemy forces. Unfortunately, in many units, the lack of quality leadership and leader corruption lowered the morale and discipline of a unit. The political leaning of the unit and the makeup of its ethnicity also had a bearing on how Laotian army units performed.[25]

Overall, the Laotian army was a light infantry defensive force, stationed near major population centers and near critical infrastructure.

The Neutralist Army—Forces Armée Neutralistes (FAN)

After the coup by Captain Kong Le was thwarted in December of 1960, he defected with his 2nd Parachute Battalion to safety and established the Neutralist Army on the Plaine des Jarres. Other elements of the Lao army throughout Laos defected and joined the Neutralist cause. This created a schism in the FAR, denying to them the troops and equipment needed in their fight against the NVA and the Pathet Lao. By December of 1962, Captain Kong Le, now self-proclaimed as the General of the FAN, had 4,500 troops in Military Region II, with another 5,500 troops in other MRs (along Route 13 in vicinity of Vang Vieng and in MR-III vicinity of Mahaxay, as examples).

In mid-1963, the NVA and Pathet Lao attacked the FAN. From that point forward there was a loose coalition between the FAR and the FAN against the enemy threat. The United States recognized the coalition and began supplying FAN forces. Soon after, the FAN resembled the FAR in uniforms and equipment, but were generally ineffective during major clashes with enemy forces.

The Irregular Forces

The Hmong guerrillas were initially considered like ADCs, and grouped into GM-B in Military Region II. When General Vang Pao's Hmong forces began organizing as special guerrilla units (SGUs) under the pay and control of the CIA (Operation *Momentum*), the Hmong military units were dropped from the payrolls of the FAR. *White Star* teams assisted in the training and advising of the SGUs. As the Hmong forces grew and became more involved in conventional-style operations in 1963, the SGUs grew into battalion-sized units and were finally organized in a series of *groupe mobiles* by 1967, beginning with the number 2, to designate forces in MR-II. Thus, GM-21, GM-22 and so forth, were activated.

In the south, a similar program was initiated, the Kha tribal guerrilla program, under the CIA's Operation *Pincushion*. *White Star* teams ran this program under the control of CIA assets. These forces were not considered as part of the force structure of the FAR. They were disbanded as a result of the Geneva agreements in the summer of 1962. In the late 1960s, the irregular forces program in the south and in other MRs was resurrected. In 1970, the countrywide SGUs were renamed as *bataillon gujerriers* (BGs).

Other Government Military Services

Laos maintained a small navy, primarily equipped with patrol boats and old landing craft. The Lao navy was used to patrol accessible areas of the Mekong, but was too small and ineffective to contribute militarily to the wider war. The Lao navy could have possibly developed a riverine warfare capability, given a robust security assistance program, but the Lao navy in this role was never considered by the military attachés in the U.S. embassy.

The Royal Laotian Air Force started as a fledgling service under the control of the Lao army, but with military assistance and the combat advisory assistance from the USAF Air Commandos, performed well until the government's collapse in 1975. The mainstay aircraft of the RLAF were the T-28, C-47 and H-34 helicopter, formed in squadrons at four major military airfields: Vientiane, Luang Prabang, Pakse, and Savannakhet (and later, a squadron at Long Tieng).

Operational Assessment

All of these historic, geographic, cultural, religious and military and political variables would dictate a war fought in remote and rugged terrain, where mobility was limited. Coalition interoperability between the French and the United States would strain military relations at the tactical level. Key roads and intersections would dictate terrain to be fought over and controlled. Lack of access to remote villages allowed the Pathet Lao and NVA to operate in some areas with impunity; these areas were often ceded to the enemy by the RLG. Command and control was limited, often to how far one could see into the jungle.

The length of operations and battles was often dictated by air assets and the provisioning of forces to keep them extended out in the field. The monsoon seasons dictated the timing of major offensives, for both sides. The fighting prowess of the individual soldier, based on his leadership, training, equipment and belief system often meant short firefights which were quickly broken off, much to the frustration of American advisors.

The RLG and the FAR were unable to convert any of their tactical gains into strategic effect; the military forces of Laos were not prepared to serve as counter-insurgency forces and prevent communist gains among the rural populace. U.S. financial and military aid, passed through the hands of corrupt politicians and the French military advisors, was failing to achieve U.S. policy goals of preventing the spread of communism in Laos. To prevent further deterioration, U.S. policymakers looked to bolster Laotian military capabilities all the while skirting the prohibitions of the Geneva agreements. The choice to deploy U.S. Army Special Forces allowed decision-makers an economy of force option (if applied clandestinely), buy time to allow American diplomacy to work, and reassure allies in the region of U.S. determination.

PART II

AMERICAN MILITARY ASSISTANCE

CHAPTER TWO

Hotfoot: Army Special Forces Deploy to Laos

"By this time, the French had pretty much pulled out of Laos, but there was still one French team left nearby and they were to monitor what we taught and ensure we did not give any tactical training to the Lao Army. This was an agreement between governments. The American 'civilians' were only to train the Lao soldiers on the equipment they'd be given by the U.S."

JAMES C. WILLIAMS (MSG, U.S.A., RET.)
A GREEN BERET'S JOURNEY

One of the contributions of SOF to achieve strategic utility is being employed as an economy of force measure when larger, and more conventional military forces are inappropriate. This was the case in Laos due to the Geneva Agreement restrictions prohibiting the use of foreign forces and denial for any foreign military bases in the country. At a low cost, the deployment of U.S. Army Special Forces into Laos in 1959 provided a solution to the French and Lao mismanagement of the U.S. Military Assistance Program administered under the control of the French military training mission. There were other strategic benefits. As noted by Colin S. Gray in his work *Explorations in Strategy*, choosing a special operations course of action in lieu of conventional forces helped to slow the pace of military failure on the part of the Laotian army, helped to reassure allies in a region confronting communism, secured support from American policy-makers (plausible deniability), and provided a "stiffener" to both the Laotian army and the Royal Laotian Government.[1]

In 1958, Brigadier General John A. Heintges provided the U.S. government a study and assessment on the security situation in Laos. Due to the poor performance of Lao army troops against the Pathet Lao, and the misuse of military aid and equipment provided by the United States, General Heintges recommended the inclusion of American military trainers alongside the French Military Mission trainers to remedy the deficiencies. This initiative was bolstered by King Sisavang Vong's desire to improve his military with the use of American trainers. Heintges, now the PEO commander in Vientiane, coordinated with the commander of the MMF, Major General Jean d'Arrivere, to develop a concept along these lines. Their proposal was forwarded through both American and French channels, but was resoundingly condemned or stonewalled by the French government, with reasonable concerns for violations of the Geneva Agreement.

U.S. concerns on the matter, and the composition of a U.S. military training contingent based on General Heintges's plan, were identified in an excerpt from Memo for Record discussions between Ambassador Houghton and Mr. Quarles conducted with Minister of Defense Guillaumat on January 13, 1959:

> I touched briefly on General Heintges' proposal to take in twelve battalion training teams in which perhaps ten Americans would be associated with four French officers and NCOs, and also mentioned the eighty or so Philippine experts now in the country. M. Guillaumat indicated a generally sympathetic attitude toward the objectives of General Heintges' program but said he understood their Foreign Office found difficulties with it in relation to the Geneva Agreement limiting the build-up of combatant forces in the area. He asked if we had opened up the subject with their Foreign Office and I indicated that we had and that we would pursue it there with any support he felt he might be able to give us.[2]

After lengthy diplomatic discussions, and French acquiescence, the two sides met in Paris in May of 1959 to outline the plan. During the meeting there was agreement by the French for the United States to provide trainers at all the major Laotian training centers, working alongside their French military counterparts. The American proposal consisted of providing eight men alongside eight French counterparts, formed as combined training and advisory teams. The arrangement took into account the rotation of the ANL's twelve infantry battalions through the four Lao national training centers and would take one year to complete. At first the French intended to limit all the training to their base at Seno (an unworkable plan),[3] but agreement was reached to utilize training centers in Luang Prabang, Vientiane, Savannakhet, and Pakse. Along with training Laotian infantry battalions, the combined U.S.–French teams would also provide cadre for artillery, armor, and NCO/officer schools.

Selecting U.S. Army Special Forces

The 77th Special Forces Group (Airborne) was part of the global response force in the 1950s. When the combined training agreement was reached between the U.S. and France, Pentagon planners first thought to fill the requirement with Army or Marine teams. Fortuitously, Colonel Donald D. Blackburn, the 77th SFG commander, was in the Pentagon and advocated for the use of U.S. Army Special Forces detachments—already organized in teams to train foreign forces in infantry skills and adept at working with other cultures. (Blackburn was well known for his involvement with a guerrilla movement in the Philippines during World War II.) The 77th SFG was subsequently selected to fill the trainer requirement in Laos.

Colonel Blackburn returned to Fort Bragg and began preparations for the mission. He chose Lieutenant Colonel Arthur D. "Bull" Simons, commanding FB-3, to lead the first deployment. (Simons had served with the 6th Rangers who conducted the famous raid on the Cabantuan prison camp in the Philippines during World War II.)

With a request from Colonel Blackburn, a team of experts from both the Pentagon and the State Department arrived at Fort Bragg to begin area, cultural, and history briefings for the men, along with a months-long training regimen to prepare the troops for the deployment. The CIA also provided subject-matter experts to provide background briefings. Thai paratroopers were sent to Fort Bragg to assist in the training.

Detachment personnel were required to read the little literature existing at the time about Laos and Southeast Asia, most notably, books such as *The Quiet American* by Graham Greene (1955). Later in 1960, detachment members read the popular book *The Centurions*, written by Jean Lartéguy about the French paratroopers' experiences combating insurgency in Indochina and later in Algeria.

OPSEC (operational security) was paramount; the mention of the word "Laos" was highly forbidden. The teams called Laos "Ooogie Boogie Land." Along with modified isolation procedures, teams conducted individual skills and cross-skills training, weapons training, PSYOP training, and medical training. Field training exercises were conducted to hone fieldcraft and tactical skills. Language training consisted of classes in French and in the Lao language. Some teams were given training in cooking classes to prepare them for living in team houses in Laos; bulldozer operations were given to one team in anticipation of the variety of ranges and training facilities which were anticipated to be constructed upon their arrival.

Team members were given a clothing allowance of $400 dollars to purchase civilian clothes for the mission; the local department stores benefited greatly.

While all these preparations were being made, Colonel Blackburn flew to Laos to meet with General Heintges to further clarify the mission. It was during those meetings he found out the secret nature of the mission—his men would deploy in civilian clothes, with diplomatic cover provided by the embassy (Special Forces team members would be classified as civilian technicians of a U.S. Geodetic Survey Team). The mission required deployment into Laotian army training areas, and in consort with the French Military Mission, to train the twelve Laotian infantry battalions in small arms and individual proficiency skills. Tactical training and employment of crew-served weapons was left to French tutelage (per the agreement). The Operation was codenamed *Hotfoot*. The program was sponsored by the embassy's Programs Evaluation Office, and run as the Laotian Training and Advisory Group—LTAG.[4]

U.S. Special Forces Field Training Teams (FTTs)—twelve eight-man Operational Detachment Alphas, the ODAs—and the battalion control team (in all totaling 107 men), began deployment to Laos in July of 1959. Two C-124s departed Pope Air Force Base with their destination as Bangkok, Thailand. However, continuing disagreements between the French and U.S. negotiators caused a delay in the arrival of the teams. The *Hotfoot* contingent remained in Oakland, California a few days, then spent a little over a week at Wake Island, followed by a week delay in northern Okinawa until the finalized agreement to field the U.S. teams was reached. (This delay caused an extension in *Hotfoot I* rotation in order to meet the agreed six months in country; *Hotfoot I* served an additional month, not leaving Laos until the end of January 1960.)

Upon arrival to Don Muang airport in Bangkok, the task force was trans - loaded onto Air America aircraft and deployed into Laos. To circumvent the Geneva restrictions on introducing additional, permanent U.S. military personnel into Laos, the contingent was placed on six-month TDY orders in order to not exceed the number. Upon arrival in-country, team members were issued embassy ID cards, some being labeled as government service employees (GS-5 to GS-11 level) and reminded they could not wear distinguishing haircuts, tattoos, dog tags, nor carry weapons, nor participate in fighting during their six-month training mission. They would perform their duties as "contracted civilian technicians" and remain in civilian clothes.[5]

This caused consternation among the military command as to what the legal status of SF team members would be if captured by enemy forces. The military preferred to wear military uniforms and identifying insignia in order to be treated as military POWs if captured by enemy forces, under the provisions of the Geneva–Hague accords. This option was disregarded in order to maintain the cover story.

The eight-man U.S. advisory and training team composition consisted of a detachment commander and his XO, a team sergeant, a weapons expert, a medic, a demolitions expert, one radio operator, and a mechanic (all mechanics on the teams were provided from the 82nd Airborne Division at Fort Bragg). Each training team was provided one or two Thai interpreters.[6] Thai interpreters were "volunteers" from the Thai army, and were usually Special Forces-trained, or a Police Aerial Reinforcement Unit (PARU) member, or were military intelligence specialists. (The Thai language was close enough to Lao to be understood during the training.)

In July of 1959, the ANL became the Forces Armée Laotienne (FAL).

The *Hotfoot* task organization consisted of the battalion control team in Vientiane (the participating SF battalion became an FC—Field Control Team for Laos) with three FTTs in Military Region I (who were involved mostly with building and opening up a new training center and Ranger school camp outside of Vientiane)[7], and three FTTs assigned to each of the training areas in Luang Prabang, Savannakhet, and Pakse. No B team command and control elements were deployed during the initial *Hotfoot* rotations (they would deploy later when *White Star* rotations began and the number of teams increased in Laos). Command and control of the FTTs ran directly from the Field Control Team in Vientiane down to the SF detachments. To handle matters of administration and control at the training centers, the senior detachment commander of one of the three FTTs at each location usually adjudicated matters. Each team established a radio base station at their locale, using the AN/GRC-109 (RS-1) radio.

Upon mission assignment, each team was given a designation as an FA (Field Detachment-A) followed by a number; on the ground the teams normally adopted the name of their detachment commander to identify themselves. (Thus, Team *Moon*, Team *Korcheck*, Team *Ipsen*, Team *Roy*, and so forth.)

The training of individual infantry skills to Lao line infantry battalions was not the only task for the FTTs. The FAs also helped to train Laotian armor contingents, artillery batteries, and helped to initiate NCO schools (in each military region), along with police training (Savannakhet) and assisting in the establishment of the National Officer's School at Dong Hene.

There would ultimately be three full, six-month rotations for Operation *Hotfoot*. The first two satisfied the agreement to provide Laotian line battalion training, for one year. When the year-long training was completed, only about sixty to seventy percent of the officer and NCO training was actually accomplished. The embassy team negotiated for a six-month extension to complete the task. However, after the August 1960 Kong Le coup d'état (during the third rotation of *Hotfoot*), the French Military Mission withdrew from the combined training initiative in protest of the American support for General Phoumi Nosovan's actions to remove Kong Le from Vientiane. This paved the way for the authorization of *Hotfoot* teams to accompany the Laotians on combat operations and to expand some of their training to the BVs as Rotation IV of *Hotfoot* deployed into Laos, December of 1960.

The initial three *Hotfoot* rotations could be characterized as:

- Rotation I: initial establishment of the training program, building of training facilities, and overcoming the animosity of the French along with cultural obstacles from Laotian commanders and troops (the *tahans*); the rotation also involved the surreptitious attempts by American trainers to train Laotians in tactical operations, through night training
- Rotation II: expansion into Military Region II (the NCO and officer school at Khang Khay) and beginnings of the unconventional warfare (UW) training with the Hmong
- Rotation III: the coup d'état by paratrooper Captain Kong Le and the involvement of *Hotfoot* teams in the counter-revolution of General Phoumi Nosovan; the withdrawal of the French Military Mission from the training agreement and the expansion of training and advice to the BVs

Rotation IV of *Hotfoot* would become an anomaly. During this rotation, *Hotfoot* teams became involved in RLG combat operations against the Neutralists and Pathet Lao, and, in April of 1961, President Kennedy ordered the establishment of a full MAAG in Vientiane. *Hotfoot* changed to Operation *White Star*, the overt military support of Laotian forces. *Hotfoot* teams donned their U.S. Army fatigues, carried weapons, and were soon on the way to accompanying Laotian forces in combat.

This also included expansion of the mission to assist the CIA with training of Vang Pao's guerrilla forces on the Plaine des Jarres, Operation *Momentum.*

The Laotian military expanded with the inclusion of five more BIs, followed by the build-up of the FAL to twenty-one line battalions (which necessitated an additional nine Special Forces teams). An additional military region was established in the provinces around Vientiane (MR-V). Lao battalions would soon be organized in *groupement mobiles* (GMs), forming regimental-sized combat teams of three battalions, along with an armor and artillery section, and associated engineer and logistics detachments, to form combined-arms maneuver formations.

The Situation in Laos, 1959

In the spring of 1959 the Pathet Lao resumed their offensive with attacks on RLG outposts in Sam Neua Province and limited guerrilla activities in the Laotian panhandle. Although it could not be documented, warnings of NVA incursions also occurred. By July, a ceasefire and an arrangement between the government and the Pathet Lao leadership to incorporate and integrate the forces of the Pathet Lao (estimated at two battalions), as well as surrender of weapons, was agreed upon. When the arrangement failed, Prince Souphanouvong was arrested and jailed in Vientiane. In retaliation, the Pathet Lao resumed their offensive in Military Region II, with attacks on Laotian army outposts along the Nam Ma River line in Sam Neua Province.[8] In this same period, the North Vietnamese began the establishment of the Ho Chi Minh Trail for supplying communist forces operating in South Vietnam. The Pathet Lao were estimated to control twenty-five percent of the country during the *Hotfoot I* rotation, although no *Hotfoot I* teams were ever deployed in contested country. There would be no American combat engagements with enemy forces until Rotation IV in 1961.

On December 25, 1959, a minor coup was launched against the government of Phoui Sananikone to protest the extension of the Lao National Assembly's mandate to delay national elections; the coup lasted until January 5, 1960. Even with these internal ruptures of civil government in Laos, the *Hotfoot* teams were not affected in accomplishing their training missions.

Hotfoot Rotation I

When the control team arrived in Vientiane, they were first lodged in huts near the airport, but moved into a team house in the city. The mission of FC-3 was to "organize, train and develop the Laotian military forces into units capable of defending their country." The FC-3 Vientiane Control Team was located in a nice, well-built house of French colonial-style construction. For convenience and coordination, the house location was chosen for its proximity to the American embassy complex; USAID employees lived directly across the street.

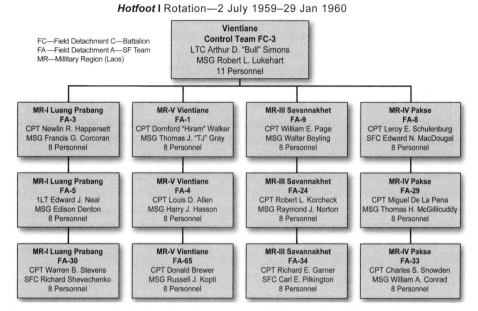

Hotfoot I Rotation—2 July 1959–29 Jan 1960

FC—Field Detachment C—Battalion
FA—Field Detachment A—SF Team
MR—Military Region (Laos)

Vientiane
Control Team FC-3
LTC Arthur D. "Bull" Simons
MSG Robert L. Lukehart
11 Personnel

MR-I Luang Prabang
FA-3
CPT Newlin R. Happersett
MSG Francis G. Corcoran
8 Personnel

MR-V Vientiane
FA-1
CPT Dornford "Hiram" Walker
MSG Thomas J. "TJ" Gray
8 Personnel

MR-III Savannakhet
FA-9
CPT William E. Page
MSG Walter Boyling
8 Personnel

MR-IV Pakse
FA-8
CPT Leroy E. Schulenburg
SFC Edward N. MacDougal
8 Personnel

MR-I Luang Prabang
FA-5
1LT Edward J. Neal
MSG Edison Denton
8 Personnel

MR-V Vientiane
FA-4
CPT Louis D. Allen
MSG Harry J. Hasson
8 Personnel

MR-III Savannakhet
FA-24
CPT Robert L. Korcheck
MSG Raymond J. Norton
8 Personnel

MR-IV Pakse
FA-29
CPT Miguel De La Pena
MSG Thomas H. McGillicuddy
8 Personnel

MR-I Luang Prabang
FA-30
CPT Warren B. Stevens
SFC Richard Shevechenko
8 Personnel

MR-V Vientiane
FA-65
CPT Donald Brewer
MSG Russell J. Kopti
8 Personnel

MR-III Savannakhet
FA-34
CPT Richard E. Garner
SFC Carl E. Pilkington
8 Personnel

MR-IV Pakse
FA-33
CPT Charles S. Snowden
MSG William A. Conrad
8 Personnel

Task organization and leadership of the first rotation of U.S. Army Special Forces deployed to Laos under Operation *Hotfoot*. *(Derived from Steve Sherman's "Who's Who in Operation* Hotfoot/White Star*" published by © Radix Press, Houston, TX.)*

While Colonel Simons, commanding FC-3, spent his time in meetings at the embassy, visiting the local FTTs, and traveling to visit teams at the outstations, he was ably assisted by Major Gordon M. Ripley, the deputy commander of the control team. (Major Ripley would return to Laos on the seventh rotation of Special Forces to Laos to command a B-team at Luang Prabang.)

Sergeant 1st Class Kenneth H. Hain remembers Colonel Simons and his leadership. It was during Hain's tour on the FTT in Pakse when he was sent to Vientiane to help out with the radio operators in FC-3. Hain said, "He was a no nonsense guy. You knew where you stood with him. He did not split hairs; he was not picky. He chose his own people carefully, so he got good people around him. He told you what to do and let you do it."[9]

As a purely training mission, the pace of *Hotfoot* did not have the long hours and chaotic nature of combat operations, requiring twenty-four-hour attention. The busiest members of the FC were the leaders and the radio operators (Sergeant 1st Class William H. McDaniel and Sergeant Tommy S. Hollingsworth), taking the twice-daily reports (or more, based on logistics requirements) from the teams in the field. The commo men were also required to travel to the FTT locations to replace the crystals in their radios.

Captain Joseph Thompson, the S1/S4, and Sergeant 1st Class Lloyd R. Fisher, S-4 NCOIC, handled the teams' logistical requests for food and supplies. Most requests were made by a line-item report from a list of items found in the embassy commissary. Occasionally, coordination was required for medical items, or USAID project materials. And, like all units in the field, the pick-up and delivery of mail was important to morale.

Resupply flights were coordinated for delivery by Air America flights. Each of the FTTs was located near good-weather airstrips, usually laterite or pierced metal planking (PSP) airstrips. C-46s and C-47s delivered supplies and logistic items once or twice a month to the outlying teams.

The embassy complex had a small base exchange (BX) along with a restaurant, both within walking distance for the eleven-man control team. The control team slept upstairs on issue cots, covered with mosquito nets. Downstairs served as the control operations room, with a radio located centrally on a table to coordinate with the embassy and the FTTs. New to the men were the geckos on the ceilings within the house.

The control team was equipped with jeep-type vehicles, but most of the team soon acquired the ubiquitous mopeds to get around Vientiane. Meals could be cooked at the control-team headquarters, but many took advantage of the local cuisine, like the Philippine or Chinaman's restaurants downtown, or the commissary restaurant run by "Hutch," the Chinese waiter. Bars and bistros were aplenty for entertainment in the evenings. Most notable to Americans in Vientiane was the bar, the White Rose Café.

FC-3 arrived during the monsoon season. It was predictable that the rains caused the Mekong River to burst its banks. Drinking water, and water for use in cooking and showers (sanitary water) was limited, or not always available as with any remote or underdeveloped country where Special Forces teams deploy. The medics and the group surgeon, Dr. Sam Skemp, were required to stay on top of the team's health, guarding against diseases and enforcing good sanitation. Diarrhea, dengue fever, and malaria were the three most occurring medical problems in Laos (followed by hepatitis). Although all the teams were given shots and medical screening before leaving Fort Bragg, the health of the men required constant supervision.[10]

Along with the FC-3 control team in Vientiane, SF teams FA-1, FA-4, and FA-26 served in the Vientiane region (soon to be labeled as Military Region V).

A Day in the Life of *Hotfoot* Trainers

FTTs began their "Laotian experience" upon arrival to Bangkok, where they met and got to know the services of Air America. It was soon to be their surrogate air transport into Laos; teams would also depend on them for travel and resupply throughout Laos. Some teams met colorful pilots like "Shower Shoes Wilson" who flew circuits regularly to bring in supplies and mail to the teams. Upon arrival to their designated field location, the teams were met at the airfield by the local military attaché or PEO representative and moved to rented houses in town. These were normally two-story structures, sometimes located in a villa. While the three training teams on location may have originally started operations in the same house, it was not long before each team separated to reside in their own team house.

Prior to initial link-up with the Laotians at their training center was the myriad of tasks to prepare for day one of the mission. These included setting up the house, hiring local cooks and house cleaners, receiving and checking over the maintenance of the vehicles provided, setting up a radio station (sometimes requiring setting up antennas on the roof), and conducting initial team meetings to organize and coordinate the training schedule and the roster of assigned trainers.

In the morning, teams sat down to breakfast (food either supplied from the local economy—the teams paid the cooks and house cleaners to shop locally for foodstuffs—or stocked supplies from the U.S. embassy commissary) and then moved out to the local training area. Transportation was either by the team jeep, individual mopeds, or bicycles depending on the distance between the team house and the local camp.

Upon arrival at the Laotian training camp, FTTs conducted scheduled military training while some members of the team worked on the construction of weapons ranges, skill courses, and classroom facilities. If fortunate, a good classroom with a generator for electricity was available. All instruction required the interpreters. Instruction was enhanced if chalkboards and chalk were available and often teams prepared their own handouts and training aids. Very few teams interacted with the Laotian officers and NCOs. No teams were billeted at the training camps and their food, water and medical supplies were carried in by the teams for their own use.

The radio operators remained in the team house for the twenty-four-hour communication watches and to send out the daily situation reports to the control team back in Vientiane. Since all three teams were colocated, often the radio operators spotted one another whenever communications training by one of them was required at the training camps, or for one of them to get a break and go to town.

Upon return from training, detachment members usually gathered around the dining table and discussed the events of the day, where to make changes and improve instruction, and review the requirements for the next day's training, followed by apportionment of duties for the team.

Social life consisted of visiting the town, eating at local restaurants, playing cards and often a chance for a drink of local beer or spirits. The "Team Bar" was a feature in many of the team houses. Surprisingly, the NCOs and enlisted members of the team had no problem off-duty socializing with French NCOs and enlisted soldiers at their local haunts in town, or by visiting the French Military Mission's team houses.

The health of the team was maintained by the medics, ensuring everyone conducted anti-malarial procedures (mosquito nets over the cots, taking anti-malarial pills) and monitoring the food and water imbibed by the team. In-house showers or portable showers were a feature of all team houses to ensure cleanliness. Although the team medics performed most of their medical care within the team, wherever possible they held sick call for the troops at the training camps and built medical huts or tents if allowed. Many friendships were made with other medical personnel in the area—notably the Filipinos from Operation *Brotherhood*, members of the Tom Dooley Foundation, and other medical humanitarian agencies—and assisted with local MEDCAPs (Medical Capability visits) where they could provide additional medical care for the local populace (a form of early civic action). If a team member became ill with malaria, hepatitis, or dengue fever they were medevac'ed back to Bangkok (often to not return back to the mission). Other medical complications experienced by the teams were diarrhea and in worse cases, contracting intestinal parasites (worms).

Daily maintenance and inventory of mechanical equipment was performed by the team mechanic who ensured the repair and good running of vehicles and generators (many of the locations did not have electricity). Washing of vehicles was most often accomplished during drives down to the riverside when water-cans needed refilling.

Often team members were required to travel to other team locations to assist or were called to the FC-3 in Vientiane, and in this way were able to experience more of Laos than just the town of their location. The teams were also required to move to the local airfield to offload monthly supplies and mail when deliveries were made by embassy aircraft or Air America. Part of their duties at the airfield was the hand-refueling of aircraft from fifty-five-gallon drums.

Almost all the teams acquired a pet of some sorts, whether a snake, gecko, parrot, bear, dog or gibbon monkey. The most notorious pet was Lieutenant Colonel Simons' gibbon, named "Charlie," who sported a military crew - cut hairstyle and drank Gimlets during the hours of relaxation.

At the conclusion of the six-month TDY, FTTs participated in local military ceremonies in recognition of their work. Team members dressed in their civilian suits and received certificates from high-ranking Laotian officers. When possible, high-ranking officers from the embassy and from CINCPAC flew in to congratulate the teams.

While a few of the FTT members in each location remained behind to assist the incoming *Hotfoot* replacement team, upon redeployment the detachments either packed their gear and flew back through Vientiane or straight back to Bangkok as part of the journey to stateside. Most redeploying teams stopped over in Hong Kong for R&R and began the tradition of buying tailored clothes and suits along with gold Rolex watches, spending their hard-earned TDY allowances built up over the six months.

Upon return to Fort Bragg, the teams were debriefed and then medically checked for any problems or diseases they might have contracted in Laos. *Hotfoot* members also helped to prepare future deploying teams by sharing their experiences and lessons learned during their tour. Clear from the veterans of the first deployment was the need for more pretraining, particularly area studies and language training. The major piece of advice offered to the next deploying rotation was to try and change the individual skills training of the Lao battalions to the next level of collective training tasks.

In time, a certificate for service in Laos was issued by the command at Fort Bragg to recognize *Hotfoot* members' contributions. Other peacetime military awards were given for achievement and service, as warranted.

FTTs in Vientiane

The three FTTs in Vientiane were initially assigned the mission of expanding the regional training facilities for the Laotian army. One of these locations was twenty-two kilometers northeast out of Vientiane along Route 13, designed for use not only as an infantry training center, but also for the training of Laotian officers, NCOs, and task force commanders. The other training facility, a Ranger and Psychological Warfare training camp, was located at Kilometer 17. The FTTs began the construction of these facilities without any cooperation or support from the French Military Mission.[11]

As this initial mission in the Vientiane region was completed, captains Lewis D. Allen (FA-4), Donald Brewer (FA-26), and Dornford "Hiram" Walker, (FA-1) began the training of Laotian soldiers.

FA-1, Vientiane

Captain Dornford "Hiram" Walker commanded FA-1, assisted by his XO, Lieutenant Bernardo "Burn" Loeffke and his team sergeant, Master Sergeant Thomas J. "TJ" Gray. The team prepared for the Laos mission maneuvering in the Pisgah National Forest, conducting cross-training and long-range communications. Lieutenant Colonel Bull Simons's philosophy and guidance for the mission was "Train and fight with the Lao." (The U.S. embassy countermanded any notion of fighting with the Lao upon *Hotfoot*'s arrival in Laos.) The team did not conduct language training, but fortunately Lieutenant Loeffke, commissioned from West Point, knew the French language. FA-1 was one of the few teams which would not have a mechanic from the 82nd assigned to them.

Upon arrival to Vientiane, the team procured a team house, hired a cook, and settled into the mission. FA-1 was not assigned a battalion to train *per se*, but rode a bus out to various training centers, including Camp Chinaimo, to train packets of soldiers. Now retired, Major General Burn Loeffke described their role and the "politics" of the French–U.S. training agreement:

> We trained Laotian infantry and the 2nd BP of Kong Le's. There was a French Detachment as trainers, led by a Captain from the Foreign Legion. I remember the French General of the French Military Mission visiting one day to observe training, and he was annoyed at the French guys using the word "OK" that had rubbed off on them from us. You know that thing about the French language purity.
>
> The French trained the Laotians in the morning and we trained them in the afternoon. We wore civvies and had no weapons. We had a Thai interpreter, but I spoke French with the officers. It seems like whatever we taught, the French taught it in the opposite way. Like the way we had the Laotians keep their fingers in the trigger guard, placed in front of the trigger. The French had the Laotians put their fingers on the trigger. We taught how to operate the M1 and they taught marksmanship. But I got along with the French pretty good; along with speaking French, I had lived in Paris. But, they weren't happy with us being in Laos.
>
> We did not train heavy weapons, like the mortars or recoilless rifles; the French may have conducted that training.[12]

Members of the team were assigned government service ranks (GS-ratings), along with issuance of embassy ID cards. They wore civilian clothes to the training sites, and were not called by their ranks; everyone was a "Mister." Along with the preparation and construction of training sites and weapons training for Lao soldiers, the team medic, Sergeant Robert B. Schultis, established a small dispensary in the team house for walk-in patients as part of their civic action program. On wider scale, FA-1 conducted MEDCAPs in the surrounding villages.

The Training Centers FTTs

The remaining nine *Hotfoot* FTTs were assigned to the regional training centers at Luang Prabang (three FTTs), Savannakhet (three teams), and Pakse (three teams). In November, members of Team *Korchek* deployed to the old French training center at Khang Khay to expand *Hotfoot* operations into Military Region II (Captain Thompson replaced Captain Korchek in Savannakhet). The mission of the team at Khang Khay was to provide trainers for the regional NCO and officer schools, under the direction of Lieutenant Colonel Kim Brabson, a *Hotfoot* advisor from the PEO office.

The *Hotfoot* regional training centers teams acquired homes or villas within the cities they were located. Usually living nearby was a member of the PEO and members of USAID, also in rented homes and villas. The teams were provided Mitsubishi-style quarter-ton jeeps for transportation, or used mopeds and bicycles to report to work. Local cooks and maids were hired off the economy; teams often ate local food or relied on supplies delivered monthly or semi-monthly from the embassy commissary. At the training sites, the French Military Mission trainers remained separated from the FTTs by time of day or training location. For instance, the U.S. trainers may have taught and instructed during the morning hours, with the French taking the afternoon period. Americans might have been using the camp's rifle and small-arms ranges for their training of the Lao, while during the same time the French used a local maneuver area to train the Lao on tactics.

The bulk of training allowed for the American "technicians" to focus on individual arms and individual soldier skills, prohibited from the French in teaching tactical subjects. Classes in field sanitation, first aid, map-reading and compass, demolitions, and basic radio and communication training were allowed. Similar classes, along with leadership subjects, were taught in the NCO and officer courses.

U.S. trainers basically taught the M1 rifle assembly and disassembly, maintenance, and firing of the weapon. Other classes included sub-machine guns, use of grenades, and firing and operation of mortars and recoilless rifles. In many locations, *Hotfoot* trainers were required to build ranges and classroom facilities prior to starting any classes. Classes such as small-unit tactics, patrolling, and emplacement and use of crew-served weapons were kept within the French training regimen (considered as *tactical* subjects).

There were several factors frustrating U.S. attempts to professionalize the *tahans* and meet expectations of the PEOs and the embassy's goals for the military assistance program. First and foremost was the animosity which existed between the French trainers and the U.S. mission in Laos. The daily training by the French consisted of a class, followed by a teabreak. The late morning, early afternoon break, *poc* time, often led to two to three hours of idleness and naptime; training often ended early in the day. Said one Laos war veteran,

> We trained alongside the French. All the stories about the hassle with the French where they reserved the right to teach French doctrinal tactics, and we could only teach individual skills, are true. So was the friction between the U.S. and French trainers. We were mostly irritated at the French and their capability to train foreign troops. They would teach a little while, drink tea, and then take a ten-minute break. They took a three-hour break for lunch, and then quit early in the day for dinner. It was not a very effective training schedule.[13]

French-trained Laotian officers and NCOs replicated the high-handed elite social order of French military culture and would not participate to train their troops, looking down on the U.S. "sergeant" trainers. Corruption in the Lao officer corps was rife, often leading to lack of pay for troops and the lowering of morale among the trainees, affecting attendance to the training sessions.

Ignorance (lack of reading and writing skills), indolence, and cultural barriers of customs and language all had to be worked through in order to have any semblance of effective training.

FA-3, Team *Happersett*, Luang Prabang, Military Region I

From Bangkok, FA-3 flew to the royal capital of Luang Prabang where they were met by local dignitaries and a Lao military major. They lodged the first night in a hotel, in the midst of the monsoon season. The following morning, Lao military personnel and trucks assisted the team for movement to the military training camp. Thinking this was their new home, Captain Newlin R. Happersett, the detachment commander, had the men move about ten kilometers out into the jungle to set up their tents and establish a base camp.

When visited by the PEO colonel in Luang Prabang, the team found out per diem was being paid so they could live in comfortable quarters, not in the jungle; they were ordered to go into town and find a team house. They soon procured a two-story, French colonial-style house, adding amenities like a water purifier and a hot-water shower system. A ferry on the Mekong delivered one Land Rover and one reconditioned Mitsubishi jeep for team transport. About a week later, the other two teams arrived at Luang Prabang, secured their team houses, and were soon ready to start the mission.

FA-3 was tasked to provide technical equipment training and weapons training to a mixed Lao–Hmong infantry battalion. The team cooperated with a detachment of French trainers, who were also there to monitor what the Americans were teaching the Lao. Initially, the battalion spent its time setting up a camp with tentage for the soldiers, constructed a mess hall, and built other structures needed to house the unit during the training. It was at this same time FA-3 assisted in the issuance of American gear: uniforms, helmets, web gear and the M1 rifle.[14]

One of the first problems encountered with many of the Lao and Hmong was the M1 rifle being too long for most Laotians, who were having problems getting a proper "stock-weld" for accurate shooting. Sergeant James C. Williams (weapons NCO) found a hardware shop in Luang Prabang which could cut down the stock, modifying the weapon, and replacing the butt plate. Important to the modification was ensuring the oiler kit well was redrilled so the Lao had some weapons-cleaning capability with their rifle.

Using innovative means of combining wood, boxes, C-ration cans, demo kit springs and cordage, and other materials, the team soon had a zero range, known-distance range, and a "train-fire" range in operation, along with appropriate target silhouettes, range posts, and firing lanes. (Apparently neither the French nor the PEO had funding for these materials; when Lieutenant Colonel Simons visited the team, he immediately corrected the situation and had the materials delivered.)[15]

Each morning, the platoons were marched to an unused portion of the ammunition storage area where the detachment helped construct some classroom sheds. To begin the day, Williams, SP5 Ray Sanchez (demolitions) or Master Sergeant Francis G. Corcoran, the team sergeant, led the trainees in physical conditioning and calisthenics. Liaison with the battalion's officers was Captain Happersett's and Lieutenant Clarence M. "Bill" Hooper's (the XO) job, ensuring the smooth running of the training and any required coordination with the French Military Mission.

The team conducted their "technical" training five days a week (the French trainers handled the tactical training). There was no training on the weekends.

Sergeant John W. Kelly, the 82nd Airborne Division team mechanic, kept the team's vehicles and generator running and repaired, but also helped to train Laotians on the maintenance of their own jeeps and trucks. Sergeant Jack G. Harper ran the communications at the team house and made the daily commo checks with Vientiane FC; if available, he also assisted in communications classes with the battalion. The medic, Sergeant Billy R. Davis, pooled his resources with the other two team medics in Luang Prabang to provide sick call for the *tahans* and to ensure the proper sanitation of the camp. The medics also spent time assisting the French medical clinic in Luang Prabang when they had spare time. The medics were also visited by walk-in villagers from the local area. Staff Sergeant Wilfred R. Mousseau, on Captain Warren B. Stevens's FA-30, helped to deliver a baby for a mountain village chief's daughter; in return, he was given a small Laotian pony as a gift. Mousseau could soon be seen riding around town in his high rubber boots, T-shirt, Australian-style bush hat, along with his medical bag slung over his shoulder, earning him the nickname "The Country Doctor."

There was never any immediate threat to the teams at Luang Prabang from the Pathet Lao. This did not mean the team thought they did not require protection. The Lao battalion commander allowed them to "shop" in his personal armory of confiscated and captured weapons. They were soon armed with rifles, carbines, and French sub-machine guns, and surprisingly, a Thompson .45-caliber sub-machine gun. These weapons were carried concealed when team members traveled outside the team house. Some of their travel by vehicle involved forays to gather information about the surrounding area, needed by the team to complete their area assessment.

After a month, the battalion was taken out of training and sent north to fight the Pathet Lao, leaving the three teams in Luang Prabang with nothing to do. Sergeant Williams took the opportunity to assist U.S. intelligence efforts with photography of the Chinese road being built in northern Laos. Williams flew with a French pilot in a Beechcraft:

> I took on the task and it wasn't bad. I got a chance to see most everything in northern Laos. We shot everything he wanted in the north of the country; a lot of small villages. We kept to the Lao side of the border and photographed the highway from an altitude of 1,200 feet, shooting out the side of the aircraft, flying parallel to the highway and shooting into China without ever crossing the border. And, south of the border checkpoint we shot the villages along the dirt road; it was an atrocious road. Sometimes I'd shoot two rolls or as many as five or even eight. Corcoran would meet me at the airstrip to collect the film and I'd keep my Army issue Leica Camera.[16]

The Agency operative at Luang Prabang began to bring in groups of Hmong about every six weeks for training (in forty-man units). The detachment considered them just young boys and kids. Apparently, this program was financed by the Agency and had none of the restrictions imposed by the French training agreement. Williams notes:

> We taught patrolling, raids and ambushes, range firing and with the ambush techniques we let them use "live fire" at night. Once you taught them the basics, they were very good at it, probably because it was similar to their experience hunting animals. We set up "killing zones" called "Fields of Fire" where we tied targets up during the day.
>
> We also started water training—how to cross rivers and streams—because although we had a lot of water in Laos with many rivers, these young kids could not swim. We taught them to use a rope to ford a river; and a poncho to wrap their weapons or supplies to carry above the water and keep it dry. The French had no objection to our teaching tactics with these folks and in fact they joined and helped us.[17]

Just before their departure from Laos, FA-3 and the other teams returned to Vientiane for out-processing. They were hosted at the home of the Lao minister of defense and awarded individual certificates, the "Order of a Million White Elephants," beautifully embossed with raised enamel symbols. Unfortunately, even this souvenir of duty in Laos was confiscated to preserve operational security.

FA-33, Team *Snowden*, Pakse

Sergeant Kenneth H. Hain was the radio operator on FA-33 in Pakse. His experience is reflective of what the FTTs faced in order to accomplish their mission. When the three FTTS assigned to the Pakse mission arrived in Bangkok, they were transloaded onto an Air America C-46 and flew straight into Pakse.

> The three team leaders with us were Captain Schulenberg, Captain De La Pena, and our team leader, Captain Snowden. Each team rented a separate house in Pakse. Ours was a two-story, large, villa type house, but very primitive.
>
> I can't recall ever receiving a mission briefing, from anywhere, or from anyone. Our team was assigned for training to the 26th Infantry Battalion of the Laotian Army. They had a compound outside of the town of Pakse, like a battalion camp. We just married up our MOS training with their requirements. We had Thai interpreters. We had a Land Rover-type vehicle (each team had one) and a couple of old trucks, maybe from the French, but they never ran really well. It kept Herlihy, the mechanic, busy. We trained the Laotians while wearing civvies—we had no weapons.
>
> The 26th Laotian Infantry had a lot of gear which did not work; it was poorly maintained. It was a mixture of French and U.S. gear. We did not train alongside the French, but we socialized with them. Rocky and I got invited to the French compound in Pakse; it had a bar and was very nice. If there was animosity between them and us, it was due to some of them being veterans of the War in Indochina and Algeria.
>
> We wore civvies to training, but everyone wore whatever headgear they wanted. If there was a basic uniform, it was khaki pants worn with a civilian shirt. We helped to build a small arms range in the jungle. We tried to teach individual camouflage and night operations. During our teaching at night, the Lao would put up a defensive perimeter, and the team would try to penetrate the defenses.
>
> When the monsoon rains were hitting, training stopped. The Mekong would overflow its banks and flood the area. Even with that, we figured out how to stretch the training for the six-month period. We were pretty much left to our own initiative as to how we conducted the mission.[18]

FA-8, Pakse

Captain Leroy E. Schulenberg led FA-8 in Pakse. Lieutenant Benjamin C. Wheat was his team XO and Sergeant 1st Class Edward H. MacDougal the team sergeant. It was an eight-man ODA, with Sergeant James W. Fulcher attached as the team mechanic from the 82nd Airborne Division. Captain Schulenberg was considered the "old man," being in his thirties and regarded as a solid soldier. He had trained the detachment well for the mission through area studies, language training, and cross-training. (Major Schulenberg returned to Laos in March of 1962 as the B-detachment commander at Paksane, and later as the B-detachment commander in Saravane for Operation *Pincushion*, the Kha tribal guerrilla program on the Bolovens Plateau.)

After landing in Bangkok, the team flew by C-46 to Pakse and procured a run-down house to establish operations. They were met by the PEO representative, an army major, living in Pakse with his wife, and provided more details on their mission. They quickly unpacked their gear, established sleeping rooms upstairs and the radio room downstairs, and prepared to meet with the Laotians to begin training. During their first night in town, some Laotian army outposts were hit by the Pathet Lao. This was the team's first introduction to the fact they were serving in an active war zone.

The team drove to the training camp and participated in a small ceremony held by the Laotians to welcome them. They found no French Military Training Mission trainers at this camp. Training was conducted in civilian clothes; FA-8 chose to wear khaki shirts and pants, even though other teams preferred straight civilian clothes. They were professionals, and wanted to present a military appearance to their counterparts. They were forbidden to carry military weapons, other than the .45-caliber pistol issued to the team's radio operator to protect the radio and the crypto items. However, it would not be long before SF "procurement" armed the team with M1s and personal pistols.

While training commenced, Sergeant Ivy C. Sanders, the team medic, established a clinic at the camp for sick call. Schulenberg, along with the team, had decided they would not run an aid station at the house, in order to not attract attention to the team's presence in Pakse.

Sergeant John H. Meadows was the radio operator on the team. He finished basic training in 1953 and volunteered for duty in an airborne unit, not knowing he was going to Special Forces at Fort Bragg, NC. Upon his arrival, he was selected for radio school, held near the airfield on Fort Bragg. After completing his MOS training, he joined others in a series of field maneuvers in Dahlonega to complete their unconventional warfare training. He was then assigned to the 10th SFG (A) in the Federal Republic of Germany. While there, he became jumpmaster qualified, learned a language, and then returned to Fort Bragg. Soon thereafter, he reported to Fort Gordon, GA for a radio repair course and the commo chief course. He was ready for a contingency deployment, joining Schulenberg's team for the *Hotfoot* mission to Laos.[19]

He had two duties in the Laos deployment: running communications from the team house back to the control team in Vientiane and assisting with communications training at the military camp. Meadows described:

> Downstairs we had our kitchen, dining room, and a place where I established our radio room. I had the AN/GRC-109, which used crystals, and the RS-1, which you would just tune. I used the AN/GRC-109 to send my messages to Vientiane. I also had a generator for the radio—the Generator 58.
>
> We trained Laotians at a military camp in Pakse. I had a little building set up to do the radio school. I taught a radio operator course—they had PRC-6s and backpack PRC-10s. I did not have the use of an interpreter, it was pointy-talky. (But, we did have a Thai interpreter, a civilian, we hired and paid him with our own money.) I would just show the Laotians how to operate the radio. Open the battery case, put the battery in, turn it on, etc. and they would follow along. They were fascinated with the workings of the radio. I also taught some First Aid. I had twenty-two students and they all had the clap! We ordered some penicillin from Vientiane; when it came in we were supposed to give them a series of three shots each, but they cleared up with one shot!
>
> The course I taught ran four weeks, and then I would get another set of students. Other team members taught their MOS skills—weapons, medical, and other military skills.[20]

During the team's training mission the Laotians were challenged by the Pathet Lao on the outskirts of Pakse. Due to the ambassador's restrictions, the team did not conduct security patrols with their counterparts, nor fly any reconnaissance missions with Air America to support Lao operations. The team was never attacked or involved in any combat with the Pathet Lao. Meadows, however, stretched the limit a bit one day when he received a mission to go up to Paksong. He said,

> One day I got a mission to help the Filipino hospital in Paksong with their communications. The Filipino Brotherhood was established by the Rockefeller Foundation, and they did medical humanitarian missions throughout Laos. The Pathet Lao were a threat in their area, and they had no radio to call for help, or report any incidents. Lieutenant Wheat and I drove up there in a jeep to provide them with a radio. It was on the Bolovens Plateau, where the trees grow crooked … While we were up there, and during the trip, Lieutenant Wheat and I did surveillance on the roads and trails in that area. One day, the Lao captured a Pathet Lao soldier on a trail. I saw him; he was tall, rugged and in uniform.[21]

Schulenberg led a good team, and they soon earned a reputation for their work. Lieutenant Colonel Simons visited them to congratulate them, as well as receiving a visit by the army attaché to commend their work. About halfway through the tour the team attended a ceremony held for them in Vientiane, where a Laotian officer praised them during his speech.

When the six-month TDY came to a conclusion, FA-8 transitioned with the incoming team of *Hotfoot* Rotation II, without any fanfare of ceremonies or certificates. Unfortunately, most of the pictures of their deployment were confiscated on departure, due to operational security.

FA-29, Pakse

FA-29 was commanded by Captain Miguel De La Pena. First Lieutenant Theodore Wilson was the detachment XO and Master Sergeant Thomas McGillicuddy the team sergeant. In preparation for their deployment to Laos, they received background classes on the country of Laos from the CIA and learned some basic words and phrases of Lao and French. They also received some training from Thai paratroopers at Fort Bragg.

The team, like all the first *Hotfoot* rotation, endured the almost one month delay to get into Laos to begin the mission. FA-29 transloaded at Bangkok onto an Air America C-46 for their flight to Pakse, along with the other two teams assigned the training mission at that location. The team wore civilian clothes and were issued ID cards designating them as civilian, GS-rated employees of the U.S. government.

They brought along their team boxes and gear, but were prohibited from bringing military weapons. The members of the team brought personal weapons, instead. Some used these to trade with the Laotians upon their departure, procuring some bows and arrows, knives, swords, and other souvenirs.

The team lodged in a house in Pakse, across the street from one of the prince's grounds where his elephants were kept. The team house was a tall white building, all of it empty, which the team dubbed the "White Elephant." All three *Hotfoot* teams assigned to Pakse initially resided in the White Elephant until finding other houses to live. The team hired a civilian cook and ate Lao-staple food. They also ate off the economy. They were provided a Thai interpreter.

The medic on the team only took care of Laotian troops, as there was Operation *Brotherhood* Filipinos and other medical NGOs performing medical care already in the town of Pakse. No MEDCAPS with the outlying villages were performed, either.

It was a quiet tour; they were never threatened by the Pathet Lao. Upon departure, a few members of the team extended to transition with the newly arriving *Hotfoot* Rotation II team.

Hotfoot Rotation II

Rotation II of *Hotfoot* basically repeated the ongoing training methodology used by *Hotfoot* I. In Vientiane, the FC-4 control team was commanded by Lieutenant Colonel Magnus L. Smith. Colonel Smith had fought in World War II as a paratrooper, participating in the airborne operation atop the "Rock" to take back Corregidor.

Upon arrival, *Hotfoot II* conducted transition and swapping of supplies and equipment with the outgoing teams, adjusted training schedules, and continued in the expansion and building of training ranges and facilities.

In the background of this deployment, the Laotian government held national elections in April. It was an astounding Rightist and anti-communist victory, incensing the Pathet Lao. Prince Souphanouvong escaped from his jailors in May, and trekked back to Sam Neua, firmly decided in his mind to launch the armed struggle as part of his political revolutionary attempt to participate in Laotian governance. Again, this had no effect on the running of *Hotfoot II*, but when *Hotfoot III* rotation began its duties, they would be in the midst of the storm of Kong Le's coup d'état, the withdrawal of participating French Military Mission teams from training, and support to the counter-revolution led by General Phoumi's Rightist elements. *Hotfoot III* teams would continue on the road to war by supporting General Phoumi's offensive against Neutralist forces in Vientiane, with SF teams beginning field advisory duties not only with the Laotian army BIs, but extended their support and advice to the BVs.

Lieutenant Colonel Simons remained for some months to coordinate deployments of FTTs into Military Region II, in hopes of including the teams in the unconventional warfare training of the Hmongs. Although Lieutenant Colonel Smith was listed as the commander for Rotation II, he served as Simons' XO until the "Bull" departed. (Of note during this deployment would be Captain Charlie Beckwith's tour, later famed for his creation of the U.S. Army Delta Force.)

FA-27 Luang Prabang—Military Region I

Sergeant Kenneth R. Bates was a radio operator on Captain Beckwith's team stationed in Luang Prabang. He joined Special Forces out of the 82nd Airborne Division. He first served in the 77th Special Forces Group under Colonel Raft, and in 1956 was assigned to the 10th SFG in Bad Tölz. Initially he served in a demolitions specialty, but due to the shortage of communications men on the teams, he cross-trained to become a commo man. Upon his return to Fort Bragg to join a UDT team (underwater demolition team), he heard that Captain Beckwith was getting up a team to go to Laos; Bates soon joined.[22]

After a period of pretraining, the team deployed on a C-124, and arrived in Bangkok. An Air America aircraft transferred the team to Vientiane, where the team was briefed on their mission in Luang Prabang. Although they had heard about the secret nature of the mission, the team was not required to turn in their military ID cards and dog tags.

FA-27 joined up with the two other teams at Luang Prabang. Two captains from the previous teams on Rotation I in Luang Prabang remained for about a month and a half to assist with the transition. Bates adds,

> There were three teams there. We were there to train Laotians—their infantry. There was a French team there and they all lived in the same house. We did not have good relations with the French; they often ignored us and treated us like it was a hassle to have us around. When

we first started training with the Laotians, we did not have an interpreter with us, so we gave the training in English. We'd hold a rifle barrel up and say, "Barrel." Then we would have them repeat this out loud. And then move on to the next part.[23]

After three months on assignment, Captain Beckwith was notified by the ambassador that he, the ambassador, had talked to the prime minister of Laos, who desired Lao troops to start receiving American tactical training vice allowing the French to teach tactical subjects exclusively. Up to that point in the mission, the team had been teaching individual skills such as weapons, medical training, and other individual tasks. Captain Beckwith chose to do the tactical, small-unit training at night to prevent the French from discovering his initiative. Upon their discovery of the ruse, the French were angered. Bates remembered, "We had an angry, drunk Frenchmen come to our house and try to make a big deal of it. One of our team members 'squared' him away in short order."[24]

The Laotians were trained in company-sized packets. The previous team had only been able to build rudimentary training facilities, so the FTT built a live-fire infiltration course. Bates described the assistance they had from Thai soldiers during their deployment: "There was also a Thai weapons training team who taught the M1 carbine and BAR. Even though I was supposed to be an instructor on weapons training, the Thais were very good at giving this training and I just went to classes and learned a lot from a Thai instructor on those weapons."[25]

Although *Hotfoot* teams were prohibited from carrying weapons while operating as civilian trainers, like most SF teams they carried personal pistols bought for the deployment while they were still at Fort Bragg. Ken Bates carried a .45-caliber pistol along with a Luger. Master Sergeant Desoto, the team sergeant, had a .357 and a .38-caliber pistol.

When the team medic, Sergeant 1st Class Herbert Forbes, was not providing medical instruction or taking care of the team and the Lao soldiers, he conducted local MEDCAPs and worked with other medical humanitarian organizations in the Luang Prabang area. Bates remarked on the medical role:

> There were no Operation *Brotherhood* Filipino medical personnel in Luang Prabang, or USAID medical support; we were the only medical capability (foreign) around. Herbie, the medic, worked with the famous Dr. Wheldon for a month. We also built a clinic locally, and went to surrounding villages to conduct MEDCAPs. We would treat sicknesses and give shots … As far as our own medical problems, these consisted of dengue fever, diarrhea. We did not have anyone contract malaria.[26]

Sergeant Bates was responsible for rotational duties at the radio base station located in Captain Garber's team house (FA-5/60) and submitting the daily reports and logistics requests. "The radios were an AN/GRC-9 (a large radio, basically used for receiving) and we had a RS-1 (Radio Set 1). The French also had the AN/GRC-9. (The AN/GRC-9 was in Group in 1959. If you add the burst device, this made it into the AN/GRC-109.) I talked during my shift to only the C-team; there was no B-team above us."[27]

The team accomplished their training mission successfully and returned to Fort Bragg after their six-month rotation. All admired the leadership provided by Captain Beckwith during the Laotian tour. Bates remarked, "Anything we had to get accomplished, Beckwith would say, 'You guys do what you have to do, and I will make sure it happens,' with respect to how we wanted to approach our mission. Beckwith was a good team leader, he let the NCOs do their work, and he was helped by an exceptional team sergeant, Sergeant De Soto."[28]

FA-5/60, Team *Garbers*, Luang Prabang—Military Region I

After alerted for deployment to Laos, the XO of FA-12, First Lieutenant John McDonald and the team sergeant, Master Sergeant James A. Tryon, loaded their seven-man A-team aboard C-124s at Pope Air Force Base, along with other contingents of the 77th SFG (A) accompanying them, and began their six-day journey to Bangkok. As was the case with all long-duration military flights, the pilots and crews of the C-124s chose to conduct a three-day crew rest period somewhere, selecting the Philippines for this break in the trip.

Upon their arrival to Bangkok, there was no reception party, so one of the officers on the flight went down to the terminal at Don Muang airport to seek information. When he returned he told the awaiting Special Forces contingent to move down to the end of the airstrip and hide in the tall grass and remain out of sight (OPSEC for the mission began early). Sometime later, an Air America C-46 arrived to fly them to Vientiane. They remained in holding in Vientiane and spent the next couple of days receiving mission briefings and conducting additional administrative requirements. Finally, they were ready for the mission, and were flown on another Air America C-46 to Luang Prabang.[29]

Luang Prabang was the royal capital of Laos and the location of the king's palace. It is located about in the middle of the northern portion of Laos astride the junction of the Mekong River with the Nam Khan River. A distinctive feature of Luang Prabang is the Phu Si hill, 100 meters in height above the surrounding ground, topped off with the famous *wat*, *That Chomsi*. It was a sleepy, quiet town consisting of a series of two village *bans* and their associated *wats*.

When the team arrived for the mission they were assigned their FTT team number—FA-5. This was a holdover from one of the previous *Hotfoot* teams assigned to Luang Prabang. Captain Edward J. Neal, from *Hotfoot I* rotation, took command of the team, but was later replaced by Captain Frank L. Garbers, who had been away on a mission in Saigon.

Halfway into their deployment, the team began a new mission training the Hmong. (The team was assigned the designator FA-60 when this occurred.)

The three teams in Luang Prabang all lived in separate team houses. Initially, FA-5 lived in the old section of town, in an old French villa across from the Royal Palace. In a short time, FA-5 moved from this team house to a new two-story house, which had been recently renovated from its prior use, a Chinese casino, which was located on the other side of town.

The teams were supplied with jeeps and trailers, along with a three-quarter-ton truck provided from the U.S. Embassy. One of the teams was issued Land Rovers; this vehicle was not very well liked due to its poor performance. The other trucks were Mitsubishi models, and were not marked in any distinctive way with U.S. markings, in order to maintain the civilian status cover for the teams (although the team jeeps bore the labeling "U.S. Army" on the sides of its hood). There is some rumor from the veterans that the later Operation *White Star* name was derived from orders given to teams to paint U.S. Army white stars on their vehicles when the military status of teams went from civilian garb to full military markings and uniforms. SP4 Rodney L. Heavrin served as the team mechanic to keep the vehicles running and in good condition, performing his duty admirably.

The teams wore only civilian clothing per the requirement of the mission. SP4 Thomas O. Humphus was the radio operator on FA-5 and described the dress:

> We wore Sarongs around the house—they are comfortable for going to take a shower or when being off-duty. For duty, we wore black baseball hats, the khaki class-B shirt with the epaulets, our green issue fatigue trousers, and issue combat boots. Later, someone had found a warehouse with French boonie hats in it, so "Bull" Simons authorized us to wear those bush hats. We had also bought some rough-looking seersucker suits downtown.[30]

Team communications were via the RS-1, the old CIA/OSS radio, and the AN/GRC-109. Radio operators used crypto one-time pads to encode their communication and then used Morse code for sending and receiving. Frequencies were assigned for communications and the range was set using radio crystals. For power, teams hooked their radios to automotive batteries.

Captain Beckwith's and Captain Garbers' mission was to train Laotian infantry at the local military compound. Captain Paul H. Combs' team was designated as an unconventional warfare training team and was assigned the mission to assist with training Hmong and Black Tai contingents.

FA-5 had the primary mission of creating a known-distance rifle range and a range for other weapons training. Although each of the three teams in Luang Prabang had their own mission, they all worked together when they had projects to do such as building ranges, instruction, and so forth. An additional duty for all teams was to travel to the airstrip and help refuel aircraft from a fifty-five-gallon drum of AVGAS (aviation gasoline fuel), using a crank handle.

The Lao military had an infantry headquarters compound with a dispensary. Members of the FTTs rode motorbikes to get to training, traveling between their team houses and the battalion training area across the river. The Lao battalion was heavily under French influence. The SF trainers never mixed with the French and were not allowed to go to the French-taught portion of the training. As noted by Tom Humphus:

> We were training Laotian infantry. We could only train them in basic, individual tasks; the French would not allow us to train them in tactics. For instance, we could not train them on machine-guns because the French said these were crew-served weapons! (The French also lived in Luang Prabang; they had a pet bear at their house.) We had intended to teach land navigation and basic patrolling, so we trained and prepared for this before we left Fort Bragg, but when we relieved the 1st rotation team of *Hotfoot*, they warned us that the French were bad and hard to get along with.
>
> We built our own ranges in spite of the French (who did not want us building ranges). These were the known distance range (KD), and then a transition range.
>
> The French military training mission personnel were a pain in the butt! We spent a lot of time correcting what the French taught the Lao. They constantly spent their time trying to override our U.S. training methods.[31]

About halfway through FTT-5's mission, they were assigned to train the Hmongs (called Meo by the teams at the time; although now considered a derogatory term, it was in common use at the time and many Hmong did not seem to mind its use), mostly in light weapons training.

Team *Van Strien*—Military Region II Khang Khay (PDJ)

Captain James M. Van Strien was the detachment commander leading the mission to Khang Khay, on the Plaine des Jarres, established earlier by Captain Korchek during *Hotfoot I*. Assisting him with the eight-man detachment was First Lieutenant Franklin D. Hicks, his executive officer, and the team sergeant, Master Sergeant George W. Sevits. The team continued training classes for the NCO and officer schools, and training for a Laotian BI, all overseen by the PEO advisor assigned to Khang Khay. Additionally, the team became one of the first designated UW teams in Operation *Hotfoot*, conducting this mission without interference from the French. (This may have been due to the CIA running the operation to assist Hmong forces, blocking the French from any say over the mission.)

The UW mission represented the desire of Lieutenant Colonel Simons to expand the training tasks of the *Hotfoot* operation; this was one of the reasons for his extension as Vientiane team control commander into the *Hotfoot II* rotation (the need for increased coordination with the PEO and the Agency with respect to a covert operation).

While on the PDJ, Team *Van Strien* trained and advised local Hmong on weapons training, patrolling, and demolitions. A controlled American source (CAS) asset named Herr Hasey was a familiar face to the team. He was a Frenchmen who spoke French, English, and Lao. Hasey had a Lao wife and daughter and lived on a farm on the PDJ, where he grew fruit and vegetables to sell in the local markets. He also worked as a hunting guide on the PDJ to assist in the tiger hunts in the region. To perform all these tasks, he owned and flew a de Havilland Beaver aircraft, which he kept at his lodge on the Plaine des Jarres.[32]

Captain Van Strien flew with his team from Bangkok to Luang Prabang, and then on to the assignment at Khang Khay. Khang Khay was a garrison town located on the eastern side of the Plaine des Jarres and had an old French military camp, now occupied by the Laotians. There was a French Military Mission team at the base living in one of its villas, but upon arrival of the Americans, they moved to the east/southeast of the town of Khang Khay. Van Strien and his team were one of the teams told by "Bull" Simons that their job was "to run the French out."

Van Strien had been the detachment commander going over, but was replaced by Captain Thompson at Khang Khay; Van Strien became the XO for a short while. When Thompson left, Van Strien once again became the detachment commander, with Lieutenant Franklin D. Hicks as his XO (who came over to Laos when Thompson left).

The Pathet Lao were active in the area and the Lao battalion occasionally tangled with them. About halfway through the team's tour, there was contact between the battalion and the Pathet Lao at a bridge sited near the camp, although the detachment was not involved in this contact; they were not allowed to patrol with the Laotians per the French–U.S. training agreement. When questioning the Laotian soldiers about the Pathet Lao, a way the team used to elicit information on the enemy, they were told the Pathet Lao could be recognized among the populace because they wore white socks!

The team established their operational site in one of the villas on the camp. It was a large building, about ten rooms, with a central hallway down the middle. There was sufficient room to establish living quarters on the south-facing side, along with the radio room and weapons room. The north side held the kitchen, dining room, living room and supply closet. Four fireplaces warmed the villa in the colder months. Outside, the team kept two pet bears, one with a white "V" around his neck. (Later, members of the team had heard their replacement detachment shot him because he was throwing the tiles off the roof of the team house villa.)

The location of the team at Khang Khay put them as the most remote asset in northeast Laos, far away from support. Fortunately, they were located near a fixed-wing-capable airstrip which allowed food and supplies to be flown in from the control team in Vientiane. Meals were augmented by buying buffalo. The meat was plentiful; so plentiful the team set up a lucrative trade with the FC in Vientiane for buffalo steaks.

The team had a jeep and trailer for their use, and a generator for electricity, maintained by their mechanic Sergeant Lawrence R. McGirr. They wore civilian clothes, and carried personal pistols. Some had acquired long guns, like Sergeant George W. Sevits, who carried a .30-.30 Winchester.[33]

The medic, Sergeant 1st Class Ronald W. Klinker, set up a dispensary in the camp to care for Laotian troops. The medic and other members of the team also conducted medical calls in the village of Khang Khay, treating elderly patients. Older Laotians came into the village to see him, not because they were sick, but because they had never seen a Westerner.

George Sevits described the role of the team: "We went to train a battalion in small arms, first aid and demolitions. We had a classroom and made a firing range with pop-up targets. The Laotians were regular infantry troops. We trained them every day, in one big classroom."[34]

Tom Humphus, the radio operator on FA-5/60 in Luang Prabang, was sent to the PDJ to assist Captain Van Strien and provide some relief to the captain's radio operator. (*Hotfoot* team members were allowed to take R&R during their six-month TDY, with many going to Bangkok for a week.) Humphus described the utility of Herr Hasey as an area "Asset":

> I went up to the PDJ to help Captain Van Strien and to relieve his radio operator (who was going on R&R). This was up at Khang Khay. The team was a UW team. While I was up there, I met Herr Hasey while he was delivering vegetables and strawberries. The team said an aircraft was supposed to deliver ammo for training, but it got weathered in. Herr Hasey asked, "What do you need?"
>
> Hoskinson, the demo man said, "Demolitions." Herr Hasey said he could get his hands on some British plastic explosive from World War II, known as PE-3 (yellowish-brown sticks like dynamite, wrapped in paper, but could be molded). Hoskinson told him that would be OK. Hasey said he had demolitions and weapons stashed in one of the caves in the area. We wondered about that. "Are we training Hasey's Gs?" we pondered.[35]

It was to be an introduction of SF teams to the peculiarities of UW in Laos, which would rapidly expand in future deployments of FTTs into Military Region II.

FA-54 Team *Farell*, Savannakhet, Military Region III

FA-54 was an eight-man FTT with duty in Savannakhet, led by Captain Joseph H. Farell, Jr. His XO was First Lieutenant Bruce D. Simnacher; the team sergeant was Master Sergeant Paul C. Payne. The mission of FA-54, along with the other two teams assigned to Savannakhet, was the training of Laotian infantry conscripts at the French-controlled base at Seno.

Like other *Hotfoot* teams, the FTTs procured team houses in Savannakhet. Embassy PEO officers also lived in the town and provided direction to the team leaders. To conduct training at Seno, jeeps were issued for the thirty-kilometer drive east, on dirt roads, to the air base at Seno.[36]

The teams soon set up living arrangements in their team houses (two-story, colonial architecture) and prepared for the mission by setting up team operations rooms and establishing radio base stations.

The teams, prohibited from bringing in long rifles, carried personal pistols purchased prior to deployment. This "armory" was augmented with foreign weapons and pistols discreetly purchased once they arrived in-country. There was great skepticism in dependence on the French and Lao military protection while conducting training.

The Laotian airborne school was located at Seno along with associated training facilities for airborne refresher courses. One of the Laotian *bataillon parachutistes* was stationed at the base. The French Military Mission trainers at Seno were French Marines, and many had previously been Legionnaires.

Although relations between the French and the U.S. trainers were stiff at the training camp, the NCOs and enlisted men of the two teams often met at lunch for drinks and a meal at a French café outside the base, leaving politics to those who outranked them.

Some of the recruits of the Laotian battalion were previously trained as artillerymen and did not gain much in ground-pounder proficiency as other Lowland Lao infantry recruits. All the factors affecting other teams were present at Seno: lack of good-quality Lao officers and NCOs, low pay, low morale and corruption which impacted daily attendance for training. These factors would spell the doom of the Lao battalion's performance on the battlefield. The battalion was used later in the battles against Neutralist forces under Kong Le, north of Vang Vieng, and were defeated by accurate and heavy artillery barrages and with the flanking maneuvers by the FAN (Neutralist Army Forces) at Pho Tesao.

Upon the completion of their *Hotfoot* deployment, First Lieutenant Simnacher and other members of FA-54 were chosen to remain behind and assist the transition of the three new incoming teams to Savannakhet.

FA-36, Pakse

Captain Charlie W. Brewington was one of the detachment commanders leading an eight-man FTT in Pakse, along with his XO, First Lieutenant Richard T. Terry, and team sergeant, Master Sergeant Howard E. Bostwick. He noted, "We prepared for Laos by getting ready to teach weapons and tactics. We did some area studies. It was a real hush/hush program. We were prepared to do special weapons training; we did not know what we would find."

Brewington continued, "There were two teams going to Pakse; the other team was Captain Mallory's. Each team had a house. We had a cook, she was part Vietnamese and part French, Ms. Lee. Her husband cooked for the USAID. We transitioned with the outgoing team led by Captain Shulenburg."[37]

"Mr. Woods" was the PEO representative in Pakse and spoke fluent French. He became the immediate command and control element for the teams, with Captain Philip L. Mallory serving as the senior team leader among the two teams. Each of the teams in Pakse had a different assignment; FA-36's assignment was training Laotian infantry. The French Military Mission trainers in Pakse were overbearing on the teams. Noted Brewington: "The French always stabbed us in the back, but Mr. Woods took pretty good care of that. We worked with Johnny Wah, a Frenchmen who did the interpreting. We had to coordinate all our training with the French."[38]

FA-36 taught the Laotians in the morning, and then left at *poc* time. Training from the Americans consisted only of small arms (and even at that they found themselves having to repair the weapons ranges the French had let fall into disuse, providing no help to the team); the afternoon was relegated to tactics training, taught by the French team. Training was conducted out in a wooded area near the military camp; no night training occurred. The U.S. team did not participate in any crew-served training with the mortar teams or recoilless rifle. The team medic, "Doc" Gerald Wareing, was allowed to establish a troop clinic at the camp to take care of the *tahans*, since this did not violate any training agreement.

Other than the French intransigence to allow the American trainers to do more, it was a pleasant tour. There was no threat and the team wore civilian clothes and never had to carry weapons to training. The Filipino ECCOIL contractors took care of the team's maintenance and logistics, which primarily was in securing food from the commissary. At the team house, the detachment kept a pet gibbon that provided much entertainment one day when he urinated on "Mr. Woods."

The Summer of Discontent

On May 20, 1960, the 77th Special Forces Group (Airborne) was redesignated as the 7th Special Forces Group (Airborne), at a ceremony at Fort Bragg, North Carolina.

Per the French and U.S. agreement, Operation *Hotfoot* was scheduled to last for one year, expiring on September 1, 1960. The training program, expansion of the PEO, economic and military funding, and USAID efforts were all instruments of Eisenhower's foreign policy decision to show a commitment to the defense of Southeast Asia against communism.

There was a glimmer of hope going into the summer of 1960 that the U.S. measures taken in Laos might just work. The Rightist elements, backed by General Phoumi Nosavan, won the elections handily in April. This electoral effort was also boosted by the support and funding by the CIA through various political action steps to ensure the subversion of the Neutralist and communist positions. Prime Minister Khou Abhay stepped down as the king presented his candidate to be the new head of government, Prince Somsanith. The Prince's anti-communist position, bolstered by General Phoumi Nosovan's "control" of the government since the December 1959/early January 1960 coup, gave the Eisenhower administration hope that things were finally starting to go well in Laos. The pieces were in place to ensure that no communists could possibly threaten the government. Now that the political solution was stable, and the military leaders were on board under General Phoumi's direction, U.S. economic and developmental aid could work to strengthen the country.

With this change in the air of optimism, the French government sent its director of Asian Affairs to the U.S. Department of State to deliver President de Gaulle's intention to fully "reclaim" the military training mission in Laos. Although there had been previous discussions on the subject in the spring, Ambassador Smith and the PEO chief, General Heintges, disagreed with the French assessment on the readiness of the FAL; CINCPAC and the Pentagon heartily concurred. Nor did anyone on the U.S. side think the French had enough trainers and money to deliver on their proposal. A new date for extending *Hotfoot* was proposed to Etienne M. Manac'h, the French foreign ministry representative, as June 30, 1961, a nine-month extension. William J. Rust, author of *Before the Quagmire,* captured Heintges's extreme discomfort on the proposal to withdraw American trainers from Laos before that date from a message to CINCPAC:

> On June 7, 1960, PEO Chief Heintges, the architect of the U.S.–French program, warned his superiors at CINCPAC and the Pentagon that removing U.S. training teams "could well result in disaster" in Southeast Asia. Suspecting French intentions to eliminate American trainers ever since the recall of General d'Arrivere, Heintges observed that the FAL, though greatly improved, was still inadequately trained in weapons, communication, logistics, and medical procedures. The FAL "training in anti-guerrilla and anti-terrorist tactics [is] especially inadequate," he wrote. Heintges declared that it was not possible to forecast accurately when the training mission would be completed, and he had "grave doubts as to whether the Lao would accept a purely French training mission if the Americans withdrew from the field."[39]

The use and employment of Special Forces teams had now just become a critical and essential pillar to achieving foreign policy objectives with respect to the situation in Laos. And, American diplomats and military leaders had just shown their hand to the French that they had little confidence in the French military training mission, or in their stewardship and use of the millions of dollars of American military gear being sent to the Laotian armed forces.

French position on this policy held firm, with no decision provided to the U.S. State Department on the extension of the *Hotfoot* program. The French were unwavering and firmly committed to ending the role of U.S. trainers in Laos by September 1, 1960. Even an attempt by the U.S. to change the extension to January 1, 1961, shortening it by six months, was ignored. Amidst this political bickering, Ambassador Horace Smith completed his tour in Laos and was replaced by Ambassador Winthrop G. Brown. Ambassador Brown had met with Etienne Manac'h prior to assuming his duties at the U.S. embassy in Vientiane and attempted to break the deadlock on the *Hotfoot* extension. And then political discontent in Laos erupted, putting the issue on the backburner. The clash of the superpowers in the game of the Cold War came to Laos.[40]

In the morning hours of August 9, 1960, Captain Kong Le led his SF-trained parachute battalion on a coup, advocating neutrality and for ridding Laos of U.S. military assistance. On the day of his march on Vientiane, Prime Minister Somsanith and General Phoumi (now minister of defense), along with other prominent members of the cabinet, were in Luang Prabang having discussions with the King.

While Vientiane was captured and secured by Kong Le, the cabinet remained in Luang Prabang while General Phoumi flew to Bangkok to talk with Prime Minister Sarit Thanarat about plans to retake the government. Phoumi needed money to pay his troops and military aid and assistance from Thailand to conduct the operation. Prime Minister Thanarat decided to not get involved militarily in Laotian affairs, only offering moral support. The Thai prime minister later agreed to conduct an economic blockade against Vientiane, and closed the northern border to trade.

General Phoumi flew back to Savannakhet, his base of support, and began to rally MR-III and MR-IV military forces to his venture. Meanwhile, Kong Le assisted in the efforts to declare Souvanna Phouma once again as the leader of Laos. To prevent a complete breakdown of the government, the National Assembly blessed Phouma's nomination and formed a new government, effective on August 16, 1960. When offered a position in the new government, General Phoumi refused to participate and began plans to form a counter-revolutionary government. With Prince Boun Oum as its provisional head, the "Revolutionary Committee" announced their new southern government on September 10, denouncing the Lao constitution as invalid. Amid this fracture in Laotian affairs, the United States suspended its aid to Laos, recommending reconciliation amongst the parties. Stipulations for resumption of aid required adherence to American foreign policy objectives for Laos: no communists would be in any government in Laos. With lack of progress, the U.S. responded with the cutting off of all aid to the Laotian government in October.

Few predicted what would happen next. With U.S aid now cut off, Souvanna Phouma opened talks with the Soviet Union and the Pathet Lao to obtain external aid. The Soviets began assistance efforts to help turncoat Captain Kong Le militarily, with the provision that Neutralist and Pathet Lao forces must work in consort as allies.

The U.S. chose to back Gen Phoumi using the embassy assets of the PEO. Approximately forty personnel of the PEO moved to Savannakhet and established a deputy PEO (called by FTT members as the "rebel" PEO), to assist General Phoumi with funding, material aid, and campaign planning experts to develop operations to retake the government. Air America began resupply operations to the Phoumists in support.

In late November, General Phoumi's forces pre - staged in Thakhek, and then began their march up Route 13. Assisting in this effort would be Team *Ipsen*, the *Hotfoot* team at Pakse. Initially rebuffed by Kong Le's and Souvanna Phouma's loyalists at Paksane, Phoumi's forces soon fought their way to the outskirts of Vientiane.

On December 12, Prime Minister Souvanna Phouma was ousted by the National Assembly and on December 13, the Battle for Vientiane began.[41]

With General Phoumi triumphant, Kong Le evacuated his Neutralist forces north along Route 13 to the town of Vang Vieng. He was resupplied with another series of Soviet air-support missions and assisted in his tactical movements by the Pathet Lao. Soviet aircraft evacuated his paratroopers to the Plaine des Jarres, where in the first week of January 1961 the combined forces of the Neutralists and the Pathet Lao drove RLG forces off the PDJ. The "allied" forces established their headquarters at Khang Khay and soon massive airlifts of military equipment began landing in Russian transport aircraft. With the United States supporting Phoumi's Rightist forces and the USSR supporting Kong Le and the Pathet Lao, the situation in Laos soon looked like a superpower proxy war.

Amidst the turmoil, the French protestations at the extension of *Hotfoot* were ignored. The restrictions against accompanying Laotian forces on tactical operations and field training were also soon ignored. With America now as the superpower protector of a free Laos, French influence over the affairs of Laos was severely diminished. In the coming New Year, *Hotfoot* teams would find themselves in combat. The newly elected President, John F. Kennedy, would be handed the first critical foreign policy crisis of his new administration.

Hotfoot Rotation III

The *Hotfoot* Rotation III contingent arrived in early June of 1960, still not knowing if they would have a three-month deployment and subsequently be required to close down the combined training mission with the French, or the United States' diplomatic alternative, extended through to the end of December. The incoming and outgoing FTTs conducted their transitions and fell in on the tasks previously conducted by the first two rotations of *Hotfoot*.

FC-4 provided command and control in Vientiane and employed only two FTTs in the newly named Military Region V. A feature of the third Rotation of *Hotfoot* was in the reorganization of teams from eight-man detachments to additional, smaller detachments, building the new four- and six-man teams to provide additional coverage by gleaning personnel from each eight-man team.

Team *McCormick* conducted training at the Ranger school established at Kilometer 17, attended by 200-man student detachments from the 1st and the 2nd Bataillon Parachutistes. The second FTT in Vientiane conducted training west of the city, alongside French MMF members assigned to a Laotian infantry battalion. The two American SF teams lodged in team houses in Vientiane. In May, just before the arrival of the third rotation of *Hotfoot*, the FTT mission at Camp Chinaimo (assisting with the officer's school) was transferred to the newly opened school at Dong Hene.[42]

All other *Hotfoot* missions remained the same in Luang Prabang, Khang Khay, Savannakhet, and Pakse.

Team *Derby*—Khang Khay Military Region II

In 1959, Reuben "Ben" L. Densley joined Special Forces and was assigned to a scuba team in FB-1. "I found out about the TDY to Laos from a lady at the bar in the NCO club; some officer's wife had spilled the beans during a wives' association meeting."[43]

After completing six months of country studies and language training to prepare for the mission, the team flew on C-124s to Bangkok, and was immediately transported by an Air American C-46 straight to the Plaine des Jarres (PDJ). The plane was flown by Art "Shower Shoes" Wilson. "I only knew what the mission was going to be when we got off the plane. We were assigned as instructors to the NCO and officer schools at Khang Khay."[44]

Team *Derby*, a seven-man FTT was commanded by Captain William S. Derby along with his team sergeant, Master Sergeant Stanley S. Rubin (Sergeant Reuben L. Densley was the demolitions man on the team). The newly arriving FTT conducted a three-day transition with the previous team at Khang Khay (Lieutenant Hicks). Lieutenant Colonel Brabson, the PEO officer was also there to recieve them. Out of the mainstream of political manuevering, the FTT at Khang Khay performed a standard training rotation. Ben Densley soon met two of the most important actors to emerge during the secret war in Laos:

> We spent a couple of days in Bangkok and then flew into Laos on an Air America aircraft, I'm not sure if it was a C-47 or C-46, but we landed on the Plaine des Jarres and were met by the team we were to replace. We were in civilian clothes and had fake ID cards, which fooled no one, and even the other passengers who were with IVS [International Voluntary Services] asked if we were military. One pax was "Pop Buell" whom I got to know quite well. He wrote the book *Thanh POP*.
>
> We spent approximately three days with the team that we replaced and were introduced to the French military team and the instructors for the officer and NCO school we instructed in weapons and demolitions. It was quite a challenge because most didn't read or write; however they were willing to learn and were eager to learn how to blow things up. One of the unit commanders was promoted to major, his name was Vang Pao.[45]

Khang Khay was a small village. The FTT lived in a large house while the members of the French MMF lived in another large house. The large house included sleeping rooms, a kitchen, and a commo room. To round out the ambience of the place, the team adopted the pet bear named "Sam" from the previous *Hotfoot* team.

The team wore civilian clothes; khaki shorts or pants, a shirt, and a bush hat. The team did not deploy into Laos with weapons, but they did acquire weapons once they arrived at the training site. Various arms were carried: Thompson .45-caliber sub-machine guns, M1s, and shotguns.

The MMF contingent was made up of French Foreign Legionnaires who gave all the tactical training. The American trainers were only allowed to teach skills classes. Sergeant Densley taught demolitions and weapons. Ben Densley described the training:

> We had classrooms with some of their soldiers also as instructors—the previous A-team had everything set up for giving classes and had gotten the training facilities built. There were roughly twenty to thirty men in each class. It was like the "Train the Trainer" philosophy. Once the Lao knew the class, we let them give the classes. I had trouble once when one of the instructors had taught field stripping the M1 down, but once he had it into all its parts he could not remember some of the reassembly, and I had to step back in.[46]

The team was a bit perplexed at the lack of security, given the location of Khang Khay. Densley said, "There was no apparent security at the camp—the Pathet Lao were sixty or seventy kilometers away. We never had any contact with the enemy. Our interpreter was a bit naïve but he knew multiple languages. He was fierce. His name was Thang Sar. We used him to get situational awareness." The team was kept aware of the fighting in the region between government troops and the Neutralists and Pathet Lao. "Things went along quite well until the unit at Sam Neua was cut off, and we made airdrops from Air America C-47s to deliver rice and ammo to them. I made one trip and watched as the rice bags floated down and hit the drop zone. A few weeks later the garrison surrendered and they allowed the soldiers to leave their weapons and walk back to Khang Khay."[47]

Although the FTT did not conduct MEDCAPs in the village, the team medic, Sergeant 1st Class Willie J. Foster, built a medical tent to handle the team's and the trainees' health problems; families of the soldiers were welcome as walk-ins.

The FTT also ran into the differences between training techniques used by them and those used by the French contingent, as related by Ben Densley:

> The troops, officers, and NCOs of the school were Royal Laotian Army. There was animosity between the French and us—they always seemed to keep us from doing what we wanted with the training. The French had a tactical field test for the students. Once, they needed to use our grenades (they used the old pineapple grenade that fizzed as the fuse burnt, so you would know when to throw it). They ignored our advice for training on the U.S. grenade. I gave them some of my concussion grenades, but during instruction they misused the grenade. A French guy blew his arm up. They would carry their grenades on LBE, held with a rubber band. When they were ready to throw a grenade, they just grabbed it and pulled until the rubber band broke. When he did this with the U.S. grenade, it pulled the pin. He was waiting for the sound of a fuse burning.[48]

Due to their distance and remoteness from Vientiane, the ramifications of Kong Le's coup did not disturb the activities of the FTT. Densley said,

> The only impact in the fall of 1960 with the Coup d'État of Kong Le in Vientiane, which did not affect us, was that Sam Neua was surrounded by enemy during this time. Our team was involved coordinating the dropping of supplies with Air America aircraft. When the Agency

dropped those 1,000 rifles to Vang Pao's guerrillas, for instance, there were no bolts! We helped to try and fix that problem.

While we were there our resupply was cut off, because Cpt. Kong Le took over the capital of Vientiane, and for thirty days we waited for resupply or the "bad guys" to come on down the road; we were only about forty to fifty miles from North Vietnam. We maintained 24-hour radio contact and kept contact with the IVS."[49]

Khang Khay would not remain quiet and out of sight for much longer. It would later have to be evacuated under duress during the beginning of *Hotfoot* Rotation IV, as the Pathet Lao and Kong Le's Neutralists chose the location in January of 1961 for their headquarters on the PDJ.

Captain Kong Le and the Coup d'État

In July, the 2nd Bataillon Parachutistes moved out of Vientiane into the Kilometer 22 camp. Without much rest, and still lacking pay, the unit was ordered to conduct a sweep around Vang Vieng and clear the area of Pathet Lao. This act of over-extending the battalion, along with disgust of the political process in Vientiane, sparked Kong Le's decision to rebel and take over the government and declare a neutralist path for Laos along with the ouster of all foreign forces.

Team *McCormick* headed out to the Kilometer 17 camp the morning of August 8 from their team house in Vientiane, loaded aboard their jeeps. As they drove north up Route 13, they were stopped by a roadblock of armed men from Kong Le's parachute unit and were told to return to town.[50]

On August 9, Kong Le launched his coup. The United States and the French immediately withdrew their support for continuance of the military training mission agreement. This act effectively ended U.S. trainers' restrictions imposed by the French Military Mission, and soon SF teams were back in the game they knew best and began expanded training to include tactical subjects and field training, often accompanying their units to the field.

In adherence to Eisenhower's policy, the United States would not abide with any attempt to create a Neutralist government, and particularly one with communist representatives. Thus, diplomatic and military support was thrown behind General Phoumi's efforts to replace the government, committed firmly to an anti-communist stance. Army Special Forces teams would assist as combat advisors to bolster and stiffen Lao resolve in eliminating the Neutralist threat.

Along with the deputy PEO (Colonel Albert Brownfield) in Savannakhet, the CIA had placed one of their agents in the town to work directly with Phoumi. A covert airfield was built near the town and soon Air America STOL aircraft were flying in boxes filled with cash to finance the General's venture. Thai covert agents from the Kaw Taw (the Thai covert activities organization) followed and began training commandos and saboteurs for Phoumi's use. The newly trained Lao covert contingent, under the supervision of Thai border police and the PARU, were soon running raids by early September against Vientiane, utilizing 60mm mortars aimed at the capital.

Kong Le's forces responded in late September by routing pro-Phoumi forces in the town of Paksane. In Military Region II, they drove government forces out of Sam Neua. Next threatened was Xieng Khouang, but Phouma loyalist forces plans were soon thwarted by Major Vang Pao, declaring his forces anti-communist and their loyalties as pro-Phoumi.[51]

Meanwhile, in the south, American military aid, primarily in the form of parachutes, was delivered to Pakse and Savannakhet to prepare for the 1st BP and the 3rd BP airborne drop near Vientiane. Team *Ipsen* at Pakse deployed on August 16 to Paksong to prepare BI-4 with communications training, prior to BI-4's deployment to Savannakhet to reinforce Phoumi.[52]

Additionally, there was the need to bolster and retrain the defeated forces of Colonel Bounleut Sanichanh, who had retreated south after battles with Kong Le's paratroopers in Paksane. Upon Team *Ipsen*'s return to Savannakhet, the deputy PEO ordered the team north to Thakhek on October 27 to assist in the preparation of General Phoumi's forces for their march on to Vientiane (and to be the eyes and ears of the PEO). Major Eleazar Parmley IV, the senior FTT commander at Savannakhet, took over operational control of the team on October 20. (Parmley had been assisting the rump PEO with planning, along with Major Robert McKnight, the FC-Vientiane operations officer.)[53]

It is not known what unique support and training *Hotfoot* teams in MR-III and MR-IV provided to prepare the Laotian battalions and paratroopers from the 1st and now 3rd Bataillon Parachutistes; certainly with the PEO contingent in Savannakhet providing direction to the FTT team leaders, they at least expanded their training subjects to prepare the Rightist forces for combat.

Sergeant Ned L. Miller was the team medic for FA-47 (Captain Ipsen's team) assigned to Pakse. The team arrived from Bangkok via Air America C-46 and rented a two-story French-style house. They were given the mission to train Laotian infantry for a *groupement mobile* and were provided one Mitsubishi-style, 1953 jeep for transport. Like other teams, FA-47 had a mechanic assigned from the 82nd Airborne Division.

Ned Miller recounts the team was strengthened with four additional men, perhaps gleaned from the other *Hotfoot* teams in Pakse:

> During *Hotfoot*, we wore civilian clothes with Department of the Army civilian ID cards. We had M1 Garands and grease guns. We started out with a split-team and one mechanic from the 82nd. Later this built up to a 12-man team and interpreter. When the coup went down, the three teams at Pakse stopped the individual training and began tactical training of the forces General Phoumi was preparing for his retaking of the capital. I was not there when they moved, but the FTTs accompanied some of those forces north, then on into Vientiane.[54]

On October 24, Major Parmley moved to Thakhek and began an initial inspection of training and field fortifications. In his new role, he became the SF combat advisor to General Boun Leut, the ground commander of General Phoumi's GM-1. After discussions with General Phoumi, Parmley assisted General Boum Leut's staff with planning the attack plans to cross the Nam Ca Dinh River in order to capture Paksane. As a combat advisor, Parmley had use of a liaison aircraft, which he used to help transport Lao wounded from the battlefield. SF medics assisted with combat medical care.[55]

When the team moved north to Thakhek, they also began training for the fledgling Lao Special Forces (designated Special Battalions). The team was approached by Major Siho Lamphoutacoul to discuss a series of special operations initiatives. Major Siho was an intelligence officer and leader of the 60mm mortar raid earlier on Vientiane; his forces were some of the nascent and growing Lao Special Forces. At Thakhek, it is certain the team began to train with his newly formed Groupement Mobile Spècial 1 (GMS-1), with two *bataillon speciales*—BS-11 and BS-33.[56]

Captain Ipsen was then ordered farther north to assess the state of affairs on the front lines north of Thakhek, near the village of Ban Bok.[57] He was soon to be the first of U.S. Army Special Forces to become involved in combat. Meanwhile, *Hotfoot* teams hunkered down in Luang Prabang as the military leadership of MR-I swayed back and forth between decisions to support Kong Le or Phoumi. The matter was settled when pro-Phoumi forces seized the town; when Kong Le later attempted to recapture the town with militia and Pathet Lao, the militia commander broke contact and joined the pro-Phoumi faction. By mid-November, even the commander of all military forces in Vientiane, General Oudane, declared for the countercoup forces.

The first step in seizing the initiative would be the retaking of Paksane and the securing of Route 13. To seize Paksane, Kong Le's forces blocking the route and the river near the village at Ban Sot would have to be eliminated. The land route was blocked with FAL units, employing artillery. The river route was blocked with four naval patrol boats from Loyalist units of the River Flotilla Force. A small commando team was formed to eliminate the threat. Captain Ipsen, along with a Thai PARU officer and ten others (from the "new" Lao Special Forces) crossed into Thailand and moved to occupy an ambush position to break the maritime blockade.[58]

On November 21, General Phoumi launched his three task forces north out of Savannakhet, and soon gathered at Thakhek. Captain Ipsen, an artillery officer by branch, was extracted from his ambush site along the river to join the 105mm artillery battery in the column. In response, Kong Le then launched forces to reinforce the Paksane front, but in doing so weakened his military hold over Vientiane.

By the end of November and into the first week of December of 1960, *Hotfoot* Rotation III was being replaced by Rotation IV. The stay-behind cadres of Special Forces personnel conducting the transition with the incoming teams were certainly viewed by the PEO as additional assets for use. In some cases, FTTs were stopped

The U.S. Army initiated its counterinsurgency capability with the formation of the Psychological Warfare Center in 1952 at Ft. Bragg, North Carolina. The Psychological Warfare Center (first termed the U.S. Army Psychological Warfare Division & School) and the 10th Special Forces Group were initially established in the Smoke Bomb Hill section of Ft. Bragg. After U.S. Army Special Forces became the predominant activity at this site, the School and Center name was changed to the Special Warfare Center in 1956 (originally titled the U.S. Army Center for Special Warfare). (*U.S. Army*)

Brigadier General William P. Yarborough commanded the U.S. Army Special Warfare Center at Ft. Bragg, North Carolina, in 1961. It was his bold act to wear a green beret during President Kennedy's visit to Ft. Bragg in the fall of 1961 which helped to solidify the headgear as official, and thus the naming of the U.S. Army Special Forces as "The Green Berets." (*Photo courtesy of the USAJFK Special Warfare Museum*)

An early Field A-team (FA) conducts guerrilla warfare training with "partisan" role-players in the Pisgah National Forest. Guerrilla warfare was a subset of unconventional warfare and one of the Green Beret roles in Special Warfare. (*U.S. Army photo via Alfred H. Paddock, Jr.*)

Typical lowland Lao houses on stilts. (*Photo courtesy of USAJFK Special Warfare Museum, LTC Keravouri collection*)

Mist, clouds, and haze confronted 21st SOS helicopters en route to evacuate the Thai survivors and SF advisors at Moung Soui, 1968. Weather conditions worsened during the wet monsoon season. (*Courtesy of the Arnau family*)

An example of the slash-and-burn agricultural style of rural Laos. After burning the slashed materials to ash, nitrogen could be released into the soil upon the next rain. During burning season, the smoke of these fires created adverse flying conditions. (*Courtesy of the USAJFK Special Warfare Museum, LTC Keravouri collection*)

Karst formations were found all over Laos. The "Tom's Thumb" karst formation is a unique landmark near Vang Vieng. (*Courtesy of Dennis W. Lid, Project 404 ARMA*)

A remote Lima Site (landing strip) on the Bolovens Plateau. (*Courtesy of the Arnau family*)

A group of *bonzes*, or novice monks. This is how they typically appeared to American advisors—shaved heads, orange or yellow-saffron-robed, and carrying alms bowls to beg for food or money. Young monks were typically naïve concerning the spread of communist ideology. They were often misled to spread socialistic tenets of solving egregious conditions in society. (*Photo courtesy Sobichevsky family*)

Highlands village and family. Note style of house built on the ground. Colors of clothing were chosen to reflect the various tribes. (*©William E. Platt, Raven 43 collection, via John Garrity collection*)

SFC Ernie Tabata conducts training for a Laotian infantry battalion (BI) mortar section at Camp Chinaimo range. The twelve Lao infantry battalions and the twelve Lao volunteer battalions (BVs) were predominantly equipped with American military gear and weapons as part of the Embassy's Military Assistance Program. (*Photo courtesy of Ernest K. "Ernie" Tabata*)

Members of the 12th BI, GM-17, fire American-supplied weapons on a range in Phong Hong. (*Photo courtesy of the USAJFK Special Warfare Museum, Lt. Col. Aito Keravouri collection*)

A typical volunteer battalion (BV) near Attopeu. Note the variety and mix of uniforms and equipment. (*Photo courtesy of Sobichevsky family*)

A company of Kha tribal guerrillas (100 men) at training camp under the instruction of *White Star* FTTs, somewhere near the Bolovens Plateau. (*Photo courtesy of Gene M. Gavigan, White Star advisor*)

A Laotian Royal Artillery 105mm howitzer battery provides fire support to troops in contact. (*Photo courtesy of Albert Slugocki*)

Lao T-28s at the Long Tieng airstrip (LS-20A). The T-28 became the mainstay fighter/bomber capability of the RLAF by the mid-1960s. (*Courtesy of Mike Lampe*)

Gunboats of the Laotian River Flotilla Force on the Mekong River. The Lao navy was small, consisting of ex-French patrol boats and American-made landing craft. This gave the Flotilla Force around thirty to forty vessels. Their mission was security along the Mekong River. They never became an effective riverine warfare force outside of that task. (*Courtesy of R/K*)

The Pathet Lao flag. (*VVATT*)

Hotfoot Rotations I–IV, Operation *Momentum*, and FID

COL Blackburn (commander of the 77th Special Forces Group) chose LTC Arthur D. "Bull" Simons, commanding FB-3, to lead the first *Hotfoot* deployment. (Simons had served with the 6th Rangers where he participated in the famous raid on the Cabantuan prison camp in the Philippine campaign during World War II.) Shown while hunting wild boar in Laos. (*Courtesy of USAJFK Special Warfare Museum*)

In 1955, the Lao Royal Army was supported by the United States Operations Mission (USOM) with money from the Military Assistance Program (MAP). French forces in Laos administered the training program and the issuance of U.S. military gear and equipment. The Lao army experienced a series of failed efforts to fight the communists, sparking the intervention of American trainers in 1959. (*Courtesy of NARA*)

Upon arrival in Bangkok, teams and equipment were transloaded from C-123s onto Air America C-46s or C-47s for further flights into Laos. (*Courtesy of Sam Skemp, MD*)

Hotfoot team house in Luang Prabang. *Hotfoot* teams were normally equipped with ¼-ton Mitsubishi jeeps and a trailer provided by the MAP from the U.S. Embassy, Vientiane. Each *Hotfoot* team was augmented with a mechanic attached from the 82nd Airborne Division. (*Courtesy of Thomas O. Humphus*)

(*Above*) French trainers at Khang Khay. *Hotfoot* trainer can be seen standing in the background. The French insisted the American trainers could not conduct any training of a tactical nature. *Hotfoot* trainers focused on training Lao forces on American-supplied military equipment. (*Courtesy of SGM, Retired, George W. Sevits*)

(*Left*) Team commo set-up in Luang Prabang (RSO-1). For static sites, these radios were powered by automobile batteries, or if a team was equipped with one, a generator. Wires lead to antenna placed on the roof. (*Courtesy of Thomas O. Humphus*)

Sergeant Robert G. Daniel gives instruction near Kiou Ka Cham, FA-65 on *Hotfoot* Rotation IV. He is dressed in U.S. military khaki shirt, without insignia, a black baseball hat, and olive green military fatigue pants. Advisors normally wore their issue GI boots. (*Courtesy of Albert Slugocki*)

SP4 Tom Humphus (communications) with pet bear "Sam" on the PDJ helping in support of Team *Van Strien* at Khang Khay, during *Hotfoot* Rotation II. In the background is Sergeant Hoskinson, the FTT demolitions man, and Sergeant 1st Class Roy M. Batton, the FC-4 control team S-4 NCO. Humphus returned to Laos later to serve in Operation *White Star*. (*Courtesy of Thomas O. Humphus*)

Hotfoot personnel were considered civilian technicians and trainers as part of their cover story for being in Laos. Referred to by the title of "Mister," some detachment members dressed the part. Others tried to at least wear khaki shirts and pants, with black baseball hats, to look a little more military. One such trainer above, in 1959, wears shorts, a cap, and no shirt. (*USAJFK Special Warfare Museum*)

SP4 Hoffman at the Savannakhet team house, with the Mekong River in the background. He is wearing army khakis, with no markings, and sports an M1 carbine and his holstered .38-caliber pistol he bought for the mission. (*Courtesy of Irving Hoffman*)

White Star radio operator, Art Walker, at the Ban Pha Khao clandestine Hmong radio station. This radio station supported PSYOP broadcasting for actions against the Pathet Lao and for bolstering the morale of the Hmong forces. The Hmong clandestine radio station was called the "Union of Lao Races Radio." (*Courtesy of Arthur F. "Sparky" Walker*)

Captain James E. Ipsen, detachment commander for FA-47 (Team *Ipsen*) on left in white shirt, stands with Sergeant Thomas B. Baldwin (light weapons) on the right, with two French Military Training Team members in Pakse. Captain Ipsen is recorded as one of the first Special Forces operators to go into combat with Rightist forces in 1960, during the retaking of Vientiane. Ipsen, an artillery-trained officer, accompanied General Phoumi Nosovan's forces on their march from Savannakhet to the capital. (*Courtesy of Ned L. Miller, Medic, Team Ipsen*)

Rotation IV activities during the transition from *Hotfoot* to *White Star*. Members of Team *Chance* prepare for airborne combat drop with Laotian forces to begin the battle of Moung Kassy. (*Courtesy of Albert Slugocki*)

FA-65 advised Laotian forces in the vicinity of Kiou Ka Cham. (*Courtesy of Herb Brucker*)

A rare photo of Bill Lair in the field during the war in Laos. Bill Lair was the originator of the Unconventional Warfare program, Operation *Momentum*, the training and employment of Vang Pao's Hmong guerrillas. In this picture taken in the late 1960s, Bill Lair observes an attack on enemy positions east of the PDJ (in white shirt, looking through observation scope). Atop the hill is Dick Secord, the CIA air operations officer, seconded from the USAF. To the rear of Bill Lair is an unknown army assistant attaché advisor, an ARMA. (*Courtesy of retired MG Richard Secord*)

FA-27, Team *Chance* camp site. In the photo are Master Sergeant William E. Patterson, the medic, and Ken Bates (fourth from left). Others cannot be identified in the order. Sergeant Jan Janosik, weapons man, is in the picture. Captain Chance, sitting on the right, is just to the left of Ken Bates in the T-shirt with his back to camera. (*Courtesy of Kenneth R. Bates*)

Ken Bates shown at right with North Vietnamese Montagnard, who was fleeing communism and passed through the camp at Padong. (*Photo courtesy of Ken Bates*)

SFC Thomas B. Baldwin (weapons) moves with column over rugged mountain trails. (*Courtesy of USAJFK Special Warfare Museum, Herb Brucker collection*)

Making commo at the camp. It was necessary to employ a hand-cranked generator to provide the electricity during radio transmissions. (*Courtesy of the USAJFK Special Warfare Museum*)

First Lieutenant Al Paddock with guerrilla troops. After duties at Kiou Ka Cham, on June 29, 1961 Paddock began a reconnaissance for a new camp site with his split-detachment, FA-65A, to conduct Hmong guerrilla training as part of Operation *Momentum*. He settled on a mountain area called Phou Ka Sak near the village of Kiou Ya. The new camp was dubbed "Paddockville." (*Courtesy of the USAJFK Special Warfare Museum, Herb Brucker collection*)

Fred Sass was an Air America H-34 pilot who flew support for operations of the CIA and Special Forces at Padong and Pha Khao. He is pictured here standing with Colonel Vang Pao at Houei Sa An, preparing for a flight to provide payroll to guerrillas; money is in duffle bags on the ground. (*Courtesy of Fred W. Sass*)

The UW team at Moung Oum was retasked to conduct a three-week Hmong Ranger course as FTT-59. Here, the team sergeant, Master Sergeant Dick Meadows, briefs a Hmong platoon on patrol techniques; Captain George Stewart stands behind him, recording student performance. (*Courtesy of George F. Stewart*)

Detachment *Faistenhammer* (B-detachment) along with members of the A-teams (1962). Major Faistenhammer led the final mission of SF teams supporting Operation *Momentum* in Military Region II by consolidating all SF-sponsored *Momentum* teams at Sam Thong. The teams trained Hmong recruits and also ran a small airborne school. Major Faistenhammer is in the first row of standing personnel, at left of the row, in short shirt-sleeves. (*Courtesy of USAJFK Special Warfare Museum, Lt. Col. Keravouri collection*)

Sergeant Norman E. Johnson instructs at the Site 20 (Sam Thong) firing range. (*Courtesy of Norman E. Johnson, via Richard Sutton*)

Dong Hene officer's candidate school headquarters and FTT-38's marker at the compound. One of the foreign internal defense (FID) missions for Army SF teams was supporting both NCO and officer schools and courses. (*Courtesy of Robert G. "Bob" Willis*)

Sergeant Robert G. "Bob" Willis advises Lao officer students on patrol. (*Courtesy of Bob Willis*)

Smith, Rivers, and "Elmo" Clark pose at the team bunker. (*Courtesy of Bob Willis*)

Sergeant Bob Willis points out the bullet hole from the night he was shot at while manning the .30-cal machine gun at the guard post. (*Courtesy of Bob Willis*)

Lieutenant Kubza from the MAAG supported the artillery MTT and was assisted by Staff Sergeant Robert Colvin from Captain Mountel's A-detachment. Here he instructs Lao artillerymen on lay of weapons and fire direction techniques. (*Lt. Col. Keravouri collection*)

FTT-36, NCO academy MR-V, Camp Chinaimo. NCO academy graduates are formed up for the ceremony. Major General Reuben Tucker reviews Lao NCOs, accompanied by camp commander and Lieutenant Colonel Radow from the MAAG (in shorts). Lieutenant Hazen and members of FTT-36 prepare to receive General Tucker and VIP party. To the left in the ranks, left to right, are Lieutenant Hazen, Sergeant 1st Class Dowdy, and Sergeant Loggins. (*Lt. Col. Keravouri collection*)

The airborne course at Seno, GM-15. Students are jumping off the 34-foot tower and practicing on the swing trainer, used to train paratroopers on how to control swinging in their parachutes and prepare for landing. (*Lt. Col. Keravouri collection*)

Split team FTT-43A commanded by Lieutenant William E. Kellenberger (XO of Detachment FA-43) provides instruction on field tactics to a volunteer battalion (BV) company at Camp Chinaimo. (*Courtesy of Ernest K. "Ernie" Tabata*)

Lieutenant Kellenberger hands out graduation certificate to a BV soldier (*Photo courtesy of First Lieutenant William Kellenberger*)

from redeploying to support General Phoumi's operation. Team *Ipsen* was extended a further six months into Rotation IV.

In Vientiane, Colonel Kouprasith Abhay, the commander of MR-V, gathered a small force of his loyalists and on December 7, 1960 launched a drive into Vientiane to confront Kong Le paratroopers; the Neutralist forces wore red armbands and the countercoup forces were seen wearing white armbands. Kong Le was forced to pull his forces back from Paksane to address the threat. General Phoumi's forces then easily took Paksane and launched an airborne drop into Camp Chinaimo to bolster Colonel Kouprasith's contingent. The two leaders soon held an offsite meeting to coordinate the countercoup. And then an alarming escalation occurred which did not bode well for the citizens of Vientiane: the Soviets delivered artillery and heavy mortars, manned by NVA artillerymen, to Kong Le's forces.

The battle of Vientiane began in earnest on December 13. Author Shelby L. Stanton noted in his work *Green Berets at War* that, "On 13 December 1960, Special Forces soldiers jumped into the critical communications crossroad of Ban Tha Deua with the 1st and 3rd Bataillons de Parachutiste and pushed aside light opposition."[59]

Phoumist forces entered the streets and were confronted with artillery and mortar barrages from Kong Le's gunners. In response, and within days, Phoumist forces had up to two batteries of their own artillery for use.

Key areas of Vientiane were left destroyed and burning, including hits on the U.S. embassy and the wing of the building used by the CIA; employees scurried to destroy documents. The staff of the U.S. embassy sought safety at the ambassador's residence.

The two *Hotfoot* teams in Vientiane hunkered down in their team houses during the battle, as described by Kenneth Conboy, in his work *Shadow War*:

> Inside Vientiane, the pitched street battles were providing a fair share of close calls for two [*Hotfoot*] teams trapped in their quarters. As the artillery barrage reached a peak, both teams withdrew to the PEO compound, only to find it deserted. Moving to the team control headquarters [FC-3], they found a decapitated woman on the front lawn. The Special Forces advisors then hid as shells rained nearby and a marauding Kong Le patrol knocked on the front door, but stopped short of searching the premises.[60]

Mervyn Brown, the deputy to the British ambassador in Vientiane, may have seen Captain Ipsen, along with some of the *Hotfoot* personnel and PEO officers during the battle. As the artillery duel began, he and other families were trapped in their embassy lodging, called the MIC site. The site had been purchased from the Manufactures Indo-Chine (MIC), a French cigarette company. In his book, *War in Shangri-La: A Memoir of Civil War in Laos*, he describes the passing back and forth of red arm-banded Kong Le troops and the arrival of Phoumist troops:

> Perhaps a hundred "white" troops passed through the MIC site garden, keeping pace with the armoured cars and tanks on the road. They were followed after a short interval by more troops coming along the road, mainly on trucks but some walking, and also by more armoured cars and tanks. On several of these were perched lightly skinned, fair-haired soldiers who were

obviously American "advisors"; and we subsequently learned that the attacking troops also included a number of Thai "volunteers."[61]

The battle ended on December 16, with Kong Le's forces pinned into their last stronghold at Wattay airport followed by the triumphal arrival into the city of Prince Boun Oum and General Phoumi. Kong Le rallied his forces and escaped before any concluding action for control of Vientiane; Souvanna Phouma had fled earlier in the month. As the Rightists under Phoumi regained control of the government, Neutralist forces were soon retreating north up Route 13 toward Vang Vieng, hauling their Soviet artillery with them.

Incoming Rotation IV of *Hotfoot* would prove to be different and unique from earlier *Hotfoot* rotations as American foriegn policy objectives changed as a result of the coup's impact. *Hotfoot* teams would soon go into the field as combat advisors to stiffen Lao army forces, amidst a civil war and a communist-inspired insurgency, all in the shadow of a looming superpower confrontation between the USSR and the United States.

CHAPTER THREE

Hotfoot to *White Star*: Rotation IV and the Transition to Combat

Now Rann the Kite brings home the night
That Mang the Bat sets free –
The herds are shut in byre and hut
For loosed till dawn are we.
This is the hour of pride and power,
Talon and tush and claw.
O hear the call!—Good Hunting, All
That keep the Jungle Law!

RUDYARD KIPLING, THE JUNGLE BOOK

Hotfoot Rotation IV deployed to Laos at the end of November 1960 and began their transition with the previous rotation. As they were settling in to their new duties, the political and military situation in Laos changed dramatically. As noted earlier, in November General Phoumi Nosovan began his efforts to oust Kong Le's Neutralist forces from the capital, resulting in the concomitant battle of Vientiane.

Lieutenant Colonel John T. Little commanded Rotation IV, along with his deputy commander, Major Charles B. Lewis; Sergeant Major James L. Hallford was the senior FC NCO.

Lieutenant Colonel John T. Little enlisted in the 508th Parachute Regiment during World War II. He was awarded a Bronze Star for his actions in Belgium where he maneuvered with his armored force and tank destroyers to save an infantry unit under pressure. After World War II, he entered the officer corps as a second lieutenant. He later volunteered for the 77th Special Forces Group.

Hotfoot Rotation IV would be characterized by breaking the teams free of the limits and restrictions of garrison training duties imposed upon them by the French Military Training Mission. Their tactical actions on ground would contribute to the success of U.S. foreign policy to prevent the inclusion of the communist Pathet Lao from participating in any attempt by the RLG to form a tri-partite government. Other achievements in strategic utility would include helping to slow the pace of military failure on the part of the FAL, participating in the attrition on communist forces, and begin the conduct of unconventional warfare (guerrilla warfare) with irregular forces to expand options for American foreign policy objectives and help the RLG in shaping the course of the war. Opening up the guerrilla warfare front imposed an additional cost to the NVA and Pathet Lao in Military Region II. These activities helped to achieve the two important "master claims" of SOF's strategic utility, as explained by Colin S. Gray: (1) economy of force and cost effectiveness (using SOF when conventional military forces are unsuitable), and (2) expanding choices and options available to political and military leaders.[1]

The French government pushed the United States to complete the *Hotfoot* mission by September 1, 1960. French plans called for a complete takeover of FAL training through an increase in the numbers of their own military trainers. No one in the American Mission believed the French could pull that off, not economically (military equipping,) nor militarily (manning sufficient trainers). The August coup by Kong Le froze U.S. military teams from *Hotfoot III* in place as a possible hedge for any upcoming contingency, and the deadline for the American withdrawal was ignored. As the crisis worsened, an additional rotation of Special Forces teams (Rotation IV) was called forward to transition into Laos. Also clear to the Americans was the unpopularity of the French Military Mission by Souvanna Phouma and General Phoumi Nosovan (Phoumi running the "rebel" government); they both wished the French gone.

With French influence waning, and indecisiveness on the part of French diplomats to extend the *Hotfoot* mission, the U.S. ambassador and PEO chief authorized SF teams to deploy out from garrisons and training camps to serve as combat advisors with their Lao counterparts.

William J. Rust captured the frustration and reasoning of CINCPAC, Admiral Felt, to make this decision in his work *Before the Quagmire: American Intervention in Laos 1954–1961*:

> While State Department officials stalled for time in hopes that Souvanna might be deposed politically, Admiral Felt, the commander of U.S. forces in the Pacific, sought to strengthen Phoumi's military position. Convinced that "at least one Phoumi military victory" was a precondition to a political solution in Laos, Felt ordered PEO officers in Savannakhet to encourage offensive operations by Phoumi north of the Nam Ca Dinh River, the ceasefire line between the general's forces and Souvanna's. Although he chafed at State Department restrictions on military activity in Laos, the admiral was acting under authority granted to him when Souvanna appeared to be preparing to retake Luang Prabang.[2]

Soon PEO, U.S. para-military experts, and Army Special Forces switched from training in garrison to advisory operations in the field. The requirement for an increase in Laotian forces grew to an additional nine more BIs (for a total of twenty-one), as a response to the increasing strength and activities of the NVA and Pathet Lao.

In January of 1961, PEO chief Brigadier General Andrew Jackson Boyle requested nine additional Special Forces field advisory teams (LTAG—Laotian Training and Advisory Group—"L-Taggers") to handle the increased military assistance requirements. In order to provide enough FAs to cover all the BIs, plus the training centers, Rotation IV would begin the practice of deploying SF teams by split detachments. This began as the nine additional SF teams began arriving in batches, spread between February and March. (This needed increase in SF team strength was termed *Monkhood* in official traffic.)

Rotation IV would also become involved in Operation *Momentum*, the use of SF teams as trainers alongside the CIA's support from the Thai Police Aerial Reinforcement Unit (PARU) and case officers deployed with the Hmong guerrillas, led by newly promoted Lieutenant Colonel Vang Pao.

On April 19, *Hotfoot* Rotation IV transitioned to Operation *White Star* upon President Kennedy's approval to transform the PEO to a full MAAG (and now under no agreement with the French for the United States to leave or remain based on the earlier arrangement with the French military training teams). In addition, U.S. military trainers and advisors switched from civilian clothes back into military uniforms, under arms; the diplomatic pretense and cover was over if the NVA were going to continue to operate openly in Laos. Transition of the SF teams to overt combat status was one of the expansion of military choices for the new president. It sent a clear message of American policy to confront the communists and helped to stiffen the resolve of the RLG and other Southeast Asian allies.

Rotation IV also included some of the first U.S. combat deaths and prisoners of war taken by the Pathet Lao.

Kong Le's Operational Moves

After his rout from Vientiane, Kong Le and his forces successfully slipped north up Route 13, escaping any engagement with Rightist forces. Expecting to be pursued, he blew the Nam Lik River bridge behind him and continued into Vang Vieng, where he halted. The Russians soon began to resupply him by air, followed by landing IL-14s at the Vang Vieng airfield. The Pathet Lao moved a 1,000-man contingent into Moung Kassy to reinforce and protect Kong Le's northward movement.

The American country team at the embassy became nervous at the possibility of the FAN combining forces with the Pathet Lao and NVA. Diplomatic messages flew between the embassy in Vientiane and U.S. Department of State at Foggy Bottom. Simultaneously, PEO military planners strongly urged the FAL to strike Kong Le and his FAN while Neutralists combat forces were still in flight, but the leaders of the FAL appeared to be more worried about who would control newly recaptured Vientiane than concerned with mounting an offensive. To sweeten the pot, the United States provided the first of four H-34 helicopters to Vientiane to assist with troop movement.

Finally convinced to do something and under pressure from the embassy in Vientiane, General Phoumi Nosovan and his Rightist forces (with help from the

PEO) developed a campaign plan to employ three task forces to strike Kong Le at Vang Vieng. The first task force was designed to maneuver south from Luang Prabang, following Route 13. The second task force was designed to attack westward out of the PDJ, following Route 7 to the road junction at Sala Phou Koun, then turn south on Route 13 toward Vang Vieng. The third task force, to be named GM *Vientiane*, was designed to attack north from Vientiane, up Route 13.

Major General Oudone Sananikone described the task organization and goals of the plan:

> I was summoned to headquarters and ordered to relieve Kouprasith Abhay as commander of the 15th Mobile Group which at that time was fighting Kong Le at Vang Vieng, on Route 13 about 75 miles north of Vientiane. I was very pleased with these orders …
>
> The 15th Mobile Group was a light infantry regimental combat team composed of three very under-strength rifle battalions, an armored platoon of light tanks, an artillery battery (l05-mm howitzers), an engineer company and a small administration and logistic element.
>
> My orders were to push Kong Le and his allied Pathet Lao force north to Sala Phou Khoun where the road forks; Route 13 continues north to Luang Prabang, while Route 7 leads east to Moung Soui, the Plain des Jarres and eventually to North Vietnam at Barthelemy Pass.
>
> While my 15th Mobile Group pushed north, Brig. General Kham Khong was to advance with his larger mobile group from Paksane north along Route 4 to Moung Soui, then to attack Sala Phou Koun along Route 7 from the east. The Americans in Vientiane and the NLA [National Laotian Army—the term used by Laotian military at that time for the FAL] staff were making wagers on which task force would be the first to reach Sala Phou Koun. The overwhelming odds favored Kham Khong, according to the bettors in Vientiane. Another task force was to attack south along Route 13 from Luang Prabang. This was GM 11 with three BIs and a battery of l05-mm howitzers.[3]

Kong Le headed north. After a small feint up Route 13 beyond the Sala Phou Koun junction, he led his forces east on Route 7 and pushed FAL forces out of Moung Soui, assisted by Pathet Lao and NVA advisors performing rearguard actions at Vang Vieng and Route 13. As an additional benefit, capturing a key airfield on the PDJ would allow for increased FAN resupply from the Soviet Union.

Added to the mix, the Pathet Lao crossed into Laos from the North Vietnamese border sanctuary on December 31, 1960 to attack the garrison at Nong Het, reinforcing Kong Le's movements east on the PDJ. In reaction, FAL forces around Ban Ban, Khang Khay, and Xieng Khouang began a retreat south along Route 4. One of the government forces remaining on the PDJ was BI-10, a mixed Hmong and ethnic Lao unit, led by Major Vang Pao.[4]

Hotfoot Khang Khay, Team *Bernshausen* (FA-32)

Team *Bernshausen* was initially commanded by Captain Clellan C. Thrower during his assignment to the 77th Special Forces Group at Fort Bragg, NC. Captain Thrower was a Field Artillery officer by branch; when the group planned to form an artillery MTT for Laos, he along with other Field Artillery qualified personnel in the group were formed as a specialty MTT team and prepared to deploy to MR-III

(Savannakhet). Other personnel on the FA included First Lieutenant Fred D. Brown (detachment XO), 1st Sergeant Harvey W. Dezern (team sergeant), Master Sergeant Dennis C. Kidd (weapons), and Staff Sergeant Lawrence R. McGirr, a mechanic from the 82nd Airborne Division.

Captain Fritz Bernshausen was assigned to replace Captain Thrower. To fully man the eight-man FA, Sergeant 1st Class Horace Ford (weapons) also joined the team. First Lieutenant Charles H. McLendon served as the detachment XO and Master Sergeant Robert V. Miller was the team sergeant. The team was alerted for an upcoming deployment to Laos and continued preparation for the mission with language training, weapons training, and country orientation studies. The team was scheduled for *Hotfoot* Rotation IV, deploying into Laos on 28 November 1960 as a six-month TDY rotation. They were informed that their mission would be training weapons proficiencies to Laotian infantry alongside the French military trainers. Lieutenant Charles H. McLendon deployed as a member of the ADVON (advanced echelon party) sometime in early November, ahead of the team.

McClendon related his activities as ADVON upon his arrival in-country:

> We wore civvies, and carried civilian passports. I had an ID card that said I was a GS employee. We were told to not call each other by military rank titles. We landed in Bangkok, and then went to the JUSMAG-Thai hotel. Fortunately, the team sergeant, Master Sergeant Stanley Rubin from Captain Derby's team, the team we were replacing up on the PDJ, was there on R&R, so we had a chance to get together and talk about the mission and the situation.
>
> The next day, Air America flew us into the PDJ. I had not received any type of mission briefing from anyone. The team had a house on a hill at Khang Khay we were going to occupy; the French had a house on another hill. There was a market town about halfway to the PDJ airstrip from Khang Khay: Phongsavan. At Khang Khay, we had a clearing which STOL-type aircraft could land in, along with helicopters. Air America mostly flew the U-10 Helio Couriers in there.[5]

Lieutenant McClendon conducted activities to transition with the team at Khang Khay, a seven-man *Hotfoot III* FA led by Captain William S. Derby. Khang Khay, a large military training center, had a PEO advisor assigned, Colonel Brabson (U.S. Army). Brabson drove Lieutenant McClendon on a reconnaissance tour of the PDJ and stopped along the way to meet with the Laotian forces stationed there. During their foray, McClendon had the opportunity to become familiar with Major Vang Pao, the deputy commander of Laotian forces on the Plaines des Jarres. Brabson had prewarned him that the Hmong and the Laotians did not get along with each other.

Three weeks into McClendon's role as the ADVON, the remainder of Team *Bernshausen* arrived (it is thought they may have been titled as FA-32; the records are not clear). The team was aware of Kong Le's forces headed their way, but Colonel Brabson had convinced them Kong Le's forces were at least sixty days away, based on the road conditions and the weather. The FAL near Moung Soui were also felling trees on Route 7 and destroying bridges to impede the Neutralist forces' advance. Unfortunately, they did not take into account the industriousness of the Neutralists to cut away felled trees and repair bridges.

The SF team became frustrated in the beginning of this tour, not only with the French trainers' insistence they not conduct tactical training, but also at the lack of response of the Laotians to attend training; as a result, the team trained no Laotians. McLendon noted, "When we were up at the PDJ, the French did things their way with tactics. After the incident at Khang Khay, the French were out, and the Americans were responsible for all the training."[6]

The only "training" the team was able to accomplish was when one day they saw some Laotians having a problem with their .50 calibers; the team members stopped what they were doing and fixed the weapons so they would fire properly. They spent most of their time constructing firing ranges.

With the now combined Neutralists and Pathet Lao headed toward the Plaine des Jarres, everyone at Khang Khay soon knew they were going to have a problem. McLendon noted, "We could see the roads from our team house. One day, in late December, we saw a large group of people coming from the west on the road heading east. In the other direction, we could see people fleeing from the east heading west. They were passing each other on the road and not telling anyone what they were running away from."[7]

The Neutralists and the Pathet Lao relentlessly cleared trees and repaired bridges and began to approach government forces holding Moung Soui. After shelling the garrison, the FAL withdrew in retreat. Meanwhile, BI-10 and BV-21 grouped their forces at the PDJ airfield, apprehensive of being caught in a pincer movement between Kong Le's force in the west and the Pathet Lao approaching from the east. Air America began delivery of mortars and ammunition, along with disassembled 105mm howitzers.

The MR-II commander, Colonel Sourith, soon arrived from Xieng Khouangville. Colonel Brabson and Captain Bernshausen, along with the *Hotfoot* team, met him; they had driven to the airfield earlier to make an assessment on the situation and assist in the downloading of the artillery pieces. When the FA team tried to unload the second 105mm artillery piece, it proved impossible. It was loaded back aboard the aircraft and returned to Vientiane.[8]

McLendon described the situation:

> Captain Bernshausen and Colonel Brabson went down on the PDJ to check the situation. They soon sent us a message that a couple of pieces of artillery were being flown into the PDJ, disassembled, and to bring the whole team down to help unload and reassemble the guns. I told the team to pack a small emergency bug-out bag with some overnight toiletries, stuff like that, and the team weapons.[9]
>
> … Once we got to the PDJ where they were off-loading the guns, Brabson and Bernshausen both left to go back to the team house at Khang Khay so they could pack their stuff. I was told that when our job rebuilding the guns was complete, or the Laotians no longer needed us, to move the team to Phongsavan to be evacuated.[10]

An Air America Helio Courier landed and the pilot reported he had seen the Neutralist column headed their way. The Laotian army troops soon began to leave.

Shortly thereafter, mortar shells began to land in the vicinity of the airfield. About that time, Vang Pao arrived. Vang Pao loaded his jeep with discarded demolitions scattered at the airport and drove to the Nam Ngum bridge in order to blow it in place and impede the Neutralists. Returning to the airfield, he then set up 4.2-inch mortars and started counter-fires on the Neutralists. Vang Pao ordered his own 105mm howitzers to move to the airfield as reinforcements.[11]

It appeared an evacuation was imminent. Brabson and Bernshausen ordered the team to reassemble at the airfield in Phongsavan; the two of them were both headed back to the team house in Khang Khay to destroy classified materials and retrieve any remaining sensitive items. Meanwhile, Lieutenant McLendon was left in charge of the team:

> We got the artillery pieces assembled. Then we started taking mortar fires on the airfield; they were trying to hit the airplanes. The airplanes departed and the Laotian troops split! I told the team, "Well, there is no one to advise. I guess they don't need us anymore!" So I moved the team to Phongsavan. Bernshausen and Brabson were still at the team house. We had some crypto and team gear and classified documents still at the house (thinking that we would return). Bernshausen put a thermite grenade in our safe and closed the door, but he did not hear the detonation. He opened the door and the thermite grenade was spewing and turning, burning him. He was evacuated by U-10 and was sent to Thailand for his treatment. When he was released back to Laos, he spent time in Vientiane with the FC, supporting them, and then came back to the team.[12]

With his forces retreating and the capture of the airfield imminent, Colonel Sourith returned to Xieng Khouangville. The last Air America C-47 diverted to the airfield at Phongsavan to pick up refugees, along with Operation *Brotherhood* Filipinos and the FA team, departing at last light. Upon the detachment's safe return to Vientiane, they were ordered by Lieutenant Colonel Little, FC commander, to move to Paksane to advise the resident GM.

By January 1, 1961, Kong Le and the Neutralist forces owned the PDJ. Kong Le established his headquarters at the abandoned camp at Khang Khay. Much to the protestations of the French, U.S. *Hotfoot* advisors elsewhere now began combat advisory duties with their Lao counterparts, breaking the agreement of SF to serve only as technical trainers at the major training centers.

President Eisenhower responded with four military initiatives. After putting TF-116 on alert (a regional, joint U.S. Task Force), the president ordered C-130s to fly in additional military supplies to Wattay airport in Vientiane. The United States coordinated with Thailand to provide the RLAF a T-6 strike aircraft capability. RLAF pilots were soon training on six modified T-6s at Kokatiem RTAB. Last, four B-26s were ordered to Thailand for potential bombing missions at Vang Vieng and the PDJ (this initiative was named Operation *Millpond*).

After skirmishing with the remains of FAL in the eastern regions of the PDJ, Kong Le's FAN pursued the FAL as they fell back south on Route 4, where government forces established a new defensive line at Ta Vieng. A new MR-II headquarters was established behind the front lines along the Mekong River at Paksane.

Meanwhile, the long awaited offensive against the Pathet Lao began at Vang Vieng, Moung Kassy, and the Sala Phou Koun junction. Colonel Kouprasith Abhay led GM *Vientiane* (GM-VT) up Route 13. U.S. Army Special Forces detachment members participated in the effort to get the task force across the Nam Lik River, after the bridge was blown by the retreating Neutralists.

After softening up the enemy at Vang Vieng with the RLAF's new airpower capability (the strike T-6 aircraft using rockets, and machine guns, and flown initially by Thai pilots), Kouprasith's forces occupied the town on January 16. For some unknown reason, he was replaced by Colonel Oudone Sananikone before the push continued.

Colonel Sananikone departed Vientiane and pushed north to Vang Vieng to assume command, with two security companies as escort. They fought through some minor ambushes between Hine Heup and Vang Vieng and arrived at the command post in Vang Vieng to find Colonel Kouprasith already gone.

From the north, the task force out of Luang Prabang initially had good luck reaching the Sala Phou Koun junction, arriving by January 17. They were soon ejected by Pathet Lao forces who were reinforced with artillery and the northern task force retreated back up Route 13 to Kiou Ka Cham. Inexplicably, the task force from the east never gained any initiative.

Major Parmley, working with Team *Ipsen*, was assigned to assist this push. Parmley described enemy activities against the Luang Prabang forces in his diary entry on January 10: "Enemy 120 mortar fire in on our position—fire ½ hour—all around but not on us or artillery—w/in 300 yards—stuff going in and out right overhead."[13]

On the 29th, he wrote:

> Up early—forward with LT In Pang slow cautious going around tortuous curves and w/ bulldozer removing obstacles. Excellent work. Came around one bend, enemy opened with machine guns—all hit bank and returned fire for 15 minutes recoilless rifles and mortars. Good reaction—envelop—drove enemy off—continue on—one really rough mess of trees only 15 minutes to move. During lunch heard blasting—found terrific landslide in face of steep cliff. Infantry 1km. beyond. Slept between jeep and cliff. Artillery in and some out all day.[14]

Now newly named GM-15, TF *Vientiane* (under Sananikone) reached Moung Kassy on January 25, and then moved on to the Sala Phou Koun junction by the end of the month. Sananikone was astonished to find out U.S. Army Special Forces trainers were involved during these combat operations:

> The fighting was heavy during the weeks I held this command. It was during this campaign that I first became aware of a new form of American involvement in the war; the White Star teams. As I visited my forward combat elements I saw some foreigners among them. As I asked around no one could tell me who they were except that they were Americans who helped with air support and intelligence. When I asked my headquarters for an explanation I was told that these were the White Star teams. It was not until later that I discovered that the teams were made up of U.S. Army Special Forces officers and NCOs."[15]

Perhaps expecting onward movement of the FAL and their potential to attack east toward the PDJ, the NVA began moving reinforcements into Laos. In Washington DC, President Kennedy began his administration.

Elements of the PAVN's 335th and 316th divisions, along with the 120th Independent Regiment and the 359th Border Guards deployed to support the Pathet Lao. They were followed by the 270th and 148th independent regiments.[16]

PSYOP Augmentation Team, *Hotfoot/White Star* Rotation IV, January 28, 1961–July 27, 1961

Ray Ambrozak graduated in 1959 as a second lieutenant from the OCS Infantry School, where he and three of his classmates received orders to report to the Special Warfare Center at Fort Bragg, NC. Second Lieutenant Ambrozak was assigned to the 1st Loudspeaker/Leaflet Company, in the 1st Loudspeaker Battalion. Once there, he received no formal training for his PSYOP job, but rather learned on his own and through mentoring from the more experienced captains in the unit. He then became a platoon leader in a mobile printing unit. (This unit was capable of producing a million leaflets a day.) He remembers how he found his way deploying to Laos on a twelve-man PSYOP team:

> One day about thirty to thirty-five of us were selected to go attend a briefing. We reported to the briefing room, and there was a Lieutenant Colonel and a civilian, Agency-type. The first item was: you are going to a foreign country. The tour is six months. If you don't want to volunteer, leave the briefing room (we did not know the country). Some guys left right there. The second item: You are going to support Special Forces teams in the field. There will be good guys and bad guys there. More left, leaving twelve of us! They told the remainder of us they were looking for technical skills, like radio broadcast and printing skills. Then they told us we were going to Laos! Nobody had ever heard of it before. We were told we would be leaving in six weeks.[17]

The twelve men were put into an old mess hall on post, located among some dilapidated and condemned buildings. The PSYOP provisional team began their area studies on Laos, along with some language training (they were taught Lao by an SF NCO, 200 to 300 basic words). First Lieutenant George Daley, a PSYOP information specialist, taught what French he knew. During their mission planning, Lieutenant Colonel "Bull" Simons visited to give them background on their mission. Laos veterans also stopped by to update them on their previous experiences in the country.

Their deployment was delayed five months due to the August 1960 Kong Le coup in Vientiane. Just before deployment (January 1961), Major Mosley, the team chief during the training, went off to C&GSC (Command & General Staff College). Lieutenant Colonel Charles A. Murray became the new PSYOP team chief; Sergeant 1st Class Lemt Greer was the team sergeant.

Upon their arrival to Bangkok, they received briefings, intelligence updates, and other necessary instructions. The team had a course of action (COA) for employment which was developed back at Bragg, but the authorities in Bangkok had their own COA, not anticipated by the team, one being permanent PSYOP advisors in three of the military regions. (The team COA was to have training on PSYOP in a central location. The Special Warfare Center had never submitted their COA to MAAG–Thailand; this is where the apparent breakdown occurred for employment.) Ambrozak related, "It didn't matter; we were dedicated to doing a good mission whatever it took. We were the first PSYOP guys going into Laos, so we knew we would be representing our community. So, Colonel Murray said, 'It's OK, we'll adapt.'"[18]

Ambrozak was assigned to MR-I. "I ended up in MR-I, Luang Prabang. George Daley went to Savannakhet, and Lt. Rindon went to Pakse. I got more briefings in Vientiane, and then two days later I was in Luang Prabang. I was the Information Officer to the commander of MR-I, like a consultant (General Bounlouk). My business card said he and I were basically good buddies, which got me a lot of access. He gave me access to all military and civilian matters going on."[19]

Ray did not serve with the SF teams in Luang Prabang. He lived with the USIS representative, Frank Corrigan, who was energetic and knew his business. Ray found Corrigan to be going flat out in his efforts to administer psychological warfare. "There were some in USIS who frowned on that, leaning more toward Public Diplomacy and such, so they had a problem with us administering it."[20]

As to how the PSYOP task was to be performed, Ray said,

> We had PSYOP objectives and themes. I was in his house in Luang Prabang, a villa-type affair. We hosted newspaper correspondents, guests of influence. But, Frank Corrigan was not my boss. This arrangement did not last too long. We were planning a leaflet campaign. He had leased a Tri-Pacer aircraft from the "Dragon Lady Airlines." It was colored blue and white, and had fourteen patches over bullet holes![21]

The day of their flight, a bad storm blew in, so they awaited takeoff. Instead, Second Lieutenant Ambrozak got on the Air Lao flight to Sayaboury with his PSYOP materials (it was an L-20 Beaver). It had fifty-five-gallon drums of fuel loaded on board, and the pilot was a Frenchman. (It was customary to prestage drums of fuel out at the airstrips; the drums were being delivered to Sayaboury for this purpose.)

The two flew through a part of the storm still around them, with clouds covering the terrain. After an "adventurous" trip, they landed on the grass strip in Sayaboury safely. While waiting for Frank Corrigan to arrive behind them, they learned he had been killed in an airplane crash. Ray went on to deliver the PSYOP materials, without the leaflets. Said Ray, "I later escorted Frank's wife to a ceremony in Luang Prabang where the king gave him a posthumous award."[22]

Unfinished back at Luang Prabang was Corrigan's project to erect a radio station. The materials arrived in Vientiane the next week and were sent on up to Luang Prabang. Sergeant Frank Howard arrived to help set up the radio station portion.

Once completed, Ray and Frank worked on the antennae, using local prisoners as their labor force. Ray found them eager to get out of the prison confines for the day and rewarded them each evening with beer before their return to confinement.

Ambrozak worked alone in Luang Prabang for the remainder of his tour, never once seeing the PSYOP team chief. He had been asked by the USIS director to replace Frank Corrigan and run the office at the Luang Prabang posting.

The radio station was the Luang Prabang local civilian radio station, but was run by PSYOP personnel from Vientiane. It was used for PSYOP/counter-propaganda along with local items for broadcast. Every program had a PSYOP theme or message. A Lao captain ran the unit with twenty men from the Lao PSYCH Warfare staff. They also produced leaflets. The radio was on three or four hours a day, went off the air, then repeated another time later. Ray described various PSYOP activities conducted:

> We really did not have a good system of metrics to measure how effective we were. I would go visit with the SF guys out in some of the outlying villages, just to get familiarization. I was surprised to see a lot of radios in Lao populace hands—it was very surprising to me. That is one measure of effectiveness, were the populace in range and were they listening? We also used the SF to elicit themes for the PSYOP. We then took them handbills, books for the schools, etc.
>
> Our effort started small in Luang Prabang. We started a small government newspaper. Leaflets were the most direct method, targeted for operations. We printed safe conduct passes for units in contact with the enemy. We utilized a Beech C-45 for those drops. There was a problem; the pilot would not go down below 10,000 foot—he said he did not want any more holes in his aircraft. This was a problem dropping leaflets from that high, they would scatter everywhere. But, he refused to go lower. I had an idea: leaflet bundles tied with a squib igniter fuse. We were constantly trying to figure out the physics. For instance, the blasting caps would shred some of the leaflets, so, we smashed beer cans flat and put them between the blasting cap and the leaflet bundle to prevent damage. We used cigars to light them. The pilot flew slow. We took the side door off and I sat in the opening, with feet propped on both sides. I had a tether to keep me in the aircraft (a web belt). Light the thing with a cigar, and kick it out.[23]

Most PSYOP products were produced in Vientiane and also manufactured in Thailand (by the Agency). The Thai occasionally flew a PSYOP aircraft into Laos; Second Lieutenant Ambrozak also helped them out with his aircraft to make a few runs. A further PSYOP technique was the showing of films on the wall at the villa. To draw a crowd, the movie always began with *The Three Stooges*. Government-sponsored films followed, with PSYOP themes embedded such as supporting the government and the Lao army.

The value of PSYOP is normally derived from measures of effectiveness (MOE). Ray commented on the difficulty for PSYOP analysts to determine whether or not a program was working:

> We did not have an MOE list. It was difficult to say how effective our efforts were. It was hard to get into some remote places. For instance, in a village, if nothing is going on, like the Pathet Lao coming in and trying to recruit, then maybe you are having an effect. We could always ask the populace, "Are you listening to the radio?"

> The SF guys working with Hmong asked me why there weren't any Hmong language-related items on the radio broadcast. We found a person who could speak the language and added them for a few minutes of each broadcast. That's kind of like MOE feedback. [24]

Ambrozak's most memorable task was doing a live, national broadcast of the king's funeral in April 1961, which to this day has been seen widely.

Other members of the PSYOP team in Laos were Bill Dixon, a media analyst, working in Vientiane with Lao artists to produce leaflets and designing handbills. (Bill had worked with Fitzburger Press and also worked with the Lao press.) Fred Ardor worked a Lao radio station in Vientiane for USIS. Colonel Murray worked in the FC Control and with the USIS offices in Vientiane.

The remaining team members included Captain Richard Gunsell (commo officer Pakse), Staff Sergeant Ray Fitzberger (printer), Staff Sergeant Fred Harder (commo), Sergeant Bob Crookham (analyst), Sergeant Howard Holliman (intel specialist), SP4 Neil Lien (media), and Sergeant Frank Howard (radio station/broadcast).

The PSYOP team departed Laos in July of 1961. They were replaced by the next PSYOP augmentation team to Vientiane (eight men, led by Captain Desmal G. Smith, Jr.), arriving on June 15, 1961; the PSYOP team served through December of that year. The last contingent of PSYOP, a twelve-man team, served in Laos from the spring of 1962 to September 1962.

Ray Ambrozak served eleven years in the PSYOP field and retired as a major. He was the project officer for Kennedy's visit to Bragg. Following that tour, he served with the U.S. Broadcasting and Visual Command in Okinawa. In 1964, he was in Vietnam with the SOG's Voice of Freedom radio—a white PSYOP program. Ray completed another tour to Vietnam in 1967, as the S3 with the 6th PSYOP Battalion. He returned to Bragg and was an instructor at the SWC PSYOP Center for three years. He reflected, "This was a period of good changes for PSYOP—getting a PSYOP unit officer's course developed and a PSYOP staff course instituted."

In 1971, Ray served as a district senior advisor in Pleiku, II Corps, after graduating from the Foreign Service Institute. "After that, I went to Europe, working in the Corps G3 office."[25]

The *Monkhood* Teams

On January 31, 1961, PEO chief Brigadier General Boyle requested nine additional *Hotfoot* FTTs in response to FAL's raising of nine more BIs—giving the FAL a total of twenty-one infantry battalions. The initiative was approved (message cables referred to them as *Monkhood* teams); the nine additional SF teams mentioned earlier deployed between February and March. The new BIs were being raised in Vientiane, Kiou Ka Cham, Tha Thom, Paksane and Thakhek.[26]

Hotfoot now had the mission to cover twenty-one BIs and the major training centers. This would force the FC in Vientiane to begin deploying split detachments to cover all the ground. During this period, the FAL reorganized into permanent *groupe mobiles*. GM-15 was redesignated as GM-12 while it occupied Sala Phou Khoun.

On March 9, the Sala Phou Khoun road junction fell into the arms of the Pathet Lao; they continued their attacks against the FAL south along Route 13 to Moung Kassy. GM-15 (now GM-12) was forced to evacuate Moung Kassy, retreating just south of the town to the village of Ban Thieng.

GM-12 counterattacked, inflicting heavy losses on the Pathet Lao, but were unable to push through to retake Sala Phou Khoun. After another strong attack by Neutralist and Pathet Lao forces, GM-12 retreated to Vang Vieng. When infiltrating enemy units slipped south of the town to cut off Route 13 behind GM-12, the unit was forced to conduct a withdrawal to the Nam Lik River line near Hien Heup, fighting a rearguard action to delay Kong Le's advance. The defense stabilized at Hine Heup.[27]

There was a growing lack of confidence by the Americans in the ability of the FAL to prevent a major attack on Luang Prabang, or down Route 13 to Vientiane. On March 6 President Kennedy met with his security advisors to discuss strategies concerning the condition in Laos. A series of initiatives to bolster the military effort in Laos emerged from the meeting.

The Road to Widen American Involvement in Laos

With the U.S. reinforcing Poumi's military coup to replace the Neutralist government of Laos, and the USSR reinforcing Captain Kong Le and the Pathet Lao forces, the situation in Laos teetered on bringing the United States and the Soviet Union into a proxy conflict. Kennedy sought a de-confliction by declaring he could now live with a "neutralized" Laos.

TF -116, comprised of U.S. forces in the region, was hastily formed by the JCS and readied for action (also increased military supplies to Thailand, along with helicopters, the repositioning of three aircraft carriers, and forces put on alert in Japan and Okinawa). However, this approach would be for naught as the Pathet Lao forces in Laos were gaining ground and Moscow, China and North Vietnam had nothing to lose.

President Kennedy then addressed the American people:

> My fellow Americans, Laos is far away from America, but the world is small. The security of all Southeast Asia will be endangered if Laos loses its neutral independence. Its own safety runs with the safety of us all—in neutrality observed by us all. I want to make clear to the American people and to all the world that all we want in Laos is peace, not war; a truly neutral government, not a cold war pawn; a settlement concluded at the conference table and not on the battlefield.[28]

In March, the remaining FAL forces at Tha Thom were routed and began their retreat south along Route 4. The FAL was now being considered by the embassy as only capable of being a "trip wire" for intervention, pending the fall of Luang Prabang or Vientiane.

The Moung Kassy Operation—April 1961

On April 5 the PEO designed an ambitious airborne assault north of Moung Kassy. Operation *Noel* began with a parachute drop, followed by the air-landing of troops and equipment via helicopters. Captain Billy J. Chance and his radio operator, SP4 Gordon J. Turpin, performed one of the first combat jumps by U.S. forces in Laos, accompanying BP-1. The insertion of forces was muddled, and BI-26 and the 1st BP evacuated and foot-marched back to Luang Prabang.

Kennedy's list of increasing military aid continued. An additional twelve to fourteen H-34s were sent to Thailand for transfer to Air America to provide for the needed increase in troop and resupply requirements. Kennedy approved an increase in the raising of additional Operation *Momentum* Hmong guerrillas. Once again, JTF-116 was put on alert. Operation *Millpond* (now six B-26s in Thailand) was tasked to prepare to bomb enemy positions on the PDJ, but after the tragic results of the Bay of Pigs operation, and the loss of the Cuba invasion's B-26s (due to lack of fighter air cover), President Kennedy now balked at their use in Laos and the operation was cancelled.

The most forceful signal sent by Kennedy was ordering the change of the PEO to a full-time MAAG, with additional orders for all *Hotfoot* teams to begin serving openly in military uniforms, under arms, and provide combat advisory assistance in the field. Operation *Hotfoot* was renamed Operation *White Star* on April 19, 1961. On the FAL side, the temporary forming of GMs was now made permanent.[29]

Sergeant Richard L. Largen was serving as the radio operator on Team *Metcalf* in Savannakhet. The team's mission was to train NCOs of the police academy. He remembers the order to change into military clothes as somewhat surprising to the team: "We were in civilian clothes and the last of the teams dressed in civvies. We were given the order to get into uniform about three weeks before our rotation date, which was stupid, and most of us could not get to them anyway."[30]

In late April, the Pathet Lao began to enlarge their operations north of Luang Prabang and farther into Military Region I. They seized Moung Sai, along the Nam Beng River valley, while a company of Pathet Lao occupied Nam Tha.

FA-65, Kiou Ka Cham, GM-16—On the Front Lines in Combat

Captain James E. Ipsen returned to Laos for a second tour, leading FA-65 at Kiou Ca Cham. He was assisted on the team by First Lieutenant Alfred H. Paddock and Master Sergeant Elbert T. Bledsoe.

Lieutenant Alfred H. Paddock was the team XO. He was an OCS graduate and had served as a rifle platoon leader in Korea for thirteen months. He joined the 7th Special Forces Group and had about a year in service with Special Forces before his tour to Laos. Hearing about an upcoming deployment to Laos, he volunteered to be the XO on Team *Ipsen* (he knew Ipsen had served earlier in Laos and was considered a solid soldier). They only had a few days in isolation before deploying. During the deployment, Lieutenant Paddock kept one of the most detailed notes and logbook on the operations of GM-16.[31]

The team conducted mandatory briefings and area studies, including reviewing political intelligence. After a brief time in isolation, the team deployed to Bangkok, where they were met by a battered Air America C-47. Curious about the pilot who wore dirty overalls and shower shoes, they came to find out he was the famous Art "Shower Shoes" Wilson.

Upon their arrival in Vientiane they were issued weapons and equipment to pack in their team boxes (the mission was still being conducted in civilian clothes). The team chose the M1 rifle and .45-caliber pistol, and also took along a couple of .30-caliber Browning automatic rifles (BARs). They remained dressed in civilian clothes, were issued embassy ID cards, and took the title of "Mister."

After the poor performance of the GMs fighting the Pathet Lao and Neutralists along Route 13, FA-65 was assigned the mission to serve as advisors and trainers to GM-16, holding in place at Kiou Ka Cham, located southwest of Luang Prabang.

While awaiting deployment to Kiou Ka Cham, the team performed live-fire demonstrations for senior Lao military and political figures stationed in Vientiane as a display of the type of training they could provide Lao army units.

Al Paddock described the initial move of FA-65 to Kiou Ka Cham from his field notes:

> In February of 1961, Captain Ipsen took a few team members and initiated contact with GM-16 at Kiou Ka Cham (KKC). GM-16 was opposed by about a brigade of Pathet Lao, equipped with artillery pieces. Both sides entrenched facing one another. Along with discussions between him and the commander of GM-16, Colonel Boun Chan, Captain Ipsen also spoke with the local Hmong chief about organizing defense units in the region. There was some trepidation on the part of headman due to possible Pathet Lao reprisals; the Pathet Lao had already targeted the local villagers with communist propaganda, some of it warning them not to participate with the government troops.[32]

The remainder of the team arrived on location April 3, 1961 and began the mission to advise and provide training to GM-16; training the local Hmong villagers was set aside. The team set up their base of operations in an old schoolhouse, with a dirt floor and a tin roof, within the defensive perimeter of GM-16.

There was an airstrip at the site used as both a landing zone and a drop zone. The airstrip was carved by widening the dirt road (Route 13) running along the mountaintop from north to south.

The team established good rapport with Colonel Boun Chan, who was appreciative of the advisory mission. FAL logistic support to GM-16 was poor; it was only through FA-65's assistance the unit was able to procure arms and ammunition, spare parts, and supplies to run and defend the camp. Convinced they could do more if allowed to visit front-line units, Colonel Boun Chan gave the FA his blessing, and soon the team was involved with improving front-line positions, repairing weapons, and training the battalions on small unit tactics (SUT—patrolling, reconnaissance, and other tasks); accompanying BI combat patrols soon followed.

The unit's performance was plagued by bad leadership. Leaders in the FAL, especially GM commanders, were often chosen based on family or political connections. There was also a lack of institutional knowledge on basic fundamentals of combat and tactics; most of the leadership had not attended formal military schools. When Captain Ipsen split the detachment after only spending a few weeks with GM-16 (for him to move away and establish a training camp for local Hmong as part of Operation *Momentum*, the training of Hmong guerrillas with the CIA), Lieutenant Paddock became the primary advisor to GM-16 with the remaining half of the team (FA-65A). He was now faced with the challenge of advising Colonel Boun Chan. Not helping matters, Colonel Boun Chan began to drink heavily, neglected his senior officer duties, and mistreated his men and subordinates. Paddock related:

> As a result, I spent a good bit of my time attempting to counsel Boun Chan. Here's an example of my recommendations: build a large bunker for an operations center and commo, build a large bunker for the aid station, build at least two more ammo supply points and give them overhead cover if possible, improve field sanitation, move tents off and away from the air strip, begin training for front-line medics (we helped in this, of course), and make plans for training in rainy weather—basic stuff that a senior commander in combat should not have to be advised to do.
>
> I wrote a recommended plan for phases of training, which included (1) an orientation squad in attack demonstration by us, (2) movement into bivouac area, (3) initial training, and (4) advanced training, with detailed steps under each major phase. I wrote a detailed training schedule for night and combat patrols, with daily activity periods. I presented a recommended organization for a reconnaissance platoon, to include its equipment. As I wrote in my journal: "The intelligence collection of this command is ridiculous!" To address this deficiency, on May 24, I presented Boun Chan with a detailed memo of intelligence recommendations applicable down to company size. This shortcoming was largely the fault of Boun Chan who, for some reason, had an aversion to recon patrols. The Pathet Lao, on the other hand, probed our front-line units regularly. Our intel weakness was one of my constant concerns.[33]

As the end of April approached, Paddock's efforts seemed to pay off; he noticed improvements in the defense of the camp and the men being treated better.

The men of the SF split detachment were not just advisors and trainers, they were combat advisors; they were under regular artillery shelling and ground attack from the Pathet Lao. Paddock explained in his field notes:

> We received enemy artillery regularly, sometimes fairly accurately. On one occasion two of my team and an interpreter went up on a hill in the front lines to train Hq Co, 3rd Bn, in the 81 mm mortar. Here's an entry from my journal: "I came up about 0945 to check training + look at positions. At 1018 first round of artillery landed about 30 yds from us. We all hit the holes and worked our way down the trench to other side of hill. Rounds continued to come in until 1118. Total of 19 rds. About 5 or 6 landed on hill, rest went over saddle where 3rd Bn Hq is. One or two rounds landed vicinity 3rd Bn Hq. Bn C. O. feels that it was we who drew

enemy fire. No casualties from fire." Probably the Pathet Lao had pre-registered their fire on our position and used this when they saw Americans on the hill. I should have anticipated this.[34]

One day, Lieutenant Paddock made an attempt to find the location of the source of the enemy artillery. When a Helio Courier flown by Air America arrived on the airstrip, Paddock convinced the Air America pilot to fly him around on a reconnaissance mission. Accompanied with a staff officer from GM-16, the pilot flew nap of the earth along a road behind enemy lines. They spotted two camouflaged trucks; suddenly, they began to receive enemy machine-gun fire. Al vividly remembers, "The aircraft was hit on the left wing, but the pilot took immediate evasive action by diving down a draw and lifting up at the last minute. He was cool throughout the action, and I was impressed. This was typical of the outstanding air support the CIA gave us."[35]

On April 22, two companies of Pathet Lao, supported by artillery and mortar fire, attacked one of the front-line BIs. At least fifty artillery rounds landed in the camp. GM-16 responded with artillery counter-fires, putting out over 1,600 rounds of 105mm howitzer shells, assisted by FA-65 loading the rounds. The 3rd BI conducted a limited counterattack to restore the defense and was successful in the operation. Unfortunately, GM-16 never conducted large offensive actions of their own; as Paddock emphasized, "It wasn't in its commander's nature to do so."

On May 16, Lieutenant Paddock helped Captain Richard E. Thomas transition in for advisory duties with the 3rd BI. (Thomas's FA-74A was a four-man split-team; the other half of the detachment went to Luang Prabang under Major Carl F. Bernard and Master Sergeant Donald E. Peterson.) The two split detachments worked together a short time, with FA-74A being groomed also for duties at GM-16 command level. Paddock's FA-65A was being moved out to establish an additional training camp for Hmong guerrillas under the Operation *Momentum* program.

Team *Moon*—The First SF Casualties in Laos

The incident with Team *Moon* confirmed in everyone's mind that Special Forces were now fully in combat. FA-30, which would become Team *Moon*, deployed at the end of November 1961 to Vientiane, with training duties at Camp Chinaimo and additionally training for FAL units quartered around Vientiane. The team was led by Lieutenant (P) Edwin M. Pulley, with First Lieutenant Harold J. Fraley as the detachment XO, and with Sergeant Major John L. O'Donovan as Team sergeant. At some time during the mission, First Lieutenant Pulley was replaced by Captain Walter H. Moon.

The team lived in a team house near the area called "Dogpatch," a run-down and poor section of Vientiane. The house had been occupied previously by an earlier FTT; their team sergeant remained behind for a week to help transition FA-30 into their duties. Next to the house was a motor pool and commercial vehicle and privately owned vehicles lot. Like all *Hotfoot* teams, the team wore civilian clothes, some in khaki pants and short-sleeved khaki shirts. Everyone had a personal weapon, whether it was a pistol or a hunting rifle.

FA-30 began their training classes at Camp Chinaimo in early December. The training sub-optimally consisted of weapons training and some individual skills, as the team was prevented by the French trainers from conducting tactical classes. FA-30 pushed some limits to this restriction and were able to fit in some fire and maneuver classes. During this period, they were caught up in the December battle of Vientiane.

Sergeant 1st Class John W. "Ranger" Roy, the weapons sergeant on the team, and a Korean War veteran, described the hectic nature of the times:

> We were near the airfield when the battle for the city went down. We got trapped in our team house and could not make contact with anyone. We circled around to the embassy/PEO compound to avoid Kong Le's troops and the Rightist troops fighting in the city. No one was at the compound. Our commo operator got on an SSB radio and called to Bangkok to get instructions … We were told to stay where we were located. We then checked the embassy— there were no guards. We checked the civilian dependent housing, and no one was there either; they later came back after the battle.[36]

Between April 3 and 7 the enemy position at Vang Vieng was reinforced with Kong Le's paratroopers jumping into the area. Lieutenant Colonel Little came to the team house to give FA-30 a new mission: advising and assisting GM-12 for their attack on Vang Vieng.

The team was newly designated as FA-54, a seven-man team, for the mission. They went forward with a total of six operators, leaving Sergeant Major O'Donovan behind to support them from the team house. Master Sergeant Roy L. "Beetle" Bailey, from Captain Billy Chance's team (who were also living in the team house) replaced Sergeant Major O'Donovan for the operation with GM-12.

The team procured a Land Rover and rode out to the Lao battalion, linking up with them prior to the operation's beginning north up Route 13; the battalion was riding in vehicles, with some of them walking. GM-12 consisted of a few BIs with some separate light infantry companies attached, three 105mm artillery pieces, and about six tanks and armored cars, formed into a mobile column. During the initial movement, Team *Moon*'s medic and radio operator were both sent back to rest; they were replaced by Sergeant Bischoff and Sergeant Ballenger.

Sergeant Roy positioned himself with the unit's mortar section located in the rear of the column. Approaching the edge of Vang Vieng, the column was ambushed with artillery and small-arms fire. The BI-6 commander had not heeded the advice to put out flank security, preferring the safety and comfort of the road over dealing with what was unknown in the dense woods to each side. Roy said:

> When the attack from the Neutralists and Pathet Lao came just as the column was entering Vang Vieng, I was behind the column in a jeep with a .50 caliber. We were ambushed and the bad guys started coming down the road (April 22, 1961). When I got close enough to the

ambush site, I saw bodies, and then started firing the .50 caliber. I saw Moon (in the distance) step out and put his hands up. Ballenger dove into the bushes on the side of the road. That was the last time I saw them. It was about 100 yards up the road from my position. Bischoff and Biber were killed.[37]

Captain Moon was captured; Ballenger evaded capture until a Pathet Lao patrol found him the next day. Sergeant Roy joined the forces retreating back to the airfield. They were shelled along the way, knocking him down, and resulting in a shrapnel sliver in his eye. He arrived at the airfield to find other *Hotfoot* members awaiting him. Upon hearing of the incident, Sergeant 1st Class Donald E. Stetson (the team's radio operator), Master Sergeant William E. Patterson (medic from Captain Billy Chance's team), and Captain William B. Radcliffe, the FC surgeon, joined Sergeant "Beetle" Bailey at the airfield outside of Vang Vieng to reinforce the remnants of Team *Moon* and provide medical assistance. Dr. Radcliffe attended the wound to Roy's eye.

Laotian units came and went through the airfield. The AVGAS and ammo dump were destroyed to prevent its capture by the enemy. John Roy described the SF's last few days there:

> The Laotians had some 105mm howitzers emplaced there. We were on one side of the position, and the Lao were on the other side. They were always shooting illumination over our position, which was giving us away to the enemy. I went over to complain to them. On my way, I saw some Pathet Lao lying in a ditch. We ran out of there! But they did not fire on us—they looked worn out and were lying back on their packs.
>
> Colonel Kouprasith told us the column was going to push out. He put a bulldozer in the front of the column. He ordered me and "Beetle" Bailey to get on one of his choppers and leave. He said, "I already lost Americans today, I don't want to lose anymore."[38]

Sergeant Roy returned to Vientiane and had his eye wound treated. Captain Chance arrived with the remainder of his team and moved into the team house (just prior to his movement to Padong to support Operation *Momentum*). With the team basically dissolved, Sergeant Roy and Sergeant Major O'Donovan remained at the team house to take care of the house and the vehicles, running the "motel" supporting other SF teams which came and went through the house. GM-12 retreated to the Nam Lik River to establish a defensive line.

Captain Moon and Sergeant Ballenger were moved to a prisoner of war camp on the eastern PDJ. Captain Moon apparently had suffered wounds to his head and shoulder during the ambush. He was executed by his Pathet Lao guards when attempting to escape from his cell. Sergeant Ballenger was held along with three other Americans: Ed Shore, Air America H-34 pilot; John McMorrow, aircraft mechanic; and Grant Wolfkill, news cameraman for NBC.

Also in April, Ban Nam Bac, astride the classic invasion route from Dien Bien Phu to Luang Prabang (Hou River), fell to the Pathet Lao. In the south, NVA border guard units attacked in the upper panhandle east of Thakhek. In one of the first interventions of Thai forces, GM-14 was reinforced with several batteries of Royal Thai artillery, flown in by Air America to prevent the Laotian unit's rout.

Operation *Hotshot*, the American supply of military arms and equipment for the newly formed BIs, began on April 25. C-130s landed continually at Wattay airport in Vientiane, disgorging enough cargo to equip the new battalions (*Hotshot* ended on April 28).

After the United States was approached by a joint Soviet and British proposal for a fourteen-nation peace conference, Kennedy agreed on the measure. The proposal was announced on April 24, with the conference to be held on May 12 in Geneva. President Kennedy shifted his policy on Laos from one of Laos being pro-Western alignment over to a policy of support for a "neutral" Laos. He was faced with few choices. His military advisors warned him against outright intervention (lack of sufficient strategic forces and airlift) nor would the Allies in SEATO commit to the defense of Laos; a policy of neutralization appeared to be the only apparent and feasible course available to the president.

A ceasefire was coordinated along the lines throughout Laos, and by May 3 was in nominal effect, per verbal orders from both sides to their units. There were two exceptions: the continuing attacks by the Pathet Lao on Vang Pao's redoubt at Padong, and on May 3, the Pathet Lao attack in the south against FAL units at Moung Phalane, along with seizing the airfield at Tchepone.

The ceasefire delegations initially met at the village of Ban Hin Heup, situated along the banks of the Lik River. The decision to hold lengthier, formal ceasefire talks in Ban Namone, in Pathet Lao territory, was worked out and agreed upon. On May 11 the opposing delegations, along with the ICC, met to work out the details; by May 13 the ceasefire papers were signed. The opposing delegations would continue negotiations down into September.

In late April to early May, *White Star* Rotation V began its deployment into Laos, supporting President Kennedy's muscular approach to at least keep Laos a neutral country and giving him a military option to buy time for a diplomatic solution.

American policy and diplomatic decision-makers accepted the notion of neutrality for Laos, under a coalition government, guaranteed by the superpowers.

Other Rotation IV Activities

The increase of BIs in 1961 opened up new deployment areas for the field advisory teams. In MR-I, First Lieutenant Hugh M. Fisher deployed with a split-team to Sayaboury. (As noted earlier, Team *Ipsen* deployed to Kiou Ka Cham with GM-16, and later supported Operation *Momentum*.)

Captain Bill Chance's team operated first at Padong, and later Pha Khao with Vang Pao's guerrillas, in support of Operation *Momentum*.

Captain Derby led a team to Thakhek in MR-III, along with Captain Rozon's FA-68. In MR-IV, Captain Garrison and FA-36 served as advisors in Pakse and Paksong, and FA-34 under Captain Grimmet served in Paksong and up on the Bolovens Plateau. Captain James D. Herndon led his split detachment to Pakse.

Finally, when Captain Bernshausen's team evacuated Khang Khay in MR-II after initially being pulled back into Vientiane, they were soon tasked to support and advise the GM located at Paksane (MR-V).

FA-68, Thakhek, BI-19

PFC Irving Hoffman was assigned to the 82nd Airborne Headquarters Battery, 377th Artillery, at Fort Bragg as a colonel's orderly in September of 1959. He had heard about the Special Forces over at Smoke Bomb Hill, but there was a freeze on all transfers from the 82nd. His unit commander assisted him in getting an approval to join Special Forces in October of 1959.

After transferring, he was first trained in demolitions. In 1960, he attended medical specialist training for eleven weeks at Womack Army Hospital. In 1961, he completed radio operator school. One day in February of 1961, he reported to his B-team as ordered and was told he was selected for a special mission. Only after extending his enlistment was he then told he was going to Laos.

He joined Captain Alan E. Rozon's full detachment as a demolitions man; plus, he had two other specialties (radio operator and medic). His team would be designated as FA-68, with duties in Thakhek upon arrival to Laos.

In a procedure a bit different from other teams, FA-68 had their military IDs and civilian IDs taken away from them at Fort Bragg. They were then issued Department of the Army IDs, AAA international driver's licenses, and a PEO Laos identification card, with their photos attached. They flew on March 20, 1961 via a KC-97 to Manila, then to Bangkok, where they transferred to a DC-7 for the flight to Vientiane; they quickly turned the aircraft around and were flown straight on to Thakhek.

Captain Alan E. Rozon led FA-68 with the assignment to train BI-19. He was assisted by his XO, First Lieutenant Ronald R. Coleman and team sergeant, Master Sergeant John N. "Jack" Coats. FA-68 was an eleven-man team. Captain Rozon volunteered for Special Forces out of Korea in November of 1959. SF rotations to Laos had been ongoing for over a year and a half and Captain Rozon's team was chosen for Rotation IV.

FA-68 arrived at Don Muang in Bangkok with two other teams. The detachments were flown to Vientiane with their team boxes via C-47, then further transported to Thakhek. Captain Merlen G. "Pappy" Lamar's team was assigned a mission east of Thakhek; Rozon's team would work out of the team house to train BI-19.

They were the first *Hotfoot* team to be assigned to Thakhek. They were billeted in an old French motel-like building, prepared for them by an advance party. The first task was to secure the building and set up operations. Hoffman described their activities upon arrival:

> I was given the job to set up the radio antenna and the radios. I was also given the job to place explosive charges around the perimeter to use in case we were attacked. I never thought much about how effective that would have been. We still had not been issued any weapons. There was a cache of old weapons in Vientiane—M1, Carbines, etc.—and we scrounged from those weapons. I bought a .38 police special from a guy who was leaving and going back to the States; I had a holster made for me in Thailand—across the river from Thakhek.[39]

The team's mission would be organizing and training battalion-sized combat units. They had use of Lao civilian interpreters and some French interpreters, who claimed they had been working in Laos as civilian contractors for an oil exploration company (none of the team believed this unlikely story). Other than the personal pistols owned by the team, no U.S. Army weapons were issued the detachment for the mission. They soon solved this problem from a cache of old World War II weapons stored in crates in Vientiane. The team armed themselves with additional Thompson sub-machine guns and a 12-gauge trench gun.[40]

The team wore their civilian clothing while performing their duties, mainly khaki pants, T-shirts, and short sleeve khaki shirts—basically, the U.S. Army summer uniform without the starch and insignia.

The training took place on a soccer field in Thakhek, not a Lao military base. Using a POI developed at Fort Bragg before departure, the team set up a series of round robin stations along its edges, using the center of the soccer field as an assembly area. There was no enemy threat. They were provided with the Thai interpreters and an interpreter who spoke French loaned to them from Captain Lamar's team. Fortunately, the battalion commander spoke some English.

The battalion was also being reequipped with new gear and weapons, a task the team incorporated into their training. Sometime after six to eight weeks of instruction, FA-68 took the battalion out along the Se Bang Fai River to give them a shakedown. Captain Lamar told Rozon of an enemy 120mm mortar which needed knocking out near Mahaxay, and this seemed to be a good objective for the maneuver. The unit patrolled in the direction of Numerach, following a small river to the northeast. (The mortar was never found.)

Radio operators were always in high demand, and SP4 Hoffman was also skilled in communication and radio operations. During his tour, he additionally worked comms at Luang Prabang, supporting the PEO (MAAG) contingent assigned there. Later, he worked in the FC headquarters in Vientiane as a fill-in for their regular radio operators, and provided commo support on combat patrols in MR-V:

> When I was assigned to Vientiane, I went out on combat patrols as a field radio operator. On several occasions, it was me and one other SF operator who was a Sergeant. We would

accompany a Laotian infantry company on combat patrols and operations. We came under fire several times, and once a sniper took aim at me and missed me by about an inch or less, because I felt the bullet pass in front of my face. As for location, all I can tell you is that it was jeep distance outside of Vientiane.

While on combat patrol I did encounter one enemy prisoner. I was alone on this patrol with a company of Laotian troops. We entered a small village and several of our Laotian troops had a black-clad, pajama-type clothed prisoner in custody. One of the Laotian troops was an NCO and they were mistreating the prisoner—smacking him around. I went over to them and told the NCO to stop and to take the prisoner to the command post—I had learned rudimentary Laotian sufficient to communicate. The NCO was not happy that I had intervened and especially in front of his subordinates, but I did what I thought to be right and was not intimidated by the NCO. Anyhow, he did as told. Later, when the operation was over and I got back to our rendezvous point, the prisoner was there with our operations officer and intelligence Sergeant. The intelligence Sergeant took a photo of me and the prisoner and showed it to me later back at headquarters. It was a dramatic photo. I asked him for a copy, but he laughed and said, "It's classified."[41]

BI-19 was deemed ready for operation and was transferred to Savannakhet. Captain Rozon stood the team down from the mission, but was required to send half the team to accompany BI-19 to continue the training and advising of the battalion while they were in Savannakhet. Remaining idle at the team house, Rozon was soon ordered by Lieutenant Colonel Little to report to Luang Prabang to relieve Captain (now Major) Carlton F. Schafford and First Lieutenant Robert T. Cooper. (Later, the remainder of the team was transferred to Vientiane to assist with operations.)

He took Sergeant 1st Class James P. Drouillard (intel) with him. Upon their arrival to Luang Prabang, they were met by a contract Agency case officer who told them they were eventually going to go to Nam Tha to the north. Rozon, along with Master Sergeant Noah F. Davis (demolitions), Sergeant 1st Class Drouillard, SP5 Ronald H. Neely (radio operator), and Master Sergeant Miles (medic) deployed to Nam Tha.

The new mission was to try and organize the FAL at Nam Tha. One of the tasks was the training of the local militia. The four set about putting the militia into shape, getting some weapons from the local commander (who had been storing them under his house).

The militia was employed for special raiding projects. They conducted raids into the mountains east and west of Nam Tha. Once, Rozon was informed of a Pathet Lao tax collector working on the island off of Ban Houei Sai to extract funds from people crossing back and forth to Thailand. The militia conducted a raid and eliminated the problem.

On another mission, Rozon (with Davis and Neely) moved with the militia into the mountains of Phong Saly Province, using four Mongolian ponies to move weapons and equipment. They established a small forward operating base (FOB) and conducted operations. While on that mission, Captain Rozon was contacted by the Agency to return to Nam Tha; they were going to conduct a raid to rescue the governor of Phong Saly Province.

The task force launched with two H-34s. Upon arrival at the HLZ, the second helicopter in the chalk hit one of the trees, which had been demolished to clear a landing zone, leaving its trunk at about six feet high. (The helicopter hit it with its tail-boom.) Then the raiding force began taking fire. Rozon assembled a reaction force at Nam Tha and flew out to retrieve the raiders.

FA-68 was relieved by a new team and eventually flown to Bangkok, where Rozon once again linked up with Ipsen and Schafford. After stopping in Hong Kong for R&R, they returned to Fort Bragg, just in time for the "dog and pony" show for President Kennedy's famous visit.

Paksane, FA-32, Team *Bernshausen*, GM-13

While Captain Bernshausen was being treated for his thermite burn, his team was instructed by Lieutenant Colonel Little to deploy to Paksane.

The team deployed to Paksane. McLendon said, "I sent one of the NCOs back to Vientiane to get some training materials for the mission. First Lieutenant Williams and his team arrived in Paksane later to assist in the training [FA-73A, arriving the end of April, as part of *White Star* Rotation V]. They were told by the FC team (Lieutenant Colonel Little) that they would be advising a GM in the field. We all lived in a big house in Paksane, with other SF teams."[42]

Colonel Brabson directed Lieutenant McLendon to work up a one- to two-week course of instruction as a training schedule for the GM at Paksane, given what could be done with the Lao rotating in and out from the field. Later, when Captain Bernshausen arrived back to the control team in Vientiane, he developed a formal nine-week POI program, but Colonel Brabson adapted to the conditions found with the unit at Paksane and left the course as a two-week period of instruction. The teams built training areas and a reaction course in preparation. Team *Bernshausen* remained in the civvies they deployed into Laos with, but the new team wore military uniforms per the directive of the MAAG. There were no French trainers at Paksane.

The threat from the Pathet Lao was on GM-13's front line, near Phou Tinpét, north of Paksane. There was never much of a threat from Pathet Lao in the town itself.

The team medic, Sergeant 1st Class Richard E. Duck, soon became revered and worshipped by the population in Paksane. He established sick call for the local population, taught basic health programs, and instituted a malaria prevention program with his limited resources. To ensure the lessons would stick, he got the village leaders involved. McLendon remembers the work-arounds "Duck" had to do because of the local cultural beliefs:

> He also did dental work [extractions] as many older Laotians had severe tooth decay of their chewing the betel nut for years. One older dental patient was given a shot to deaden the pain before the extract of an abscessed tooth. He had been informed of the effect of the shot; however, when the shot started to take effect and deaden his jaw, he went into cardiac arrest! Sergeant Duck worked tirelessly and finally brought him back. The old man then told Sergeant Duck if he would get the *phi* [ghost] out of his mouth, he would go away and never bother him again. When he was able, he departed and never returned.[43]

FA-38, Dong Hene and Tchepone

Captain John E. Williamson led an eight-man detachment, FA-38, for duties to train a Laotian BV at the old French officer's school at Dong Hene. The BV's mission was the conduct of security patrolling and establishing defenses around the Tchepone area along Route 9. First Lieutenant John A. Anderson was the detachment XO, and Sergeant Major Philip J. Hoffman the team sergeant. After premission training at Fort Bragg, the detachment arrived in Bangkok and transloaded their team boxes into Air America C-46s and C-47s. They were flown to the airfield at Seno, near Savannakhet. From there, the team was provided vehicles for the drive to Dong Hene, about thirty-five kilometers away. They arrived around noon, and began transition with the departing SF team. The transition lasted only one or two days. FA-38 occupied the team house, a nice old house built in the French colonial style.

Staff Sergeant Robert F. Mulcahy was supposed to be assigned as the second weapons man on the team, but since the team did not have a mechanic attached to them from the 82nd Airborne (as was the practice on other FAs), Sergeant Major Hoffman recognized Mulcahy's talents in maintenance (from Bob's previous army assignments) and Mulcahy became the new team maintenance man.

Sergeant Mulcahy started his military career in the Massachusetts National Guard in a tank unit as a maintenance mechanic for the 182nd Regimental Combat Team. As a sergeant in the unit, he served as the recovery NCO. In September of 1952, he enlisted in the regular army. He became airborne qualified, and served in the 82nd Airborne Division. He went on to serve tours in the 174th Regimental Combat Team at Fort Devins, duty in Iceland, and then the Infantry School at Fort Benning, GA. He joined the 77th Special Forces Group in September of 1957, and conducted further training in HALO and scuba. He was alerted one day to join a team forming up for deployment to Laos.[44]

In Laos as the team's maintenance sergeant, Mulcahy had his work cut out for him to prepare the generators and vehicles for team operations, as he described:

> I went to work on fixing the place up (as did all the people on our team). My "motor pool" was about four or five jeeps, a 2½-ton truck, trailers, and a water trailer with a Briggs & Stratton pump on it. There was an old semblance of a water tank left over from when the French were there. I found an old square tank that held water, took it and rigged it up as a shower for the team house.
>
> They issued us a Japanese jeep. I painted that thing grey and called it the "Grey Ghost." That jeep was to be personally mine as the maintenance guy. No one on the team could use it unless I green-lighted them for permission. One of my jobs was also to run into Savannakhet with 55-gallon drums to get gas to run our vehicles.[45]

It was only when they got to the site the team first learned the nature of their mission as explained from the outgoing team. They were assigned to train a *batallion voluntaire* from Tchepone (BV-33), composed of ethnic Lao (Hmong and Kha). For the conduct of the training, the team had two Thai interpreters, who were brothers. The trainees from Tchepone came to Dong Hene in company batches, and wore a hodge-podge of mixed uniforms, including old French military clothing. One of the first orders of business was to order smaller fatigues for each soldier. The troops were also equipped with M1s and mortars. The men of FA-38 named them "*Sua tahan*"—Tiger soldiers.

The SF trainers wore civvies the entire time, a mix of army-issued short pants, long pants, civilian shirts, jump boots and baseball hats. They wore their personal weapons during training; military weapons consisted of M1s, carbines, a 60mm mortar, grenades, and a .30-caliber machine gun. Mulcahy carried a "Bulldog" M1, cut down to make a military carbine version.

To handle the Pathet Lao threat in the area, a reinforced BV company provided security at the camp. They were of the same ethnic composition as the battalion, but were a step above in training and professionalism. The team regularly received messages with intelligence notices indicating Dong Hene was going to be overrun by the Pathet Lao. (After the battalion graduated and departed, only the security company was in place for force protection.)

The security company's job also included the conduct of patrols around the camp. One day while the company was out on patrol, they received a message that they were going to be overrun. That night, the security company snuck back into camp and occupied their firing positions around the team house. The team did not participate in this defense, but Mulcahy and Sergeant 1st Class Sanchez took the precaution to set up the machine gun.

When the attack came, the security company, as Mulcahy says, "Kicked ass, handled themselves well against the Pathet Lao." Mulcahy came under fire. "I came within three inches of being hit and becoming a casualty by an armor-piercing bullet. It hit on the wall beside me, and I hit the floor. I still have the double-jacket bullet I dug out of the wall."[46]

The team adapted to the unique requirements of training a BV, as described by Mulcahy:

> I only got involved in the small arms training at the rifle range. We all were involved in this training. "Buffalo" [Sanchez] instructed on the 60mm mortar. He picked a small segment of the troops to be mortar men, and somehow without knowing the language, and them not knowing English, used a method to teach them some rudimentary math numbers to get them firing proficiently. We went to a live fire one day to shoot and fire all the weapons, and Buffalo got his mortar crews together and they put on a very impressive show of firing HE and illumination. They were right on target. For the rifle firing, we just laid the *tahans* down and set a box of ammunition next to them, and told them to start shooting at the targets till they hit them.[47]

The team medic, Master Sergeant Zaky, ran a dispensary for the camp. The village where the *tahan* families lived was right behind the team area. Doc Zaky took care of them while also running a daily sick call for the soldiers. Some days there were twenty, thirty, and up to sixty patients for sick call, requiring others on the team to pitch in and handle the traffic.

It was the practice of the team to drive the newly trained BV company back to Tchepone after graduation. On one trip, the team had heard that five or six of the nuns working in Tchepone had been captured by the Pathet Lao. The team knew them; the nuns traveled by bus to Savannakhet and stopped at the team house regularly to share a meal and get medical supplies from the team. When the convoy got to Tchepone, the sisters were missing. The team broke in the door of their house and left them medical supplies, not knowing if they would return or not. They noticed a garage across the street, with a Mercedes. Surprisingly, it had North Vietnam license plates, and had probably been brought down the Ho Chi Minh Trail to Tchepone.

The four team members returned to Dong Hene. Lieutenant Colonel Little visited to check up on things. While he was there, the team proposed a concept to split into a three-man element to move forward to Tchepone and continue to advise the battalion in combat patrolling. Little was very emphatic and said, "Not only no, but hell no."

The second time they tried to get involved in combat operations was when Sergeant Ballenger and Captain Moon were captured. The team volunteered to go to Seno, don parachutes, and jump into northern Laos to look for the two SF operators. Once again, they were told to stand down. Mulcahy notes, "That was unfortunate and left Ballenger living in a hole as a prisoner of the Pathet Lao for one year."

FA-38 continued to train additional troops as other groups of soldiers came in to the camp. Some of the new troops now came from Seno.

Just before the team's departure from Laos, Tchepone fell to the Pathet Lao. The team regretted not being able to send advisors with the battalion they had trained; it may have changed the outcome.

The new replacement team sent two members ahead as their ADVON and began their transition with FA-38. FA-38 was packed and ready, and on a four-hour notice, caught an aircraft to Bangkok.

Mulcahy took thirty days' leave, and went home to Massachusetts. His father asked him where he had been, and did not believe him when he found out Bob had been in Laos. His father then showed him an article in *Time* magazine about the fall of Tchepone.

The results of diplomacy and fighting over the summer of 1961, even with a ceasefire presumably in place, resulted in the Pathet Lao and NVA controlling most of the highlands of Laos and the FAL in control of major cities and areas along the Mekong River valley. This geographical positioning between the two opponents would basically remain as the status quo throughout the future years of the war in Laos.

PART III

OPERATION *WHITE STAR*: GREEN BERETS AT WAR

CHAPTER FOUR

Operation *Momentum*: *White Star* Begins Unconventional Warfare

"Vang Pao made it explicit. The Hmong had two alternatives, either flee to the west or stay and fight, and he and his people wanted to stay. He had 10,000 men, he said. Adequately armed and trained, they could hold the mountains in most of Xieng Khouang and even Sam Neua Provinces, harassing enemy activity along the roads and in the valleys. He described the distribution of the Hmong population throughout the area, and it appeared to Lair that he might well command the manpower he claimed."

THOMAS L. AHERN, JR., *UNDERCOVER ARMIES*

One of the unique missions performed by Army Special Forces is the conduct of unconventional warfare. The purpose of UW is to provide support, training, and military advice to insurgents (guerrillas) or a resistance movement to help them overthrow a totalitarian or repressive government, or an occupying power. It is a strategic course of action if chosen by U.S. policy-makers, in that its end-state is the overthrow and political replacement of the repressive regime, or occupier. If successful, UW provides the highest payoff in strategic utility.

Unconventional warfare is also employed by friendly forces to reinforce conventional force maneuver. Friendly irregular forces can be employed as an economy of force to operate against the enemy in inaccessible areas, prolonging the conflict for the enemy (buy time for diplomacy to work), and applying friction, fog of war, and attrition on enemy forces.

With Kong Le, the Pathet Lao and NVA effectively in control of the Plaine des Jarres, the RLG initiated a series of attacks with the FAL, most ending in defeat and retreat of their forces. Near Xieng Khouangville, enemy attacks forced the retreat of the FAL off the Plaines and south to Ta Vieng (January 8, 1961). Major Vang Pao commanded BI-10, a mixed unit of Lao Theung and Hmong, and was among the retreating column headed toward Ta Vieng. As a mixed tribal unit, BI-10's families had no choice but to join the retreat. At Ta Vieng, over 4,000 Hmong fighters, guerrillas, and family members assembled on the new defensive line.

The FAL continued to retreat even farther south to areas near Paksane, but Vang Pao stubbornly refused to give up his position at Ta Vieng.

The embassy in Vientiane, along with the army attaché, Brigadier General Boyle, looked to a solution for the poor performance of the FAL; the PDJ could not be surrendered to allow the enemy free reign. The earlier work of the Hmong ADOs and guerrillas in the PDJ area to harass enemy forces gave promise to opening a new paramilitary front, not reliant on FAL presence. The Americans had heard of the intrepid Vang Pao and wondered if he could be the charismatic leader needed to unite the guerrillas. The CIA sent their agent, James William "Bill" Lair, to scout the prospect.

Operation *Momentum* was the brainchild of Bill Lair, "Colonel Billy." Lair was a World War II veteran who joined the CIA in the post-war period. He received his first Agency posting to Thailand in 1951. He was a Cold War warrior, extremely patriotic and a staunch anti-communist. Among the first of his duties in Thailand was his assignment working with the Thai Border Police Unit (formed as a response to the communist movements in Thailand). One of the Border Police's initiatives for counter-guerrilla operations was the development of an elite unit within its ranks which could work with the indigenous Meo tribes in northern Thailand to counter Chinese-sponsored communists. In a fortuitous agreement between the Agency and the Thai government, helped by the ambassador to Thailand (William Donovan of OSS fame), Lair was chosen to organize and lead a unit raised solely for counter-guerrilla, counterinsurgency, and guerrilla warfare, named the Police Aerial Reinforcement Unit—the PARU. In order to solidify his role as the commander of the unit, the Thai government asked that he be "seconded" into the unit as a Thai police captain.[1]

It was a successful venture; in little time the unit achieved great success, for the most part, in defeating the communist insurgents within Thailand. Casting about for newer roles for the unit, the PARU began to advise the FAL in their operations against the Pathet Lao and NVA as a hedge against any future communist advances north of Thailand. The weak pursuit of Kong Le's Neutralist army after it was driven out of Vientiane in December of 1960 made it apparent to all concerned that the FAL were not capable of taking on the triad of Neutralists, Pathet Lao, and NVA, even after being stiffened with PARU advisors. With the enemy now in charge of the PDJ, threatening both Vientiane and Luang Prabang, and the U.S. hesitant to put boots on the ground and intervene in ground combat, another solution to thwart enemy expansion was needed, at least until the FAL could be further professionalized and strengthened into something other than just a "tripwire."

The resistance by the Hmong against communist forces around the PDJ had been noticed, and Lair was tasked to assess the unconventional warfare potential of using the Hmong as a paramilitary force which could enable FAL conventional operations to hold territory. The Hmong were warriors, skilled at operating in the hills and mountains, hated the Vietnamese and the communist way of life, and were led by two charismatic leaders: Touby LyFoung and Vang Pao.

Lair found Vang Pao at Ta Vieng and flew up to meet him on January 11. After a discussion with Vang Pao, the CIA had found their man. Vang Pao agreed to fight with his Hmong, if armed and trained. General Boyle agreed to fund the initiative to train and equip up to 2,000 guerrillas. The guerrillas would be formed into 100-man companies and operate like the ADCs; additionally, the guerrillas would be used to harass and interdict enemy forces around the PDJ and along routes 6 and 7.

After Lair met with Vang Pao, it was estimated the Hmong could recruit up to 10,000 guerrillas for this role and could operate to achieve the following objectives:[2]

- Deny the communists access to the PDJ and a route to the lowlands of the Mekong
- Gain territory or hold territory of the RLG in light of any future negotiations
- Harass, interdict, and tie up enemy forces
- Provide intelligence on enemy activities

Lair returned to his office in Thailand, briefed his bosses, and gained approval to initiate Operation *Momentum*—the Hmong guerrilla program.

Two days after Lair's and Vang Pao's meeting, the Pathet Lao forced Vang Pao's forces from Ta Vieng; he retreated westward with the Hmong to Moung Cha. (There was not enough airlift to move the recruits to a safe, government area for training.) Besides, none of the Hmong combatants would move and leave their families behind to the mercy of the enemy. Vang Pao recommended the hamlet village of Padong as an initial site to commence training. Thomas L. Ahern, Jr., in his work *Undercover Armies,* explained the choice of this site: "Training would have to take place under the enemy's noses, and Vang Pao proposed bringing the first 300 volunteers to Ban Pa Dong, a tiny Hmong hamlet about 8 miles south of the Plain of Jars. The rugged terrain would prevent any instantaneous enemy reaction, and he promised at least three days of training before Kong Le or his allies could attack."[3]

Lair was directed to initially train up to 1,000 guerrillas. A few CIA operatives, along with their PARU teams, were deployed to begin the training course at Padong. Padong had been an old French opium trading center and the site held an airstrip on the plateau along with some rough, wooden buildings to use as a camp. USAF Air Commando Heinie Aderholt arranged the Air America drops of guerrilla warfare kits—weapons, ammunition, uniforms, and other supplies—from covert equipment stores held in Okinawa.

The PARU used the training template they had earlier developed with the indigenous populations in northern Thailand as the program of instruction with the Hmongs—a three-day crash course in weapons familiarization along with small-unit tactics for patrolling and ambush. (The Hmong already had skills in hunting and operating with stealth in the jungles of northern Laos.) Immediately after the training course, the guerrillas successfully repelled a Pathet Lao probe against their position on the mountain.

Padong could be defended; it was south of the PDJ with an intervening ridgeline occupied by a few Hmong villages between it and the enemy on the Plaine des Jarres. This ridgeline was soon outposted and reinforced with mortars as part of the Padong defenses. As time went on, Padong was reinforced with entrenchments and more outposts, along with trip wires and booby traps planted on routes into the position. A large mountain overlooked the position to the south, which was also occupied with Hmong outposts. With Padong as a central base for the establishment of the Hmong guerrilla program, additional satellite training areas were established.

Guaranteed by the U.S. to receive arms, equipment and training, Vang Pao immediately began to visit Hmong villages and recruit guerrillas for the new program. He knew he could not take on Pathet Lao and NVA forces directly on the Plaines, but he did hold the positional advantage in the rugged terrain surrounding the PDJ.

With CIA assistance, he opened up a series of seven outpost locations ringing the PDJ. Agency operatives, with PARU trainers and military equipment, deployed to each site. The seven Hmong guerrilla camps were located at Ban Na (March 1961), then Phou Nong Py, Tha Lin Noi, Phou Vieng, and San Tiau. In April, Moung Ngat and Houei Sai An were opened.

With Padong established as Vang Pao's headquarters, Lair operated out of his Operation *Momentum* control center at Wattay airport in Vientiane.

Initially, three companies (soon known as special guerrilla units—SGUs) were trained and put onto the battlefield. They experienced their first success against the Pathet Lao on January 17. By mid-February, a total of five companies had been trained, two more companies were in training, and four companies of recruits were awaiting training. By early May 1961, 5,000 guerrillas had been trained.

White Star Begins Unconventional Warfare

Although not desired by the Agency to have U.S. Special Forces trainers in the program, the DOD funding of the first 2,000 guerrillas gave the MAAG and the U.S. Army leverage over the participation of *White Star* FTTs in the guerrilla training program. Lieutenant Colonels Little and "Bull" Simons were huge advocates of using Special Warfare in this manner, consistent with how SOF should actually be applied to the best of their capabilities. Subsequently, there were two initial Special Forces forays into Operation *Momentum* during April of 1961: the FTT at Kiou Ka Cham followed by an ODA assigned to Padong.

Captain James E. "Jim" Ipsen conducted his second tour to Laos leading FA-65 during *Hotfoot* Rotation IV. In February of 1961, he took selected team members south of Luang Prabang and initiated contact with GM-16 at Kiou Ka Cham (KKC).

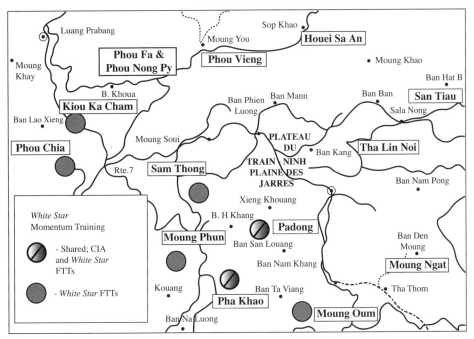

Momentum and *White Star* Hmong guerrilla training camps, circa mid- to late 1961. Derived from a map printed by the Army Map Service. *(Courtesy of George W. Sevits)*

In the month of April, "Mr. Little" (Lieutenant Colonel Little, the *Hotfoot IV* commander) was successful in his attempts to get his teams into Operation *Momentum*, beginning with Captain Ipsen, employing half of Ipsen's detachment (FA-65). Soon, Little had succeeded in coordinating the raising and training of an additional contingent of Hmong in the area, and tasked Lieutenant Paddock (FA-65 XO) with the mission.

On 29 June 1961, Paddock began a reconnaissance for a new campsite, settling on a mountain area called Phou Ka Sak near the village of Kiou Ya. The new site was named "Paddockville." Al Paddock described the activities in those initial days as gleaned from his journal entries:

> On July 3 Meos began building huts and a dispensary of bamboo and thatch at Paddockville, and July 9 I received a message relieving me of GM-16 advisory duties and putting Thomas in my place. My journal entry for that date read, "At last!" We moved the team on two helicopter loads the following day, where we found that the "New area now has addition to dispensary, another barracks going up + mess hall being built." The CIA directed and funded our new mission, with the coordination of Lieutenant Colonel Little. That day I had a talk with our team about duties, plans, current situation, and priority of subjects. I also talked with several Meo chiefs and "emphasized the importance of working together to fight communists." [4]

Once the camp was erected and organized, the call went out for recruits. Hmong villagers began arriving soon thereafter, reporting in with as little as sixteen men in the early days and forty to fifty recruits on other days. By July 15, a hundred Hmong were present for duty. The Hmong were immediately armed as they reported in for training.

The recruiting and arming of the villagers did not go unnoticed by the Pathet Lao. Although they probed and sniped at the camp's security outposts, fortunately no larger attacks or enemy shelling occurred to disrupt the mission.

Paddock's team organized the Hmong guerrilla company with a commander and his headquarters (an XO, 1st sergeant, supply and communications chief, and a senior medic with four platoon medics). The company was divided into three rifle platoons (twenty-two men each) with three rifle squads (three- to five-man squads). There was an additional weapons squad armed with automatic riflemen and their ammo bearers.[5]

A weapons platoon of about twenty men was formed to man a 57mm recoilless rifle, a 60mm mortar section, and two light-machine-gun sections. Al notes from his journal: "All weapons were U.S.-made: M1s, carbines, BARs, LMGs, 60mm mortars, 57 RRs, and .30 cal LMGs, provided by CIA and airdropped by Air America (we did not have an LZ for fixed wing aircraft; just a DZ that also served as an LZ for helicopters). This was a lean organization in which we put maximum emphasis on using small units for ease of communications and maneuver. I had names assigned to each position on the company roster."[6]

The following is verbatim from his journal: the concept for future operations and organization of the Hmong. Paddock used this concept, and other details on logistics and propaganda when briefing CIA operatives on his team's operation:

- Mobile guerrilla force (the 95-man company) cadre capable of directing, training, & organizing area consisting of series of ADCs, or home guard. Guerrilla force will consist of volunteers who will go anywhere, anytime. Will be considered the "elite." These men will consist of troops already on hand plus volunteers picked up as we travel from area to area.
- ADC, or home guard—will be given 2 or 3 week basic tng course in wpns, ambushes, raids, medic, etc. Cadre will be used for majority of tng. Units will be organized as much as possible on village level with chiefs organizing as they see fit. After training, people will return to their normal lives, being called upon in event of enemy in their areas of responsibility, or when area commander calls them for coordinated mission, or when local C. O. calls for tng. These ADCs, or home guards, will be under the overall command of the mobile guerrilla force.
- Offensive operations:
  (A) Know locations of 3 or 4 villages & areas where PLs [Pathet Laos] and/or Khas are armed. These people are in our area—consider it important as show of strength & confidence to do something about them. These people must be

eradicated before thinking of going somewhere else (east). Will give our troops confidence & prestige & will help in recruiting drive.

(B) American should accompany troops on first combat mission to ensure success & instill confidence of the troops in Americans. A failure on first mission would be disastrous to morale.[7]

On July 20, Vang Pao visited the camp to encourage the men in their endeavor to arm themselves and defend their villages. It was a tremendous morale boost for the unit, signifying the importance of Vang Pao's prestige and influence in the area.

As the capability of the unit increased, the unit began wider area patrolling in addition to their security duties in the villages. Paddock's team took this opportunity to conduct civic action through the conduct of sick call with the villagers and building rapport for support to the Hmong self-defense unit initiative. One of the tasks for the team was countering the ever-annoying Pathet Lao communist propaganda effort. Paddock noted:

> Our concerns with the effectiveness of Pathet Lao propaganda in the villages continued. In response, I talked to the "psywar man" in LP [Luang Prabang] about developing leaflets emphasizing unity + evils of communism + cut out petty tribal rivalries. I also asked him for leaflets with Vang Pao's picture on it. He said he would "get on it right away." I began conducting armed patrols to the outlying villages to do sick call, distribute leaflets, and build support for our efforts.[8]

FA-65A departed Laos in August of 1961. Upon their departure, they had armed and continued to train the ninety-five man company, had begun building a set of barracks for the ADC with a goal to house 360 men, and were in the process of arming and training these additional men with the assistance of the cadre from their company.

After his return from Laos, Lieutenant Paddock was assigned as a battalion S3 in the 1st SFG. He later commanded a Special Forces team in Vietnam (1962 to 1963) and served as a Major with Special Forces again in Vietnam from 1967 to 1968, with MACV–SOG. He would remember his time in *White Star* as one of the foundational experiences in his Special Forces training. (Retired Colonel Alfred H. Paddock, Jr. is the author of *U.S. Army Special Warfare: Its Origins*. He holds a Ph. D. degree in history from Duke University.)

Padong

With the urging of Lieutenant Colonel Little to incorporate his *White Star* teams into the Hmong *Momentum* program, the second Special Forces team to deploy and begin training the Hmong guerrillas was Team *Chance*, FA-27. Captain Billy J. Chance, a West Point graduate, led the seven-man team, assisted by First Lieutenant Eugene A. Fisher, his XO, and Sergeant Roy L. "Beetle" Bailey, the team sergeant.[8] Other team members included Staff Sergeant Jan Janosik (weapons), Sergeant John M.

Retterer (demolitions), SP4 Gordon J. Turpin (radio operator) and Sergeant William E. Patterson (medic). The team deployed into Laos in late February and was assigned the advisory UW mission at Padong, sometime in early April 1961.

Team *Chance*'s initial mission in Laos was the training of Lao infantry at Camp Chinaimo. The team lodged in the prince's house in Vientiane, along with another Special Forces team. Much of their training consisted of teaching the Lao the M1, machine guns, pistol firing, and the use of demolitions. The team used the ranges at Camp Chinaimo to teach these fundamentals.

Captain Chance also conducted a combat parachute operation into Moung Kassy with the 1st BP during this time. About a month into their duties, they were transferred to Vang Pao's position at Padong, arriving in late April. They began to experience the "difference" in advising guerrillas vice the Royal Laotian Army troops. It appeared that Vang Pao controlled everything; a sure sign of his control over everyone was the footlocker he kept in his quarters with paper money notes to pay the troops and for use in obtaining supplies. There soon appeared friction between the SF military advisors and the Agency paramilitary advisors as to how to run the operation. It was important to the Agency operatives to not interfere with the decision-making of Vang Pao and his subordinates, even to the extent of hesitating to suggest defensive improvements to the base. The Special Forces operatives felt the advisory training should be more active.

Sergeant John M. Retterer was cross-trained as both a medic and a weapons man on the team. He primarily served as a weapons trainer for the maintenance and use of the mortars and artillery at the site. When he arrived, the Hmong were using the old M2 chemical mortars with the square base-plate. Later, this situation would be improved with the arrival of newer, M632 mortars.[9]

The team found the defenses of the camp haphazardous. There was no wire, but the Hmong did have outposts. Retterer noted: "We tried to organize the defenses better, but Vang Pao took total charge of running that site—so, we did not interfere. He basically would tell us what he was going to do."[10]

The team members were armed predominantly with M1 carbines, but Sergeant Retterer preferred the M1 rifle. He also noted the difficulty of the Hmong carrying the M1 rifle, due to their size. "To the size of a Lao, an M1 was a crew-served weapon!"[11] Team *Chance* did not have any automatic weapons. The team initially wore civilian clothing, mostly black in color, in some sort of way to look like villagers or enemy troops. (This could have been a measure taken in case the team was forced to escape and evade, but like other *White Star* teams, they changed into military fatigues with the directive from the MAAG to do so in late April.)

The team was supplied through Air America deliveries of food and rice, either landing H-34 helicopters or airdrops of rice bundles, which as usual, resulted in the killing of a few Hmong guerrillas who hastily ran out to catch them. The team lived on the heights of the plateau, near the Hmong chain of command, but as the constant daily shelling of the position endangered their location, they soon moved down the hill. Retterer described the reason for the move: "Yes, we were always under Pathet Lao fires—we suspected from 75mm artillery. They must have had someone close in as a spotter. Whenever we would walk across clear areas, the fires came down. They tore up the hootch area with artillery strikes. We moved down the hill to the escape ravine to get out of the impact area."[12]

Although they could move around to monitor and observe fighting positions, they were frustratingly prevented from patrolling with their counterparts (as was also the case with the Agency operatives; Vientiane feared the ramifications of U.S. personnel being captured and paraded by the communists to reinforce enemy claims the United States was conducting combat in Laos). Captain Chance's advisory efforts were limited to sitting with Vang Pao and his commanders and suggesting sound tactical advice during their planning efforts, such as recommending patrol routes and times.

Retterer noted the deficiencies in their indirect fire capability, as well as the use of innovative tactical techniques to provide counter-fires against the daily, and increasing shelling from Pathet Lao and NVA mortars and artillery:

> I trained them to shoot mortars. They also got in some Pack 75mm artillery pieces. Vang Pao always tried to help us with the training, but he just got in the way. The Hmong were basically shooting H&I [harassment & interdiction], not shooting at any definite targets.
>
> After we got the newer version of mortars, the Hmong would carry them on raids. They would go down into a position, set up, fire onto trails suspected in use by the Pathet Lao, and then they would tie vines to the pieces of the mortar and hoist them into the trees (to hide them from the Pathet Lao). In this way, they did not have to hump back the mortar, tripod, and base-plate, and the mortar was there for their next attack.[13]

Sergeant John Retterer would not be at Padong the day of the big attack launched by the Pathet Lao. He left immediately after witnessing the crash of an Air America H-34. He was sent to Paksane, and then Yat Mu (along the Mekong River) near the Thai and Lao border. He remained there for the rest of the tour with another FTT and with the job to help square away the weapons owned by the Lao, primarily helping them with maintenance of their mortars.

Sergeant Kenneth R. Bates served as the Team *Chance* radio operator. This would be his second tour to Laos; he had previously deployed during the *Hotfoot II* rotation at Luang Prabang. He initially deployed with FA-34 in Paksong, but did not remain with the team long before being pulled back to Vientiane to support the FC team, serving there for two months. He joined Team *Chance* at Padong, along with Sergeant William E. Patterson, a medic, and Sergeant Jan Janosik, a weapons man (also on his second tour in-country).

Ken Bates provided another of the few eyewitness accounts to the first of the SF teams on Operation *Momentum*:

We were working with Vang Pao and about 1,300 Hmong troops, along with an Agency advisor. There was also a Thai PARU team there.

The Hmongs built me a radio shack. The Agency gave me a radio with a big antenna. I found out later it was a beacon of some sort. They provided me with a generator and two civilian radio operators to talk to Udorn and to talk with Air America. I also talked once a day with the C-team. I was the only building in this camp! So I had a great place to sleep every night; all the rest of the team and Hmongs lived in the woods and emplacements, under ponchos.

Vang Pao would not let us or the Agency rep go on missions; he was very adamant about this. We did help defend the camp; we had 4.2 mortars. We also had two .50 calibers.

We were taking 122mm rounds and artillery from Pack 75s; we could not fire back due to range and reach out to them. We tried to get the helicopter pilots once to fly our 4.2 mortars out further so we could engage the Pathet Lao, but they refused, causing some "inter-service" arguments![14]

(Ken Bates later continued to serve in the 7th SFG and joined the 5th SFG as the Vietnam War intensified. He spent a total of four and a half years' worth of tours in Vietnam.)

Lieutenant Colonel (USAR, Ret.) Fred Sass flew his H-34 in support of the SF and Agency during these operations. He was an Army helicopter pilot who "sheep dipped" with other Army and Navy pilots to join Air America in 1961. He was on active duty in the army in early 1961 at Fort Benning, GA, and was called one day to attend a meeting with other unmarried pilots. He volunteered for Air America duties after receiving a classified briefing on Laos.

He joined Air America and arrived in Bangkok, noticing the Marine helos positioned there still in OD green paint scheme, with the USMC insignias overpainted; however, he could still see traces of the insignia through the paint. The "picked" pilots met at a hotel in Bangkok and received their briefings. "We got briefed there that our mission would be resupplying SF troops in Thailand and Laos. We would fly into Vientiane, in civvies, and then get our mission for the day. We were also supplying Hmong."[15]

They then flew the H-34 helicopters to Udorn, after fueling at Korat. Fred noticed that the crew chiefs were a mixed bag, most of them Marines.

One of his first important missions was a flight to Luang Prabang where he was met by an Army Special Forces team. There was a large airborne operation going on, supported by Air America C-46s and C-47s for the Lao paratroopers. The Lao BP initially refused to jump, but eventually conducted the operation. Fred flew that day with an ex-Marine Air America pilot in his H-34 (the Moung Kassy operation).

The airborne operation was planned to be conducted about forty miles east of the royal capital. Upon landing his H-34, Fred noticed there were parachutes lying around on the drop zone. Suddenly, one got tangled up in his helicopter rotors and damaged the H-34. The pilots left the bird at the landing zone, returning via another helicopter to base. They attempted to return the next day and repair the H-34, but found the chopper totaled and unrepairable.

Fred remembered the dangers of flying into the Padong area during the base camp's engagements with the NVA and Pathet Lao:

> Our missions were posted every night. No one wanted to go to Padong [Vang Pao's headquarters and training camp]; it was considered a hairy place. It was hostile, always under attack.
>
> I flew there, then later into Pha Khao. I also flew into Savannakhet and Pakse area. In those early days, it was pretty disorganized. No one knew all the LZ/DZs, what they were numbered, etc. The SF were out at these sites, running ranges, training, etc. We often hauled troops to satellite sites. I met Captain Nagle, Colonel Little, and Colonel Simons while operating out there. I met Captain Moon at Vang Vieng.
>
> Flying in the mountains was tough; the weather was often bad, and navigation capability was piss poor. We initially used road maps; one over Asia type maps! I took fire, but was never hit. I think the enemy did not know how to engage one—a helicopter was a strange machine to them in 1961.

Part of Fred's duties was flying Vang Pao around to deliver payroll to the guerrillas. During these flights he became familiar with the SF teams on Operation *Momentum*, delivering their supplies or transporting them around. He also ferried Colonel Little to other sites where *White Star* teams were working around Savannakhet and Pakse. During the peace negotiations, Fred's job included the transport of VIPs to the peace negotiations site; he remembered the duty was good because there was great food and eating at the site. He, along with other Air America pilots, noticed the Russian helicopter transporting the Pathet Lao and NVA delegations, but the Americans were not allowed to talk to the pilots or go near the aircraft.

Sass' most vivid memory was to support the evacuation of Vang Vieng, after the incident with Captain Moon and Sergeant Ballenger being captured. (Fred Sass ultimately flew missions in Laos from March of 1961 to October of 1961.)

After the March agreement between the superpowers to begin negotiations on the neutrality of Laos, the inevitable "talk while fighting" strategy of the communists continued. To claim more "liberated" areas pending a ceasefire, the Pathet Lao and the NVA planned to remove pockets of Hmong resistance, especially the *Momentum* headquarters at Padong.

Enemy forces moved artillery and men to capture the interceding ridge between Padong and the PDJ, soon opening up on the Hmong outposts with artillery barrages. Captain Chance moved forward to one of these positions, bringing the 4.2-inch heavy mortar with him, and began counter-fires, which seemed to have a good effect in reducing enemy fires (or at least shifting them from his mortar position). But he clearly deduced that at some point the position would be untenable; guerrillas are not designed to hold and defend ground against superior forces. Captain Chance and his team advised Vang Pao on the evacuation of the ridge, but they were not successful in their endeavors. Vang Pao did take one thing into account, at least understanding there would be a prolonged battle at Padong; non-combatants were evacuated from the area.

On May 13, Moung Ngat fell after Hmong defenders repulsed several waves of attack from NVA during a day-long battle. On May 15, enemy forces now focused their attacks on the ridgeline before Padong, and it soon fell, with the defenders and remaining refugees retreating to the Padong position. NVA and Pathet Lao moved artillery to the back side of the ridge, where 4.2-inch mortar fires could not reach them, and began a sustained bombardment of Padong. Simultaneously, reconnaissance patrols and probing attacks began as the precursor to a larger attack. Team *Chance*'s positions, covered in discarded parachute canopies, were soon riddled by artillery fire.

For some unknown reason, the Hmong at the outpost on the southern hill overlooking Padong evacuated their positions and came back to Padong, leaving the position to infiltrating enemy forces. A small effort was made to go back and ambush enemy forces on the hill, but the effort was unsuccessful. The sound of entrenching, movement, and the activities of stringing communications wires on the overlook position foretold its use against Padong.

The enemy began digging entrenchments up the slopes toward Padong, inexorably progressing upward even with mud and slippery slopes from the days of rain from the monsoon. The first artillery rounds began impacting the site on May 15, and continued throughout the month, reaching up to 400 rounds one day near month's end.[16]

Reinforcing Padong became dicey with the fog and the rain and clouds of the monsoon. Some Air America pilots refused to risk their lives to resupply the Hmong on Padong. On May 31, an Air America H-34 crashed into a karsk mountain formation while trying to land at the site, which was covered in fog and clouds, resulting in the first loss of life for that organization. Two pilots were killed: Charlie Mateer and Ed Wyzbowski, both Army pilots. The surviving crew chief was Dale Klock (Army).

By the beginning of June, three companies of the 148th Independent Regiment of the NVA, along with nominal support by the Pathet Lao and Neutralists, were prepared to begin operations for a final assault on Padong (with approximately 1,200 men). They were reinforced with 85mm guns moved off the PDJ and situated closer to the site. Heavy, incoming fires were a daily event for the defenders of Padong. Captain Chance spoke of his efforts to keep Vientiane informed of their dire situation, during an interview with Ken Conboy (as described in Conboy's work, *Shadow War*): "The enemy appeared to have gotten above and behind Padong, and we were taking a beating. Every day we contacted Vientiane to give an update for the ICC, and I was supposed to report the exact number of rounds that had fallen over the previous 24-hour period. Vang Pao came to me one day with a set of ears as proof the North Vietnamese were the attackers. I asked him how he knew they were Vietnamese, and he looked at me serious and said, 'Because they're pointed.'"[17]

During a three-day absence of Vang Pao (off flying around visiting other camps, and could not return due to the bad weather), combined forces of Pathet Lao and

NVA used the period of fog and rain to conduct their final attack. CIA intelligence sources in Vientiane passed their warning of an imminent attack on the camp for June 6, 1961. Surprisingly, Edgar "Pop" Buell arrived the day of the attack to coordinate refugee affairs.

The bulk of defending forces at Padong were moved to the back side of the hill, prepared for evacuation, while a small group of rearguard defenders manned the heavy weapons in preparation for the enemy assault. It came; after an afternoon defense by the forward positions, the outposts were rolled up, resulting in increasing Hmong casualties. Firing their machine guns and assisted by Team *Chance* helping to site and lay-in the mortars, the defenders were forced to withdraw by 1800 hours. Captain Chance and his team, along with the fleeing rearguard, did their best to sabotage the weapons, artillery and ammunition stores (setting fire to the buildings), along with laying grenades as booby traps, and evacuated south.[18]

The group moved all day toward Pha Khao, stopping in the middle of the night, exhausted from traveling in the rain. Due to lack of light and noise discipline, the pursuing enemy soon mortared this position and Chance and his team lay in the mud of a rice paddy, fortunately not hit.

The next day, Air America H-34s picked up Captain Chance and his team, along with the Agency operatives, and flew them to Pha Khao. Pha Khao would serve as the new base and training site for Vang Pao's headquarters, but everyone knew a safer, inaccessible place would be needed. In the summer of 1961, after searching for alternative sites, Vang Pao chose the position at Long Tieng for his new base. The nearby village at Sam Thong would support the refugees.

Team *Chance* was replaced at Pha Khao by Captain Carl J. Nagle, FA-63A, a split-team. In August, Major Jimmy Johnson deployed to Pha Khao with a five-man B-detachment (unofficial) to command and control the expansion of *White Star* teams conducting *Momentum*. Captain Nagle and the B-detachment remained at Pha Khao. They did not move with Vang Pao when the new Operation *Momentum* headquarters was established at Long Tieng.

Operation *Momentum* Project Headquarters, Vientiane

To coordinate the activities of Operation *Momentum* in the field, the CIA, along with Vang Pao, established a project headquarters in Vientiane near "Meo Alley" to put them closer to supporting aircraft and logistics for the mission. The Vientiane headquarters utilized a warehouse located at Wattay airport for the storage and shipment of food and supplies transported by Air America out into the field. Along with CIA and PARU operatives, a representative from Air America flight operations, and Vang Pao's Hmong staff officers, Lieutenant Colonel Simons posted two Special Forces officers in October/November of 1961 as liaison and operations officers to the headquarters: Captain George F. Stewart and Captain Charles "Chuck" Judge.

The two would perform a variety of duties until Captain Judge was pulled out to conduct the *Momentum* mission at Moung Oum.

Captain George F. Stewart was a Korean War veteran, serving in the 17th Infantry Regiment of the 7th Division during the invasion of Inchon. After returning home, he served in the Pennsylvania National Guard and did service later in Germany. He attended OCS at Fort Sill, Oklahoma, and upon graduation was assigned to the 761st Field Artillery Battalion. He attempted to volunteer for Special Forces, but was told he had to complete his tour in the Army—five years—before he could apply. He was not deterred: "Exactly five years to the month that I had applied to go into Special Forces, I went to Fort Bragg, but had to go into the 82nd Airborne for jump school and training. I was then assigned to the 7th SFG."[19]

Stewart had not yet completed the UW portion of his Specialty Code "3" designator when he was asked to volunteer for a classified mission to Laos.

After some brief language training in preparation for the mission, he joined Major Johnson's B-team as they flew to Bangkok, departing out of Pope AFB on a C-124. After flying to Vientiane, escorted on the flight by an Agency paramilitary operative, the B-team was split up; Captains Stewart and Judge were chosen to remain in the city as UW liaison officers to the Operation *Momentum* project headquarters. They moved to "Meo Alley" and began their job. Stewart said:

> We lodged in a civilian housing area near the airport. We did not receive any mission briefing or instructions, it was a bad setup. We decided to wait in our room until we received instructions. Soon, we began receiving little flimsy strips. On them was like a SITREP of the Auto-Défense du Choc (ADC) companies. It had the ADC number, coordinates, name, and description of their activities. We went back to *White Star* headquarters and got maps. We returned to our house and made a map-board, and started plotting all of these activities. The best maps of those days were 1:250,000. Some of the areas of Laos were whited-out on the map and had never been recorded. Some of the pieces of the map were made up from aerial photos.[20]

Captain Stewart completed his duties, now "experienced in" and qualified on the subject of UW in the field, and after a forty-five-minute flight, replaced Captain Judge on the B-team at Pha Khao. Captain Judge would serve as the A-detachment FTT team leader for *Momentum* activities at Moung Oum.

B-Det at Pha Khao

As the number of *White Star* teams increased to support *Momentum*, Major James L. "Jimmy" Johnson deployed to Pha Khao in late September of 1961 with a five man B-team to provide command and control over the teams. Sergeant Major Ralph G. King served as the FB sergeant major, along with Sergeant 1st Class Jerrie Richardson, the medic, Sergeant 1st Class Otis L. "Pappy" Scofield (weapons), and joined later by Sergeant Marvis Engram as the radio operator.

Sergeant Major Ralph G. King was serving in the 7th SFG at Fort Bragg during Rotation V of *White Star* in Laos and helped to ship over military uniforms to the teams (when the decision was made in April to switch from civilian clothes to military uniforms). When he deployed with Major Johnson, they flew in civilian clothes, but changed into military fatigues for the mission. The B-detachment was equipped with M1 carbines, and most wore a personal pistol of some sort (Sergeant Major King's favorite was the Walther P-38).[21]

They deployed to Bangkok, then Vientiane, and then were flown up to Pha Khao on the PDJ. The site was controlled by the Agency operatives. The B-detachment made their camp separate from the Hmong guerrillas and deployed the teams, some in split detachments, to train the Hmong. Part of the work at Pha Khao was to continue the construction of training ranges out at various locations where the Hmong guerrillas were located. In some of these locations, they found the Hmong guerrillas living in caves. The B-detachment had a Thai major for an interpreter.

The teams used their own food, flown in by resupply. If the weather was bad, the teams went without sufficient rations. The FTT at Moung Oum got so low one time, King remembered they were down to eating one meal a day.

The men did eat with the Hmong, however. If there was some sort of celebration, they were invited to attend, which may have been often, since the Special Forces normally provided the whiskey. On these occasions they would feast on glutinous rice and buffalo meat. Pigs were also available for the Hmong diet.

A partial airstrip was constructed near the B-team location. There was difficulty in trying to get Air America planes to land there, so the SF operators worked to smooth it out, remove rocks, stumps, and other work to make the strip serviceable. The Hmong were supported by Air America airdrops and helicopters. The B-detachment could get their own supplies and materials a couple of times a week using this system.

The detachment medic built a hospital to treat slightly wounded Hmong and also trained a few of them to be unit medics. Sergeant Major King remembered the introduction to the local custom concerning medical care. "One day the team medic's prized Hmong medic did not show up. The man's baby was sick and he took him to a medicine man instead of letting our medic look at him!"[22]

Although surrounded by the Pathet Lao, there were no enemy probes during the B-detachment's time at Pha Khao. The B-detachment had no vehicles, but were able to travel via air to support their teams. The men of the detachment also assisted efforts during refugee evacuations.

Although being stationed near the captivity location of Captain Moon and Sergeant Ballenger as the two were being held as POWs, the B-detachment and SF teams were frustrated that Vang Pao would not help support a rescue plan. The FTT at Moung Oum drew up a plan with the B-detachment, but were informed that Lieutenant Colonel Simons could not get permission to conduct the raid.

Along with the teams at Pha Khao (possibly two, but cannot be identified with lack of existing records of the operation), the B-detachment also included split detachment FTT-33, commanded by Captain Hugh R. "Mike" Burns operating near the PDJ, with the other half of his detachment, FTT-33A under First Lieutenant Clinton L. Allen, Sr. and Master Sergeant Paul C. Payne operating to the north of the PDJ (this was probably the team operating at Moung Huon, in Sam Neua Province, but cannot be confirmed). Additionally, Captain Rolf W. Utegaard had a split-team (FA-73) west of Pha Khao (March to October 1961) at Moung Phun.

In a rare attempt to provide an "antiaircraft" capability at the site, Command Sergeant Major (Retired) King described FTT-33A's attempt to shoot down a suspected North Vietnamese resupply craft: "Paul Payne was on a team out there. He contacted us and said there was a plane flying over his area every day. Maybe it was from North Vietnam. His team was training a different group of Hmong. He requested a .50-caliber machine gun to shoot it down. We went to the motor pool and made a tripod for him. He told us later that they used it and after firing one burst, the gun did not work, but the plane never came back!"[23]

Captain Charles W. Judge and Captain George F. Stewart (the two alternated duties between the FTT and the B-team) ran the FTT at Moung Oum, with their team sergeant, Master Sergeant Richard J. Meadows. It was the Moung Oum FTT which would have the only casualty during the *Momentum* deployments. George Stewart explained: "Berlett was killed [Meadow's team]. He was teaching 3.5-inch rocket-launcher training, but without using the tubes. They would put them on boards and set them off with batteries. You had to stand off about fifteen feet to do this. Berlett had his troops standing off at an angle about forty feet. When the round malfunctioned and blew up, Berlett was kneeling and got a sliver into his heart."[24]

Moung Oum

Moung Oum was located on the southern edge of the PDJ, southeast of Pha Khao, and just southwest of Ta Vieng. Captain Judge led a full A-team, FTT-59, to the site to conduct training for 100-man Hmong ADCs. Sergeant Richard J. "Dick" Meadows was the team sergeant (he led the team until the arrival of Captain Judge).[25] They had two Thai PARU to serve as their interpreters. The team soon found that a 100-man company was a fictitious number; there were never 100 men forming the companies, sometimes forty-three, or seventy-six, and so forth.

The FTT issued the recruits HBTs—herring-bone twill fatigues –and boots, a hat, M1 rifle, and a rifle belt for the M1. The SF advisors soon noted the Hmong could not be taught with scientific principles—there was no unit of measure with them, no written history, no medical system, and, they were animist in their religious beliefs.

To take cultural adversities into account, training soon had to be modified. When the Hmong could not hold up the M1s on their shoulder, the team gathered them all up and shipped them out via the H-34 helicopters, replacing them with M1 carbines.

The Hmong ate glutinous rice and the team lived, worked, and ate with them until they could get *White Star* to ship food out to them; they were disappointed when they often received little food, but amazed that the *White Star* S-4 ensured beer and brownies from the commissary were sent. (At times, the team would be reduced to one meal a day until resupply.)

There was also the phenomenon of the families living with their men. Stewart recalled, "The men in the ADCs could not stand to be away from their wife (s) and families overnight! They wanted their wives to go out on patrol with them. This custom severely curtailed our military operations. As was the Lao custom, they offered wives to the Americans, but we politely refused and told them we were too busy."[26]

Vang Pao made it a point to visit the men at all the sites. He commanded a lot of respect and readily intervened in training. Stewart observed his style one day:

> Vang Pao was a politician first. He was considered the military leader of the Meo. I witnessed him walk up to a training site where mortar training was going on; they were having a problem adjusting fire. He listened, and then walked in front of them and said, "The solution is simple." He talked some more, then went up to the mortar and kicked the bipod. The fellow out on the OP said the round was a direct hit on the target![27]

During the mission at Moung Oum, the team chanced upon some intelligence which might help them rescue Sergeant Ballenger, held as a POW near Khang Khay since April. Stewart described their attempt:

> One day a kid walked in and told Taylor someone was being held at the old USOM building on the Plaines des Jarres (about twenty or thirty miles from our location). We thought it might be Ballenger, and reported this to the *White Star* headquarters. The S-2 there also felt like it was a sighting of Ballenger. We talked to *White Star* about conducting a raid to free him, but we thought we could not depend on the ADCs; we would need help from other *White Star* assets. The headquarters told us, "Come up with estimates for ammo and demo."
>
> While we were doing this planning, the USAF flew over the suspected area and took overhead pictures. We looked at these with stereo glasses—overheads, approach pictures, etc. We could see every face of the Pathet Lao there, every weapon. They were holding a formation.
>
> We got the raid planning pretty well laid on. We were going to hike there. I was going with a small body ahead to do the recce, and if it looked good for the raid, high-sign with a hand signal for the others to commence the raid. All of a sudden we got a message from the *White Star* headquarters. Ambassador Brown s#*%-canned the mission![28]

During his last days before retirement from the Army, George Stewart met Ballenger personally at Smoke Bomb Hill. "I recognized him and asked him if he knew during his captivity the story of us trying to conduct a raid to free him. He said he had never known."[29]

Upon completion of the ADC training, which lasted about two months, the team was ordered by Johnson's B-team to conduct a twenty-one-day Ranger-style school for the Hmong.

UW West Operations

In unconventional warfare Operating Area–West (UWOA–West, guerrilla activities west of Route 13), two FTTs were located between Kiou Ka Cham and Phou Chia (one of these was Team *Ipsen*); the teams operated through September and were replaced by one ODA at Phou Chia and one ODA now operating between Phou Chia and Sala Phou Khoun (the road intersection); this was possibly First Lieutenant Robert J. Moberg's team. However, the teams were driven out by Pathet Lao incursions to the area in November of 1961.

At Kiou Ca Cham, Team *Ipsen* was replaced by FA-74A during *White Star* Rotation V. Major Carl F. Bernard split his team, taking his section to Luang Prabang to train Lao infantry and ordering First Lieutenant Richard E. Thomas to Kiou Ka Cham to continue the training of Hmong ADCs.

In the panhandle region, Captain Sid Hinds operated with a split-team near Thakhek, to participate in an Operation *Momentum* initiative to raise Lao Theung guerrillas for reconnaissance and interdiction operations along the Ho Chi Minh trail.

Operation *Momentum* in the Northern Panhandle

By April of 1961, the RLG had ceded the mountainous areas of the panhandle to the Pathet Lao. In addition, communist offensives throughout the spring and into the summer resulted in Pathet Lao control over Moung Phine and Tchepone, threatening Route 9. By June 29, the embassy assessed the potential of opening a southern front of Operation *Momentum* using Lao Theung (and some Hmong) tribes located in the panhandle region to thwart and harass any further enemy encroachments. President Kennedy authorized the raising of this new guerrilla force. The force would be under the command and control of the FAL commander in Thakhek, Colonel Sounthane.[30]

The concept initially called for the formation of three twenty-seven-man reconnaissance platoons operating northeast of Thakhek near Napé and the Na Kay Plateau. The operation was run on a shoestring: one CIA case officer, one Thai interpreter, and Captain Sid Hinds with half of his SF team. There were initially some good results, with the impetus to expand the amount of guerrilla teams, particularly the use of Hmong guerrillas around the vicinity of Route 8. However, with the pending formation of a coalition government in October, and the choice of Souvanna Phouma once again as prime minister, RLG support for any such initiative waned and the project eventually ceased.[31]

In December, the CIA began the transition of Operation *Momentum* to an entirely Hmong-run training program, with the Hmong assuming their own command and control over operations. (This would preclude the need for the increased number of Agency operatives and PARU special operations teams employed.) A select group of Hmong guerrillas were chosen to become Hmong special operations teams (SOTs), based on the PARU model. In February of 1962, 160 of these men were sent to Thailand, Hua Hin camp for training. In this same period, the Hmong special guerrilla units (SGUs) were created, becoming more light infantry and conventional-like in their operations. There was no longer a need for *White Star* teams to create 100-man ADCs, and all the participating FTTs were consolidated to open a central, major training camp at Site 20, Sam Thong.

Site 20—Sam Thong

With the growth of the special guerrilla units requiring battalion-sized training, the PEO directed *White Star* teams to begin the construction of a large training base with equipment warehouses and a communications center at Sam Thong (LS-20). The existing airfield would also have to be improved to handle larger cargo aircraft to support the operation. In March of 1962, three *Momentum* FTTs transferred from their training camps to the site at Sam Thong to begin the transition project.[32]

There was not much at Sam Thong; a small village and a barely usable dirt airstrip (suitable for STOL aircraft only). The FTTs would have to not only build their own living and operating facilities, but also weapons ranges, a clinic, and improve and extend the airstrip so it could become at least C-123 capable. It was an enormous task. SF teams on other missions would continually rotate in and out to assist the effort, some only spending a few weeks at a time. Individual augmentations (medics, logistics officers, radio operators) taken out of *White Star*'s hide would additionally rotate in and out to also assist. This endeavor took almost two months for the camp to become operational.

When the 11th BP was scheduled to leave their garrison at Seno to go to reinforce Nam Tha, FTT-19 was pulled from their advisory mission with the BP and returned to Vientiane for a debriefing concerning their battle with the 11th BP near Tchepone, including their brief escape and evasion at the end of battle (see exploit in later chapter). Lieutenant Colonel Keravouri retasked the team to go to Sam Thong (Site 20). The 1st SFG team at the site needed help during the construction and the improvement of the airstrip at the camp, prior to Major Faistenhammer's arrival with the B-team. First Lieutenant Richard O. Sutton led the split detachment until he broke a leg during a crash-landing in an Air America Helio Courier. The remaining detachment members served at Sam Thong until September of 1962.

There was one recorded engagement with the Pathet Lao at Sam Thong. Captain Raymond K. Carter's team supported the Hmong in a defensive engagement between May 17 and 21, 1962. The Hmong were being attacked by two companies of Pathet Lao. Captain Carter also directed artillery fire against the enemy, with decisive effects. For this action under hostile fire, Captain Carter was awarded a Bronze Star.

In order to provide command and control of the project, an additional B-detachment was created to handle the enterprise. In May of 1962, Major Ludwig Faistenhammer Jr. deployed with a twelve-man B-detachment and two teams from the 7th Special Forces Group to command and control Site 20. Major Faistenhammer began his career in Special Forces in the 77th SFG, after graduating the Special Forces officer course. He had a tour to Formosa, and then joined the 10th SFG in Bad Tölz, Germany, where he spent ten years. He returned to the 7th Group at Fort Bragg and prepared to deploy to Laos. Ludwig Faistenhammer described his experience:

> I was selected by Lieutenant Colonel Keravouri to go to Laos, and Colonel Russell, the Group Commander approved. My mission was to go to a remote place called Landing Site 20, at the village of Sam Thong. There was nothing but hills and rough, wooded terrain. Our first project, our priority, when I got there in June 1962, was to get an airfield built before the Hmong troops and their families arrived for the training. We used both our teams' and local labor to build a 2,000 foot runway, with PSP (the PSP was airdropped to us.) We had a Navy bulldozer dropped in for us to help clear the field. The first one augured in! But, we got a second one.
>
> The first Air America pilot to land on this strip was "Red," flying in a C-123. He used the whole runway, and stopped at the edge of the PSP with his nose wheel sticking off of it in the dirt! It took us quite an effort to get him free.
>
> When I arrived, I brought two A-teams; there was already one team there from the 1st SFG. The C2 was from me to Lieutenant Colonel Keravouri. "Arthur" was on site from the Agency. We would coordinate and discuss the mission with him, but he never directed us. I also had a Laotian Colonel counterpart.[33]

B-Detachment *Faistenhammer*'s mission was the training of Hmong ADC companies. Additionally, Vang Pao requested a platoon of airborne troops be trained, presumably for prestige reasons alone, but could never satisfy Faistenhammer with a good answer on why he needed guerrilla paratroopers. The B-detachment S3, Captain Jim Palcer, developed a training program prior to the arrival of the first trainees.

There was still work to be done on the camp prior to beginning the training. Faistenhammer noted, "We started the site with nothing, and built sheds for the camp; we used parachutes for most of the roofs, initially. We had a kitchen built, and got supplied everyday by rice airdrops."[34]

When all preparations were made, Major Faistenhammer, along with members of the B-detachment staff, visited the local mayor and asked him to have all capable men report to the airfield. Faistenhammer also requested that the mayor search for any Hmong who had been previously trained as soldiers. As the troops reported into the Sam Thong site, their companies were formed and broken down into four platoons. At its peak, there were about 3,000 Hmong at the site, the troops along with their families, who all had to taken care of, fed, and paid by the B-detachment. Faistenhammer described some of the training:

> Training consisted of weapons, patrolling, small unit tactics, as well as communications and medical classes. Weapons training covered both light and heavy weapons. A number of ranges

and exercise areas were developed around the surrounding hills to encompass all these tasks. As far as the airborne platoon, one of the SF NCOs and the rigger conducted this training. It was a three week basic airborne course, with one additional week of parachute jumping, using Air America H-34 helicopters.

We conducted patrolling as part of the training. We would go out to check the Tom Dooley clinic to the east near the PDJ; we also did reconnaissance and surveillance on Route 6 as part of the training. The only incident we ever had was three rounds of artillery landing near us. That was it; I have no idea what that was about. But there was nothing else the rest of the tour. We had a graduation parade. Vang Pao and the CIA station chief came for the graduation, along with the Military Attaché.[35]

There were three SF teams and one Hmong SOT on the site to conduct the training for the Hmong ADO companies. Captain Raymond K. Carter from the 1st SFG commanded a ten-man FTT, along with his XO First Lieutenant Fredrick G. Terry, Jr. and team sergeant Master Sergeant James Stover. First Lieutenant Andrew T. Uswa commanded a split detachment of six men.

Captain Richard O. Sutton arrived on site after his earlier mission along the Se Bang Fai River. Master Sergeant Raymond F. Flaherty was his team sergeant, but was replaced by Master Sergeant Moore (who had been on a *Hotfoot III* rotation), after the escape-and-evasion escapade down south. Others on the team included: Sergeant 1st Class Francis E. Bushong, Sr., (demolitions), Staff Sergeant Charles G. James (medic), Sergeant Thomas W. Pettit (weapons), and his radio operator, PFC Norman E. Johnson.

(Although it is not clear from the record, Captain Albert A. Desprospero and his team may have been at the site prior to his move to the Bolovens; or another team may have been formed with First Lieutenant Gardner leading the FTT.)

As the Geneva Agreement was signed in July, the Americans began preparations for an eventual withdrawal. In July, FTT-3, FTT-19, FTT-33, FTT-40 and FTT-41 were serving at Site 20.[36]

Detachment *Faistenhammer* ultimately trained nine ADO companies, along with the airborne platoon. All Special Forces were withdrawn from the camp by mid-month September. Much to the dismay of the Americans, the Hmong immediately looted the camp for items of worth.

Operation *Momentum* in Northwest Laos—Training the Yao

In early 1962, two new programs to recruit local tribes were approved by Washington. One, which actually began in December of 1961, was recruitment of Loven tribes around the Bolovens Plateau (this would be named Operation *Pincushion*—see later chapter). In the north, a guerrilla program was needed to offset the expansion of the Pathet Lao into Nam Tha Province and other areas in Military Region I.

The Yao tribes had migrated into Laos from southern China, and were mountain tribes. Fortunately, they had a war-experienced, capable and charismatic leader,

Chao Mai, who along with the tribesmen hated the communists. Chao Mai fought against the Japanese in World War II and was considered a "Warrior Chief" by the Lao government, as well as the titular leader of the Yao (approximately 5,000 in population) in Nam Tha Province. Chao Mai assured the CIA he could easily raise more tribal warriors among the other tribal groupings and the Hmong, scattered throughout the province. The only opposition to opening up of this new guerrilla front was predictable: General Boun Leut, commander of Military Region I. However, seeing the growing communist threat around Nam Tha, he acquiesced to provide his support to the initiative.[37]

The Yao were equipped with the issuance of three 100-man guerrilla kits from the Agency, and then received some training from an SF FTT, prior to fanning back out to defend against the Pathet Lao. Bill Young was the Agency paramilitary operative detailed to this program and operated on both sides of the Mekong River near Ban Houei Sai. Captain Henry L. Ellison led FTT-2 at that location with the primary responsibility to train Laotian infantry stationed in the river town. Ellison (later reaching the rank of colonel before retiring) related his involvement with the training: "Bill Young, from the Agency, was with me a lot. He lived across the river. On the Thai side, there was a small village, a monastery, and a hotel, where Bill lived. He had two interpreters, but one was later suspected of being a double agent. Later, we trained some men from one of the hill tribes; there were about seventy-five to eighty of them. The Agency equipped and armed them. The course lasted from around April through May."[38]

Momentum's End

After the signing of the peace agreement in July of 1962, part of the American down-sizing was the removal of *White Star* teams participating in Operation *Momentum*. As a result, by the end of June weapons and ammunition supplies for the Hmong ceased to be delivered. Training of other Lao army units, however, continued until all *White Star* teams were evacuated from Laos in October 1962.

CHAPTER FIVE

White Star Rotation V: The Ineffective Ceasefire

"The rainy season is just about over and when it is over there is supposed to be all out war. Last time the P. L.s [Pathet Lao] didn't bother the Americans, but this time they are going to kill all of the Americans. The Lao soldier will stand and fight against equal forces so when the Viet Minh and Chinese come back the Lao soldier will run off and leave the Americans. That is why Capt Moon and the other got captured."

SFC KENNETH N. COX, TEAM *HINDS*, THAKHEK, IN A LETTER TO HIS WIFE

White Star Rotation V was a staggered deployment of FAs and FTTs, which resulted from the staggered deployments of Rotation IV's additional nine teams (*Monkhood*). Company A, 7th SFG, supported the bulk of this rotation, since they were the deployment-ready force in the group (becoming FC-1 in Laos). The majority of the teams would be employed as split-teams. They operated alongside the nine in-place Rotation IV teams, until Rotation IV completed their mission in the fall of 1961. Five of the late deploying teams of Rotation V (deployed in August) remained until mid-January of 1962.

The period between May and November of 1961 was relatively quiet as the ceasefire went into effect and negotiations began in Geneva. In the north, defensive operations continued along Route 13 between Vientiane and Luang Prabang in MR-I. In the Borikhane Province (MR-V) around Paksane, GM-13 conducted limited offensive operations to establish control over key valleys between Paksane and Tha Thom. Two spearheads, each consisting of two battalions each, pushed north, one along Route 4 and the other to the east, moving up the Nam Sane valley to Ban Man. The western column was halted at Moung Huong; the eastern column stopped at Ban Man. By October, this situation remained static and became the new front line north of Paksane. *White Star* advisors supported GM-13 forces near Phou Tinpét, north of Paksane.

MR-III saw one of the few major offensives conducted by Lao forces. The FAL conducted operations to reduce enemy activity at Mahaxay, Moung Phalane, and Ban Nhommarath, supported by *White Star* teams. GM-14, retrained in Thailand, returned to take responsibility to clear enemy forces around Mahaxay and the Se Bang Fai River area.

From the summer of 1961 to the early fall of that year, MR-IV military forces were often used to reinforce other military regions, for the most part leaving BVs to conduct limited operations. The Pathet Lao continued to harass FAL forces near Saravane and Attopeu. GM-15 (airborne BPs) focused their efforts on the Moung Phalane sector (between Pakse and Tchepone along Route 9). Additionally, newly formed GM-18 began operations in this area, assisted by *White Star* team FTT-30.[1]

In September 1961, the FAL was renamed as the Forces Armées du Royaume (FAR).

As *White Star* Rotation VI teams began arriving at the end of the year (October, November), operations in MR-III would take campaign-like dimensions, centered on the Mahaxay and Se Bang Fai River operations.

Farther south, in MR-IV, *White Star* teams began the early development of the Kha tribal guerrilla program, centered on the Bolovens Plateau and Saravane. This would grow into a major UW effort, named Operation *Pincushion*.

The Pathet Lao and NVA increased their activities in northern MR-I to seize more "liberated" territory as the Peace talks continued. Normally a fairly quiet area of Laos, by early fall of 1961 Pathet Lao were in Nam Tha, in control of the Nam Beng valley as far as Moung Huon, and the NVA and Pathet Lao garrisoned the town of Moung Sai. Rotation VI *White Star* teams were supplied to the Northern Command as they planned an operation to retake the Nam Beng valley, Ban Namo, and Moung Sai.

Team *Hinds* serves as representative example of the increase in combat tempo experienced by *White Star* teams in MR-III.

Team *Hinds*, Thakhek, April 24–October 23, 1961

Captain Sidney R. Hinds, assisted by First Lieutenant Homer S. Mapp (XO) and Master Sergeant Joseph A. Mancuso, deployed as an eleven-man team to Thakhek to work with the 33rd BI. The team lodged in a house in town outside of the military compound. Each member paid room and board; the house was like a motel and another team shared the facility (Captain Derby's team from Rotation IV and Captain Chuck Darnell's FTT-15, who replaced Derby), but the bulk of those teams were out in the field. Although the ceasefire was supposed to be in effect, few believed in it since fighting continued.

Sergeant 1st Class Kenneth N. Cox, Team *Hinds* intelligence sergeant, was not impressed with the caliber of Laotian troops, and found most of them to be lazy. While awaiting the team's mission to begin formal training with the 33rd BI in June, he served duty to guard the two helicopters at Thakhek which were being used to fly Lao officers to Hein Heup for the ceasefire negotiations.

Air America also flew helicopters out of Thakhek to support the teams at Padong, and later Pha Khao, during Operation *Momentum*. On May 30, during one of these flights, two pilots were killed in an uncontrolled crash. On board, Sergeant Jan Janosik from Team *Chance* leapt clear, but was injured seriously and medevac'ed (with a broken back). The two pilots' bodies were transported back to Thakhek, where Sergeant Cox assisted in loading them onto fixed-wing aircraft.

Captain Hinds met with the team and conducted planning and preparation to run a ten-week training course. Each of the detachment members prepared their individual lesson plans and gathered materials to set up training at the Lao military compound. Sergeant Cox's portion of the military instruction revolved around scouting and patrolling. After preparing 480 hours of potential lesson plans, the team established an operations center on the compound, June 7.

BI-33's strength was 435 men. One of the first actions of the team was a battalion full-field layout inspection in order to assess the capabilities of the unit (June 8), prior to beginning formal training. It was not a great showing.

It was not the best of times to train; the monsoon rainy season set in. On top of that, BI-33 moved out of the compound, about eight miles outside of Thakhek. This seemed a bit peculiar to Captain Hinds and the team, since the unit was supposed to receive at least nine weeks of training before deploying into combat operations. The team adapted; they drove out to the field site every day to conduct training. Captain Hinds focused the lesson plans on appropriate skills needed in the field: patrolling, raids and ambushes.

There were Pathet Lao operating in the area. The team had already heard there was a $25,000 bounty for the capture of an American soldier. The team was assigned a ten-man bodyguard. For their own protection, they placed a Thompson .45-caliber sub-machine gun in each jeep. On their person, they carried M1s, grenades, and each had their own personal pistol.

In preparation for their transition to conduct training in the field, Captain Hinds ordered Lieutenant Mapp and Sergeant Cox to conduct an aerial reconnaissance to find suitable training sites (June 18). By June 28, the team was conducting 24/7 operations. The *tahans* were trained during the day, and officer and NCO classes were conducted in the evening.

Sergeant Cox provided extensive patrolling training. It was arduous, with the rain, heat, humidity, and jungle terrain. Cox tried to limit the weight he carried, stripped down to just his Thompson with 120 rounds, two grenades, and a canteen. On one of these night patrols (in the first week of July) the unit took fire around 0200, with shots ringing out from the trees about 100 yards from the road they were traveling down. Cox stopped the jeep, and fired a thirty-round clip from his Thompson. The enemy faded away.

Just a day or two later, while in their jeep, the detachment members were fired upon (receiving about eight rounds) from a suspected Pathet Lao village. Lieutenant

Mapp, Sergeant Cox, and SP5 Michael G. Hollingsworth were driving down a trail, about seven miles from the BI camp, reconnoitering for an additional training site. When fired upon, they left the jeep and jumped into the jungle. Again, it was quick and the unit suffered no casualties.

On July 12, Lieutenant Mapp was accompanying a Lao squad when he became pinned down by Pathet Lao automatic fire; nothing resulted from the clash. Later, Mapp and the squad were maneuvering back in the area of the Pathet Lao village when another squad from the 33rd BI received automatic fire; the squad returned fire and killed three Pathet Lao. These incidents were reported higher, and as a result the teams were told by Lieutenant Colonel Little not to write home about the engagements, in order to not worry the wives. (This tactic did not work, as can be seen throughout Sergeant Ken Cox's letters to his wife.)

In his letter to his wife dated July 18, Ken Cox wrote: "We are still quite busy. I got a helicopter this morning and flew over the area that we have been shot at twice. They didn't shoot at the helicopter and we got to see what we were looking for."[2]

Everyone in the command soon had enough from the harassing engagements near the Pathet Lao village. The commander ordered the entire BI-33 to conduct an attack. The concept of the operation involved a two-company attack to seize a hill near the village; Lieutenant Mapp and other detachment members would accompany the third company, to maneuver around the hill into a blocking position. The attack was scheduled for the July 27, kicking off at 0530. There were two suspect villages: Bo Kene and Na Tham.

Ken Cox, writing on July 25, outlined the operation:

> The rest of this letter will be classified, don't talk about it to anyone, I just want you to know in case something happens to me. If anything does happen to me, you will know it long before this letter gets there, as it only takes 24 hours or less to send a twix back. Tomorrow we are going out for 3 days to attack the P. L.s. I am leading 2 companies to assault a PL hill. The same place that we were ambushed and where Lt. Mapp and a squad were hit with automatic rifle fire. Behind the hill is a P. L. village, Lt. Mapp is going to use a company to surround it, while I use the two companies to take the hill and Hylton [Sergeant 1st Class Roy L. Hylton, radio operator] will have a company off to the left along the river to prevent reinforcements from coming across the river.
>
> I am going to start the attack about 5:30 AM 27th July. After we take that village we are going to hit two more, moving through the jungle in the day time and hitting them at dawn. Bo Kene and Na Tham. With the amount of men we have it won't be any problem and probably the PLs won't even fight and will just fade away or pretend to be farmers working in the rice paddies. They don't wear uniforms and look like any other civilians, until they start shooting at us.[3]

On July 30, Ken Cox wrote his wife with the results of the attack:

> Well our attack against the PL village was a success. I probably should have written you about it, didn't want to worry you, just wanted you to know in case anything happened. We had a nice little war, but had them so outnumbered that they didn't have a chance. They used mortars and Russian machine guns, but no one got hurt (our people). I captured 2 P. L.s and Lt Mapp captured one and 20 some odd slipped into the jungle. We wounded 2 of them. We spent 2

nights and 3 days in the jungle, seeking out other P. L.s but didn't come in contact with any more, guess they got the word …

On the second day in the jungle we came across a P. L. platoon area, with sleeping quarters, mess table and food. We ruined the food and burned the P. L. huts. Next time we will send a platoon out to locate their new place and raid them. Oh yes, when we took the village, we also captured some of the Russian machine guns, and Chinese hand grenades. The Colonel and other people were quite pleased with our operation, and it looks like we will continue to be quite busy.[4]

Another incident occurred on August 16, even though it was thought the village was cleared of Pathet Lao. Ken wrote:

We have been quite busy. I have been giving quite a few classes through an interpreter, but August 12th I took a 9 man patrol out to recon the village that we attacked on the 27th of July. Getting close to the village, one of the men said that we were being observed by a civilian in the jungle. I went back and could see a man in a black beret watching us. I crept up to about 50 yards to him, to see if he had a weapon. (Didn't want to shoot an innocent civilian.) He brought a carbine up and started shooting at me. I jerked my Thompson Sub Machine Gun up and had him in the sights. The damn gun misfired. I jumped down, pulled the round out and started firing, he was still shooting at me. The machine gun jammed on me 3 more times, so I had the patrol charge into him. (Meanwhile, there was automatic fire and grenades being thrown to my left.) When we charged toward the enemy, he ran into the jungle and another jumped up and ran. We didn't catch them, just got a hat that had been shot off of the other one.[5]

Ken determined after input from one of his patrol members that the enemy in the beret had fired at least fifteen rounds at him, given that the enemy soldier was observed changing a magazine before running away. He then wanted to maneuver to the left to see if others in the patrol had contact. "But one of our patrol men that was on that end said that it was 2 enemy squads (16 or 18 men) who were firing at the left end of our patrol and was trying to get in behind us. So only having 9 men, I pulled the patrol out and we went back to the camp in a hurry."[6]

On August 30, a Lao military unit was ambushed near the Mekong River. BI-33 was tasked to take two companies and conduct a security sweep of the area. In mid-September, the unit spent six days on a sweep. Three Pathet Lao were captured, and others wounded as they fled. The unit had a small rest in a village, and then returned to their camp.

On September 18, the SF team received their initial guidance for returning home, with R&R in Hong Kong en route. To keep busy, they accompanied BI-33 patrols, but there were no significant results or contact from the effort. In October, they hosted Admiral Felt, who was traveling throughout the area to visit SF teams and to hand out awards. Almost home free, and with their replacement team (Rotation VI) arriving in October, Sergeant Joe Mancuso's patrol was attacked by a NVA unit.

Team *Hinds* stopped patrolling when its replacement team arrived during the first week of October. The team relaxed, gained weight, and prepared to depart.

FA-68, Captain Rozon (a Rotation IV team) and FTT-15 commanded by Lieutenant Charles B. Darnell, Jr. would begin what turned into a series of team field deployments starting in March of 1961, near Savannakhet, Thakhek and the Se Bang Fai River, to contest Pathet Lao control of Moung Phine and Mahaxay. These operations are characterized as the "Mahaxay and Se Bang Fai River" campaign.

FTT-15 and Se Bang Fai River Operations, MR-III

Lieutenant Charles B. "Chuck" Darnell's ODA was split upon their arrival in Laos in August. Darnell took command of FTT-15, a five-man team, and was assisted by Staff Sergeant Lewis R. Taylor, the senior NCO on the split-team. The split-team assumed advisory duties with GM-14 at Thakhek. (Lieutenant Darnell's team replaced Captain Derby's team.) They moved into the team hotel in Thakhek, living alongside Captain Hinds' team. (Hinds and three other of his detachment members split off to work with the CIA, training Lao Theung recon units for the "*Trailwatch*" program. This training was conducted at the nearby airstrip. Hinds was replaced by Captain Othar J. "Shali" Shalikashvili, during Rotation VI.)

Darnell enlisted in the army at Los Angeles and took his basic training at Fort Ord. Awaiting classification, he met with a Special Forces recruiter and decided to join the force. He was assigned to the 10th SFG while it was still at Fort Bragg, and trained to become a radio operator. He served with the 10th SFG in Germany until 1955 and returned to the States, where after some time he applied to attend OCS, was accepted, and graduated at Fort Benning in December of 1957. He was then assigned to Fort Ord, in the 3rd Battle Group of the 1st Brigade. After serving a thirteen-month tour in Korea, he volunteered to serve again in Special Forces and was assigned to the 7th Special Forces Group upon his return to the U.S.A.[7]

Once the detachment arrived in Vientiane, they offloaded and remained a short time in the city while receiving their mission. Lieutenant Colonel Little told them, "You will join Colonel Soun Thong at GM-14, or else!" Apparently, there had been friction and lack of progress with the mission to date, and Lieutenant Darnell was tasked by the FC control to "fix the problem or not come back."

The split detachment became FTT-15 for the mission. In Vientiane, FTT-15 picked up their Thai interpreter, Bong Chong Sichuan; the team shortened his name to Bo John. Throughout the mission they would come to admire him as being extremely sharp and very good tactically. (Later, Darnell found out he was from the Thai Rangers in Lopburi, and Bo John later became a major in the unit. In 1970, Darnell served as the S3 of the 46th SF Company in Thailand which trained with the Thai Rangers.)

FTT-15 flew to Thakhek via Air America C-47 and was met by Captain Derby, driving a Land Rover vehicle. Derby drove them to the team house, the French villa "Hotel" situated along the Mekong River. There, they also met Captain Hinds and his team. (Even when in the field, Captain Hinds' stay-behind men ran a medical clinic at the house.)

After settling in, Captain Derby drove members of FTT-15 down to the Se Bang Fai River. The river was situated just about along the line of the district/provincial boundary, and ran northeast to southwest. The headquarters for GM-14 was along the highway road, with units spread all over the jungle. Captain Derby introduced Darnell to the commander, who spoke French and a little bit of English. It was a good meeting, with good rapport established by Lieutenant Darnell. The commander ordered a bamboo hut built for the team in preparation for their advisory mission.

GM-14 had the mission to retake the town of Mahaxay, currently under the control of the Pathet Lao. To accomplish this, GM-14 consisted of the 7th, 8th, and 9th BIs, plus a headquarters company, and were equipped with M1s and 75mm recoilless rifles. The military camp was situated near a little village at the river bridge. To the north, the 5th BI occupied a blocking position, east of Thakhek, as a permanent defensive posture against Pathet Lao in that area.

It was not long after their link-up with the unit when FTT-15 began combat patrols with them. Darnell found Colonel Soun Thong's BIs good in the field, but was frustrated by their movement techniques. For daily patrolling, the colonel moved most of the morning, and then would stop for lunch. After lunch, the unit moved again. Apparently, his tactical skills were the result of French doctrinal training. Darnell said, "Their maneuver for combat operations was to get an order in increments. Not like our combat orders where you get the objective and whole mission, then plan how to get to that point. First order for Laotians would be to move from point A to point B, then wait for word of what to do next. Then another order would be written up for the next place to go. I was very aggravated by this method and not knowing what we were going to do next."[8]

The team ate, lived and slept with the unit. Daily fare was rice, fish or crawfish, and water buffalo. Usually teams in the field were given great support by the field control team in Vientiane and Air America; Darnell's team only received one airdrop during their entire tour: beer and liquor! (While at the Se Bang Fai River bridge, the team paid a bus driver to deliver a small block of ice daily on the bus travelling from Thakhek to Savannakhet.)

The SF medics out in the field were indispensable. Darnell described the work of SP5 James W. Gualtieri:

> SP5 James "Jim" W. Gaultieri was a tremendous guy (our medic). Every village we stopped at he would set up a MEDCAP. That was worth anything else we did. The Buddhists tried to keep us away, but after treating the first couple of patients, the people would line up.
>
> Penicillin was great for most of everything we had to treat. Once the word was out that we had a MEDCAP, people would come down the river in canoes to get help. We also gave basic hygiene and teeth-brushing classes. (I guess we got this stuff from USAID.)[9]

Inevitably, it was time to begin the operation against the Pathet Lao occupying Mahaxay. GM-14 designed the operation to follow the Se Bang Fai River, heading north to Mahaxay. Darnell remembers:

> The first day we went out on patrol, the 7th Battalion got shelled with indirect fire, which scared the Laotians. The battalion fled, which caused us to start a withdrawal. When we were first withdrawing, we were going downhill. I heard the whop, whop, whop of a helo, and an H-34 appeared and hovered over our position. At that time we were in a line of troops. It was Lieutenant Colonel Little, the "*Shark*"! We were able to load up the heavy equipment stuff and ammo on the helicopter to lighten the load.
>
> There were two Laotians wounded in action from small arms fire and two Laotians wounded from shrapnel during this operation. We got the wounded out fast so the other Laotians could not see how bad they were, and get spooked. We cut out an LZ to get them out. We started to call for chainsaws when an H-34, with a pilot in civilian clothes, appeared from NKP.
>
> I was sent in an H-34 helicopter to go pick up the stragglers of this battalion. Because of this, my entire team was ordered to go to the 7th Battalion, along with three other teams brought in from Okinawa, to go and work with this battalion.[10]

FTT-15 moved to Ban Keng Thao, and set up training for the 7th Battalion. Darnell again:

> Part of the problem in combat was that the Lao did not like to kill; they were Buddhists. They were also too small to carry enough combat load and heavy weapons. We set up a firing range, defensive positions, and conducted combat medical training. Later, the 7th Battalion received extensive mortar training to help defend themselves from the Pathet Lao. According to what they had been taught under French doctrine, if the enemy has a big gun, get a bigger gun. The GM procured a 75mm pack howitzer and a 105mm U.S. artillery piece. An American Field Artillery lieutenant came along with the guns. A helo brought in a 106mm from the GM warehouse in Savannakhet; 1st Lieutenant Sam Liberatore was attached as an artillery advisor to the unit from the MAAG and flew in with the artillery piece.[11]

Lieutenant Darnell was later awarded a CIB (combat infantry badge) for his actions along the Se Bang Fai River. A description of the intensity of the engagement is found in a supporting paragraph to the orders awarding his CIB:

> FTT-15, advising GM-4 Hqs and the 7th BI, began an offensive operation on 29 and 30 September 1961 when GM 14, consisting of the Hq, 7th, 8th, and 9th BIs crossed the Se Noi River (WD1187) in an operation designed to regain control of Mahaxay (WE2225) and Ban Nhommarath (WE1946) area. On 2 October 1961, while moving into Ban Na Xoi (SD2392), elements of GM 14 Hq, FTT-15, and 1st Company of the 8th BI were attacked by an estimated company (-) from the vicinity Ban Kham Teui—Ban Thap area (WD2494) with small arms fire and small caliber mortar fire. Action lasted approximately thirty minutes at which time the attackers withdrew. Ban Kham Teui—Ban Thap was taken by our units. The GM Commander, having no further plans to move ahead, chose to move to a ridge (Phou Xoi) just west of Ban Thap and await further orders. On 5 October 1961, while in defense positions along Phou Xoi (WD2197—WD2294) we received large caliber mortar—105mm shells as part of an approximately 300+ shells fired on positions occupied by the 7th BI (WE1403). The 7th BI broke and fled leaving most of their equipment and our left flank exposed.
>
> The GM 14 Commander decided to withdraw, which we did, to Ban Na Than (WD1288). While there, WSMTT ordered my team to assist the 7th BI in reorganizing and to stay with

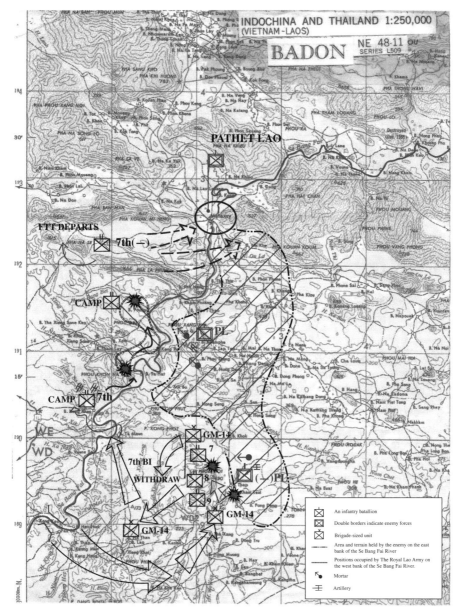

A sketch of the battle action along the Se Bang Fai River, as described by Charles Darnell during his interview. (*Derived from map provided by Charles Darnell*)

them as advisors. Our mission was to clear the area of any infiltrators. FTT-15 with the 7th BI moved to Ban Keng Khen (WE0303). Operations during this period (late October 1961 to late December 1961) were conducted by companies. My FTT was split among the three companies.

I remained with the BI Commander. We moved daily from Ban Ta Hat (WE1407) north to vicinity Ban Poung (WE1515). On several occasions during this period, FTT-15 was subjected to large caliber mortar and artillery fire from the enemy.

On one occasion (I do not recall the date) near Ban Poung, four rounds landed within our defensive perimeter. Also, during this period GM 14 Hq, 8th BI, 9th BI, 75mm pack howitzer Battery, 105mm Howitzer section and one company of the 24th BI moved into this area of operation. In early January 1962, the 7th BI minus two companies moved to the high ground (Pha Na Se Pass WE0422) and prepared defensive positions. Plans were being made for a major attack on Mahaxay. The 7th BI, minus one company attached to the 5th BI, was to take Ban Na Se (WD0723) and attacked from the west. During this stage, my FTT was replaced on 19 January 1962 by another FTT.[12]

During the relief-in-place by the incoming ODA, FTT-15 only had a few minutes with the new detachment commander. The teams exchanged weapons, and FTT-15 flew back to Thakhek, picked up their footlockers and team gear, and boarded a C-47 for the flight to Vientiane, and then home.

White Star Redeployment Procedures

By the end of 1961, the Headquarters *White Star* Mobile Training Team (WSMTT) had developed an extensive procedure to ensure the efficient and quick redeployment of teams upon completion of their mission. Much of the procedure was learned earlier through trial and error.

Redeployment of a *White Star* SF team began with an alert notifying the team when to report to Vientiane, with movement instructions usually published two weeks prior. If lucky, and still in the field, an ADVON of one or two personnel from the incoming team arrived to conduct orientation, briefings, crypto accountability and transfer, and weapons and equipment sign-overs. The two teams also conducted an inventory of all classified items. Supplies, and the equipment, were handled by transfer of hand receipts. All forms were signed, copied, and sent to the B-team, or if a B-team was not present in the military region, on to the S4 in Vientiane. All MAP property remained in Laos (jeeps, trailers, and other equipment).

Medics were required to give the team shots of 0.1cc typhoid–cholera vaccine two weeks prior to departure. They were also advised to take primaquine one week prior to departure, and for two weeks thereafter.

Along with movement instructions, the teams also received enclosures for movement instructions, instructions to the medic on how to handle medical supplies and controlled drugs, an individual checklist, a checklist for each OIC of the movement serial (teams usually moved in three-detachment increments), and a certificate signed by the detachment commander that he had searched all baggage for unauthorized items.

In Vientiane, personnel cleared their postal accounts along with any outstanding commissary accounts. On departure day, personnel were instructed to fly in civilian clothes until reaching Hong Kong; once departing Hong Kong, and in flight, all were ordered to change into military clothing. Certificates were issued for the flight indicating the individual had non-availability of quarters and mess while traveling.

Individual weapons, such as pistols, knives, and other weapons were packed in a footlocker. Upon landing at the first U.S. military base or port of entry, the departing serial was required to undergo a customs check.

The contributions made by *White Star* were not only in conducting combat advisory missions with their assigned unit. *White Star* teams also conducted technical MTTs, proficiency courses, and leadership training schools and academies. These efforts were just as important for improving FAR proficiency as accompanying them on combat operations.

CHAPTER SIX

White Star Rotation VI: "Fighting While Talking": Expansion of Combat Missions

"Meanwhile, the Geneva delegates were becoming impatient with the Laotians. The diplomats had finished drafting the necessary documents; all that remained to be done to reach a final agreement was the seating of a new Lao government ... Washington, which at the urging of Ambassador Harriman now backed Souvanna as prime minister, began to apply diplomatic pressure on the Vientiane government. When this friendly persuasion failed to work, the United States cut off economic aid to Boun Oum. Four days later, the prime minister consented to new discussions; the aid was resumed. Boun Oum and Phoumi, nevertheless, continued to reject Souvanna's control of the defense and interior portfolios. The talks deadlocked. The situation in Laos then took another turn toward superpower confrontation."

TIMOTHY N. CASTLE, *AT WAR IN THE SHADOW OF VIETNAM*

White Star Rotation VI deployments began in October of 1961 and lasted until its assigned teams departed in June of 1962. The events and activities of this rotation would set the tempo, parameters and pace of combat for the remainder of the *White Star* program, until its culmination and U.S. military personnel withdrawal in October of 1962 (the seventh and final rotation of the operation). When *White Star* concluded, over 400 Army Special Forces members would be counted out of the country by the ICC.

Since President Kennedy's decision to employ more military force in Laos (April 1961), the *White Star* mission expanded across the entire country of Laos. First and foremost in his policy goal was to thwart communist expansion during the period of negotiations for peace. Special Forces were used to stiffen the Royal Laotian Army and improve their proficiency and capability to stand their ground as well as to conduct offensive operations to roll back Pathet Lao gains; protracting the conflict for the NVA and Pathet Lao was used to buy time for diplomacy to work (the goal being the formation of a Neutralist country). Using SOF as an economy of force gave diplomats in the embassy and in Washington more choices to achieve U.S. policy objectives.

The Field Control Team (FC-3)—Vientiane

Lieutenant Colonel Arthur D. "Bull" Simons returned for a second tour in Laos to command the FC in Vientiane. Over forty-plus teams were deployed, almost all of them as split-teams of four to six men; there was one exception, the eleven-man team deployed at Moung Oum in support of Operation *Momentum.*

The FC team commanded the SF detachments and B-detachments, supported them logistically, and served as the interface between the chief, MAAG Vientiane and the American ambassador. The FC also provided liaison to CIA control teams conducting *Momentum* and *Pincushion* guerrilla training programs.

Captain Alvin H. Buckelew was the S-1 adjutant for FC-3. He joined the 7th Special Forces Group (Airborne) after serving as the G2 of the Army Training Command, and then the S3 of the 3rd Brigade, Fort Benning, GA, under Colonel Hanks. He was assigned to the 7th's mission contingency deployment company, followed by attendance at the six-week SF officer's course at the Special Warfare Center. He was put on deployment orders for Laos to serve on Lieutenant Colonel Bull Simons' field control team in Vientiane.

Captain Buckelew was looking forward to working with the "Bull" in the field: "LTC Simons was the battalion commander. He was the finest commander I ever worked for. His philosophy of leadership was, 'You guys know the job, go do it.' Simons did not put up with B. S. He shipped out screw-ups."[1]

There is a saying among junior officers in the Army that states: "Mice don't play where elephants dance." Buckelew watched from a distance the dynamic between Lieutenant Colonels Little and Simons during the turn-over of the field control command: "He replaced LTC Little—the relationship between he and LTC Little was rough during the week of transition. LTC Little tried to brief him and pass on lessons learned, but LTC Simons brushed him off and went on to do what he wanted to do."[2]

In his interview, Buckelew explained the variety of jobs he performed as a staff officer on the control team:

> I flew all over. I was the TS-SCI control officer, so I had to go out to the teams with the one- time crypto pads and to pay TDY money. I flew with Air America and Bird and Sons. Sometimes I RON'ed [remained overnight] at the various outlying sites. I visited with Jesse Ramos up in Nam Tha; Lieutenant Moberg was also a friend of mine.
>
> One of the special assigned projects I had was to go to Bangkok and to help with the recruitment of the PARU for duty in Laos. We had an office in Bangkok where the Thai would sheep dip their PARUs to work with our teams. It was manned by an SF NCO. I also picked up gold to pay the PARU teams. I went to the office of the City Manager of Bangkok (Dr. Randy Hamilton) to pick up gold.[3]

One of the major events performed by the FC and its staff was in support of the evacuation of refugees from the Nam Tha airfield during its siege by the Pathet Lao.

The staff worked with Captain Jessie Ramos and his FTT on the airfield, ensuring a smooth operation.

Incoming Rotation VI teams covered down on expanded operations in every military region, as listed:

- Military Region I: about eleven teams, located at Nam Tha, Kiou Ka Cham, Luang Prabang, Ban Houei Sai, Sayaboury, and the Sala Phou Khoung road junction
- Military Region II (*Momentum*): at least six teams, located at Pha Khao, Moung Oum, Moung Phun, PDJ, Xieng Khouang, and Sam Thong
- Military Region III: about ten teams, located in Thakhek, Seno, Savannakhet, Moung Phalane, Mahaxay River region, Pak Lay and Moung Kao
- Military Region IV (includes Operation *Pincushion*): about eleven teams, located at Pakse, Champassac, Saravane, Paksong, and Bolovens Plateau
- Military Region V: at least two or three teams, located at Vientiane (Camp Chinaimo), Paksane, and Phou Tinpét

One of the distinctive features of Rotation VI of *White Star* was the first use of B-detachments to command and control the increase in forces. FB-B under Major Patrick J. Marr commanded teams in Military Region I (with thirteen men); FB-C under majors Warren B. Stevens and Charles E. McCrary were at Savannakhet for Military Region III (with twenty-four men); and FB-D under majors Edgar J. "Coach" Albrick and Joseph L. Beasley at Pakse for Military Region IV (with twenty-five men). Although the B-team for Operation *Momentum* at Pha Khao only consisted of five men, it was considered as FB-A.

Rotation VI also would be the introduction of SF teams from the 1st SF Group on Okinawa due to the increased growth of missions.

If there was a ceasefire in place, very few believed it was holding. In Military Region I, the FAR focused on the defense of Nam Tha against what was building up to be a growing siege of the town by Pathet Lao and NVA. Skirmishing continued along Route 13, with the front lines south of Luang Prabang at Kiou Ka Cham, and north of Vientiane at the Nam Lik River line.

Vang Pao's Hmong special guerrilla units continued fighting the Pathet Lao and NVA on the Plaine des Jarres and farther up north in Sam Neua Province. In August, President Kennedy approved the increase of guerrilla strength to 12,000 men. Vang Pao and the CIA had moved earlier to establish *Momentum*'s field headquarters at Long Tieng (LS-20A, the "Alternate"), where it would remain until the end of the war in 1974. South of the PDJ, along Route 4, FAR units defended north of Paksane at Phou Tinpét.

There were two pockets of contested territory in Military Region III. The first area was bound by Thakhek, Mahaxay, and the Se Bang Fai River, where Pathet

Lao blocked the FAR from the enemy occupied town of Mahaxay. This area would experience constant contact between FAR and Pathet Lao over control of the region and resemble campaign-like dimensions (in scope, intensity, and length).

From Savannakhet and the airfield at Seno, the FAR pushed east along Route 9 to hold back increased operations from Pathet Lao and NVA forces around Moung Phalane. The NVA readily fought in this area to prevent any encroachments against the expanding Ho Chi Minh Trail network, particularly near Tchepone.

South in Military Region IV, an unconventional warfare program opened up on the Bolovens Plateau region, named Operation *Pincushion,* to try and replicate the successful program of guerrilla warfare in the north. This program focused on the Kha tribal forces.

This was the combat picture throughout Laos in the late fall of 1961, and it would basically remain the same (except for the fall of Nam Tha) as Rotation VII entered Laos in March of 1962. The game-changer in the conduct of war would be the eventual signing of a peace agreement in July of 1962, freezing *White Star* teams in place, followed by their subsequent phased withdrawals down into October.

Activities in MR-I

Up until the ceasefire agreement, north and northwestern Laos (Military Region I) had remained relatively quiet. So quiet, only BV-13 stationed at the provincial capital of Nam Tha was needed to defend the region. There were three main towns in Houa Khong Province: Nam Tha, Moung Sing (and old French military post, to the northwest of Nam Tha, with a serviceable airstrip), and Ban Houei Sai, the river town to the west on the Mekong River border with Thailand. The situation changed upon the ceasefire declaration in May and the anticipated follow-up negotiations for a final solution to the ongoing crisis in Laos. Again, communist forces employed the "fighting while talking" strategy, pursuing operations to expand control over additional terrain; they could then announce more "liberated territory" and redraw favorable, and new, ceasefire lines pending conclusion of the talks in Geneva.

In late summer of 1961, the FAL reoccupied Nam Tha, driving out a company's worth of regional Pathet Lao troops. To the south, government forces controlled the Nam Beng River valley up to Moung Houn, blocking any attempts by the NVA and Pathet Lao garrison at Moung Sai to drive any farther down the river line. Elements of GM-11 and the Nationalist Chinese Bataillon Spéciale 111 were stationed at Ban Houei Sai.

The thorn in the side of General Phoumi's military posture during this period focused on ejecting the enemy garrison at Moung Sai, and regaining government control of the Nam Beng River valley. While the RLG was hesitant to conduct major offensive operations during the ceasefire, they did intend to reoccupy and roll back communist forces in instances where the enemy had violated the ceasefire lines (much to the chagrin of the U.S. mission who did not want to upset the current state of diplomatic affairs).[4]

The concept of the operation consisted of a two-prong attack to envelop the NVA and Pathet Lao garrison at Moung Sai. The northern pincer would depart from Nam Tha, head east to Ban Namo, reset there, and continue south to Moung Sai. The southern pincer would move northeast up the Nam Beng valley directly to Moung Sai. Both task forces were required to be in position by the end of December and then coordinate their attack as a double envelopment.

To set the force for the operation, GM-11 and BV-13 re-occupied Nam Tha by October. GM-11 had a two BI task force: BI-1 and BI-2. In support, *White Star* FTT-2 was assigned to GM-11 at Nam Tha. In the south, the Chinese Bataillon Spéciale 111 pushed the Pathet Lao out of Moung Houn, and occupied the town. Some local Pathet Lao would remain in the area, harassing the force with mortar fires. BS-111 was then reinforced with BI-3, BV-3, six volunteer companies, and five ADCs grouped together to form Groupement Tactique 2 (GT-2), a temporary field organization for the operations. The commander of BI-3 assumed overall command of GT-2.

In September, FTT-40 arrived at GT-2 to begin combat advisory duties. They assisted in the training of the various elements of the force over the months of October and November.

Meanwhile, in November GM-11 pushed out of Nam Tha headed east toward Ban Namo, and after light contact with local Pathet Lao, occupied the area. The commander of the unit decided to remain in that position for over a month, waiting to coordinate his movements with the southern pincer of GT-2. While in position at Ban Namo the unit was reinforced with its 3rd Battalion and FTT-3 on December 2, 1961.[5]

The enemy garrison at Moung Sai did not sit passive. In December, Soviet airlift brought supplies and the 4th Battalion of the PAVN 216 Division to the garrison, in response to the anticipated two-pronged attack from the FAR.

About mid-December, GT-2 began its push up the Nam Beng valley. They reached the halfway mark between Moung Hun and Moung Sai where they clashed with enemy forces as the PAVN and Pathet Lao counterattacked on Christmas Day. During the battle, FTT-40 maneuvered alongside BI-3 that was out on a ridge to their west. BI-3's position collapsed under pressure, and they fled back toward Moung Houn. FTT-40 was abandoned, now only fighting on with a volunteer militia company. Soon GT-2's position on the eastern ridge collapsed and the remaining BI elements also retreated, leaving only BS-111 on the battlefield. BS-111 conducted an orderly retreat, taking FTT-40 into their safety. Appalled by the conduct of GT-2, BS-111 headed west to the Mekong River rather than linking back up with the demoralized force. Upon reaching a place of safety, FTT-40 remained with BS-111 till the last day of the year. FTT-40 was evacuated by helo and returned back to Luang Prabang. BV-13 was moved out of harm's way to Ban Houei Sai.

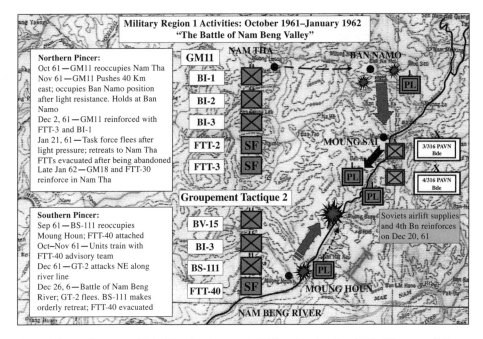

Military Region 1 Activities: October 1961–January 1962
"The Battle of Nam Beng Valley"

Northern Pincer:
Oct 61—GM11 reoccupies Nam Tha
Nov 61—GM11 Pushes 40 Km east; occupies Ban Namo position after light resistance. Holds at Ban Namo
Dec 2, 61—GM11 reinforced with FTT-3 and BI-1
Jan 21, 61—Task force flees after light pressure; retreats to Nam Tha
FTTs evacuated after being abandoned
Late Jan 62—GM18 and FTT-30 reinforce in Nam Tha

Southern Pincer:
Sep 61—BS-111 reoccupies Moung Houn; FTT-40 attached
Oct–Nov 61—Units train with FTT-40 advisory team
Dec 61—GT-2 attacks NE along river line
Dec 26, 6—Battle of Nam Beng River; GT-2 flees. BS-111 makes orderly retreat; FTT-40 evacuated

Derived from silk map published by the Aeronautical Chart Service, Jan 1951. (*Courtesy of George W. Sevits*)

The anticipated attack from GM-11 on Moung Sai began on January 21, 1962; it was never completed. On the day of the attack, while under light enemy pressure, BI-2 fled, causing the collapse of the position at Ban Namo. Soon the rest of GM-11 followed the withdrawal on the route back to Nam Tha, abandoning FTT-2 and FTT-3 alone on a nearby hilltop. The detachments called for evacuation. An Air America helicopter flew in to extract the teams; after receiving some enemy fire on his H-34, the pilot identified the signal smoke from the teams. They were safely evacuated and moved back to Nam Tha.

To stiffen the resolve of GM-11 at Nam Tha, General Phoumi ordered GM-18 to reinforce the garrison. GM-18 was accompanied by their FTT advisors, FTT-30, commanded by Captain Thomas J. Stanford.[6]

White Star Rotation VI, FTT Sayaboury, September 3, 1961– March 2, 1962—"Riverine Warfare!"

Sergeant 1st Class Richard D. Ellmers was in the Korean War in the 3rd Infantry Division, serving in the Rangers. He was in a recon platoon and did two tours, the last with the 7th Infantry Regiment, 3rd Battalion (in a rifle company). He landed with the 3rd Recon at Wonsan in North Korea in the fall of 1950, and transferred to the 3rd Ranger Company when they arrived in the spring.

After the Korean War, he was serving in the 82nd Airborne Division at Fort Bragg, NC, and was jump-qualified. When he heard about Special Forces, he decided to join. Ellmers just missed going into the 10th SFG as they went off to Bad Tölz, so he was assigned to the 77th SFG at Smoke Bomb Hill, serving as an intel/operations MOS (he also went to heavy weapons training.)[7]

He was on Captain Jesse Ramos' A-detachment. Master Sergeant Robert D. Larson was the team sergeant, and First Lieutenant Robert R. Page, the detachment XO. When his team was nominated to go to Laos, they conducted some French language training in preparation. Ellmers recalls:

> We boarded up a C-124. I know we traveled at least through Hawaii and Wake Island, and arrived at Don Muang airport in Bangkok. We transferred over to Air America—maybe a C-47 or C-46—and ended up at Luang Prabang. Sergeant Major T. J. Gray was there. We took a Helio Courier or C-47 to Sayaboury, I don't remember, but Sayaboury had a good airfield which could take larger aircraft. The team had split before we went to Sayaboury; Captain Ramos and some of the detachment went north to Nam Tha up by the Chinese border. I never visited Nam Tha, but went to Luang Prabang a few times. Our split-team was led by Lieutenant Page, the Detachment XO.[8]

The FTT's mission was to train and assist the Laotian battalion at Sayaboury. The Lao battalion was garrisoned at the airport. The split detachment did not have high regard for them, after observing them in the first weeks of the assignment. Ellmers said, "It was a messed up battalion, just sitting around doing nothing. They had a Laotian Colonel for a commander. We thought that they were about at the level of Boy Scouts and could not do much in the way of fighting."[9]

The military camp at Sayaboury had no firing ranges. The FTT conducted weapons firing training out in the forest outside of Sayaboury. The tactical training was conducted in platoon-sized elements, again, while they were in the jungle. Patrol training was also conducted down along the river. From Ellmers: "The Laotians did very poorly."[10]

Most of the detachment's work was with the local tribes. The FTT was able to contact some of the local tribes around Sayaboury, first to procure any useful intelligence and information, and then helped the tribesmen with weapons training and village defense. The tribal affiliations to the north of Sayaboury were Kha; to the south and west of the town were Meo (Hmong), who were considered more warlike by the team. The team's biggest ally in this venture was a Christian missionary, George Tubbs, who lived with his family in Sayaboury. Tubbs lived in a house near the airstrip and became a big asset to the team; he knew everything about the local situation in the province. He also assisted the team during their visits to the outlying villages, as he spoke the local languages.

The Lao military unit was not very helpful in absorbing the team's attempts to train with them, but the team was at least able to get them to patrol and conduct reconnaissance.

The Mekong River was to the east; Sayaboury lies on a tributary river from the Mekong, so one could travel over water all the way to Luang Prabang. When the team traveled this route, they tried to feel out the sentiments of the tribes and whether or not the Chinese were trying to influence them. However, the threat in the area was from the Pathet Lao, who operated on the east side of the Mekong River.

For the most part, the detachment members conducted foot patrols in the woods and over the mountains. The patrols along the Mekong were conducted by the Lao battalion with the team in accompaniment. During the patrols, the Lao unit took time to visit the Meo (Hmong) and Kha villagers; on the SF-only team patrols, the Lao unit provided a few men to work with the FTT.

Ellmers described a patrol to the Mekong:

> I went over to the Mekong with the medic to visit with villagers and to link up with a Lao Navy Patrol Boat. I made contact with them. They had an old, twenty-five-foot French-made gunboat, with a turret and .50 caliber machine gun. They also carried a 57mm recoilless rifle. I went with them when they patrolled the river. They would escort a troop transport, which was a three-story paddle boat, which could carry about 100 men. We would get ambushed when going through enemy territory.
>
> We were ambushed twice on the river. The first time, we were going down the river flowing with the current. This had to be about the time of the beginning of the rainy season (spring) because the Mekong was not that flooded. The first ambush that occurred from the Pathet Lao along the banks was not very effective. There may have been some casualties on the big river boat, but our gunboat had no casualties. We fired all of our weapons. I saw bullet splashes from enemy fire in the water alongside our boat. I had to report to Vientiane and LTC Simons on that incident.
>
> The second ambush was when we were going up the river, against the current, so it was slow going. The Lao took casualties on this one. We docked and stayed at a village. We had to radio for MEDEVAC.
>
> The Lao battalion, or at least elements of the Lao army, had outposts along the river and out in the villages. We never crossed the river into Pathet Lao territory. It was kind of you stay on your side and we will stay on ours. When we were in the villages, our medic helped to treat villagers and treat the wounded. When we went out, we stayed in the Lao troops' tactical positions. Conrad was the medic—a very intelligent, young man. It was very important the medical aid given to the villagers. Conrad also ran a medical clinic at the camp for the soldiers and their families. (He had received advanced medical training at the U.S. hospital at Bragg.)[11]

Corruption and Mutiny

There was one small incident at the turn of the year which highlighted the endemic corruption of senior officers in the FAR. After FTT-40 (First Lieutenant Mike Layton) was evacuated and pulled back upon the defeat of Groupement Tactique 2 near Moung Sai, the FTT's new mission was to train and advise Bataillon Volontaire 17 at Xieng Lom, a small and remote village located in southwestern Sayaboury Province near the hook of the Mekong River. (The team was renamed FTT-2.)

On January 31, a company of the unit entered the camp one morning in a rebellion over lack of pay. The SF team was disarmed and put under arrest, along with the BV-17 commander.

After the FTT missed the daily communications checks, the B-detachment commander, Major Marr, along with Lieutenant Colonel Simons, gathered a rescue force which included the newly arriving FTT-1 under Captain Charles L. Johnson. Lieutenant Colonel Simons and Major Marr, along with some C2 elements of the B-team, a senior Laotian military official, and with the help of three Air America H-34s (outfitted with machine guns and protected with sandbags), flew to the outpost with FTT-1 and resolved the issue. Sergeant Ned L. Miller, the medic on FTT-1, remembered the sequence of events:

> Lieutenant Colonel Simons was quickly forming a rescue force and FTT-1 was included. Three helicopter loads of us flew down to Xieng Lom and landed behind some trees just to the north of the fortified position. LTC Simons then flew on in and set down in front of the wall of the camp. O'Rourke, the junior demolitions man on FTT-1, was prepared with demo charges to breach the wall. So we planned with the B-team to go out on a rescue. My job was to be loaded down with ¼ kg blocks of C-4, and when we conducted the raid, place them in the berms around the camp to blow a hole for our forces to attack the camp.[12]

Ned continued, "Simons went in to talk with the Lao lieutenant company commander and promises were made to correct the situation. We then flew up to his helicopter location and FTT-40 personnel came out very happily and climbed aboard. The three choppers then flew back to Luang Prabang."[13]

Paksane and Phou Tinpét

As part of the defensive line north of Paksane in Military Region V, GM-13 deployed two BIs thirty-five miles north of the city up the river valley to a position at the mountain of Phou Tinpét. Phou Tinpét is an 8,500-foot mountain. One battalion was positioned on the northwest sector of the mountain and the second BI held a position to the west of the mountain. Two SF split detachments supported the effort, one at each BI (the eastern BI was supported by First Lieutenant David P. Williams, FA-73).

The mission for both the BIs was to sit astride the infiltration route down Route 4 to Paksane and hold and contain the Pathet Lao. The western-positioned BI was a 650-man-strong infantry battalion commanded by Colonel Bou Noi. Captain William J. T. Leuders' split detachment, FA-75A, was assigned to train and advise the battalion during the summer of 1961, as part of the earlier *White Star* Rotation V.

The battalion CP was located on the top of a hill along the ridge of the mountaintop, facing northwest, where they could observe Pathet Lao hilltop positions across a valley. A 4.2-inch mortar section with three tubes was sited just below the CP, and much lower in the saddle formed by two ridges sat the helicopter LZ, situated out of the line of fire. Defensive positions were dug all around the hill, most sited within the heavily forested area.

The battalion support area lay two kilometers below the mountain and also had a DZ/LZ for resupply drops and incoming helicopters. Four hundred yards away in the surrounding jungle, Captain Leuders' team established their camp out of danger and harm's way. (There was strong pressure from Colonel William "Skip" Sadler, the MAAG representative in Paksane, for WSMTT teams to not get involved in combat action with the unit or get themselves killed as a result of enemy fire.)

The battalions were armed with M1s and M1 carbines as the standard infantry weapon, along with 3.5-inch rockets and World War II M1 grenade launchers. They also carried a variety of old hand grenades, and had a bunker with anti-personnel mines and demolitions to be used for protection of defensive positions. There was also a scattering of .303 bolt-action Enfields. For automatic weapons, the battalions were equipped with air-cooled .30-caliber machine guns and a .50-caliber heavy machine gun. Fire support included 60mm, 81mm, and 4.2-inch mortars.

A radio base station served the battalion CP, but the troops out on positions had only the old banana-style walkie-talkies, many of them non-operative.

The opposing Pathet Lao carried AK-47s and were supported by captured American 105mm field howitzers. The Pathet Lao were observed to be dressed in cream-colored, khaki-type uniforms or a drab hue of olive green, and wore the "Mao"-style cloth cap. Although the Pathet Lao conducted patrolling and ambushes in the area, surprisingly, they never conducted a deliberate attack against the GM position during the tenure of *White Star* teams.

The lack of heavy combat, and Lao apprehension to engage in any large offensive action, resulted in a fugue-like state with the deterioration in combat proficiency and capability of the BIs. Positions were improperly sited; none of the anti-personnel mines had been emplaced; there was no launcher for the 3.5-inch rockets (the "bazooka"); several weapons were broken or not maintained; and ammunition stocks were growing low.

Morale was down, due to lack of leadership from officers who were politically appointed and who did not have a sound grounding of tactics. Many were corrupt (taking pay from the men during their payroll or through gambling with the men). Drinking among the leadership was also a problem. Water and food atop the mountain was scarce. On top of all that, the position was shelled daily by the Pathet Lao 105s. Responding with only what was available to the GM, the 4.2-inch mortars could not reach enemy artillery positions and were basically ineffective for counter-fires.[14]

FA-11, commanded by Captain Edward R. Frank Sr., with his XO, First Lieutenant Jimmy Jones and team sergeant, Sergeant 1st Class George E. Yosich, departed with FC-3 in October as part of *White Star* Rotation VI. Upon arrival to Bangkok, they transferred to an Air America-piloted C-47 for the flight into Vientiane. The team was dismayed to find out they were being split for separate missions. Captain Frank took the senior NCOs of the team south with him to Saravane with his mission to support a major training camp for the Kha tribal guerrilla program—Operation *Pinchushion*. First Lieutenant Jimmy Jones, with acting senior detachment NCO Staff Sergeant George W. Hill, was ordered to support the GM at Paksane. The SF split-team was designated as FTT-11A. Other detachment members of FTT-11A were Sergeant Charles "Huk" Heakukulani (medic), Sergeant Joe R. Garner (radio operator), Sergeant Robert H. Young (junior weapons), and SP5 Bobby L. Gregory (junior demolitions).

(It is from Retired Sergeant Major Joe R. Garner's autobiography, *Code Name: COPPERHEAD, My True Life Exploits as a Special Forces Soldier*, that A-11A's story is told.)

Joe Garner enlisted in the United States Air Force in 1951, and after basic training and skills training, deployed to serve in the Korean War. He was assigned to the 51st Fighter Wing, south of Seoul, Korea. After the war, Garner left the USAF but in 1954 enlisted into the Army. He attended the engineer school at Fort Leonard Wood, Missouri, in January of 1951. Upon his re-enlistment, Garner opted to join Army Special Forces. He was assigned to the 77th SFG in 1958, then under the leadership of Colonel Blackburn (Joe was a corporal in rank at that time). Just prior to his detachment's deployment to Laos in October of 1961, Garner was serving on A-detachment FA-11, in Lieutenant Colonel Simons' FB-3 Company.

FTT-11A flew to Paksane aboard a C-47. The team moved into town to the MAAG district headquarters, a two-story building with several rooms. Both the senior MAAG advisor, Lieutenant Colonel Sadler, and the A-teams shared the building, paying rent to occupy the rooms. At the house, FTT-11A met with another split A-team whose mission was supporting the other half of their team deployed out to the battlefield. A third additional SF split-team was also operating out in the field. While FTT-11A got settled, Garner overheard a deployed split detachment at Phou Tinpét radio in for an extraction; they emphasized they were in danger and would not last the night.

Lieutenant Jimmy Jones was immediately ordered by Colonel Sadler to replace the team. FTT11-A grabbed their team gear and weapons, boarded an H-34 helicopter at the airfield, and flew to Phou Tinpét.

As FTT-11A landed at the base of the mountain in the BI support area, they were rushed by three of the detachment members of the outgoing split-team who were attempting to board the outbound helicopter. FA-75A, under Captain William T. Leuders and Master Sergeant Joseph F. Seyer were assigned to the BI during the summer of 1961 (*White Star* Rotation V). Armed Laotian infantry stood around the HLZ, glaring at the threatened team as they left, but indicating no attempt to harm or stop them.

A Lao security detail escorted FTT-11A to the outgoing team's camp, situated in the jungle. They found, and met with Captain Leuders for a brief transition orientation; also at the camp were SP5 Alvin H. Young (FA-75A medic) and Sergeant Daniel J. Deliz, the radio operator.

The two transitioning team medics went off to conduct an inspection and tour of the camp's medical facilities and to visit patients under current medical treatment. There had been an ongoing severe medical problem in the camp; men were coming in with bloated bellies, and were dying. Meanwhile, Garner took the opportunity to orient himself to commo operations with Deliz.

Lieutenant Jones soon learned the nature of the "emergency extract." In some way, Captain Leuders' team had lost rapport with the battalion commander of the BI, who ordered them to leave. Leuders wrapped things up with Jones, and he and his two men departed on the H-34 when it returned back to the site for their extraction.

FTT-11A got down to business, assessing the tactical situation and improving the position. They built a new hut with beds off the ground, made a mess area with an oven for meals, and constructed tables and chairs. Security positions were selected in the event of an emergency. The team then began inspection tours of the BI positions and began to advise and train the *tahans* on weapons maintenance and sighting of fires. Sergeant George W. Hill, weapons NCO of the team, led the tour.

Hill served previously in Laos on *Hotfoot I* in 1959 assigned to FA-1 in Vientiane. He was appalled by the condition of the unit, nowhere near comparable to the units he saw during his earlier tour; this BI was short of ammunition, had bad ammunition, and some defensive positions were situated such that they would fire on one another during an engagement. During his walkabout, incoming shells from Pathet Lao artillery landed near the battalion CP. The team promptly built a bunker as an immediate priority, after this introduction to the combat zone.

To fix the weapons problem, Garner radioed in a request for arms and ammunition. Training began immediately, starting with the light and heavy weapons sections to improve their proficiency. Suggestions on how to improve fighting positions soon remedied that problem.

Meanwhile, Sergeant "Huk" Heaukulani correctly diagnosed the problem with the dying *tahans*. Whenever there was a rice shortage in Laos, the USAID delivered husked rice from their stocks. Laotians had a diet of glutinous rice, with husks, which provide their only source of Vitamin B.

This was the source for the sickness and deaths in the camp. The deficiency was corrected by flying in stocks of the correct rice, along with supplements of fish oil. "Huk" saved over twenty men, administering Vitamin B pills from his medical stocks until the proper rice and Vitamin B fish-oil supplements arrived. The treatment method soon spread to other teams throughout Laos, saving countless lives.

Daily shelling from the Pathet Lao became a fact of life, with about fifty rounds fired on the position each day. When the team reported this to Colonel Sadler, the MAAG representative in Paksane, he refused to believe the count and intensity of the fire.

Reestablishment of rapport at the senior leader level was key for success of the team's mission. Lieutenant Jones climbed the mountain each day to meet with the battalion commander and reestablish a good working relationship. With his efforts, the detachment was soon accepted by the unit as partners, particularly in light of saving the men who were sick and getting new arms and ammunition supplied. Lieutenant Jones was a superb advisor, not telling Colonel Bou Noi and his lieutenants what to do, but "suggesting" ideas on position improvements and tactical actions. In only weeks, significant improvements were seen.

After one month, the team was invited to establish their camp at the top of the mountain, near the LZ and just below the rim of the battalion CP. This position was even more remote than the base camp helicopter landing zone, and involved a tricky approach for the H-34, exposing the helicopter to Pathet Lao fires. The Pathet Lao were keen to destroy a helicopter, so any landing also invited artillery shelling. The team admired the skill and bravery of Air America pilots, who never balked at the mission.

In relating the team story in his book, Garner recites Lieutenant Jones's words as he came back down from the mountain one day. "We had been in position a month when Jimmy Jones got back from another meeting at the battalion CP. He was just smiling and chewing his Red Man." Jones told the team, "Boys, we're going up on the hill. The Colonel has just 'invited' us to join him for the duration. And they're going to build hootches for the team."[15]

The team transferred their gear and equipment to the top using a helicopter. The transfer operation attracted Pathet Lao artillery, but no one was hit. The detachment moved into their new team hootch and built a bunker alongside. Now settled, Lieutenant Jones sent two men back to Paksane with the task to support the team with logistics and to coordinate supporting air from the airfield. The two team members were Sergeant George W. Hill, supporting from the MAAG building, and Sergeant Robert H. Young, who would work at the airfield.

In time, as rapport and trust improved, Lieutenant Jones "suggested" the unit conduct some limited offensive action in the form of ambush patrols, to take the fight to the Pathet Lao. His suggestion was accepted. The team capitalized on Lao cultural norms to make the patrols successful. They knew that contact in the jungle was fast, with whomever firing first and making more noise probably winning the engagement. Therefore, the team trained patrols on quick reaction drills to fire immediately with all the arms they carried. They also found that if any *tahan* on the patrol were blessed by "Good Buddha" amulets, others would follow them into combat.

One day the bazooka launcher arrived. It was put to immediate use, firing on Pathet Lao positions on the opposing hills. There was a pesky bunker in the valley blocking the BI patrols; a direct hit from the 3.5-inch soon solved the problem. The team put the .50 caliber back into operation. The only problem was it fired once and stopped. Attempts to fix it were in vain, but it at least could be fired with single shots. The *tahans* soon took turns sniping at the Pathet Lao.

One day Garner noticed four Pathet Lao standing within the perimeter of the camp. Apparently they had infiltrated up a small trail, unobserved by anyone. Garner used his pistol to defend himself while the troops of the BI opened fire. The Pathet Lao escaped.

In response, Garner worked with the unit to emplace mines and booby traps along trails leading into the position, and in the valley before them. He found a vast load of unused mines and demolitions in a bunker. After training soldiers on their use, he taught them how to emplace the explosives on the trails, using trip wires. One of the novel ideas he used with the 3.5-inch rockets was to demonstrate to the soldiers on how to dig them in alongside the trails, as a form of anti-personnel mine. An unfortunate result from one of the new minefields was the killing of migrating elephants. The battalion ate well for several days, however.

The team's deployment at Phou Tinpét lasted five months. The BI held a small celebration for the team atop the mountain prior to the arrival of the extraction H-34. FTT-11A was presented with an elephant tusk, with the battalion commander's name etched onto it.

The team returned to the MAAG house in Paksane and served a small time as a mini-support detachment for the new teams arriving from 1st Group. Huk, the medic, spent his time working at the hospital in Paksane. The team got to meet the King during his visit. They also had an opportunity to attend a wedding across the river in a Thai village, invited by the mayor of the village. They crossed over the Mekong River on inflatable mattresses to attend the ceremony.

When relieved of their mission by the new teams, FTT-11A returned to Vientiane for a short spell, spent their R&R in Bangkok, and flew home on a C-124 aircraft.

Military Region IV—Attopeu

Attopeu is the provincial capital of Attopeu Province and was located in one of the remotest portions of southern Laos, Military Region IV. The town was built along an ancient trading route from Vietnam to the Bolovens and Mekong River, and was noted for its gold and timber trade. It lay along a curve of the Se Kong River confluence with the Se Kaman River.

There were three major roads leading into Attopeu, often impassable in the monsoon season. Route 18 ran through the town as its main street. Route 18 began as an intersection at Route 13 along the Mekong, going east through Attopeu and continued farther east into Vietnam (Route 18B). Headed north out of town, following the Se Kong River valley, ran Route 16, which circled around the northeast side of the Bolovens Plateau on its journey to Saravane. In relation to other major

Lao cities, the distance from Attopeu was about 162 kilometers to Paksong and 212 kilometers to Pakse.

The town sat in the valley of the Se Kong River, surrounded by the mountains of the Bolovens Plateau to its north and west, 1,000 meters higher than the valley floor. There were approximately thirteen different ethnicities living in the area, with the Lavae, Nge, and Talieng as the most predominant. There was also a mix of Lao Loum, Vietnamese and Chinese mixed into the population.

Attopeu's significant importance during the war was that it sat near three branches of the Ho Chi Minh Trail. About twelve kilometers southeast of the town, the trail split: one portion headed south to Cambodia, named the Sihanouk Trail, one portion headed easterly toward South Vietnam, and the northern portion of the trail ran alongside the eastern border of Laos.[16]

A FAR unit garrisoned the town, usually with a BV, but the battalion rarely ventured out into the countryside to take on the feared NVA operating the trail. Pathet Lao forces operated outside the environs of Attopeu, but seemed to have a loose agreement with the FAR: if not antagonized then they would not bother the FAR.

FA-14A was the first Special Forces split detachment to operate at Attopeu. Captain Leon M. Hope and Master Sergeant Robert D. Hede were running the team in Company A, 1st SFG in Okinawa, when they were selected to go to Laos for Rotation VI of *White Star*. Upon arrival to Laos, the B-team in Pakse split the detachment: Captain Hope took his half to run an NCO academy at Paksong, while Captain Richard N. "Sam" Lewis got the mission to train and advise the BV at Attopeu. Assisting him was Platoon Sergeant William D. "Billy" Waugh. (Others on the split detachment included Sergeant 1st Class Benjamin F. Fitch (intel), Sergeant Peter G. Morley (medic), Sergeant Thomas D. Pahel (weapons) and Corporal John McKay, the radio operator).

U.S. Army Special Forces (Retired) Sergeant Major Billy Waugh graduated high school, and after one year of college in West Texas, joined the Army to be a paratrooper in the 82nd Airborne Division. He volunteered for Special Forces, serving in the 77th SFG from 1956 to 1957. Tired of the lack of training money and pettiness of labor details at Fort Bragg ("picking up pine cones"), he volunteered in 1960 for the 1st SFG on Okinawa.

FA-14A flew from Pakse to Attopeu aboard an Air America H-34. The mission for FA-14A was to train the 46th Bataillon Volontaire. The team landed at the airstrip in town, a decent field capable of handling C-46s and C-47s, and rented a house in town about 400 meters from the airstrip. A jeep arrived for their use, delivered via sling load under an H-34 helicopter. Training for the BV would be accomplished out in a field camp where BV-46 was located.

The detachment was informed there was not much activity or known threat from the Pathet Lao, but, they were vaguely aware that the Ho Chi Minh Trail cut through the area. BV-46's mission did not include running operations against the trail or attempting its interdiction.

Upon arrival to the 46th's camp, the detachment was surprised to find out it was a "ghost" unit. The payroll rosters were padded with non-existent troops. It became frustrating to the team to accomplish training as very few members of the battalion ever attended. Waugh explained: "Our training courses we had prepared consisted of weapons training, tactics, and firing weapons at the ranges. We did not have any French trainers alongside us; there were some up at Pakse, mainly Foreign Legion rogues. There was never any full battalion which showed up for training, some days about seventeen or eighteen people only. This was due to bad leadership and corrupt leaders who were padding the books to make money.[17]

While out in the field camp, resupply for the team was para-dropped or sent via C-47, carrying commissary stores ordered from Vientiane. Waugh even noted watching an indigenous para-drop resupply; "Some of the tribal forces used to have cows para-dropped!"[18]

About three months into the TDY tour (January 1962), Captain Hope completed the mission at the NCO academy and was ordered south to reinforce the efforts in Attopeu. His split-team, however, was sent to a different location in a remote field camp and he did not see the other members of the team until their departure from Laos.

Captain Hope and FA-14 flew into the remote jungle camp with no roads leading in or out, about sixty to seventy miles northeast of Attopeu. They knew of other SF teams operating in the area, but never saw them during their assignment, other than Waugh and Captain Lewis, who occasionally passed through the other teams' locations.

Colonel (Retired) James W. Kraus, Captain Hope's weapons NCO at the time, described the Lao military unit located at the remote camp:

> They did not have uniforms; I think they wore black pajama-like clothes, but I don't remember. The battalion was commanded by one we called a "Major," so I am guessing that was his rank. They were only equipped with M1s; they had no mortars or crew-served weapons. Those kids were shorter than the M1s when they held them at their side with the butt-plates on the ground! The battalion of irregulars never went into combat. They did pretty much low-key patrolling. This may have been a function of shortage of ammunition. My view of our mission was to baby-sit them, give them some training.[19]

Due to the extreme remoteness of the position, all supplies were air-dropped or landed by helicopter. Meat was procured from the jungle. The diet for both the team and the battalion consisted of rice, augmented by whatever could be hunted in the jungle. However, game in the local area was scarce.

FA-14 did their best to train and advise the irregular unit until their redeployment in April of 1962. Kraus summarized: "It was a pretty quiet tour. The mission ended pretty quick; I was in Pakse when we got the order to bring everyone out. The team extracted by Air America helos. We redeployed on the same route in, but I don't think we went to Bangkok; instead we went through Hong Kong, where we spent one week on R&R. It was a good time to get the 'Rolexes' and 'Blue Sapphire' rings!"[20]

Other Major Operations during Rotation VI

In Military Region II, Operation *Momentum* continued around the Plaine des Jarres and near Phou Bia and the Sala Phou Khoun junction. In Military Region III, the earlier orchestration of operations in the Thakhek, Se Bang Fe River, and Mahaxay region would grow, reaching a campaign-like quality and involving several Special Forces FTTs and FAs.

A large, ambitious program during this *White Star* rotation was the development of the Kha tribal guerrilla program in Military Region IV. The program was located on the Bolovens Plateau and also near Saravane. It was a CIA-sponsored program, and at its peak involved about eleven supporting SF teams. The operation was codenamed *Pincushion*. The command and control requirements necessitated the formation of another B-team, under Major Schulenberg in Saravane.

(The Thakhek, Se Bang Fai and Mahaxay campaign, along with Operation *Pincushion*, are covered in a separate chapter due to the scope and magnitude of the program.)

CHAPTER SEVEN

Operation *Pincushion*:
The Kha Tribal Guerrilla Program

"As with the Momentum Program, the Lao Theung maquis companies consisted of
headquarters with two officers and 14 enlisted men, and three platoons of one officer and
27 enlisted men apiece. To outfit the companies, Pincushion used Momentum's 5,900-
pound Standard Weapons Unit, palletized into 11 bundles fixed with cargo parachutes."

KENNETH CONBOY, *SHADOW WAR*

The unconventional warfare initiative to develop a tribal resistance movement in
southern Laos differed from Operation *Momentum* in the north. With the Hmong,
the CIA developed and ran the program, with U.S. Army Special Forces assisting as
trainers. The Hmong were raised, organized and armed to take the fight to the enemy.
In Operation *Pincushion*, the reverse would be true. Lieutenant Colonels Simons and
Little had convinced the ambassador that U.S. Army Special Forces could run the
program with nominal assistance from the Agency, but the role of the tribes would
be one of local and civil defense. *Pincushion* illustrated the use of UW to support
conventional force maneuver and gave the RLG an economy of force option for
southern Laos.

The potential for any guerrilla warfare program in this region centered on key
prerequisites. The population had to be one of strong character, cohesive and with a
strong warrior-hunter ethic. Second, the terrain had to be favorable for the conduct
of irregular warfare, rugged and remote. The guerrillas could not outmatch the NVA
and the Pathet Lao head on. The operational area would need to be located in places
under weak control of the Pathet Lao, where the tribes at least had a chance to win
over or win back the support of the population. Last, any resistance movement was
going to require capable, strong, as well as charismatic leadership. It was assessed
that of all the tribes in southern Laos the Loven tribes in and around the Bolovens
Plateau region would have the best potential.

Ultimately, the Kha tribal guerrilla program would not live up to its full
potential. The ambassador, the RLG, and even higher Lao military authorities did
not understand the application of UW as practiced by the Army Special Forces.
The Kha units ultimately resembled uncoordinated village militia rather than an

operational tool to harass, interdict, and create friction against the enemy. The capability to serve as an adjunct and supporting operation to FAR maneuver in the south did not materialize.

The southern guerrilla warfare program was designed initially on a plan to form twelve companies of Kha. The Agency and the MAAG were authorized to begin this program on March 5, 1961 (via an interagency special group message), giving the MAAG operational control and authority to use *White Star* teams for as long as U.S. military advisors were present in the country. The program also required RLG and FAR sponsorship and not be under unilateral control of the Americans, such as the program with Vang Pao and his guerrillas in the north.

This requirement would be difficult to implement, given the lack of cohesion among the Lao Theung tribes in the south and their disdain for hierarchical tribal leadership. An overall charismatic clan leader for this program could not be found; Prince Boun Oum assumed the mantle as the connection between the tribes and the RLG.

General Kot Venevengos, the Military Region IV commander, would also be in the command loop, even given the mistrust in his performance. These command and control relationships would also contribute to the confusion experienced by SF teams implementing the program. Later, there would be talk of doubling the force to twenty-four companies, but this initiative would fall apart in the face of the ceasefire and negotiations in late June of 1962.[1]

The Bolovens Plateau is situated in northeast Champassak Province, Military Region IV, at the southern edge of the Annamite mountain chain. Bolovens (also spelled Bolaven) means "home, or place, of the Laven," the largest Lao Theung, Mon-Khmer ethnic group inhabiting the region.

In its eastern half are the indigenous tribes of the Sayasila. Other ethnic groups include the Alak, Katu, Tahoy and Suay. Historically, these ethnic groups were labeled Khàa, a derisive term meaning "slave" or "servant," because of their role as corvée labor and indentured servants over history. Some of these tribal ethnicities differ from other Lao tribes in the region because they build their village structures in a circle (the Katu and Alak). The plateau tribes are spirit worshipers, ancestor worshipers, and animists.

The Bolovens Plateau covers about 10,000 square kilometers. The plateau itself consists of mixed, deciduous forest, gentle rolling hills, and is drained by its predominant river, the Se Set, which flows west toward the Mekong. The area is known for its magnificent waterfalls. The climate is cool and moderate, and the soil is highly fertile. It was in this area the French colonials built plantations and began farming in coffee (Arabica blend), bananas, and rubber trees.[2]

It is a very remote and unimproved region, with few roads. It is oval shaped, with mountains ringing its central region. Its largest town is the city of Paksong (the center of the coffee industry); to its west lies Pakse, to its north Saravane, and to its southeast Attopeu. It is bounded in the east by the Se Kong River valley. The major road on the plateau was Route 23 from Pakse to Paksong, which then turned north to Saravane. At the fork in Paksong, the route became 232, east to Ban Houei Kong, then further connecting to the north–south Route 16 from Attopeu.

Its primary importance during the war was its role as the intersection of many branches of the Ho Chi Minh Trail. By the end of the Vietnam War, the Bolovens Plateau would be one of the most heavily bombed areas of Laos.

It was this strategic importance which caught the eye of Lieutenant Colonel John Little, the *White Star* commander in the spring of 1961. Seeing the success of the guerrillas under Vang Pao in the north, it was worth considering whether a successful guerrilla program could be developed in the south to harass the Pathet Lao, and, as well, to conduct attritional battles of interdiction against the NVA operating the Ho Chi Minh Trail. Captain Robert Mountel, serving as one of the staff officers on the field control team in Vientiane, was tasked to conduct an area assessment of the region and determine the feasibility of opening another guerrilla warfare campaign, based on the ability of the local tribes to form as maquis. After Mountel's study of the area, he returned to Vientiane to report it was highly feasible to initiate a UW program. (Captain Mountel would later lead one of the last *Pincushion* Teams near Saravane in 1962.)[3]

The RLG was leery of opening another guerrilla front. The loyalty of the hill tribes in this region was questionable. The worst case for the RLG would be the newly armed tribes defecting to the Pathet Lao. Lao government largesse did not reach very far into this region; therefore it would pass to the Americans to fund any such initiative, given the reluctance of the Laotian government. The CIA took up the challenge to fund and equip the tribes, but required manpower to conduct the training.

Lieutenant Colonel Bull Simons returned for his second tour as the Vientiane control team commander in the fall of 1961 (*White Star* Rotation VI). Without a doubt, he saw the opportunity to include more of the Army SF teams in this unconventional role. With funding in place, and teams available, Operation *Pincushion* began. There was only one problem: the Pathet Lao dominated the Bolovens region and would have to be cleared to create safe guerrilla zones for the program. GM-18 was given the task in November to clear the area from Paksong in the west to Attopeu in the southeast.

Captain Thomas J. Stanford's *White Star* FTT-30 maneuvered with GM-18, and after GM-18's skirmishes with the Pathet Lao, the unit swept into Attopeu. (Stanford had a split-team consisting of Master Sergeant Lupe F. Rodriguez, Sergeant 1st Class James C. "Jimmy" Dean, Sergeant Richard G. Lahue, and Sergeant James O. Wells.) The FTT was assigned to the Savannakhet-based GM-18 in September of 1961, and remained with the unit until March of 1962, when GM-18 was deployed to participate in the battle of Nam Tha.

To direct the program, the CIA procured two experts: PEO officer Roy Moffitt, known for his knowledge of Lao Theung dialects and culture, and Jean Cadeaux. Cadeaux was a French-Vietnamese *métisse* plantation owner (and a big-game hunter) who was familiar with the Bolovens and its people. Cadeaux would become the primary liaison with the tribes. He had a loathing for the communists: his son had been murdered by the Pathet Lao.[4]

Kha Tribal Guerrilla Program

Captain Elliot P. "Bud" Sydnor was tasked by Lieutenant Colonel Simons to establish the first FTT for Operation *Pincushion*. Captain Sydnor's detachment was split during their tour in Laos, arriving in October of 1961. Sydnor ran a five-man FTT in Attopeu (FTT-43), while his XO, First Lieutenant William E. Kellenberger, took the other seven men to conduct training at Camp Chinaimo, near Vientiane (FTT-43A). The mission at Attopeu consisted of training and advising one BI and one unit of volunteer militia, who resembled a Maquis or Choc unit (BV).

Sydnor explained the receipt of the task. "We kept on this mission [Attopeu] until it was changed. I went to Vientiane to complain to Lieutenant Colonel Simons about pay for our interpreters. We had two Thai interpreters who were about to lose pay. They were converting their pay from Thai Bhat to Laotian Kip, which gave them a reduction in pay. But Lieutenant Colonel Simons told me he had something new for me to do."[5] Sydnor moved his split-team from Attopeu up to the district headquarters on the eastern Bolovens, the town of Ban Houei Kong. From there, the team moved east to find a suitable piece of terrain to establish a guerrilla training camp. Sydnor said, "Our new mission was on the Plateau de Bolovens, we went there in late 1961. I think the SF team number then was FTT-43. There was an asset there, Mr. Cadeaux, who was half French and half Vietnamese. He told us, 'I'll help you raise a 100-man company, guarded by the Old Militia [the former Maquis], armed by the French [with U.S. carbines].' The security for this venture seemed good since no one messed with the old Maquis."[6] (The old Maquis were village defense forces used by the French during their earlier conflict in Indochina.)

The team made camp and soon met up with some local Hune tribesmen who had previously served in the Auto-Défense organization. Sydnor and Mr. Cadeaux pitched the guerrilla warfare program, to which the old militiamen agreed, and they tribesmen went off to recruit more men (now convinced and armed with new rifles as gifts). In the meantime, the five men of the SF team began construction of the training camp, with buildings made of local materials to serve as barracks and team hootches, along with the clearing of a field to serve as a landing strip.[7]

The organizing principle for the Kha guerrilla training program was equipping and arming 100-man units to provide local security and presence patrolling in their tribal region. The task organization for an irregular company consisted of the commander and his headquarters group, along with three guerrilla platoons, each led by a platoon officer. Captain Sydnor's program of training was designed to last four weeks, thereupon another 100 locally recruited men would begin their respective train-up. The companies were simply labeled K-1, K-2, and so forth (Kha Company 1, Kha Company 2, and so on).

The guerrillas were lightly equipped, using the successful template used by the Agency with the Hmong guerrilla program of 100-man companies. Once the recruits were processed-in and organized, the SF team issued uniforms and equipment, airdropped from Air America, using eleven pallets under cargo chutes (a CIA standard guerrilla load). The pallets contained uniforms, web gear, and M1 rifles for each man. Other pallets contained ammunition and grenades. For heavy weapons, the guerrillas were equipped with Browning BARs (three each), one 60mm mortar, and one 57mm recoilless rifle.[8]

Sydnor described the equipping and initial training:

> The troops we were training wore a shirt and trousers of standard type. We adopted the ROTC system of rank using pips, diamonds, buttons, etc. We had a shipment of weapons for them—a basic regular infantry company's worth; M1s and some mix of carbines. However we did not have any rapid-fire weapons like machine guns. We spent time on the range teaching basic weapons stuff and marksmanship, how to adjust fire, etc. They were good with weapons! They had skills from hunting little birds with crossbows."[9]

The camp was austere, all supplies and food for the team were delivered by Air America H-34 helicopters or cargo-parachute-dropped from C-46s and C-47s, along with bags of rice to feed the troops. Mr. Cadeaux was a big-game hunter and augmented the diet by hunting wild gaur, an undomesticated ox. Sydnor recalled:

> Some background about the area. It was brother leading brother. Some were in the enemy formations and some were in the friendly formations; some were Viet Minh. There were no markers between enemy and friendly territory.
>
> We had a little camp for training. We roughed out adequate training areas, cut down some trees. We had to deal with the "spirited" trees, from their Animist beliefs, which required holding a banquet or celebration before we could cut them down.
>
> We were near a little airstrip, used by Air America. This was used mostly by H-34 helicopters, which were piloted by Marines who were "seconded" for a few months.
>
> For security, we had stand-to every morning at the camp. We would come to an agreement between us and the leader of the group for how we conducted that. We were under the command and control of another group for our directions. We were working in their area. The closest town was Ban Houei Kong, at the end of the road coming out from the town along the Mekong—Pakse.[10]

As the time drew near to begin the training of the second Kha guerrilla company, Captain Sydnor realized he would eventually need more help, not knowing how many companies would ultimately be raised. He coordinated to unite the other half of his detachment serving under Lieutenant Kellenberger at Camp Chinaimo. Kellenberger would be tasked to train K-2.

K-2 Company

Lieutenant William E. Kellenberger was drafted into the 7th Special Forces Group after completing a tour in Korea as a combat engineer platoon leader. The FTT at Camp Chinaimo was his first overseas deployment as a Special Forces officer. In the middle of the mission at Chinaimo, he and his split-team received a new mission from Simons to reinforce the effort at Houei Kong. They flew down to Pakse on an Air America C-47, and from there, were flown by H-34 helicopter out to the training site. They linked up with Captain Sydnor and received his guidance and orders along with an orientation to the Kha tribal guerrilla training program. They immediately began the mission to train the K-2 company. Kellenberger recalls:

> When we got there, there was one company in training. We gave the big people among them M1 Garands; the smaller people we issued M1 carbines. My job was to line them up and issue gear and stuff. The training lasted, I think, about four weeks; there was no FTX [field training exercise] at the end.
>
> We moved into Sydnor's established site. We had 100 people to train. The place we were at on the Bolovens was at 4,000 ft. altitude—it got very cold. We had to change our sleeping bags to adjust to that and mountain-type sleeping bags were sent in.
>
> I think Mr. Cadeaux knew how to pick the leaders of the Kha companies—the first formation was like lining up plebes at West Point, but without the hair-cuts. He probably took input from the village elders on who was strongest leader, and so forth. The indigenous tribal men did not live in the camp, since they were from the local village. They just went home after training. We were not responsible for feeding them.
>
> The camp was in the jungle. The nearest light bulb was ninety miles away in Pakse! It was very primitive. It was in the middle of nowhere. We lived in lean-tos. There was a clear field we used for the rifle range. The tribal people we were training were from the local vicinity.[11]

There was little threat from the Pathet Lao in this area. However, the team still took precautions. Foxholes were dug and stocked with ammunition and grenades for immediate use. A twenty-four-hour guard watch was established. One of the security measures used by the team was patrolling the surrounding area, taking some of the tribal fighters with them, often stopping at villages to converse with the tribes to assess the threat situation. Whether a detriment to the patrol, or a benefit to further civil relations, these forays into the villages often involved the traditional rice-wine-drinking ceremony to establish personal relations.

Occasionally, the team could hear firing off in the jungle; upon investigation they found it was local hunters tracking down and shooting the small reh deer found on the plateau. As a means of building the rapport with the locals, the team hired their hunters to provide them with venison, with a simple payment of ten bullets for each deer delivered.

Sergeant 1st Class Ernest K. "Ernie" Tabata was the assigned demolitions sergeant for Kellenberger's split-team. Tabata had served in the 11th Airborne in Germany as an engineer sergeant before joining the 7th Group. His remembrance of the K-2 training mission was that it was in a very remote area with primitive conditions:

Captain Sydnor welcomed us, gave us a situation briefing on the training of the "Kha" tribesmen before we started. The volunteers came in dressed in loin-cloths, with crossbows and arrows and their personal belongings, which were very minimal. Very primitive life-style. We requested logistical supplies consisting of rice, rations, individual light weapons, crew-served weapons, and some heavy weapons; for instance, the 57mm recoilless rifle.

Since there were no roads near us to get supplies on, we got some radio messages through Morse code method and eventually coordinated aerial resupply bundles. After receiving the bundles of the rations, rice, arms and ammunition, and clothing, these air-dropped materials were issued to the tribal forces.[12]

K-2 Company would not complete the training program due to its internal leadership problems and dissent among the tribesmen. Soon, half of the unit deserted. Unfortunately, as was all too common when living in primitive conditions in Laos, both Lieutenant Kellenberger and Sergeant Tabata fell ill from hepatitis and were evacuated. A new K-2 was raised and a new FTT began.

As Operation *Pincushion* continued to grow, Captain Albert A. Deprospero's twelve-man A-team arrived as part of the *White Star* Rotation VII deployment to assist with the efforts at Houei Kong. Sydnor and Deprospero ascertained the need to open a new site and found one southeast of Houei Kong near a village named La Ta Sin. Deprospero split his team and moved to the camp. At the same time, he sent his XO, Lieutenant Maples, to Paksong to open a third camp. All of these new camps required the construction of barracks, weapons ranges, and an airstrip.

The site at La Ta Sin was near the largest concentration of Hune tribesmen and recruiting 100-man companies was easy to accomplish. To handle the load, another split A-team arrived at La Ta Sin to assist Captain Deprospero, bringing the strength of the SF advisors there up to twelve men.

In April, Captain Sydnor's deployment ended and he was replaced by Captain Joe Hicks, coming in with a full A-team. Both Captain Sydnor and Lieutenant Colonel Simons extended for three months to continue supervision over the *Pincushion* effort. Lieutenant Maples' team was replaced at Paksong by another six-man split-team.[13]

The New K-2

Captain Charles W. Murphy commanded FTT-11 at Saravane, training FAR units. His XO was Second Lieutenant Berton E. Spivey, one of a batch of second lieutenants assigned to Special Forces in 1961, even though the manning documents called for a first lieutenant. Master Sergeant James V. Hanks Jr. was the team sergeant. The 7th SFG team deployed from Fort Bragg to Laos on November 30 1961. In January of 1962, Captain Murphy was directed to move his team down to the Bolovens Plateau to train a newly organized K-2 company.

Sergeant Eugene M. Gavigan was the junior radio operator on FTT-11. He was assigned to FB-2 of the 77th SFG, transferring from the 82nd Airborne Division, 307th Engineers. After his break in service in 1959, he re-entered the Army to serve in the 18th Airborne Corps, 618th Engineer Company (LE). He attended Ranger school while awaiting a security clearance background investigation for his request to transfer to Special Forces. He barely missed being assigned earlier to Captain Moon's team in Laos, due to a delay in getting his top secret clearance. (He later attended OCS at Fort Benning, got commissioned as a signal officer, and would serve tours in Vietnam.)

The team deployed from Fort Bragg on a flight with two other A-teams. Upon arrival to Bangkok, the team was flown to Vientiane and lodged in the Continental Hotel. Later, they flew to Pakse, and then flown further onward to Saravane. It would not be long before the mission to replace Lieutenant Maples at Paksong arrived. Gene Gavigan describes the beginning of the mission:

> People were brought in from the villages. We set up a base camp, got our supplies, did surveys, emplaced security, etc. People came in wearing loin-cloths, piecemeal uniforms. We photographed them. Frye stuck a weapons clip in their hands during in-processing—he made them fire their weapons right off for familiarization, so there were no mistakes. Uniforms and arms were brought to us via parachute drop. The weapons were 1903 Springfields, still in cosmoline, packed in barrels. These were too long for some of them, so we got them shorter carbines."[14]

To prevent a repeat of what transpired with Lieutenant Kellenberger's group, the SF advisors organized the unit leaders instead of the Kha self-selecting their duty positions. This was accomplished through interviews with those Kha who Mr. Cadeaux felt had potential.

Prior to the arrival of the team, Captain Murphy took time to develop a good POI of approximately nine weeks, adapted to the local conditions. Along with small-unit tactics and firearms proficiency (assembly and disassembly of weapons, cleaning, dry fire, and so on), the team also conducted heavy weapons training, including both night fires and live fires. A raid on an old leper hut served as the field training exercise, along with a night ambush scenario. For translation, the team had four interpreters: Otel, Vivat, Trail, and Sokol (all Thais).

The area was known to have Pathet Lao and NVA operating nearby. For defense, the team carried Thompson .45-caliber sub-machine guns, a .30-caliber machine gun, and had 60mm mortars, along with a 57mm recoilless rifle. For security of the camp, the Kha platoons and squads were deployed along the likely avenues of approach (AA). Booby traps were emplaced and heavy weapons positions were sited along the approaches. One night, the unit thought they were being probed when a trip wire went off at 0200. Much to their surprise, and upon later inspection, they found the paw prints of a tiger.

One of the missions for the Kha company was reconnaissance and scouting to find a suspected NVA company presumed to be operating to the north of their position. The SF advisors patrolled with the irregulars, carrying what they needed in rucksacks. If available, an elephant was hired from locals to pack additional gear and ammunition. Patrolling through a village always included a stop to perform a ceremony, but it was an excellent means to elicit information on enemy whereabouts.

It was on one of these patrols the team and the Khas came into contact with the NVA. Gene Gavigan had just recently left the team, but was told the story later by one of his teammates:

> Just before my leaving, we went through a large, deserted village that showed some recent signs of contact. The story later (all hearsay from Wallace), after that village, was that the patrol kept on moving when suddenly "Bertie" Frye [Staff Sergeant Bertram E. Frye, radio operator] shouted out, "Lock and load. Get your ass over here!" to the troops. He always kept troops on the perimeter. The troops felt like they were being led too far out of their range, when they had been promised they were being trained for the defense of their village, and had sort of rebelled and quit patrolling. Murphy and Spivy tried to talk them out of their rebellion and made a deal with them.
>
> The Kha leader had military experience with the French. He agreed that they would continue on, but if there was no contact, the patrol would return to the village. The team called "Cowboy Red," our Air America chopper pilot to bring bread. The team was leery of going back into a village, because one time a village had invited Captain Murphy for a ceremony, but we found out later they wanted to kidnap him because the NVA had promised the villagers a reward. Wallace had heard from someone that the NVA had asked around as to why they hadn't killed any Americans.
>
> But there was contact and all hell broke loose. Spivey took out an NVA guy who was standing on a small mound above the grass everyone was lying in, to see if he could spot anyone. Sergeant Wallace told me he was the one in the brush pile and an NVA type stood on a log above him raising hell because no Americans were dead. The NVA never looked down, Wallace said, "I had my .45 on him."[15]

Second Lieutenant Berton E. Spivy was one of the second lieutenants the Army levied to go into Special Forces. This initially caused some confusion when he and other second lieutenants in-processed at Fort Bragg, no one really knowing why second lieutenants were being sent when manning documents required first lieutenants. There was doubt among some of the older veterans in the group as to how the brand-new second lieutenants would perform.

On the combat patrol mentioned earlier, he performed well, even though receiving wounds for which he was later awarded a Purple Heart. After the engagement, and after the team was scattered, he and another team member had to escape and evade through the jungle. Fortunately, Lieutenant Colonel Simons sent out searches and retrieved them.

Training K-3 and K-5

Captain Billy R. Wilson's ODA was split to operate as two FTTs in Savannakhet. They arrived in Laos on November 30, 1961 as part of *White Star* Rotation VI. The mission for the two split-teams was training Lao infantry. In the spring of 1962, the split detachments received orders and instruction from Lieutenant Colonel Simons on their new mission: supporting Operation *Pincushion* near Captain Sydnor's operation. Captain Wilson reformed his team back into a full ODA and moved to the field site where they would train the K-3 and K-5 units.

Sergeant James F. Everett was the radio operator for the team. Everett began his career in the Army assigned to Company A of the 76th Tank Battalion, 11th Airborne in Germany. On a field exercise, he participated as a role-player guerrilla with some Special Forces and decided then and there he would reenlist for Special Forces upon his discharge. In 1957, he volunteered to serve in the 14th Special Forces operational unit out in Okinawa, and spent thirty months on that tour. In November of 1961, he was back at Fort Bragg and put on orders to go to Laos; there was an urgent need for radio operators (he was hoping to in-process to serve in a demolitions specialty). Everett remembered the team's mission before being tasked for Operation *Pincushion*, describing his team's activities:

> The camp was already established when we got to this mission area. The troops lived in pup-tents made from two ponchos, or made lean-tos. The SF teams were all together at the end of the DZ/LZ. Arriving SF teams first met with Lieutenant Colonel Simons and Mr. Moffett and were in-briefed on the mission. The next day, training began. It was the smoothest operation I have ever seen; everything worked like clock-work precision. We got everything we needed and every training event scheduled was done on time.
>
> The team area was located along the major airstrip there—it was about a mile long. We were on the west side of it, next to the river on the plateau. There was no village there.
>
> We received 100 troops, processed them in, gave them uniforms, photographed them and then took them on to weapons training. We had one day to get this done! While this was going on, we set up a security detail.[16]

He described further the running of the camp and its daily activities:

> I was there for the training of Kha unit 3 and Kha unit 5. The uniforms of the Kha were like our basic fatigues. We equipped them with M1 rifles. They also had .30 caliber machine guns. We broke the 100-man unit down into platoons. We went on patrols with them out on the eastern edges of the Plateau, over by the border with North Vietnam. We only got into combat when they had contact and would rush back into the camp. The camp would set up a rear ambush, and we would have to radio ahead so they would not ambush us. There was English spoken there, but we used our two Thai interpreters.[17]

Around the same time, early spring, Operation *Pincushion* grew and spread to include the Loven tribes north of the Bolovens near Saravane. With this new initiative, the two efforts began to be called respectively the Northern Zone (Saravane) and the Southern Zone (Paksong and Ban Houei Kong). By June of 1962, the following Kha tribal guerrilla units trained in the Southern Zone were K-1, K-3, K-4, K-5, K-6, and part of K-8 (and retraining of K-2 after the desertions).[18]

Northern Guerrilla Training Zone—Saravane

The northern effort of the Kha tribal guerrilla program centered around the Saravane region where a sufficient number of Loven tribesmen readily provided recruits to develop additional Kha company units.

K-7

The first *Pincushion* team deployed to this area was FTT-11, commanded by Captain Edward R. Frank Sr., with his XO, Lieutenant Jimmy Jones and team sergeant, Sergeant 1st Class George E. Yosich. The team departed the States with FC-3 in October 1961 as part of *White Star* Rotation VI. Upon their arrival to Bangkok, they transferred to an Air America-piloted C-47 for the flight into Vientiane. The team was dismayed upon their arrival to find out they were being split for separate missions. Captain Frank took the senior NCOs of the team south with him to Saravane.[19]

In April 1962, one Special Forces A-team began construction on a camp southeast of Saravane, at the foot of the Phou Kate Mountain (Site 106). There were more than sufficient recruits for a company or two of tribal guerrillas; three more A-teams worth of instructors and advisors joined the effort to train four companies (K-7, K-9, K-10, and K-11). Elements of K-8 would also be trained at Phou Kate, with their main body remaining at Paksong.

K-8

Sergeant Robert G. "Bob" Willis was serving on an FTT at the Dong Hene officer's academy when he was ordered to Saravane to reinforce the team with another commo asset (or to replace a radio operator). He joined Captain Walter J. Nagorski's team located near a river at Site 106. Captain Nagorski had the mission to train some of the elements of K-8 (from Paksong) at Phou Kate. Sergeant Willis described the location and living conditions:

> The team lived in longhouses, separated from the training area. I had a small radio shack section off to the side of one of these. One of the customs of the Lao tribal people was to let the defecations from their livestock lay on the ground below the longhouse—the more that piled up, the more "affluent" you were regarded! We did not follow that custom. The Laotians would help me with commo duties. I had a DY88 powered by a generator; I had a Laotian crank the hand generator while I made commo. We ate local food, mostly. We had no vehicles. We had a local cook and Thai interpreters. We were making $15.00 a day in per diem."[20]

Although the Pathet Lao patrolled in the area (the team could hear their small-arms fire occasionally), the enemy chose to never attack the camp. The tribesmen pulled security for the camp, augmented by the SF detachment's weapons men, among these, Sergeant 1st Class Calvin Thompson. A strange thing noted on the security patrols was the tribal irregulars' local custom that they could not fire over a river, based on their spiritual beliefs: someone had apparently drowned in the river, and his "ghost" was to be avoided. Another local custom plaguing the team was the offer to the Americans of a wife, or several wives. Of course, the team made appropriate excuses and did not partake in this custom, telling the tribesmen they preferred to remain "single."

(Sergeant Willis departed before Captain Nagorski's team completed their mission and returned to his own team at Dong Hene. He was later awarded the CIB for actions on the Bolovens.)

The SF teams for the northern guerrilla zone were under the command and control of Major Leroy E. Schulenberg's B-detachment, FB-A. When Lieutenant Colonel Simons and Captain Sydnor departed in the summer of 1962, Schulenberg moved his twenty-three-man B-detachment from Paksane to serve as a forward command and control base in Saravane. Schulenberg reported directly to Lieutenant Colonel Keravouri in Vientiane, as a compartmented program. In the southern zone, Captain Deprospero moved back to Houei Kong to replace Captain Sydnor in the role as the senior SF *Pincushion* coordinator.[21]

First Lieutenant Richard A. Iori was on Schulenberg's B-team. Rich A. Iori served on the division staff of the 25th Infantry Division; he was an infantry officer, both Ranger and airborne qualified. He saw a directive from the CINCPAC commander asking for volunteers to go into the 1st SF Group on Okinawa. He was assigned to Company A somewhere around September–December 1961. Company A was commanded by Major Leroy E. Schulenberg, and was picked to form a B-team for Laos. Lieutenant Iori was assigned as the S-4 of the B-detachment.

Schulenberg's detachment flew via C-130 to Bangkok on March 11, 1962, transiting through Kadena, then to Clark AFB Philippines, and arriving 0900 into Bangkok the same day. They were met by representatives of the FC team from Vientiane. After setting up their commissary account and postal accounts, they flew aboard an Air America C-46 to Paksane. With the help of Captain Stanleigh K. Fisk, the split-team detachment commander operating in Paksane, they settled into a large team house.

Captain Fisk's team was deployed with Laotian troops on a mountaintop north of town. The Pathet Lao and the FAR were at the base of the mountain, on either side. Rich Iori remembers the situation when they arrived:

> This was during the ceasefire and funny, odd things happening on the battlefield. There was an agreement that, for instance, the Pathet Lao could get water from a source in the morning, and then the FAR could get theirs in the afternoon, but, the Americans were restricted from getting water at the water source, so we kept busy getting water into Fisk's location. The Pathet Lao would fire their mortars at a certain time, and then the FAR would fire back, at a certain time.[22]

On April 15, General Yarborough, General Rosson, Colonel McKnight, and Lieutenant Colonel Little visited Schulenberg in Paksane. (Lieutenant Colonel Little was escorting General Yarborough.) Major Schulenberg told them his B-team was underutilized, with no mission. He said to the VIPs, "The B-team should be reassigned or given a mission, or sent back to Okinawa." On April 17, General Richardson and his entourage from CINCPAC visited, received a briefing on activities in the "Central Region of Laos," and had lunch. Schulenberg apparently also got the message through to General Richardson with respect to the wasting of the B-team and the inactivity in the Paksane sector.

Shortly thereafter, Schulenberg received the mission to serve as the B-team for Operation *Pincushion*. Schulenberg and his detachment transferred to Saravane and set up a command-and-control headquarters. He appointed Lieutenant Iori and his S4 NCO, Sergeant 1st Class William H. Caison, along with SP4 William L. Tapley, the S3 NCO, to go serve as a *Pincushion* liaison cell at the embassy in Vientiane.

Iori explained the job there:

> Our job was to monitor the message traffic and get things for the teams—ensure their supplies got out into the field. Another one of my duties was to get the pay for the guerrillas out to the field. I would go to the MAAG compound, and visit the CIA building there. I gave them our estimates on numbers, ranks, and so forth of the guerrillas, and they gave me the appropriate amount of pay in duffle bags. I then went to a bank in Vientiane and converted the dollars to Kip. I flew out to Saravane and sat with the S-1 of the B-team, and worked out all of the payroll. We brought all twelve companies of payroll to Saravane.[23]

During Iori's time at the embassy, he participated in monitoring the message traffic and coordinating assets for Second Lieutenant Spivey and his men after they were ambushed on the Bolovens Plateau and their subsequent escape and evasion until being found by Lieutenant Colonel Simons.

K-9 and K-12

SP4 Michael B. Donohue was a demolitions man on Captain Robert J. Arkley's FTT-16 (First Lieutenant John A. Hixson joined the team in Laos as the detachment XO; Master Sergeant Earl A. Higgins was the team sergeant).

Donohue volunteered for Special Forces out of HHC, 502nd Infantry at Fort Campbell, KY, where he was serving as the company armorer. (As was usual with the times, the company "lost" his paperwork volunteering for SF, forcing him to travel to Washington DC and the Pentagon to get it sorted out.) He was first assigned into the training company of the 7th SFG, but was transferred to Company A, again as a company armorer. His entire unit at that time was gone to Laos. He pushed to be assigned to Company C, for the next deployment to Laos, and after mission preparation on Arkley's ODA (Det A-736), they were on their way. They flew into Bangkok, and transferred to Pakse with the B-team, via Air America C-47; shortly thereafter, they flew on to Saravane to participate in Operation *Pincushion*.

Donohue stated,

> After two days there, we choppered out to site 106. This site was due east, or southeast of Saravane on the top of the hill. I was told if you stood on the top of the hill you could see Saravane. There were three teams on that hill. The first was a team from Okinawa commanded by Captain Robert A. Mountel. His team (six personnel) operated as a B-team, in overall control of the operations. He was at the northwest end of the base on the hill. His team was

also responsible for site security. Part of the time we would do a three-way split and conduct security and reconnaissance patrolling out to the west.[24]

Lieutenant John A. Hixson joined the 7th SFG (A) in August of 1961, following completion of the field artillery basic officer's course. A group of approximately seventeen to eighteen second lieutenants (volunteers) were selected out of this class and sent to the 7th SF Group. (Second lieutenant volunteers for SF were being sought at this time; twenty-one was the desired number.) He served in the group training company and with the public affairs office. One of his duties was assisting in the artillery training of an A-detachment scheduled to deploy to Laos to train Laotian troops in field artillery gunnery and fire support operations. He then completed the Special Forces qualification course and was assigned to Major Lancelot W. Krueger's B-detachment, training teams at Eglin AFB in Florida. Upon his return to Fort Bragg, Lieutenant Hixson was assigned to Detachment B-8, which was preparing for their mission in Pakse. While serving at Pakse, Hixson was transferred to FTT-16, Captain Arkley's team, to become the executive officer. He remembered:

> We were assigned to Site 106 on the Plateau des Bolovens. Our MTT established a base camp, in conjunction with two other A detachments (captains Jerry Kilburn and Bob Mountel).
>
> These camps, which were separate from each other, were very temporary and basic in nature with individual hootches, constructed from bamboo, ponchos, with a rough kitchen/mess area and a storage hootch. These camps were laid out around a large clearing on a hillside which served our common DZ and helicopter LZ. We also laid out training areas and firing ranges.
>
> The Kha tribesmen, recruited by others (non-SF, as I understand) in their home villages located away from Site 106, were moved to Site 106 and the detachments organized them into individual security companies to enable them to secure their home villages and local areas from the Communist Pathet Lao (I assume there was a common TOE for these companies, but I don't recall seeing one). Upon completion of training, the FTT generally moved with their respective companies to their assigned operational areas. (As I recall, we did not move with K-9 or K-12, the companies FTT-16 organized and trained.) We were sent to Thateng and told to conduct reconnaissance, security and surveillance operations with the Kha companies and to support them, for example, K-11 in that local area. While at Site 106 and at Thateng, we were probed a couple of times by whom we assumed were the Pathet Lao—neither action amounted to much, with no casualties on either side that we knew of.[25]

Also at Phou Kate was Captain Thomas P. Harkins' twelve-man ODA (deployed to Laos from May 9, 1962 to September 28, 1962). A group of tribal recruits was assigned to Captain Harkins (this may have been K-9 to K-10 iteration); there were about 100 to 120 of them. Four or five days later, Captain Arkley's group walked in from Saravane (to train K-9). The Agency CAS (controlled American source) for the training was codenamed "Frenchie," found to be a pleasant man by the teams, and spoke both French and Lao (this was undoubtedly Mr. Jean Cadeaux).

To outfit the "Gs," there would be airborne drops of supplies, arms and clothing. Harkins's team was training on the northeast side of the hill. Donohue continues:

Our team designation was FTT-16. We took the bottom end of the hill—the only way into this hill base camp was with helicopters. We had our team boxes, LBE [load bearing equipment web belts], and some carbines which were issued to us by Captain Mountel. Our camp was on the south end of the hill, in what was almost like marshy terrain, running into a creek. We lived under parachutes which we recovered from airdrops. We had cots and bamboo floors. We had a central messing area. The medic was the cook; he had formerly been a Mess Sergeant (Dixie Thornton). We all took turns cooking. One of my jobs was to fill the lanterns daily. We got water from the creek, and our food and supplies were all airdropped. We had no problem getting weapons and food via this method. The rice bags were dropped full and exploded when they hit! We had food we could order from the embassy commissary, class B rations (10-in-1), 5-in-1, and some C-rations, but the C-rations were for our E&E plan if we had to bug out. We had a stove. It was a small medical stove, like a Coleman 2-burner.[26]

The team wore standard-issue fatigues and wore Ranger-type patrol caps or the French camouflage boonie hats. For commo, the team used the AN/GRC-109, but fortunately had an EGB-12 generator and two sets of batteries, so they were not forced into using the hand-crank generator. They were armed with M1 carbines and BARs. Other munitions consisted of grenades and explosives. Again from Donohue:

We only took our demo kits, but not the explosives and mines when we deployed in. We were supposed to get explosives and demo when we got in-country. When we were down range, they issued us blasting caps, which were transported separate to us by helo. The explosives were airdropped. We were airdropped the old C-3 explosive (it was a yellow color). It was wrapped in red meat paper; it would fall out into your hands like fresh dough when you un-wrapped it. We had trip flares and mines, but not the toe poppers and we were not issued claymores.[27]

Captain Mountel, as senior team leader at Site 106, coordinated the training and disseminated intelligence on the threat. An 81mm mortar was located at this position for defensive purposes. Although being told there was zero threat in the area, Donohue remembered the area getting shelled one night with five or six rounds from a 60mm or 82mm mortar. No SF advisors were injured, but the guerrillas had five WIA from the engagement.

The team had two Thai interpreters, one whom they liked for his tactical acumen, but not the other, who acted more like an administrative NCO or officer. Upon the team's arrival, the guerrilla standard equipment kit and munitions were air-delivered. The Kha were issued two uniforms, a hat, pistol belt, canteen, along with a first aid packet, and other items to keep up their health. As the training continued, the unit was given field sanitation classes and regularly checked by the medics, Sergeant 1st Class Dixie R. Thornton and Sergeant 1st Class E. G. Wofford. The medics also performed MEDCAPs into the local villages to maintain rapport and to glean situational awareness of the threat.

The FTT did not have to organize this group; they appeared to have a semi-rigid organization of leaders, company headquarters, and platoons already decided. The tribal company did not wear distinctive insignia. In clannish behavior, they did not mix with the other tribal companies training at the site.

After medical screening of the recruits, they were briefed on the training schedule and purpose for the program: they would have the mission to receive enough basic training to go back out to their homes and do local patrols, under the command and control of a Lao military soldier or officer assigned to their district, or town. (This would be a Lao sergeant; he resided in the center of the town of Thateng in an old French villa.)

SP4 Ivan E. Larson was the Radio Operator on FTT-16. He joined Special Forces while he was in the 82nd Airborne, in a rigger group. At Fort Bragg, he joined Captain Arkley's detachment. They were alerted for duty for the mission in Laos and went into isolation at Smoke Bomb Hill for pre-mission training. They flew to Bangkok, then transferred aircraft to fly to Pakse, where they lodged with the B-team for a few days. He described the role of FTT-16:

> We carved a place in the middle of the jungle, then the Lao came (Kha Tribal). We issued uniforms and equipment to those who arrived. We were in the center of the camp and the Kha were in positions all around us. We had pistols, rifles, M1 carbines and automatic weapons. I don't recall we had any mortars, but we did have grenades. Again, there was no threat there during our time. I don't remember that we put up any wire, or trenches, or bunkers. We cleared a bit more off of a small clearing to make our HLZ and drop zone.
>
> We sat them up in quarters. We then gave them basic military training. Trying to get them to be military-like was quite a feat! We tried to get them into some kind of organization. I was not too impressed; some of them went AWOL. I gave some classes, like basic military skills, small arms, etc. We wore uniforms and dressed military; we left our civilian stuff back at the team house in Pakse, in a trunk. Overall, the biggest difficulty, we had this feeling, that they didn't want to do what the Americans wanted them to do.
>
> We had no threat to our training mission and site from the Pathet Lao. We went out on patrols to little country places with primitive villages. We once had a trip wire go off when we were near Saravane, which gave us a scare, but that was it.[28]

Because of the lack of a POI for training, the team developed their own schedule to fit the skills found in the unit. Donohue explained:

> Our training for the tribal forces consisted of basic ambush techniques, weapons training (very standard and basic), the execution of jungle lanes. This training lasted 30–45 days depending on the progress. My platoon went AWOL early during the training and I had no indication this was going to happen! One night, they took off their uniforms and stacked their weapons and departed. There were no discipline problems, or griping, etc. that would have been a warning to me.
>
> We also had silk training aids. There was a weapons set, demo set, mortars, and a medical set. They came in the size of a pack of cigarettes. Very good training aids; haven't seen them since.[29]

(The platoon in fact did not go AWOL; they departed temporarily to return to their village for a traditional ceremony.) Later in the training, the FTT would accompany K-12 and other Kha companies back to Thateng and live with them while the companies conducted their area security patrols.

K-11

Captain Gerald Kilburn was the detachment commander of FTT-45, which had split to cover Fort Lao Ngan and Dong Hene. His Detachment Executive Officer, First Lieutenant Herbert R. Johnson, covered Dong Hene with the Team Sergeant,

Master Sergeant James O. Schmidt. The team deployed to Laos on 10 March 1962 and remained until the end of September. (Captain Gerald Kilburn was present at Site 106 in the late spring of 1962, but it is not known if he operated there with his whole team or with a split-team.)

K-12 Phou Kate

Captain Robert A. Mountel led SF Detachment A-314 at Okinawa. He was assisted by his XO, First Lieutenant William T. "Tom" Bayha. His team sergeant was Master Sergeant Francis J. Benbenek. The team received orders to deploy to Laos in late May of 1962. Upon their arrival, they were assigned as FTT-17 to support the Kha tribal guerrilla program at Phou Kate, near Saravane. This mission would last until September 28, 1962.

The training for the last and final Kha company began in June, when Captain Bob Mountel's team, along with his XO, Lieutenant Tom Bayha, began training the K-12 contingent. K-12 recruits were divided by the origin of their tribal locations: about half came from Thateng, down on the Bolovens, and the remainder from the village of Ban Nong Boua, about twelve kilometers northeast of Phou Kate. This combination of the tribes from two separate locations would cause some friction during the mission.

(Due to crowded conditions at the camp in Phou Kate, Lieutenant Tom Bayha later took half of the SF detachment to establish a forward operating base at Ban Nong Boua.)[30]

The team deployed in military uniform with all of their team gear and weapons. The ODA was transported via C-130 to Bangkok, then got a ride on to Pakse in an Air America helicopter, where they met the B-team. There, they received their mission to move near Saravane to train K-12 Company. Upon their arrival, they were briefed by what appeared to be Agency assets, and then moved to a training camp to meet the troops.

PFC James H. Anson was the junior radio operator on FTT-17 (Sergeant Fredrick D. Callahan was the senior radio operator). He joined the Army in 1960, attended airborne training in the 82nd and then was assigned to the 101st, in the 501st Signal Battalion, as a teletype operator. He heard about President Kennedy starting unconventional and COIN units, such as Special Forces, so he volunteered. After attending skills training courses at Fort Bragg, he was assigned to the 1st Special Forces Group on Okinawa, with duty on Captain Mountel's ODA. Anson remembered the beginning of their mission:

> The recruits moved into the camp, and hootched on the outskirts. (They were supposed to provide the security, but we also provided our own security and guarded against any of them who might have been Pathet Lao).
>
> We started training right away at the platoon level, then grew and moved on up to company level operations, like running patrols. Captain Mountel and the Lieutenant had to draw up POIs for a four-week training course.

We started in our military uniforms, but these began rotting away from the Monsoon effects. Then we wore fatigue pants, jungle boots, no shirt, and a hat. We had M1 carbines. I made mine fully auto. I had a Ruger .22 long barrel pistol. We had machine guns. I used it to try to shoot down a Russian-made aircraft that kept buzzing us at midnight (Mountel was pissed at me and told me to quit it).

There was no threat from the enemy. The guerrillas had their own outposts, but we did not trust them. There were no Agency reps in our area (April to Sep). We got our recruitment leaflets made from the B-team. We got airborne drops for our supplies. I built a supply hut to store that stuff in.

We were told our mission was to recruit and train villagers for security operations. The villagers already had experience fighting in that area. They were paid monthly. We had recruiting leaflets we used when we would go through villages.[31]

Anson was not the only person who had spotted the Russian-made aircraft. Early one evening during a period of some remaining daylight, Brown, Wofford, and Hixson from Captain Arkley's team climbed a ways up the Phou Kate. They had a clear view of the valley south of them. Suddenly, a four-engine transport aircraft, the make and ownership unknown, flew south past them headed down the valley. Its side cargo doors were open, and it was flying at top speed. Hixson recalls, "We never saw any of the crew. We never saw this aircraft again, but when we were at Thateng later, we heard aircraft engines a couple of times NE of the village probably in the vicinity of the same valley, but farther south. Obviously, someone else was receiving airdrops. Just who it was, we never knew."[32]

The K-12 Company had been already recruited and assembled; all the unit needed was their equipment issue at the camp to begin training.

A portion of K-12 was issued .03 Springfields. When Lieutenant Bayha checked one of the serial numbers, he found out later in his life it had been manufactured in 1919. There were also a few M1s and carbines. The troops were issued two sets of fatigues; all of this was airdropped out in the field; a single DZ/LZ served as the lifeline for the team; their supplies, mail, rice, and other materials were dropped to them from low-flying H-34s flown by Air America. One day, even a live pig was dropped. Additionally, the troops were issued two sets of underwear, a field jacket, a rain poncho, web-gear, and a soft cap. They immediately put on every bit of clothing. The SF Advisors had to instruct them that some was for wear when appropriate, and some was for spare to carry on patrols.

The guerrilla leaders were not issued radios, but there were maps and compasses at least for navigation purposes. For signaling, the team used the old World War II-type "cricket" clickers at night. They also made extensive use of hand and arm signals.

Captain Mountel and the Agency asset did not pick the Kha leadership for K-12; these men emerged naturally from their tribal standing. The K-12 company commander was the headman of his village and he chose his own subordinate leadership.

Lieutenant Bayha graduated from OCS in 1959, as the top graduate, thus receiving his RA commission directly afterwards as a result of earning the "Patterson

Award" during his course. He went on to the 25th Division in Hawaii after he became airborne qualified. At the division, he commanded the 25th's jungle warfare school for soldiers in the division. He then had a chance to go to Okinawa to act as an aggressor during one of 173rd's maneuvers, and while there, got acquainted with the 1st SFG stationed on the island. He visited Colonel Menard (the group commander) afterwards and told him wanted to volunteer for Special Forces duty. Colonel Menard had him transferred to the 1st Group in January of 1962, where Bayha joined Captain Mountel's team. Of note, Colonel Menard always made it a point to visit his 1st Group teams assigned to *White Star* in Laos. (Later in Bayha's Southeast Asia service, he would serve in MACV-SOG and participate in recon missions into Laos.)

When ready to begin the training, Captain Mountel briefed the unit on their mission. Tom Bayha remembered the thrust of the conversation: "The mission of the Kha unit was self-defense; that's what we sold it to them on that basis. Stand up to the enemy and say no. They had been at the mercy of the Pathet Lao who came through their villages and recruited soldiers and took their food. Our training was supposed to help them defend their own homes, like a civil guard."[33]

The ODA was equipped with light M60 mortars, but these remained in the base camps. For personal defense, they carried M2 carbines and a .30-caliber semi-auto BAR.

Bayha described the training:

> We improvised training as we went along. Basically, the team's NCOs took care of the fundamental small-unit training and the use of weapons. It was just the minimum of tactical training needed to get the job done. My part was foot patrol leadership. Sometimes we had "cavalry." We used those small Laotian mountain ponies. Mountel went to Vientiane and got some pack saddles from the MAAG. By using these, we extended the duration of the patrols, letting the ponies carry extra food, rations, etc. Also, the Kha tribesmen knew how to ride them, so they could move ahead and scout and clear areas. When not patrolling or training, they were quite good at entertaining themselves with rodeo-like events!
>
> The instruction was three weeks of basic skills and weapons training, followed by patrolling and learning more stuff through patrolling. We had a Thai Ranger as an interpreter, plus some locals when we needed them as we went out to remote villages and the dialects might change. We patrolled out near the Annamite mountain range and the Se Kong River, out near the Ho Chi Minh Trail.[34]

The split-team was issued 1:100,000 maps, which in some places had only grid lines over blank paper. During the team's patrols, they worked to fill in the maps with details of the villages they came across, terrain features, and other landmarks. Bayha continued with a description of patrolling with K-12:

> For patrols, we went to remote locations, somewhere east of Saravane. The threat in the area was minimal. We did not expect to encounter enemy units of great size. The terrain, and the Se Kong River, was very tough to navigate, so we never got near the actual portions of the Ho Chi Minh Trail on any reconnaissance patrol. We had some brief exchanges of fire, like a

hit and run, a round or two, and then the enemy broke off. That's it. It was all a tremendous physical effort. Our enemies were medical: jungle rot, amoebic dysentery, threat of malaria, etc.

To gain acceptance with the villagers and locals, and to establish rapport, we, like all Special Forces, used our best asset, the medic. Andy Andrews established a clinic, aid shed, as a top priority. We were cautious about the threat of infections from the people when we were treating them. We delivered some babies, after some time, they [the locals] became comfortable and trusted us.[35]

After about a month into the mission, Captain Mountel instructed Lieutenant Bayha to take a split-team (FTT-17A) with about a hundred irregulars to Ban Nong Boua and establish a forward outpost. K-12 (forward) differed somewhat from earlier iterations of the northern *Pincushion* effort; they did not form up into platoons and companies; the structure used by the FTT was to form them into small patrol units, like a six-man foot patrol.

The camp was not fortified; the village was the camp. The guerrillas lived in their own houses and the team rented one of these (all the houses were up on stilts), for a grand total of $1 a week, each man. (As members of the team recalled, they rented one of the nicest homes in the village. They also remember the location as very remote.)

Later, FTT-17 would deploy with K-12 back to Thateng to help advise and support the operation at that location. Upon the completion of their mission, the two split detachments recombined and helo'ed back to Pakse, then to Vientiane, where they were counted out by the ICC at the Vientiane airport. During their departure, Pathet Lao were standing around at the fringes of the airfield, laughing at them. It was to be a very bitter experience.

Everyone on the team admired Captain Mountel, remembers Tom Bayha:

> I don't know why Captain Mountel was called "Speedy the Rice Baron." But it probably came from the fact he had a sense of humor. The medical aid shed they had at the camp, for instance, had a sign that said "Mountel General Hospital."
>
> Captain Mountel made it a point to teach me not to promise something to the native tribal members that I could not deliver. He taught us how to avoid situations where the native troops might turn on us, like had happened to other teams. He stressed the need to be sensitive and trustworthy with the troops, try to learn some of their language and culture.
>
> I appreciated his leadership and guidance. He was a great mentor.[36]

James Anson added, "Mountel had a previous name, 'Speedy the Rice Baron.' He was a nice guy, but very strict. Everyone had praise for him, he was low key. He was excellent on tactics. He came up with things that amazed us. He primarily dealt with the guerrilla leadership. He had great interpersonal skills; one of the best I have seen. He told us later that we were one of the best teams he ever had."[37] (On July 5, FTT-17 also assumed advisory control of K-9.)

Upon the declaration of neutrality on July 23, 1962, FB-D (Schulenberg's "unofficial" B-team) was commanding sixteen FTTs and ATTs between Pakse,

Saravane, the Bolovens, and Attopeu. Some of the teams were conducting missions with the FAR, while the remainder were with the *Pincushion* program.

The Mission with K-2 and K-12 at Thateng

Upon completion of training guerrillas, Captain Arkley's A Detachment moved with their Kha company to its assigned operational area. This was the area of Thateng and its surrounding Lao and Kha villages, south of Site 106, on the Plateau. This portion of the Bolovens was flat, with slightly rolling terrain to the east. The entire Bolovens was a base area for Pathet Lao groups. The detachment conducted reconnaissance, security, and surveillance operations with the Kha companies K-2 and K-12.

Following the truce of July 1962, the team was ordered to cease military operations and to conduct civil affairs operations only. Specifically, the detachment was directed to construct a rice mill, to be built in the village of Thateng, and turned over to the locals for their use.

Michael Donohue describes some of the security patrolling and other activities conducted by the FTT in those remaining days:

> We had a house; it was two stories with a garage. We slept on the second floor, and had our operations downstairs. The Laotian sergeant let us use his old World War II jeep. We took the troops we trained out on live patrols—combat patrols. We would be given our task for where to patrol by the Laotian sergeant. Two of our team members normally went out on these patrols with the troops. We were shot at occasionally, but all of these shots came from long ranges, maybe 300 yards or better. The bullets might have kicked up some dirt around us, but no one on our team got hit. There were some injuries in the tribal forces, but more of hitting the ground than getting hit by bullets. We did not experience any mortar fire during these patrols.
>
> We did not have any fire support. We did have a 3.5 inch rocket with about six rounds for the team. This was issued to us by the B-team when a report came out from the C-team that the enemy had been operating T-34s up in north Laos.[38]

During a local area patrol, the FTT and its tribal forces were approaching a village and saw a tall (over six-foot) man standing near his Land Rover. He appeared to be surrounded by what the patrol at first thought were FAR troops. As the patrol approached the man, who appeared to be a minister or a humanitarian agency employee, the stranger told the patrol he was prisoner of the Pathet Lao. The soldiers standing around him were dressed in light green fatigues, but had different caps than the FAR. In surprise, the patrol recognized they were Pathet Lao. Neither the Pathet Lao or the FTT and the patrol raised their weapons. The team sergeant, assessing the situation could potentially go bad, urged the patrol to withdraw from the village. They never heard of the final fate of this captive.

The project to build a coffee mill or a saw mill by USAID, who the team never saw, evolved into what detachment members referred to as the "School House

Caper." The team skillfully massaged the saw-mill project to build what the village desired—a schoolhouse.

The detachment departed by helicopter in October of 1962, staged through Pakse to Vientiane. They were counted out of the country by the ICC (International Control Commission) and returned to Fort Bragg.

The End of *Pincushion*

At the close of the program, eleven Kha tribal companies were available for service as local security forces (it appears that K-4 was demobilized due to attrition from desertion).

On the eve of the potential forming of a coalition government and the signing of the Peace and Neutrality Agreement, Operation *Pincushion* guerrilla companies were looked upon by the RLG as a liability if they could not be advised by the *White Star* teams and Agency assets. The program was suspended in June of 1962, with Lao government representatives demanding select units be disarmed.

Major Schulenberg designed the phase-out plan. In July, he closed out the effort at La Ta Sin and consolidated the SF advisors at Houei Kong.

The teams balked at disarming the units. Tom Bayha explained their rationale.

> After the Declaration of Peace in July 1962, the pull-out of SF teams began. I received a message one day from the B-team in Pakse, who had received the message from the control team at Vientiane. It said, "Disarm the troops and report back to Pakse." I refused the order and thought it was absolutely outrageous. If we left the indigenous defenseless, after it was known they were training with U.S. forces, the enemy would punish them. We decided to leave all of the stuff at the camps to the troops, and gave them all our extra ammunition.

(Captain Arkley's team was never ordered to confiscate Kha weapons.)[39]

The CIA had other plans, however. Anticipating they would continue their unconventional warfare program after the U.S. troop withdrawal, they coordinated with the *Pincushion* teams to establish underground caches around Paksong and Houei Kong, burying equipment, ammunition, and food supplies, but allowing the guerrillas to keep their weapons and immediate combat gear.

In the northern guerrilla zone, there were only three split-teams to serve at Phou Kate and Ban Nong Boua. Captain Arkley's team was tasked to escort K-12 back to the Thateng area and serve with them until the end of his team's tour. The final remaining split-team at Phou Kate was assigned the task to assist the CIA in training a thirty-two-man stay-behind cadre to operate a resistance and intelligence-gathering cell. This included covert operative and tradecraft training, establishment of hidden caches, and a field training exercise near Saravane. This effort ended in early September.[40]

All SF *Pincushion* teams were detached from *Pincushion* training areas by September 14, 1962.

CHAPTER EIGHT

The Thakhek, Se Bang Fai River, and Mahaxay Campaign: Operations in the MR-III Panhandle

> "The Lao were very laid back. They took a nap from 12–2 PM every day. Most were not warriors. We did have a few hard chargers who welcomed combat. Those we trained extra hard. The PL were a cut above our Royal Lao soldiers, guess they were more motivated. The Viet Minh [NVA] were a cut above both the FAR and the PLs. The NVA were very good."
>
> PFC JOHN MCCALLUM, RADIO OPERATOR, FTT-13, THAKHEK

The Pathet Lao occupation of Mahaxay was a thorn in the side of the FAR. From Mahaxay, Thakhek could be overrun by enemy forces spilling down Route 12, cutting the northern panhandle in two. GM-14 was assigned to defend the area and clear enemy forces out of Mahaxay and the Se Bang Fai River region. A succession of Special Forces teams would try in vain to advise GM-14 (often reinforced with GM-15) on their operations to clear the area, often without success on the part of the FAR.

Team Shalikashvili operated as a split-team assigned to Thakhek as FTT-13. The other half of the detachment, FTT-7, under First Lieutenant Bruce B. Mcdonough, was assigned to the vicinity of the Se Bang Fai River, working with the 11th Bataillon Parachutistes.

Captain Othar J. "Shali" Shalikashvili arrived at the 7th Group in the summer of 1961, transferring out of the 82nd Airborne Division at Fort Bragg. He finished the SF officer's course in September, and with very little pre-training with his team, deployed to Laos that October.

The team arrived in Bangkok during the morning then transloaded to C-47s and flew on up to Vientiane. They did not unload there; they received their team number, FTT-13, from Lieutenant Colonel Little, who told Captain Shalikashvili, "Shali, you are going to Thakhek by C-47."

Shali was replacing Captain Sydney R. "Sid" Hinds and his team. The two officers had known one another from their service in Korea. Captain Hinds met Shali's team at the Thakhek airfield and moved them to the team house, but they had very little turnover time together.

Little gave Captain Shalikashvili a three-part mission. Shali listed the three tasks:

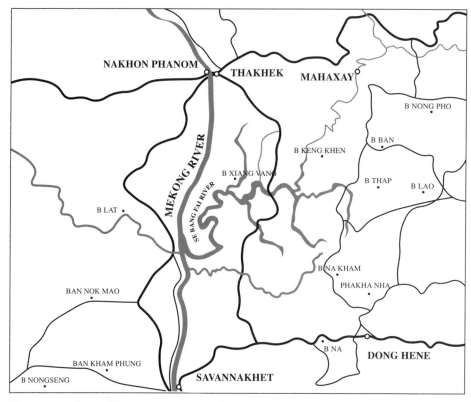

The operational area of the campaign was bounded by Savannakhet in the south, the Se Bang Fai River in the middle, Thakhek in the north, and the occupied town of Mahaxay east of Thakhek near route 12. *(Derived from silk survival map issued to Special Forces serving in Laos, courtesy of George W. Sevits)*

One. Work with the Lao government military province officer, in the subdivision of military affairs. He was a Lao LTC and spoke excellent English. I was supposed to give him advice, but I did not do it because he was very good and better than me.

Two. The second mission was to be an advisor to the 14th GM (there was only me and my radio operator available to do this). I could not do this with the team when we were assigned to Thakhek because the 14th GM was no longer stationed there. The unit was in a bit of a panic at that time due to their operations to try to take Mahaxay. However, the subdivision military officer told me he did not think this was due to Pathet Lao advances. The GM-14 had the 7th BI and 32nd BV in the field.

Three. My third mission was helping with the "Trailwatcher" program. This had been one of Sid Hines' missions before I got there. We did not call them "Trailwatchers"; we just called them guerrillas.[1]

At this time, the Pathet Lao were pushing GM-14 south out of the Mahaxay area. There were other FTTs advising GM-14's units (Lieutenant Darnell's FTT-15 and Captain Peter T. Owre's team), but Shalikashvili was the senior captain among them, and served as overall control of the three teams. (There was no B-detachment yet at

Thakhek; later, one would arrive at Savannakhet.) Local control and administration for the teams in the field was conducted by an A-team manning the team house in Thakhek.

Team *Owre*

Master Sergeant George W. Sevits was the team sergeant for Captain Peter T. Owre's FA. They were also assigned to train and advise the 10th BI of GM-14, starting the mission in November (they followed Captain Shalikashvili's deployment in October of 1961). Owre's team settled into the team house at Thakhek with the other SF teams, and once ready, went out to meet their battalion, introduce themselves, and orient themselves to the operation prior to moving out on maneuvers the next day. In a bit of culture shock, that very same day they witnessed the battalion commander holding a court martial, followed by the execution of the guilty soldier by firing squad.

The 10th BI headed east into the karst region (the Pathet Lao were known to be living in caves in this region). At one place, they had to crawl through a hole in the karst, which was about the size of a Laotian soldier, or about rucksack size, but everyone made it through.

The unit bivouacked in a volcano-like crater. Throughout this entire field deployment, the FTT could only be resupplied by air. Sevits recalled, "We patrolled out from there; we had a small passage in the crater where the patrol could go out, and then down to a field which ran alongside the river. We left one of the companies at the crater; they were very weak in their loyalty and could not be trusted. Only a couple of us went on the patrol."[2]

Prior to the patrol, the BI received fresh beef and had a BBQ. The local village militia (believed to be an ADC) were invited to partake in the feast. The militia did not forget to return the favor one day when a patrol from the unit was ambushed by the Pathet Lao. Sevits said,

> On patrol, we crossed the river into the jungle. There were six of us (Americans). We got fired upon by a small element of Pathet Lao, small arms fire only. The enemy looked tall and were wearing weird boots. Both our guys and the enemy were shooting up into the air, like they did not want to hit each other. The village militia heard the firefight and came to our rescue! Our interpreter ran off to the other side of the defense position when the firing started.[3]

Team *Shali*, near Mahaxay

When GM-14 withdrew under pressure from the Pathet Lao during their push to Mahaxay (with Captain Darnell's team), Sergeant James E. Ferguson (the medic on Captain Peter T. Owre's split detachment serving in the Thakhek region with the 10th BI) remained as part of the covering party. Armed with a recoilless rifle, Ferguson fired on the Pathet Lao to impede their progress.

Captain Shalikashvili was attached to the GM-14 command group; they withdrew down the Se Bang Fai River a short way using boats while the line battalions maneuvered overland to a new location, maneuvering west toward Route 13. Under light pressure from the Pathet Lao, GM-14 conducted an organized withdrawal. Shali and the command group left their boats and walked through the "National Forest" collecting units and putting them into a "two battalions defending forward position." As things settled down to a static defense, Shali's team moved to begin advisory duties for the 55th BP.

Shalikashvili continued explaining his other activities:

> During this time, I am doing mission one and two, splitting my time between them. (The mission with the subdivision military officer did not take up much effort or time, but it was useful to still have the mission to play it off the other two tasks when I needed to.)
>
> I divided my split-team into half again so part could stay in Thakhek and conduct the training for the *Trailwatch* program and I could spend my time with GM-14. It was very rudimentary program, there was not much commo. I left my team sergeant, Sergeant 1st Class 'Bucky' N. Smith, in charge of the *Trailwatch* training. We were advised by a CIA operative. He came to Thakhek and I had a very casual relationship with him—he mostly helped to clarify things. Bucky's part of the team trained the recon teams on basic weapons use and handling, patrolling techniques, and how to observe.[4]

(The *Trailwatch* program was developed to send Lao recon teams out to the Ho Chi Minh Trail, remain there for some time, and observe and report on NVA activities.)

Shali reported directly to Lieutenant Colonel Little in Vientiane. Two months into the deployment, a B-detachment was established in Savannakhet and C2 was switched over to Major Johnson, the B-team commander. The *Trailwatch* program eventually began to fade away after only two iterations of training by Sergeant Bucky N. Smith (intell NCO on the team). The team was once again back together to continue the mission of advising and training GM-4.

Prior to GM-14 launching another attack on Mahaxay, the team began training of the BIs. Eventually, GM-14 began their move to retake Mahaxay. The detachment armed themselves with carbines and pistols. (One member of the team carried a .45 Thompson sub-machine gun. Most of the others carried M1s, but Shali personally carried a French MAT-49.) Surprisingly, they were one of the few Special Forces teams in Laos issued maps.

During the operation, the 8th BI was attacked by the Pathet Lao, who were using a couple of armored cars. The Lao unit retreated back across the river. Shali recalls, "I was tasked by higher to go look for the SF folks who were with them, but I was too busy with duties with GM-14 headquarters. LTC Simons took a helo to go look for them." (The missing team was Lieutenant Charles H. McLendon's team.)

GM-14 lost people short of the ridge southwest of Mahaxay. As they were pushing Pathet Lao forces in that area, the Pathet Lao attacked GM-14 headquarters with indirect fires. The unit pulled back and awaited their M8 armored cars.

Shali described the FAR efforts to return counter-battery fires. "There was a Lao 105mm battery commanded by a sharp Laotian Lieutenant. After some time, the unit was assigned a U.S. artillery Lieutenant from Korea. He was not effective as an advisor. (Too young and inexperienced—Army should have been sending senior advisors for this duty.) The battery did not have forward observers, they just used maps, compasses only, but they were still good."[5]

GM-14 remained in their new defensive position, satisfied to only conduct a "presence" mission. In the March/April time frame, Shali's FTT spent one day transitioning with a new team and left the battlefield.[6]

White Star Escapes and Evades—Team McLendon

Lieutenant McClendon returned from his first *White Star* deployment to Laos (conducted in April of 1961). While at Bragg, he found out he was scheduled to return to Laos. "The Adjutant called me in one day and told me I was going to Laos again. He moved me to Company C to replace a Captain on a split-team."[7]

The team landed in Savannakhet (early December of 1961) and reported in to Major Warren B. Stevens, the FB-Charlie commander for MR-III. McLendon was given the mission to go to the 8th Battalion of GM-14; the other new team deploying with McLendon had the mission to go to the 9th Battalion, near Thakhek. The 9th BI was scheduled to attack the contiguous base area for the Pathet Lao near Mahaxay. However, for some unknown reason the 9th never executed the attack; the FAR command soon replaced them with BI-8.[8]

McLendon's team flew from Savannakhet to the battalion location via an Air America H-34. On first impression, the team found that the battalion camp appeared to be in good shape for the defense. It had foxholes with overhead cover, bunkers for heavy weapons, and security emplaced. The BI had no artillery, but they had brought their 60mm mortars.

The terrain in the area dropped into jungle, then plains to piedmont, and then to higher ground. Sergeant Thomas O. Humphus was the radio operator on the team. He had served an earlier tour in Laos on the *Hotfoot II* rotation at Luang Prabang. The first surprise for Humphus was the lack of maps for the operation. "I quote strongly, 'WE DID NOT HAVE A MAP!' When we got up to where the battalion was, they had one map only. The only other map was in the field CP. Captain Shali took us into the CP where we went over the map and looked over the coordinates of the operation. I only sketched about half of the map. With this little piece of information, the decision was made that we would advance up the river to ease navigation."[9]

Humphus continued: "We formed up into single file and went down the river with the Laotians. The Se Bang Fai River was on our right, and there was dense jungle on our left. It looked like a perfect kill-zone to me and I did not like the single file thing."[10]

Meanwhile, McLendon positioned himself with the unit S3 during the movement. He recalled, "We went up to the front lines on the Se Bang Fai River. I remember walking along the river, alongside the Lao Battalion S3, who spoke a little English. I asked him, 'Do you know what's on the other side of this river?' He told me, 'Yes, the Pathet Lao, but we have an agreement with them not to shoot one another.'"[11]

BI-8 stopped at a stream which flowed into the river. It formed a "U" at that location; the unit stopped in the middle of the "U" shape. Soon, mortar rounds started landing. One hit 100 meters long; the next hit 100 meters short. It was very apparent to McLendon's team they were being bracketed by Pathet Lao indirect fires. Then, artillery rounds started landing on the position while small-arms fire broke out. McLendon told his counterpart, "'They know where you are, let's move the camp!' He told me they were not going to move. I told the team, 'Dig a foxhole! You have to get overhead cover!'"[12]

At 0600 hours the artillery fire began again and hit at one end of the "U," then in the middle of the "U," and then at the other end of the "U." It would not be long before a fire-for-effect pinned down BI-8 at the stream. The Lao lieutenant yelled at the team, "Come, we go now!"

McLendon continued his description of the action:

> We could count thirteen to thirty rounds in the air before they landed, then small-arms fire broke out. The Lao left us. I said to the team, "It is hard to advise when no one is here. An attack is coming." We moved out and headed back in the direction of the patrol. After about fifteen to twenty minutes, we heard some voices. I had the interpreter call out to them, hoping they were Lao soldiers, to let them know it was the Americans coming in. They fired on us! But fortunately, they missed. We outflanked them to the northwest, then headed west, and went to the GM headquarters.[13]

Escape and Evasion

Sergeant Tom O. Humphus provided a detailed and thorough description of the engagement with the Pathet Lao, which eventually forced the detachment to conduct escape and evasion after their abandonment by the 8th BI, which had already fled the scene:

> We had walked about a half of the day when suddenly we took fire from the left front. It intensified until we had a full firefight. The fire was coming from the jungle, but I was also worried about what could be coming up the river on our flank. From the size of things, we had apparently run into a Pathet Lao battalion. Fortunately, from the sloppiness of their fire, I don't think they had any NVA with them. I only shot at muzzle flashes in the trees. I never saw any of the enemy.
>
> At lunchtime, I made a commo check, then heard a round pop out of a mortar. Ettman hit the hole I had dug earlier as the mortar round went overhead. I went to get the radio and the antenna down when we heard another mortar round pop as it left the tube. Everyone else was

still eating and paying no attention! Paul got out of his foxhole and headed down to alert the other people, and then, Pop! Another round

Then a lot of mortar rounds, or 105mm, came crashing down and exploding. Finally, a lull in the action. The Lao XO, carrying two bamboo cages with roosters, came up to our position and said, "We go now! We go now!" We told him we were remaining in the hole and we should wait for the artillery to stop.

When we finally got out of the hole, we walked around and saw pieces of bodies everywhere and all the Laotians had run away. We thought maybe the Lao commander had sold us out to the Pathet Lao.

Now seemingly left abandoned by the Lao unit, the team faced the decision to E&E from the area. Humphus continued:

We made the decision to E&E to the west, in the direction of Thailand. We did this for three days. On the first day, we were shot at again. We fell to the ground and our Thai interpreter gave the challenge because we thought maybe our Laotians were out there also. Whoever was out there shot at us again. (This lasted about five minutes.)

We did not have all of our TO&E weapons. I had a shotgun from Okinawa; Hemphill had a semi-automatic .22 rifle (not sure what he was going to accomplish with that); the Lieutenant had an M1 or M2 carbine. We had our .45s, and no grenades.

During this engagement, I said, "Paul, watch your right flank!" He flopped over to provide cover from that direction. The Lieutenant was lying quietly observing this, but had given no orders. Then, McLendon yelled out an order, "Fall back to the last dry creek bed!"[14]

(Missing from the engagement that day was Sergeant 1st Class Richard D. Whitehead, the weapons NCO; he had been pulled up to the B-team as the detachment's mission support element.)

McLendon ordered everyone to drop their rucksacks to make better speed, but Humphus was concerned about leaving the radio behind, their only way to communicate. But following orders, he stashed the radio in a nearby hole. Humphus then took up the rear security with his shotgun and the team continued their E&E westward. They spent the night atop a large pile of boulders, which was strange to them, to find such a thing in the middle of the jungle. There was no food; it had all been left behind when they dropped their rucksacks. Humphus had some vitamins and some amphetamines, along with salt tablets, and shared them with the team as their evening "meal."

The following day, a good-sized trail was discovered along their route of foot march. Cautiously, they followed it, walking in single file, in extended column. Hopefully, they thought, the trail led to a village; they had seen footprints on the trail so they knew people were around. They followed the trail and soon came upon the village where they met the chief of the village who relayed to them there were some Laotians who had come through earlier asking about their American advisors. The team asked, "Can you take us to the nearest military compound?" The head man replied, "Yes." Two teenage guides were provided to search for GM-14, but before the team left the village everyone had the chance to eat a good meal.

They did not know that Lieutenant Colonel "Bull" Simons was conducting an extensive search for them. (Simons was in Vientiane to oversee the Operation *Pincushion* program.)

After their ordeal, Lieutenant McLendon's team was given a break with an assignment in a quiet zone—Military Region V. The team moved to Vientiane to serve as trainers at the NCO academy, Camp Chinaimo. They replaced Lieutenant Kellenberger's split detachment (from Captain Sydnor's team) when Kellenberger took his team to reinforce Captain Sydnor on the Bolovens Plateau for Operation *Pincushion*.

Military Region III Activities

First Lieutenant Robin Luketina commanded FTT-21, a split-team assigned with duty as advisors and trainers to the Laotian 55th Bataillon Parachutistes, stationed at the airfield in Seno. The 1st SFG (A) detachment split for two separate missions in Laos; the detachment commander with half of the team remained in Savannakhet to assist the B-team.

Luketina's split-team included Master Sergeant Floyd O'Conner, the detachment team sergeant. Luketina described:

> From Savannakhet, the split-team was choppered (H-34 helicopters from Air America) into a small, remote village where we initially linked up with the Laotian 55th Bataillon Parachutistes (BP) located about two to three days walk east from Savannakhet. (The home of the paratroopers was the base at Seno, which still had French military trainers assigned.) The mission of the Laotian paratroopers was to patrol a region of Laos near the North Vietnamese border, provide presence, and disrupt Pathet Lao forces. The next day we took off on a relocation march, at a rigorous, fast pace. It was horrendous! This is why it is better to get in shape with rucksack marches in SF than running for physical training.[15]

The Seno-based 55th Battalion was deployed in a remote jungle camp about two to three days' walk east of Savannakhet, near the small river of Se Noi. It was not a mountainous area, but rather riddled with rice paddies and jungle. The nearest main trail was located over twenty kilometers away. The commander of the 55th BP was Major Southchay.

The 55th BP consisted of five companies of fifty-five-men each. When the detachment arrived they found the unit conducting light patrols throughout the area. In Lieutenant Luketina's initial assessment of the unit, he found them to be "proficient and well equipped for a Laotian unit, and very fit."[16]

The team established their camp about a hundred meters from the battalion CP. They confirmed there was a drop zone clearing, or a landing zone clearing, as this would be the only way they could receive supplies. Although not clear of the exact nature of their mission with the 55th, the team planned to train, advise and assist as soon as possible. Luketina said, "We really did not have a mission statement from higher, it was more of a guidance to do what we could to improve their performance and to hang around and provide intelligence of the area and status of the unit. We had a Thai interpreter assigned to us, a skinny guy with glasses, but he seemed to comport himself like an officer."[17]

On the second day at the camp the SF split-team attended a meeting between the battalion commander and the local village chief. Basically, the commander was urging the village chief to take his men and go over the next valley and attack a village that was known to be communist, or at least sympathizers supporting the Pathet Lao. Luketina said, "I will never forget the village chieftain's sensible reply. 'Look, we can do that, but one day you will not be here. Then that village will retaliate and come to my village and kill my people.'"[18]

The 55th BP soon began patrolling the area to keep the Pathet Lao off-balance; the battalion did not appear to desire any larger engagement or fight. Much of the time it was quiet with no activity. None on the SF team ever saw any Pathet Lao soldiers. However, there was one instance of a mortar attack against the camp. (Other dangers were landmines in the area.)

Corporal John T. Haralson extended his three-year enlistment tour in the 1st SFG (A) to participate with his A-team going to Laos. (He was the team's radio operator.) Haralson noted, "There were a few casualties killed by landmines. These people were cremated in a funeral pyre as was the Laotian custom."[19]

Even though the 55th's subordinate units were deployed throughout the jungle, FTT-21 was able to train platoons, sections, and companies as they rotated back into the battalion CP area. Noted Haralson: "We conducted small unit training (SUT) classes with them consisting of tactics, patrolling techniques, and weapons firing—basic stuff. Dick Benzel was on the team helping to conduct these classes. (He was later killed in Vietnam.) We did not conduct any airborne proficiency training with them. They did get jump pay, however. The paymaster would parachute into the camp occasionally with their money."[20]

The 55th BP was considered a top-notch unit within the FAR. However, Luketina found their biggest tactical deficiency was the use of French doctrine to establish hedgehog positions, rather than a good all-around battalion defense:

> One thing I would like to mention, and this is why the BP got defeated and scattered later at Nam Tha. When we were training with them in the jungle, the commander of the battalion would send his men out all scattered around. He had five companies of fifty-five men each. I tried to teach him the military principle of keeping your forces consolidated. I advised him to pull in the scattered companies. The Laotians just would not listen to us on this subject. After a while, I finally convinced him to pull all the people in. I guess they forget that lesson when we jumped into Nam Tha, because the battalion commander once again scattered out his companies."[21]

In the camp, the team soon learned of the strange obsession of the soldiers wearing their Buddha amulets. Haralson described the amulet tradition:

I remember something interesting about the *tahan,* which is what we called the Lao soldiers. They were Buddhist and would visit the local temple to get charms and amulets to hang around their necks in order to protect themselves. I guess we would call this "ju ju" bags. They would bring them to me and ask me to "test" them by hanging the bag in a tree, then shooting at it to see if the charm worked. I was a pretty good shot with my .38 revolver I kept in my shoulder holster and rarely missed, but then it dawned on me they wouldn't go out on patrol if the bag didn't work, so it might be a pretty good idea to "miss" the bag, thus raising morale and proving its magic![22]

In mid-March of 1962, the 55th BP was pulled back to Seno to prepare for a combat jump to reinforce the beleaguered garrison in Nam Tha. Lieutenant Luketina and John Haralson would participate, making one of the few American combat jumps recorded during the war in Laos. (Luketina later served two tours in Vietnam; John Haralson attended OCS later and retired as a lieutenant colonel in the Army.)

FTT-13—With a Batallion Parachutistes on the Se Bang Fai River

Operations continued in the Mahaxay and Se Bang Fai area into 1962. The FAR still conducted static defense, with limited patrolling, and the Pathet Lao still owned Mahaxay. Detachment A-26, 7th Special Forces Group would be another team involved in what seemed like a never-ending series of mission assignments in Thakhek.

Captain Michael T. Eldred was the detachment commander of A-26 of the 7th SFG (A) at Fort Bragg, NC. The team was alerted for deployment to Laos with departure on 10 March 1962. He was assisted on the team by Lieutenant Richard O. Sutton, the XO, and Master Sergeant Raymond F. Flaherty, the team sergeant. It was a full-up, twelve-man SF detachment.

Just before actual departure, A-26 packed their team equipment boxes and personal items and moved all of it into the isolation facility. They learned they were going to operate as split detachments in Laos, and made the split-team assignments prior to departure.[23]

Upon their arrival in Bangkok they transferred to a C-47 flown by an Air America pilot named "Red," who was the route pilot for Savannakhet. Major John T. Morgan, the B-detachment commander in Savannakhet, met them at the airport with a 2½-ton truck and trailer and moved them to the B-team compound, a walled-in area with a three-story house. Leaving their gear at the house, the team lodged in the Constellation Hotel in town while awaiting further mission guidance.

In the morning Captain Eldred moved the detachment back to the B-team to receive their mission briefing. Eldred and his split-team were assigned to the 1st BP, under GM-15. The area of operation for GM-15 was contested by Kong Le's Neutralists. GM-15 units were deployed southeast of Thakhek, with three battalions. (GM-15 was based out of Seno airfield.) Eldred would become FTT-13, taking over from the previous team at that location, FTT-17. Captain Shalikashvili, the current commander of FTT-13, met Eldred at the B-team house to discuss the mission.

From Savannakhet, the team deployed out to one of the BPs assigned to GM-15 (possibly the 55th Bataillon Parachutistes), operating along the Se Bang Fai River line.

The team wore standard army fatigues, combat boots (which lasted a very short time in the jungle humidity), and bush hats. All uniforms were sterile (stripped of patches, names, ranks).

They transitioned with the outgoing SF team, and signed for communication gear, radio crystals, supplies, and other necessary items. After transition of gear with the departing team, they were left armed with M1 Garands, a 12-gauge shotgun, one Thompson .45 SMG, along with the personal sidearms they brought for the deployment. The outgoing team introduced them to their counterparts in the BP. (They were designated FTT-13 by the FB-C in Savannakhet. The B-detachment was commanded by Major John T. Morgan Jr., and was a twenty-five-man unit.)

The main operating area for GM-15's BPs was located approximately fifty-five kilometers southeast of Thakhet along the Se Bang Fai River. The SF team's mission was to enhance Laotian unit skills to fight the Pathet Lao. There were no French trainers at this position (although some remained at GM-15's home station, the airfield at Seno).

The team lived in hootches constructed from materials in the field, mostly bamboo, with ponchos overhead. Water and washing came from a local stream. A slit trench sufficed for sanitation purposes. FTT-13 ate with the unit, the food consisting of water buffalo, chickens, snakes, and monkey, along with rice. To augment their diet, one of the detachment members traveled to Vientiane once a month to place an order for canned food (delivered by helicopter). Air America became their lifeline. At times in the jungle, the LZ was where the team could find a clear area and lay out air-recognition panels.

Given any available time, FTT-13 trained the BP in weapons, small-unit tactics, patrolling, radio procedures, and emergency medical procedures. Training was conducted at the company and platoon level. The team also ran an internal NCO academy of sorts.

The GM moved often; the team rotated through five different campsites in six months. Rucksacks were kept packed every night and at least one of the detachment's members remained awake and on guard. Later in the rotation, the transportation problem was alleviated a bit by the team acquiring a Mitsubishi jeep.

PFC John F. McCallum was the radio operator for FTT-13. He served in the 101st Airborne Division as an infantryman and senior scout, prior to joining Special Forces. He described a typical day in the field: "A typical day for me as the radio operator: I had an early morning contact so the B-team would know we were still there. Then I would conduct weapons or commo training, then, another radio contact at noon, more training or camp work, then mid-afternoon we'd usually get a BTB, then one last radio contact before evening meal. Sleep if we could."[24]

The Pathet Lao were a constant, irritating threat, and considered by the team as tactically more proficient than the paratroopers. McCallum described some of the other conditions of combat:

> We had no close air support and the only artillery support was Lao-controlled so we were a little leery about calling it in close to our position.
> We pretty much got shot at every time we visited our troops along the river. We also got a lot of mortar and artillery fired randomly into GM positions as harassing fire. We trained a Ranger Company and accompanied them on several patrols that made contact with PL troops. Lot of shooting but no serious injuries on our side.[25]

It was becoming apparent to the *White Star* teams Mahaxay would not be retaken in 1962.

FTT-19, First Lieutenant Sutton

Lieutenant Sutton's assignment, as FTT-19, was with the 11th BP. The BP was currently being advised by Captain Walker's FTT-2, at Moung Phalane. (Captain Walker also attended the B-team morning briefing to begin the transition of assignment with Lieutenant Sutton.) BP-11 had four companies deployed on the Se Bang Fai River, opposing Kong Le's Neutralist BP. The 11th BP was the center battalion of a three-battalion deployment at that location; there was one battalion to their northern flank, and one battalion to their southern flank. A fourth battalion served in reserve behind the force.[26]

Lieutenant Sutton's FTT drew their weapons. "We met one of the outgoing teams; they gave us their weapons. We had M870 12-gauge shotguns, M1s, and a BAR, grenades and our pistols: a .32 Colt, Ruger .44 Magnum, a .38 Smith & Wesson, .357, and .45 Cal military pistols."[27]

Leaving their personal clothes and duffle bags behind, the team was ferried out to their field sites by H-34 helicopter.

Sutton's team was met by the now outgoing "FTT-19" and conducted a one-day transition, which included a reconnaissance of the BP positions. During the tour, they came upon the Se Bang Fai River and observed the Neutralist forces dressed in grey uniforms, wearing berets.

The outgoing team left them three .30-caliber machine guns, which they had been using to "leverage" the battalion commander to accept their advice anytime he requested the additional firepower. They also met their interpreters, "Sam" and "Charlie." They learned from the outgoing team an H-34 serviced the site every day, to bring in supplies, mail, and food.

That night, Sutton sat with his men as they were settling down into their new camp (fixing the hootches and making beds) and discussed their E&E plan. In the event of a bug-out, the men would move by twos, dropping any heavy loads, and travel west, hopefully intersecting Route 13.

FTT-19 (Sutton) found the 11th BP a mile out of Thakhek with positions about 300 meters from the Se Bang Fai River. The battalion was arrayed with two infantry companies on line, one in reserve, along with a weapons company and the battalion headquarters to their rear. The battalion had a ¾-ton Dodge truck at the CP, for transportation. There were also two 105mm howitzers for fire support.

Lieutenant Sutton met the battalion commander of BP-11 the next day to introduce himself and the team to the operation. He described activities at the site:

> The commander of the 11th BP was a good commander—Khom Krasofrath. On the Xe Bang Fai, I met with him every day and helped in planning operations. There were three line companies and a weapons company (not really like we would envision a weapons company— some of the machine guns were World War I models). They were deployed in a two-up and one-back configuration. We helped to train the unit that was back, then the others when they rotated into that position. There might have been some mortar harassment fires, so we built a bunker at that position.[28]

As an introduction to the situation in the area, Lieutenant Colonel Khom accompanied Sutton around the battalion positions and then up to the river, where they received sniper fire from across the bank. There was also an enemy bunker sited across the river which often harassed with fires any 11th BP reconnaissance efforts. A patrol was soon sent out with a 57mm recoilless rifle to reduce the bunker.

In March of 1962, BP11 was operating ten miles east of Route 13. The Pathet Lao sprang an ambush on GM-15's Rangers and blew two bridges in the area. BP-11 was tasked to find the Pathet Lao conducting those operations. The battalion moved to secure the bridge at Phou Pongdeng and then began a reconnaissance patrol to the village of Ban Moung Ba. They swept through the village; encountering no opposition, the patrol continued their sweep into Ban Tung, where they had heard from local sources the Pathet Lao were still in the area.

Meanwhile, BP-11 elements at the bridge near Phou Pongdeng were attacked and overrun, encountering casualties. After reinforcing the bridge position, BP-11 and the FTT bivouacked near the bridge to support a detachment of engineers attempting to rebuild the structure. It was repaired the next day and the unit crossed the Se Noi River to reach the village of Ban Na Xoi. From there, they continued patrolling to Ban Sok Sa, but found no enemy forces. In each of these locations they heard from sources there were about twenty local Pathet Lao operating in the area, made up mostly of Home Guard with a few Pathet Lao regulars as advisors. At Ban Sok Sa, sources informed them the enemy had moved on to Ban Khom Phuang. Colonel Kohm then planned to intercept them at Moung Ba but the Pathet Lao unit eluded them and headed in the direction of Ban Na Deng.

BP-11 continued in pursuit. Around 1700 to 1800 hours they found the enemy and assaulted. During the assault, Lieutenant Sutton and his team sergeant chased one Pathet Lao into the woods, where the SF NCO shot him with a pistol. During the whole engagement, BP-11 killed seventeen enemy and captured three, who they searched and interrogated.

In the morning, BP-11 moved out to Ban Na Deng where they spent three days reconsolidating. The almost two-week sweep operation was over. (This operation was called the "Long Patrol" by the team.)

On March 30, 1962, FTT-19 was pulled back to Savannakhet to stand down and get some rest. (It was also thought the 11th BP would return to their base at Seno for refit.) Sutton and detachment remained in Savannakhet until BP-11 returned to Seno in April, and then FTT-19 moved onto the airbase with Captain Buck's 1st SFG (A) detachment. The team was now down to five men, with Sergeant Pettit being pulled to assist the B-team in Savannakhet. There was no need for training and advising the 11th BP while they were undergoing refit, so life soon became boring. Detachment members took the opportunity to visit the town of Seno (*François'* restaurant was the favored place) and visit with other SF teams at Dong Hene. One day, they noticed French aircraft landing at Seno and loading up gray uniforms. The planes took off east, headed in the direction of the Neutralist forces. Putting two and two together, the detachments at Seno now understood where the Neutralist BP on the river got their gray uniforms. The French were flying provisions to the Neutralists.

GM-15 soon undertook operations with BP-11 to sweep Route 9 from Seno east to Tchepone. Their plan was to capture Tchepone with a ground element of the BP, seize the airfield, and then land the remainder of the BP to reinforce harassment operations on the Ho Chi Minh Trail. Once completing that mission, the unit would pull back west along Route 9 to link up with FAR truckborne units moving east toward them. A ruse for the mission was to get the French to fly Colonel Khom into Tchephone, posing as a defector to Kong Le.

BP-11 was successful in seizing the Tchepone airfield (April 15). They marched in column farther east, and established a bivouac, northwest of Ban Dong on Route 9.

The Ambush on the Ho Chi Minh Trail

A firefight broke out at Ban Dong; eleven NVA were killed and some of their wounded captured. The 11th BP had four KIA and some wounded among the paratroopers. In reaction to the firefight at Ban Dong, the Pathet Lao moved forces to Xiangbom, about fifteen kilometers north of Ban Dong.

Colonel Khom moved his force north up the Ho Chi Minh Trail to intercept. At a chokepoint flanked by two ridges he placed one company along the trail in a blocking position, with two companies atop the ridges on each flank. It was a good

WS Rotations V–VII, *Pincushion*, and Siege of Nam Tha

1st Special Forces Group (Airborne) beret flash circa 1961–1962.

SFC Kenneth N. Cox, Team *Hinds* intelligence sergeant (on right), prepares for a combat raid on Pathet Lao positions near Thakhek during Rotation V. (*Courtesy of the USAJFK Special Warfare Museum, Ken Cox collection*)

FTT-40 participated in the battles of the Nam Beng River valley. FTT-40 poses for a team photo at one of the Lao .30-caliber machine-gun positions. On left is Master Sergeant Paul C. Payne, the ODA's team sergeant. Next, in glasses, is Lieutenant Clinton L. Allen (remaining team members unidentified). Sergeant 1st Class Gerald "Doc" Wareing was the medic; Sergeant Joseph R. Cervantes demolitions; Sergeant James F. Cevis the radio operator; and Sergeant William Burgess weapons. (*Courtesy of USASOC History Office*)

Prince Boun Oum na Champassak was selected as the overall government and paramilitary titular head of the Kha guerrilla program (*Pincushion*) due to lack of an overall clan leader. Here he is shown visiting the Bolovens Plateau to meet with Kha tribal leaders. (*Courtesy of Albert Slugocki*)

Captain Stanford's FTT-30 was assigned to GM18, commanded by Colonel Nu Phet. GM-18 was assigned to sweep the Bolovens Plateau from Paksong to Attopeu and clear out enemy forces prior to the establishment of Operation *Pincushion*. At left, Colonel Nu Phet, commander GM-18, in center with (from left) Jimmy Dean, Richard La Hue, Lupe Rodriguez, and J. O. Wells. (*Courtesy of USAJFK Special Warfare Museum, via Dottie Dean*)

Kha tribal guerrilla companies were designed to be 100-man strong. Upon arrival, recruits were formed into platoons and leadership chosen to run the company. Airdrops provided uniforms and arms. (*Courtesy of Ernest K. "Ernie" Tabata*)

Captain Bud Sydnor, commander of FTT-43, meets with K-1 and K-2 leadership to discuss training. (Captain Sydnor is on left, in bush hat and dark pullover.) Sydnor was tasked by Colonel Simons to establish the first FTT for Operation *Pincushion*. (*Courtesy of Ernie Tabata*)

Sergeant Eugene Gavigan, shown here in the camp for training a new K-2 company after the first K-2 deserted, was the radio operator for Captain Charles W. Murphy, who commanded FTT-11. (*Courtesy of Gene M. Gavigan*)

Second Lieutenant Berton E. Spivy, one of a batch of second lieutenants assigned to Special Forces in 1961, served as the team XO. (*Courtesy of Gene M. Gavigan*)

The team sergeant, Master Sergeant James V. Hanks, trains K-2 in movement techniques. (*Courtesy of Gene M. Gavigan*)

Captain Billy R. Wilson's ODA was split to operate as two FTTs in Savannakhet, as part of *White Star* Rotation VI. In the spring of 1962, the split detachments received orders and instruction from Colonel Simons on their new mission: supporting Operation *Pincushion*, where they would train K-3 and K-5 units. At left, Sergeant James F. Everett (radio operator) and Staff Sergeant Norman A. Doney, along with unidentified team member of the FTT, take a break between classes and instruction. (*Courtesy of James F. "Jim" Everett*)

As Operation *Pincushion* grew in scope and size, a B-team was established in Saravane. The SF teams for the northern guerrilla zone were placed under the command and control of Major Leroy E. Schulenberg's twenty-three-man B-detachment, FB-A. Here, members of Schulenberg's B-team at Saravane relax in front of the team house. Schulenberg is seated in center. (*Courtesy of Richard A. Iori*)

A newly recruited and outfitted Kha company stands uniform and equipment inspection in front of B-team house in Saravane. (*Photo courtesy of Rich Iori*)

One of the FTT camps at Site 106. (*Photo courtesy of Rich Iori*)

FTT-16, Captain Robert J. Arkley's detachment, established their camp at Site 106 to train K-9. Shown here are recruits practicing assembly and disassembly of the M1 rifle. (*Courtesy of Ivan E. Larson*)

Ivan Larson was the radio operator on FTT-16. (*Courtesy of Ivan E. Larson*)

Lieutenant Tom Bayha (in white T-shirt), the team XO, stands in front of camp medical clinic, known as "Mountel General Hospital." Second from far left, leaning on corner post and smoking a cigarette is Sergeant 1st Class Edward "Andy" Andrews (senior medic). Seated just inside is Sergeant Frederick D. Callahan, the senior radio operator. Sergeant John W. McIngvale is beneath sign, without a shirt. Lieutenant Bayha would later take a split detachment and about a hundred men to establish a forward operating location at Ban Nong Boua as part of Operation *Pincushion*. (*Courtesy of Tom Bayha*)

The area of operations formed by the triangle of Thakhek, Mahaxay, and Savannakhet saw constant, campaign-like fighting between the RLG forces and the Pathet Lao. This area was roughly bisected by the Se Bang Fai River. Pictured here is the imposing terrain east of Thakhek in the limestone karst mountains, near Mahaxay. Team *Shalikashvili* began initial operations in this area with GM-14 in late 1961. This is where the 7th BI of GM-14 located their camp. (*Courtesy of Sobichevsky family*)

Captain Henry L. Ellison, detachment commander of FTT-2 at Ban Houi Sai in 1962, assisted in the training of Yao guerrillas along with his team. This rare photo shows him and his team with the guerrilla formation. (*Courtesy of Henry Ellison family*)

PFC John F. McCallum, FTT-13 radio operator, prepares a meal while PFC Richard D. Osborne (demolitions) looks on. FTT-13 operated with Laotian forces along the Se Bang Fai River. (*Courtesy of John McCallum, FTT-13*)

Sergeant Vladimir Sobichevsky prepares commo check and message for transmission to Thakhek from Lieutenant "Pappy" Shelton's split team operating east of Thakhek (Lieutenant Shelton to right in photo). (*Courtesy of Sobichevsky family*)

The 7th BI battalion CP at main camp fighting position on the front lines. (*Courtesy of Sobichevsky family*)

PFC Clarence W. McCormick (FTT-40 team medic) tries out the French MAS-36 during operations in the vicinity of Thakhek. He wanted to take the weapon back to Okinawa; when firing the weapon some of the bullets were so old they turned sideways after leaving the barrel. (*Courtesy of Clarence W. McCormick, via Paul Kulick*)

Colonel Aito Keravouri, *White Star* VII commander, at his headquarters on the MAAG compound in Vientiane. The field control team in Vientiane would face three challenges during the last rotation of *White Star*: the siege and battle of Nam Tha, the Mahaxay and Se Bang Fai River campaign, and the extraction of over 400 U.S. Army Special Forces personnel from Laos in accordance with the 1962 peace and neutrality agreements. (*Courtesy of the USAJFK Special Warfare Museum, Lt. Col. Aito Keravouri collection*)

Pathet Lao and NVA shell the Nam Tha airstrip. (*Courtesy of "Too Tall" Simmons*)

Corporal John T. Haralson participated in the combat parachute operation during the siege of Nam Tha. He dropped as one of three SF advisors of FTT-21 on March 27, 1962, from a C-47 at 400 feet AGL, using a T-10 parachute. He was awarded Laotian combat wings for this mission, and later a CIB. (*Courtesy of John T. Haralson*)

Fighting and observation position of PFC Robert H. "Tex" Simmons (FTT-1 demolitions) near the front lines around Nam Tha during the siege. Shown in the photo is Simmons holding his M1-rifle with bayonet attached. The ridges behind the interpreter were Pathet Lao-occupied, as well as the ridges to the left and right outside of the photo. (*Courtesy of Robert H. "Too Tall" Simmons*)

SP4 Robert H. Simmons of FTT-1 preparing for security patrol operation at Ban Houei Sai. (*Courtesy of Robert H. "Too Tall" Simmons*)

Sergeant 1st Class Edmundson, team sergeant for FTT-1 at the advanced outpost at Ban Phoung. (*Photo courtesy of Don Valentine*)

Sergeant Ned Miller with BAR, his carbine, and grenades in a fighting position at the Ban Houei Sai airstrip. (*Courtesy of USAJFK Special Warfare Museum*)

Pictured left to right in Sayaboury: FTT-1's 1LT Robert G. Lunday, Staff Sergeant Lawrence P. Schell (light weapons), and Sergeant 1st Class Lionel F. "Choo Choo" Pinn (heavy weapons). (*Courtesy of Judy and Wenonah Pinn*)

FTT-22 under Lieutenant George Marecek advised Laotian forces at Kiou Ka Cham in 1962. Pictured left is the morning command group meeting with Colonel Wong. Lieutenant George Marecek is in center, with his interpreter to his right. PFC James W. Young, radio operator, stands behind Lieutenant Marecek. (*Photo courtesy of Major, Retired, James W. Young*)

Captain William J. Richardson's FTT at Paksong was typical of the period after the signing of the Declaration of Neutrality. The ODA was one of the last deploying teams in a batch of three teams scheduled for deployment to Laos in late June, 1962. Very little activity occurred and Laotian troops remained, for the most part, in static positions. Seen here are some of the activities of Captain Richardson's FTT, with students of the NCO academy at Paksong. (*Courtesy of William T. "Bill" Richardson, Jr.*)

Pincushion teams often spent their remaining time in Laos working on civil affairs projects. Captain Arkley's team helped to build a schoolhouse for local villagers. The ceremony to dedicate the schoolhouse was attended by the villagers and local dignitaries. (*Courtesy of Ivan E. Larson*)

Captain Rich Iori, U.S. Army Special Forces, stands before the RLAF T-6 squadron at Wattay airfield in early 1962. In October, SF teams were "counted out" of the country at Wattay airport by the ICC, while Pathet Lao soldiers lined the fences on the airfield and laughed. (*Courtesy of Rich A. Iori*)

Project 404 ARMAs and 46th SF

Left: The unofficial insignia of Project 404. Right: The Deputy Chief JUSMAG was headquartered in the Capital Hotel in Bangkok where Project 404 was administered. (*Courtesy of Retired CWO4 Raymond J. Millaway collection, Project 404*)

LAOS

PROJECT
404

An original Project 404 handbook. (*Courtesy of Retired CWO4 Raymond J. Millaway collection*)

Raymond J. Millaway receives direct warrant officer appointment from Brigadier General Richard Trefry, Deputy Chief JUSMAG, and Colonel Ronald W. Clegg in Udorn, Thailand. (*Courtesy of Retired CWO4 Raymond J. Millaway.*)

Major Reuben L. Mooradian served as a Project 404 ARMA for MR-III in Savannakhet in 1967. He served a second tour as an ARMA in Pakse in 1969. He is shown here at left as a detachment commander during his first tour to Laos as commander of FTT-24, advising GM-11 south of Luang Prabang. (*Courtesy of the USAJFK Special Warfare Museum, Lt. Col. Aito Keravouri collection*)

Lieutenant Colonel Alan E. Rozon was the Project 404 ARMA to advise General Vang Pao at Long Tieng in 1968. He spent his time there to help organize artillery units on Skyline Ridge (shown at top). Although lack of transportation plagued many of the Project 404 ARMAs, Rozon was able to avail himself of a Russian jeep, captured on the Plaine des Jarres. (*Courtesy of Al Rozon*)

Major Dennis W. Lid walks with the FAN G5, Colonel Chongsaly, at Vang Vieng. (*Courtesy of Dennis W. Lid*)

Lao and Hmong T-28s at Moung Kassy positioned to support combat operations at Moung Soui. SFC Joseph M. Bossi served as a Project 404 ARMA at Moung Soui, along with SSG David L. Pompili (artillery advisor). Both of the advisors flew with RLAF pilots to serve as observers (Pompili was also flight qualified on the L-19 artillery spotter aircraft). They both were present during the Battle of Moung Soui and were among the last to be evacuated from the airstrip. (*Courtesy of John R. Cassady, LTC, USA Retired, Project 404 ARMA*)

Major John R. "Jack" Cassady (left), MR-V Project 404 advisor, with Jack Spey, Project 404 AOC commander at Pakse under Project 404, *Palace Dog*. Cassady served as an ARMA between 1970 and 1971, first at Camp Chinaimo, and then later at Vang Vieng with the FAN. (*Courtesy of John R. Cassady, LTC, U.S. Army, Retired*)

Major John Cassady with Major Thong Kham during the FAN's Nam San Valley operation. (*Courtesy of John R. Cassady, LTC, U.S. Army, Retired*)

Lieutenant Colonel Charlie W. Brewington served as an ARMA at Long Tieng, 1970–1971. He was one of the Project 404 advisors evacuated when the Pathet Lao attacked Sam Thong. Here he stands with some of Vang Pao's special guerrilla unit members on the Plaine des Jarres. (*Courtesy of Charlie Brewington*)

Sam Thong (LS-20) destruction after NVA attack. Project 404 advisors were rescued during the attack by Bob Moberg flying the army attaché's helicopter, along with other Project 404 ARMA detailees, including Sergeant Jeff Hotujec. (*Courtesy of Steven R. Schofield, Major, SF, USA, Retired*)

The unit flash of the 46th Special Forces Company (Independent) in Thailand was black, bordered by yellow. The "bar sinister," the diagonal running from top right to bottom left contained the red, white and blue of the Thai national colors. The diagonal running in this direction indicated the unit had no parent organization, in accordance with the Institute of Heraldry. The yellow border signified its connection to the 1st Special Forces group (Airborne), with operations in Southeast Asia, and black background to symbolize the clandestine and unconventional warfare nature of Special Forces. (*Unit flash courtesy of Gary Perkowski*)

Various members of the 46th Special Forces Company (Independent) serving in Thailand during the war in Laos. Special Forces medic Sergeant William F. Rouleau (front row, third from the left, seated) served at the secret camp at Site 603 in Phitsanoluk. He, along with other members of SFT-31, trained Hmong special guerrilla units (SGUs) for use by General Vang Pao in MR-II. (*Courtesy of Gary Perkowski*)

Major Frank Jaks was the 46th Special Forces Independent Company B-detachment commander who oversaw the secret training camps in Thailand. (*46th Company Yearbook*)

As the war continued, attrition began to take a toll on the manning for General Vang Pao's special guerrilla units and guerrilla battalions. Recruits were often children and teenagers, picking up the fight where their dead fathers left off. (*Courtesy of James K. "Jim" Bruton, 46th SF, via DOD Project 404 personnel*)

Camp at Nong Takoo, where B4610 trained combat recon teams for Laos. (*46th SF Year Book*)

An unknown team member of ODA-2 instructs GM heavy weapons unit at Wat Phu, Laos, on the 106mm recoilless rifle. (*Courtesy of James K. "Jim" Bruton, 46th SF, via DOD Project 404 personnel*)

ambush position. Before him was open savannah-like terrain which would leave enemy forces exposed as they came south down the trail.

Lieutenant Sutton and Sergeant Flaherty positioned themselves with the battalion CP, located behind the blocking company on the trail. Sergeant 1st Class Francis E. Bushing (demolitions), Sergeant 1st Class Charles G. James (medic) and PFC Norman E. Johnson (radio operator) positioned themselves with the western flank company, along with the team's interpreter.

Around 1400 hours an enemy battalion of Pathet Lao approached, coming down the trail in a column which stretched for almost three kilometers. BP-11 sprang the ambush. The Pathet Lao battalion reconfigured into a "V" formation to counterattack, supported by machine guns, while maneuvering units both east and west to flank BP-11's positions on the two ridgelines.

It was a large engagement with heavy fires and use of hand grenades. The 11th BP looked to become overwhelmed, forcing them to begin withdrawing south. Lieutenant Sutton loaded and fired a flare, the team's prearranged signal for bug-out. Sutton and Flaherty moved south, then west into the jungle, where they established a RON position, hoping to link up with any remaining members of the team. (It appeared the interpreter fled early, and defected to the Pathet Lao.) What Sutton did not know was that Sergeant Bushing, Sergeant James, and PFC Norman E. Johnson had evaded southwest and were picked up by a rescue helicopter the next day.

Sutton and Flaherty moved westward, and eventually turned to the southwest to evade their pursuers, before their rescue. They had been running through the jungles for about a week. They were pulled from the mission with the 11th BP when the battalion was ordered to move to Nam Tha to help break the Pathet Lao siege.

They were evacuated to Vientiane for a new mission. Sutton and his men were moved to support the Site 20 operations (Sam Thong) with another ODA until the arrival of Major Faistenhammer's B-detachment to that location. They assisted with the training of the Hmong SGUs, helped to build the camp facilities, improved the airstrip, and provided liaison to Agency operatives at the site.

FTT Thakhek, BI-7

Captain Joseph H. Johnson's ODA would be another full team which was split upon its arrival to Laos. The team XO was Lieutenant Ralph W. "Pappy" Shelton, a well-respected operator. Master Sergeant Lonnie J. Ledford was the team sergeant. The detachment prepared for the mission, loaded their team boxes, and deployed via a C-124 to Laos on January 9, 1962. (They would be one of the *White Star* Rotation VII teams to be extended on their six-month TDY and served until all teams departed in October of 1962.)

After their arrival in Bangkok, they flew to Vientiane where they were then trucked to the team house in Thakhek. Upon arrival in Thakhek, the team was split. First

Lieutenant Shelton led his half detachment east of Thakhek to serve with the 7th BI, located in a remote camp in Khammouane Province. The camp was situated in a limestone mountain area near the North Vietnamese border. The team hiked in to this remote location, about twenty-five kilometers from Thakhek (a two-day journey).

They arrived at the camp, finding it to be sited on volcanic, lava-type rock. Many of the Laotian troops they found there had the seats of their pants worn through from sitting on the jagged and sharp surfaces.

Sergeant Vladimir Sobichevsky spent three and a half years in the 10th SFG at Bad Tölz; when his enlistment was up he left the army to try civilian life in San Francisco, CA. When he saw a newspaper article about Special Forces in Laos, he went to an army recruiter and rejoined to serve again in Special Forces. He was still in his ninety-day separation period, so he was not required to re-attend basic training, and also retained his sergeant, E-5 rank. When he got to Fort Bragg, he joined Captain Joe Johnson's team preparing for deployment to Laos.

When told by the team leader he would be remaining at the team house in Thakhek as a radio operator, Sobichevsky pleaded with Lieutenant Shelton to take him into the field; he was young and wanted to be in the combt zone, not sitting in a house monitoring a radio. He convinced "Pappy" that his communications and demolitions skills, as well as his medical cross-training, would be invaluable to the team.[29]

Lieutenant Shelton's team also included Sergeant 1st Class Donald J. Talamine (intel/opns and senior NCO), Staff Sergeant James C. Williams (weapons), SP4 Gareth E. Brookhart (medic), and SP4 Frank W. Lepp (demolitions). "Zeke," the pet Gibbon, rounded out the team roster in the field.

The FTT transitioned with the outgoing team, but only for one day. The departing team relayed to them that the biggest issue with the Lao battalion seemed to be lack of parts for weapons maintenance. After passing on gear and equipment, the outgoing team departed for their two-day hike back to Thakhek.

The mission for the team was to gather intelligence on the enemy situation, train and advise the BI in counterinsurgency, help the unit to be combat ready, and repel the enemy if attacked. It was during the period of the ceasefire in Laos, which apparently was not observed by the insurgents in the area. The camp received frequent probes, sometimes two to three a week.

The team was only armed with their personal handguns, anticipating their military weapons would be issued to them from the outgoing team. (Lieutenant Shelton was later able to "buy" a .45-caliber Thompson sub-machine gun.) The largest detriment to their operation was the lack of maps.

Sobichevsky joined the team as their radio operator, linking up with them later during an H-34 resupply flight. He recounted his initial arrival to join the team. "At that time, as I looked around, I began to understand the foolishness of youth that I worked so hard to get out there. I mean we were in the middle of nowhere! Surrounded by jungle and the enemy."[30]

BI-7 had been well trained by the outgoing team and was manned by 400 men. The commander, Major Say, had three companies; two on line (about 1,000 meters from the battalion CP) with one behind in reserve, reinforced with the battalion mortar company.

The battalion commander did not seem too aggressive; he often sat in his chair at the CP and awaited status reports from his officers and the SF team, who visited the front lines every day. The team tried a proven method to involve him in the tactical dispositions of his unit—they made a "sand table map" for everyone's use.

Sergeant James C. Williams was the weapons NCO on the team. He joined the Army on September 1, 1950. He was assigned to the training regiment of the Army Jump School at Fort Benning, GA. From there, he transferred to the training command at Fort Chafee, Arkansas, the 5th Armored Division. After a short stint working as a civilian when his enlistment expired, he reenlisted for Special Forces in November of 1953, and joined Company A of the 77th SFG (A). He then served in the 10th SFG (A) from 1953–1958. He returned to Fort Bragg and served in the newly formed 6th SFG (A), and then once again served with the 77th SFG (A) for his first tour to Laos in 1959, as a trainer on the *Hotfoot I* rotation in Luang Prabang.[31]

James Williams explained the use of the sand table:

> The sand table is a training tool or aid used by the SF to show the troops' positions on a map. It's meant to give a commander a "look" at his defensive forces at their current locations and we decided to use this device to educate the Lao commander on the configuration of his defensive positions, and the locations of his forces, with the "lay" of the ground, the elevation and relief; also the "shape" of these areas … it was open, like a child's sandbox. We used a system of "grid" lines and we used rocks to build up the mountain ranges and created a couple of termite mounds. We chipped away at some clay to create the contours of these mountains. Our scale was large, 1:250,000.[32]

In this way, the commander learned of the fields of fire for his positions with respect to enemy positions. The sand-table map depicted where his early warning systems were emplaced and possible locations to site the 75mm recoilless rifle. Dead ground and air approaches for their resupply helicopter were also outlined.

One of the first security tasks for the team was organizing an escape-and-evasion plan in the event they had to bug out. Sobichevsky explained the plan:

> So we got settled. At that time, once again, no weapons, or maybe it was later, Pappy Shelton, Talamine, began to discuss emergency procedures. We had no weapons! What would happen if we were overrun? And a primitive plan was: we would sleep with our clothes on and our boots on. We would wear our compass always around our neck and the signaling mirror on parachute cord around our neck. They figured out approximate azimuths, and it would have to be approximate, that if we were overrun, we had no weapons to fight with and we had some machete looking things, that we would cut our way through the jungle toward the direction

of the Mekong River. Once again, Thakhek was on the Mekong River. And then find our way to Thakhek. Thank God! This never happened. Thank God.

... 'Cause I don't know, yeah, we would have made it, but I don't know—water, food, I have no idea, the jungle was horrific. I guess we would have made it, but it was the best plan at that time.

When we made that escape and evasion I as the radio operator taped, or a rubber band, I don't remember, the one-time pads with ¼ lb demolition so when we had to bug-ass I would pull the fuse and the one-time pad would be exploded.[33]

Not many days after devising the escape and evasion plan the Pathet Lao began shelling the battalion position with 81mm mortar fire. Although few rounds fell near the team, "Pappy" Shelton soon organized a work party, and together with the Laotians dug a team bunker with large logs placed overhead.

The FTT did not conduct training classes; their approach was to advise and pitch in wherever the unit needed help. The team was provided with two interpreters.

Getting a good helicopter LZ was a priority. The team found an appropriate spot southwest of their position where an H-34 could approach and land out of visual range of enemy fire. Laotian troops assisted in cutting down the trees with their machetes then burning the stumps to clear the land. Surrounding jungle was burned out further to make a DZ for Air America drops. With this task complete, the BI could now receive food resupply, and most importantly, evacuate their sick and wounded to the regimental hospital in Thakhek. This proved beneficial one day when a Laotian soldier accidentally stepped on a landmine. It was the first exposure to combat for the young men on the FTT, especially Brookhart the medic and Sobichevsky.

Sergeant Williams wanted to rid the camp of the perimeter incursions by local Pathet Lao. The BI treated the harassment tactics as a nuisance and did not seem to have the warrior spirit to counterattack or put an end to the harassment. Normally when attacked or probed, most of the *tahans* fired their weapons in the air. Sobichevsky was not impressed by their soldierly skills:

Couple of comments about my impression of the Laotian soldiers. They were kids! Very young, grinning, smiling. Major Say was hard-nosed. His battalion or brigade (whatever) headquarters was a tree where he would sit on one side with a clipboard and a map. On the other side of the tree was a radio operator with a PRC-10.

... They had firefights in the distance. And it was indicative to me, the results were indicative; sometimes the firefights in the distance between Pathet Lao and Royal Laotians would last a long time! Now, how long? I don't know. If you have constant firing lasting a minute, two minutes, that's a long time! Yet the results, you would think, there would be fifty people killed. But the results were that maybe one guy would be killed and maybe one guy would be wounded and I thought about that.

I think the Pathet Lao were children just like the 7th, they were like children. When I mention that violent fight, firefight, very few casualties. I think that if the PL were NVA they would have overrun us.[34]

Sergeant Williams traveled to Thakhek and procured some white phosphorus mortar rounds, along with some parachute flares. He told the man at the ammo dump his plan:

> At the next attack or probe, we're going to light up the area with parachute flares and when they look up it will temporarily blind them. Then, we'll traverse the mortar tubes scattering the high explosive [hot steel mortar rounds] to baptize the enemy in a shield-of-steel across our defensive position, left to right. And, we'll do the same with the WP, burning everything in a 50–150 meter radius per round at temperatures exceeding 2,200 degrees Fahrenheit. The next time the enemy attacks we're going to light up the mountain; we're going to kill them all.[35]

The munitions were delivered to the camp by helicopter, taking two trips. The ammo was divided out among the mortar crews, who put it to good effect. After a couple of attempts to breach the defensive wire, and being mortared, the Pathet Lao soon stopped trying. Another technique to kill enemy forces was the use of mines along infiltration trails into the camp.

The detachment trained the BI to conduct sweeping reconnaissance patrols out to 3,000 meters from their position. Frequently, the ODA patrolled with the Ranger platoon of the BI.

During one of the patrols, team members observed a Russian cargo aircraft delivering supplies to the Neutralists east of the BI. A plan soon formed to climb to the top of a mountain and shoot down at the aircraft (it was making cargo drops at about 1,000-foot altitude) with the recoilless rifle. Williams accompanied the entire Ranger platoon with the recoilless rifle and three rounds broken down between all the men, but after an arduous climb, and out of water, it happened to be the day the aircraft did not appear. (It was just as well the engagement did not occur; it was the ceasefire period before the negotiations and would have probably caused a diplomatic incident.)

In October, the team received orders to withdraw back to Thakhek for their eventual out-processing from Laos. Many on the team sold their pistols to the 7th BI. Sergeant Sobichevsky, who had contracted hepatitis about three months into the mission, was sent to the Seventh Day Adventist hospital in Bangkok, remaining as a patient at the hospital until in better condition, allowing for his return to the States. The war was over for Sergeant Sobichevsky, and in October, for the entire Operation *White Star* FTTs.

FTT-20 Thakhek, 24th BI

Captain Melvin G. Williams commanded FTT-20 at Thakhek, arriving with *White Star* Rotation VII in late May of 1962. His team was out of the Okinawa-based 1st SFG (A). The mission for FTT-20 was training the 24th BI. Upon arrival at the unit, they found BI-24 to be an already well-trained unit, so they focused on helping new recruits by running a basic infantry course for them. The other half of the detachment split under First Lieutenant William C. Hazen and operated as FA-36 at Camp Chinaimo outside of Vientiane.

FTT-20 differed from other teams in that they did not maneuver and live out in the field with the 24th BI. Instead, they drove fifteen to twenty miles outside of town to the training camp location. To Sergeant 1st Class Clarence W. McCormick, the team medic, other than running a dispensary for the teams at Thakhek (due to the fact the town had a couple of doctors and sufficient medical facilities, negating the need for any MEDCAPS), the work was very boring. To keep busy, "Mac" took on an additional task to service the helipad near the team house. "I mostly found myself servicing the helo pad near us; helping refuel the helicopters. There was no threat in Thakhek, but I would go out to visit the teams and the training, flying with Air America pilots. We would take some ground fire, but the pilots were pretty good about knowing where the friendlies were and where the Pathet Lao were. (They could point out these areas while flying around.)"[36]

The team had a lot of free time to spend in town and to attend socials, "earning their per diem." On occasion, some of these events took place across the Mekong River in Nakhon Phanom (NKP). Other entertainment included the team pet, a gibbon named "Lefty," because he had no right hand.

During his trips to the field, some as far away as a hundred miles, McCormick could not tell that the war was even going on. "We did service outlying teams and local villagers in the areas sometimes as far away as fifty to sixty miles (chow, ammo, personnel). I personally was awed by being in a supposed war zone, the lack of infrastructure, schools and the people living out in the jungle and never seeing a major town."[37]

It was not a great introduction to the war for the team. FTT-20 turned over the mission with the 43rd BV to Captain Maurice G. Bostwick, who arrived with his split detachment in June of 1962; Bostwick and his team would remain in Thakhek as the new FTT-20 until their early departure at the end of August (with the signing of the Peace and Neutrality Agreement in July of 1962). Captain Williams and his detachment remained at the team house in Thakhek to provide support to other SF teams out in the field. They departed Laos in September.

Mahaxay was never retaken by the FAR and the Pathet Lao continued to operate from this location, despite the campaign-like efforts to evict them.

CHAPTER NINE

White Star Foreign Internal Defense (FID) Activities: Schools, Academies, and Proficiency Courses

"Foreign Internal Defense—The participation by the civilian and military agencies of a government in any of the action programs taken by another government to free and protect its society from subversion, lawlessness, insurgency, and terrorism."

JOINT PUB 1–02 & 3–07.1 (04)

There were a variety of foreign internal defense (FID) missions conducted by the Special Forces teams outside of the requirement to train and fight with the infantry battalions of the FAR. Among these were officer and NCO schools, the training of the Police academy in Savannakhet, and airborne proficiency courses run in both Vientiane and Seno. There were also Ranger-style courses and specialized military training teams (MTTs), used to conduct courses in artillery and the conduct of indirect fires.

To conduct FID in Laos required SF teams to build facilities for the conduct of training; this began with the three 1959 *Hotfooot I* teams serving in MR-V, the Vientiane region, although they themselves would not present any courses. The three teams were FA-1, under Captain Dornford "Hiram" Walker, FA-4 led by Captain Lewis D. Allen, and Captain Donald Brewer's FA-26.

Two teams went to work at Kilometer 22 outside of Vientiane and built a training facility which would also house officer schools: a battalion commander's course and a company commander's course. At Kilometer 17, an FA was involved in the construction of a Ranger school and a psychological warfare school.[1]

Two of the representative FID missions were courses taught by Special Forces teams at the NCO academy in Paksong (there were other NCO schools in each military region) and the officer candidate school at Dong Hene.

NCO Academy Paksong

Sergeant James W. "Jim" Kraus had just returned to the 1st SFG on Okinawa from his tour in Vietnam when SF Detachment 14 was already alerted to go to Laos. The team was led by Captain Leon M. Hope, the detachment commander, and Captain

Richard N. "Rocky" Lewis. Master Sergeant Robert D. Hede was the team sergeant. The team packed four boxes and flew to Bangkok, then on to Vientiane, on October 15, 1961. They did not know the exact nature of their mission, but during their predeployment period they focused on being prepared to teach and train Lao BIs on small-unit tactics, weapons proficiency, and Ranger-like patrolling. Upon their arrival in Pakse, and link-up with the B-team, the detachment was broken down into two split-team FTTs. Captain Lewis took his split detachment to Attopeu, along with his team sergeant, William D. "Billy" Waugh. CIA

Captain Hope's FTT consisted of five men with a mission to establish a Laotian NCO academy at Paksong. It is not known exactly what team numbers may have been assigned, but some evidence suggests Captain Hope was FA-14 and the Attopeu team was FA-14A, after their 1st Group team-numbering system. Now retired, Colonel Jim Kraus described their arrival to the B-team location and the subsequent splitting up of the team:

> We got our in-country mission from the B-team at Pakse. The B-team had a compound and a building in town, nothing fancy, in a residential area and not requiring any large security signature—no wire or things like that. I'm guessing the B-team was maybe about twenty to twenty-five folks at that time—not too big, but operating on a 24-hour basis. Billy Waugh and half the team were sent south to Attopeu via Air America H-34s to train volunteer infantry. We were assigned to establish a Laotian NCO Academy at Paksong.[2]

Captain Hope departed the B-Team compound driving with his men in a ¾-ton truck and followed the Route 23 black-top road to Paksong, which was located about forty-three kilometers east of Pakse. (Other members of the FTT included Master Sergeant Robert "Bob" D. Hede, team sergeant; Sergeant Patrick D. Ballard, demolitions; Sergeant Bruce E. Warner, radio operator; and Sergeant James W. Kraus, weapons.) Paksong was the site of a Laotian military camp with a building for the NCO academy. The team chose to billet on the compound. To help with the instruction, a Thai SF team of approximately six men assisted the FTT. Notes Jim Kraus, "They were a great asset."[3]

Across the street from the NCO academy stood a medical facility run by Filipinos from Operation *Brotherhood*. (Operation *Brotherhood* was a State Department-sponsored initiative to improve medical care in Laos as part of the hearts-and-minds program.) The Filipino Brotherhood often provided the team with supplies and also information concerning the threat situation in the surrounding area.

The NCO course was designed to last four to six weeks in length. There were about twenty-five Laotian NCOs in each course. Notes Kraus:

> On a scale of their proficiency from one to ten, I would give them about a two. We set up the NCO academy curriculum and training very similar to our Ranger-type doctrine, focused on patrolling and small-unit tactics. The course was designed off an existing POI we had that we had used earlier on an MTT to train the Indonesian National Police (so even though we did not know the mission beforehand, we were able to get on about the running of the course using

those POIs, adapted to the situation). Our patrolling courses were in the area around Paksong. I don't remember any combat, but once on a reconnaissance patrol with the students we observed some Pathet Lao hauling rice with animals and wagons. Since we were on reconnaissance, we did not engage and merely reported the sighting. Other than that, there was not a lot of enemy activity in our area.[4]

Although never being engaged by the Pathet Lao, there was a hidden danger to the team. The Pathet Lao were very good at agent infiltration of Lao military units in the region as well as operating an underground intelligence and support network in the Mekong valley. The purpose of the underground cells was to monitor and observe the activities of Americans operating in Laos.

The team did not realize how well this network functioned, but found out later in their tour. To relax, the team enjoyed visiting Pakse. They were able to befriend a Lao there, whose father was French and mother Laotian. The team was invited on occasion to the gentlemen's mother's house, who cooked dinners for them. They heard a story later that the Lao man was a Pathet Lao battalion commander!

After three months of serving at the Paksong NCO academy, Captain Hope and his split-team were sent to Attopeu to rejoin with the rest of FA-14. (Later in his career, Colonel Jim Kraus commanded the 5th Special Forces Group during Operation *Desert Shield/Desert Storm*.)

Dong Hene Officer's Candidate School

In early 1962 the FAR senior command decided to open a reserve officer candidate school. Its purpose was to provide a venue for higher achievement for young men and to counteract Pathet Lao propaganda attempts. The youth of the country were being lured by the Pathet Lao to better themselves by attending communist military training camps in the jungles around Vientiane. Providing an institution to better themselves through becoming Laotian officers counteracted the propaganda message.

An old army post at Dong Hene was chosen as the site for the school, astride Route 9, between Savannakhet and Moung Phine. This was also an area of Pathet Lao activity. It was hoped a byproduct of placing a military school in that location would provide "realistic" training for the officer candidates and get them involved in actual combat. It would be hard, however, to support the school logistically if the Pathet Lao ever interdicted Route 9, west of the school.[5]

General Phoumi Nosovan directed Colonel Sananikone to tackle the challenge of establishing the school. The odds were against Sananikone; there was little in terms of support, equipment and supplies to open the school. Worse, no weapons were available for issue to the cadre and the students. Colonel Sananikone coordinated with the U.S. embassy MAAG to solve most of the problems, but the MAAG had one caveat: would he use American instructors to solve the shortage of qualified Laotian officer instructors?

The deal was agreed to, and one week later *White Star* advisors reported to Dong Hene, bringing arms for the compound. Colonel Sananikone reflected on the arrival of the SF team: "The Special Forces soldiers of the White Star teams were enthusiastic trainers. For the basic subjects, such as rifle marksmanship, the Americans worked directly with the Lao trainees. When more theoretical subjects were taught, the Americans used Thai interpreters. Most significantly, the White Star teams taught a type of tactics that was new to the Lao Army schools: insurgency and counterinsurgency."[6]

Sananikone continued, "Up to this time we had followed the French practice of emphasizing conventional infantry tactics. While the Americans conducted the weapons and tactical training, Lao instructors taught the courses in military discipline, regulations, and civic action."[7]

Field training exercises (FTX) were held just prior to class graduation, often involving live combat patrols. During the six month period of *White Star* support, two groups of 120 officer candidates each, graduated.

Captain Maurice J. Healy deployed with a full detachment to Laos in mid-January 1962. His team leadership included First Lieutenant Edward J. F. Thomas as the detachment XO and Master Sergeant Robert "Moe" Frander as the team sergeant. The team was alerted at Fort Bragg, NC, for its *White Star* mission and entered the isolation facilities at Smoke Bomb Hill. They received language training and orientation briefings to prepare them for their mission. (Of note, the Company C operations officer was "Charging" Charlie Beckwith.)

FTT-38's mission would be providing instruction and advisory assistance to the Laotian officer's candidate school at Dong Hene. They would be the only foreign instructors at the camp; there were no French trainers, and there was no prior SF team to transition with. (The only exposure the team would have with French military personnel was social, in the town of Seno, when they went for a meal or to buy bread.)

The team settled into a longhouse on the compound. They were aware of the Pathet Lao threat in the area: for defense, the team carried .45-caliber pistols and M1s and some M2 carbines. They also carried Thompson .45-caliber sub-machine guns and had a .30-caliber machine gun and a 60mm mortar. Some on the team preferred to carry their own personal pistols, usually the Ruger Blackhawk of .357 caliber. The team took advantage of the weapons ranges at the camp to maintain their proficiency. They also built a bunker in the event of an attack on the camp. The team performed their duties in military fatigues and wore the typical camouflaged boonie hat favored by SF in Laos.

For communications with higher the team was fortunate; they had a gasoline generator to power the radio and RS-1, along with a DY88, in order to make their two to three daily commo checks with the B-team. Sergeant Robert G. "Bob" Willis was one of the radio operators on the team (Sergeant James Rivers was the other commo man).

Sergeant Willis had served in the North Carolina National Guard, 30th Infantry, as a gunner on a 155mm howitzer crew (1956). He completed basic training at Fort Jackson, SC, and further trained in CW (Morse code procedures). He was then assigned to the 50th Airborne Signal Battalion at Fort Bragg and completed his RTT course at Fort Gordon, GA. While in the 50th, he completed Ranger School and the Cold Weather Mountain School at Fort Greely, Alaska. He also completed airborne training and jumpmaster school, and then volunteered for Special Forces, joining Company C in the 7th Special Forces Group. He was assigned to Captain Healy's team prior to their departure to Laos.

At Dong Hene, the detachment made up their lesson plans and a POI for the officer's candidate course. With two Laotian interpreters to assist, the team began classes. Bob Willis described the overall design of the course: "We started the first class of OCS at Dong Hene; there were no USSF teams at the Academy prior to ours. We made up lesson plans, with a POI. I gave radio instruction on the AN/GRC-109 and antennas. Other classes consisted of our MOS skills (commo, demo, medical, weapons, and so forth), along with tactics. Each class of officer candidates was approximately fifty men. The training was designed for eight weeks, as I recall."[8]

The medics played a crucial role in keeping the team healthy, running a clinic for the students, and conducting medical calls in the surrounding villages (Sergeant 1st Class Elmo Clark and Staff Sergeant Donald Dougan).

The team did not anticipate combat with the Pathet Lao while serving as instructors. There was only one minor incident: one night a shot was fired at Sergeant Willis when he was manning the .30-caliber-machine-gun position while on guard duty. (No one ever knew the source of the fire.) There were also indirect threats, as described by Willis: "There was also the threat of mines on the road to Seno. The Pathet Lao would often just lay them on top of the road. We would see them and stop, then shoot our submachine guns with plunging fire to explode them! We got into no major fire-fights in Dong Hene."[9]

Sergeant Willis was transferred for a short time to assist with the Kha tribal guerrilla training program on the Plateau de Bolovens. He returned to his team before their departure from Laos.

Proficiency Courses

Many of the FTTs advising the GMs and BIs, BPs, and BVs selected some of their best *tahan* students to attend mini-courses in scouting and reconnaissance, sniper, ranger, and commando courses as a means to improve the combat proficiency of their units. Other known courses conducted by the FTTs include the following:

- A Ranger course conducted by Captain Stewart and Sergeant Meadows of FTT-59 for Hmong guerrillas during Operation *Pincushion*
- The training of commando platoons for GM-11 conducted by Captain Reuben Mooradian's FTT-24, south of Luang Prabang
- The NCO academy at Luang Prabang conducted by First Lieutenant Ammerman (FTT-2A)
- An airborne platoon of the Hmong SGU GM trained by Detachment Faistenhammer at Site 20
- The airborne course for BPs under GM-15 at Seno, conducted by FTT-21, Captain Buck's team, and followed by FTT-27, Captain Prewitt's team
- The Laotian officer's academy course at Dong Hene, conducted by Captain Zummo's FTT

FTT-24 Commando Platoons, GM-11

Captain Reuben L. Mooradian's FTT-24 was assigned to train Laotian infantry at an old French military base south of Luang Prabang. Along with training the infantrymen, the team was additionally tasked with training GM-11's two commando platoons (1st and 2nd platoons). Not all the courses worked to perfection. In FID, working with foreign forces has its own pitfalls. Mooradian describes what they had to work with: "We were in a situation we did not expect. Our assigned troops for training were Lao border squads—commandos. They were commandos in name only. They were very ignorant—they did not know how to even use a compass. We taught them mortars, weapons, small unit tactics, but it was very difficult based on their education and skill level. Again, they were called commandos, but we could tell they had not been trained very well."[10]

Mooradian continued about the training: "If you planned a week's worth of training on the schedule, it actually took about three weeks to get it done, due to the troops' education and youth. Me, Worobel and Coffey always talked over what we could do to accomplish the training. Coffey was very innovative. When we were instructing tactics, he had cut out soldier figures from the C-ration crates and used them as illustrations for how to maneuver.[11]

"We had the same group the whole time we were there; no one new was rotated in. It was an under strength battalion. We only had twenty guys at most who would ever show up for a training session."[12]

FTT-27 at Seno, Basic Airborne Training

PFC Thomas E. Holladay was the junior radio operator on FTT-27 at Seno. The team was commanded by Captain Clifford W. Prewitt. First Lieutenant George F. Harrison was the detachment XO, and Sergeant Arif R. Zaky served as the team sergeant.

Holladay and John McCallum, his friend in the 101st (and also a *White Star* veteran), were intrigued one day by a poster in the recruiter's office of an SF operator scaling down a cliff, and they both put in for a transfer to 7th SFG at Fort Bragg.

Holladay had wanted to train in demolitions, but there were openings only for medics or communications operators. He chose to be a radio operator, and after assignment to Company B in Training Group, he was sent to complete a three-month radio training course. He then completed other "3" designator-required courses and was sent to Okinawa in March of 1962. In a very short time, he was alerted and put on orders for Laos. Holladay described his team's mission:

> We replaced Captain Buck's team, who had just gotten back from the siege and battle of Nam Tha with the 55th BP. Part of our job, along with basic airborne training, was to refurbish and retrain the remnants of 55th BP after the Nam Tha battle … Our job was to run basic airborne training along with given small unit tactics classes, like night ambush, etc. All the training aids and airborne mock-ups were already there and had been provided by the outgoing team. There was no enemy threat to our operations.[13]

Camp Chinaimo—FTT-43A, *White Star* Rotation VI

FTT-43A was the other half of Captain Bud Sydnor's team; when Sydnor moved to the Bolovens to start Operation *Pincushion*, Lieutenant William E. Kellenberger remained in Vientiane with his split-team to train BV-22 at the Camp Chinaimo training center (October 1961).

Camp Chinaimo had a parade field in the center, surrounded by barracks around the sides, with a big, prominent flagpole in the center. (During the training, the team observed soldier punishment FAR style: soldiers were tied to the flagpole by their thumbs to sit out in the sun or rain, all day.)

They were provided an interpreter named "Monty" to assist with the training (they did not know if he was Lao or Thai).

Kellenberger described the POI and training during his assignment: "We built a POI for the training of the Lao. The types of classes included demolitions training, use of the bayonet, physical conditioning. The rest of the team handled their particular MOS—commo, medical, and the other SF skill sets. We also did tactics training, basic field and patrol movement, and then a live-fire exercise. I don't remember any French military trainers there—we were alone. We did not issue gear to the Laotians, we only concerned ourselves with their training. We did not have Lao counterparts attached to us during this training."[14]

Sergeant 1st Class Ernest K. "Ernie" Tabata was the demolitions sergeant on the team, and an experienced NCO. Lieutenant Kellenberger appreciated having some "old hand" NCOs to assist him. FA-43A's team sergeant, Master Sergeant Wallace L. Klink and Sergeant 1st Class Fred A. Edwards (medic) were also a part of the FTT, along with three other Sergeants E-5.

Tabata describes the training mission from his perspective:

> Our mission at Vientiane was to proceed to Camp Chinaimo, about seven kilometers out of Vientiane. Here we were greeted by a training officer, a captain, from the Royal Lao Army. He introduced us to Lieutenant Meng, one of the platoon leaders. He broke down the units into several groups by MOS. Then we had outdoor classrooms, open fields, and later the multi-arms range to conduct our training. Training was done in coordination with Thai interpreters at different locations. Subjects taught were small arms, light automatic weapons, the BAR, French bolt-action rifles, U.S. carbine M1, 57mm recoilless rifle, and the 60mm mortars. Last but not least, small unit tactics, ambush and counter-ambush, and then all of this ended up with a live-fire exercise, held at night.
>
> We trained for five weeks and at the end of the training, one of our BVs, BV-52, was called out to defend a village. They made contact with some Pathet Lao elements and were victorious in the battle. Our good training paid off.[15]

In the last part of December, FTT-43A got word to reunite with the "other half" of the A-team under Captain Sydnor, down on the Bolovens.

Special Forces conduct foreign internal defense missions to increase the capacity of a host nation to tackle internal insurgency and subversion with appropriately trained counterinsurgency forces. FID also enables host nation capabilities through improving the proficiency of internal security forces. Ambassadors used their military assistance and security assistance programs to help the RLG in its fight against the NVA and Pathet Lao. Select *White Star* teams performed FID programs as one of the means to enable the ambassador to achieve his policy goals.

CHAPTER TEN

1962: *White Star* Rotations VI & VII and the SOF Withdrawal from Laos

"The term 'political warfare' refers both to the whole of warfare directed at producing political results, and to that part of warfare that employs political means to attain the political goals of war in conjunction with fighting troops—or even without the actual engagement of fighting troops."

ANGELO M. CODEVILLA AND PAUL SEABURY, *WAR: ENDS AND MEANS*

In 1962, the final two rotations of Special Forces teams to Laos would experience three distinct phases of activity in the American goal to prevent a communist takeover of the country. From January to July, the first phase was characterized by an increase in combat for the deployed teams. After the signing of the Treaty of Peace and Reconciliation in July, Special Forces teams consolidated their positions with the Lao army and began a series of increased civic and humanitarian actions (the second phase). The third phase consisted of the withdrawal of Army Special Operations forces from Laos and their subsequent return to home stations.

White Star Activities—1962

In January of 1962, *White Star* Rotation VI had three more months remaining of their tour before the incoming deployment of their complete replacement between January and March of 1962. The *White Star* commander was still Lieutenant Colonel Arthur D. "Bull" Simons, who would be replaced by Lieutenant Colonel Aito Keravouri on March 19, 1962. The battlefield situation throughout Laos consisted of Pathet Lao jockeying to add to and consolidate their positions against the RLG in light of the Geneva peace talks in early 1961. The May 1961 ceasefire deadline (which the communists did not observe), and the deadlock of the three factions to form a coalition government, contributed to the Pathet Lao's use of military pressure to force the RLG into ensuring the communists a full share in the coalition. This was a time-proven military tactic to weaken the opposition and consolidate and enlarge gains on the ground, both geographically and amongst "secured" populations during negotiations.

An improved position on behalf of either side strengthened the hands of negotiators prior to reaching any agreement.

Minor political squabbling in Vientiane aside, the deadlock primarily emanated from the Rightists and from their leader, General Phoumi Nosavan; Phoumi disagreed with proposals for the selection of who would occupy key cabinet positions in the newly forming coalition government. In February of 1962 the U.S. government attempted to break Phoumi's intransigence and force the other two factions to settle their disagreements, cutting off cash payments to the RLG as a pressure tactic. General Phoumi tried to improve his situation by ignoring pleas to accept decisions by the other two factions. He then moved to expand his political position by currying favor with the Rightist elements of the FAR. He created two new military districts—the Northern Laos Command and the Southern Laos Command—to create new senior positions within the army as a form of patronage and also to shore up his base. Phoumi also instituted a new officer's training academy for the reserves (presumably hand-picking loyal Rightists), and additionally created two new military regions to expand the roster of commanding generals and colonels devoted to him.[1]

Northwestern Laos—Military Region I

RLG military forces deployed throughout MR-I in January of 1962 consisted of GM-11 at Nam Tha, BV-17 at Xieng Lom, BV-18 at Ban Houei Sai, and the GM and BV forces assigned to the Luang Prabang area. On the Pathet Lao side, regional forces were operating in the vicinity of Nam Tha, Moung Sai and Ban Namo, as well as in the Nam Beng valley. Elements of the NVA's 316th Brigade consolidated their positions at Moung Sai and Ban Namo, also.

The Chinese Speciale 111 unit, after leaving in disgust after the performance of Groupement Tactique 2 in the Christmas battle of Moung Sai, eventually ended up consolidated in an area north of Ban Houei Sai, along the Mekong River.

For *White Star* Rotation VI's effort in Military Region I, Detachment BB was headquartered at Luang Prabang with responsibility of several FTTs. Major Patrick J. Marr commanded the thirteen-man B-team element, controlling logistics support and providing operational guidance to FTTs in the following locations:

- Nam Tha, among them Captain Freddie H. Boyd with a split-team to train and advise the 27th BI; Captain Lewis D. Allen's split-team, and two or three other FTTs (one being Captain Jesse Ramos' split-team)
- FA-2 at Ban Houei Sai with Captain Ruben W. Shay's split-team (soon to be replaced)
- A team at Sayaboury (split detachment under Lieutenant Robert R. Page—his team leader, Captain Ramos, with the other half of the team at Nam Tha)
- Two FTTs at Kiou Ka Cham (Captain David L. Wise, with FTT-23 advising GM-16 and the 26th BI and the other half of the team under Lieutenant

William R. Beal, FTT-23A advising the 25th BI), south along Route 13 of the B-team's position at Luang Prabang

- FTT-40 (renamed FTT-2) under Lieutenant Mike Layton, just recently deployed to train Bataillon Voluntaire 17 at Xieng Lom
- Major Marr's Luang Prabang-based B-team also commanded three FTTs in MR-II to support the Hmong SGU training[2]

White Star Rotation VII began its initial batch of team deployments on January 10 and would continue to deploy the remaining teams of the rotation throughout February and March.[3] This would be the first rotation to deploy a new B-team element to handle the training of the Hmongs and SGUs at Site 20 in MR-II: Detachment Faistenhammer (named after Major Ludwig Faistenhammer, the detachment commander).

The significant activity in Military Region I during 1962 was the siege and battle of Nam Tha, which ran from January to early May, resulting in the capitulation of the 5,000-man garrison and loss of government control of the Houa Khong Province for the reminder of the *White Star* mission.

The Battle of Nam Tha

Nam Tha sits in a flat, bowl-shaped valley surrounded by ridges and at the confluence of four rivers. The town consisted of a series of connected villages that ran north–south in direction (about ten kilometers in length including the airfield—L-100), paralleling the winding Nam Tha River to its immediate east. In 1962, there were a little less than 2,000 inhabitants of the town. Nam Tha was once the administrative and economic center of northwest Laos and was a key stop for trade transiting from China to the north. Nam Tha connected to Route 13 to the east via Route 32; the town of Moung Sing was located fifty-eight kilometers to the northwest, which also had an airstrip (it had once been a GCMA French outpost).

The city of Nam Tha was connected to Ban Houei Sai by Route 3, a mere jeep track, which wound its way to the southwest through valleys and mountain passes until reaching the Mekong River (approximately 175 kilometers away).

The battle of Nam Tha, a successful attack on RLG Phoumist forces by the NVA and Pathet Lao, ran from January 1962 to May 6, 1962. The sequence of operations to prepare for and conduct the battle is a good example of one of the larger and successful operations of the combined communist forces during the war in Laos. The NVA military advisors and the Pathet Lao chose to confront General Phoumi Nosavan's build-up of 5,000 Laotian troops as a means to discredit him as a Rightist, and to also take more territory for political gain during the ongoing negotiations to form a coalition government. It was hoped by the communists that a successful defeat of government forces would help to break the deadlock in the negotiations.

In the late fall of 1961, Nam Tha was garrisoned by Groupe Mobile 11, consisting of the 1st and 2nd BIs and the 13th BV, along with their attached *White Star* teams. GM-11's earlier attempt to attack forty kilometers east in January of 1962 to defeat the Pathet Lao in Moung Sai prompted a counterattack from combined Pathet Lao and NVA forces, forcing GM-11 to retreat to the safety of their lines at Nam Tha.[4]

The North Vietnamese then chose to conduct a setpiece battle at Nam Tha. As explained by Arthur J. Dommen:

> Northern Laos appeared to be the logical setting for the decisive Pathet Lao victory wanted by the Vietnamese. A Phoumist defeat there would exclude Vientiane troops from a band of territory along the border of China, which was then building the first road into Laos from Yünnan Province under an agreement announced by the New China News Agency on January 13. Also, a triumph could be achieved there with the maximum shock but without throwing pro-Communist forces into the Mekong valley and risking American (or Thai) retaliation.[5]

The threat to Nam Tha began to grow. Concerned with NVA and Pathet Lao front lines extending west from their consolidated positions at Moung Sai and Ban Namo, and finding cached rice in the vicinity (portending a future communist offensive), GM-11 (advised by FTT-30) conducted security sweeps in the surrounding jungles to secure a wider perimeter around the town.

In what may have been a political maneuver to convince the Americans of communist duplicity during the ceasefire and discredit their involvement with the soon-to-be-formed coalition government, General Phoumi Nosavan looked to create an incident to support his theory. At the end of January, GM-18 (with its 28th and 30th BIs) deployed to reinforce the garrison. The GM had recently been retrained in Thailand under the EKARAD program and arrived at Nam Tha at full strength and well-equipped.[6]

The Nam Tha sector was commanded by Major General Bounleuth Sanichan, who was supremely confident that Nam Tha would never be taken by Pathet Lao forces.

The NVA battle plan to destroy the garrison was named "Campaign XYZ."[7] The plan called for the town of Nam Tha to be initially surrounded and isolated by three NVA brigades, supported by local Pathet Lao forces. A key element of the plan would be the denial of the airfield through indirect fire interdiction, to prevent the reinforcement of the garrison in what was to be styled as another "Dien Bien Phu" battle. The backup airfield at Moung Sing would also require capture to deny its use as an alternate line of communication to Phoumist forces.

The operation initially included two NVA infantry battalions of the 316th occupying the ridges to the east of Nam Tha, followed by the 2nd and 4th battalions of the 335th Brigade occupying siege lines to the south and north-northwest. Airborne resupplies to the NVA were packaged and flown by the North Vietnamese 919th Air Transport Squadron conducting airdrops at Ban Namo, which were then disassembled and man-portaged to communists forces at Nam Tha.[8]

The Pathet Lao task organization for the attack may have consisted of four main-force Pathet Lao battalions, ranging from a battalion strength of 150 men (the 408th Battalion of Pathet Lao traditionally operated in the Nam Tha sector) to perhaps 300–350 men in the other battalions, along with the reinforcement of two district independent companies out of the four in the Nam Tha region: the 51st with seventy men and the 53rd with fifty men.

The NVA advisors for the attack came from the three NVA advisor companies stationed in the jungle near Nam Tha. Chinese forces were suspected as participating in the attack and later confirmed when men from Laotian government forces who were captured during the battle (and later released) spoke of their capture and move by Chinese forces to prisons just across the border.

In the latter part of January, NVA and Pathet Lao forces began building a series of trenchworks on the heights east of Nam Tha. The RLAF began close air support operations with T-6 aircraft in an attempt to disrupt the buildup (with one T-6 pilot credited with potentially shooting down an IL-14 resupply aircraft, which was presumed to be damaged and later crashed trying to return to North Vietnam). After probes by combined Pathet Lao and NVA patrols overran some FAR outposts, the besieging communist force advanced a series of trenches to within twelve miles of the town. In fright, armed civilian militias were mobilized by the officials of the town.[9]

FTT-1 Nam Tha

FTT-1, commanded by Captain Charles L. Johnson, arrived in Laos at the end of January. The team was split between Sayaboury (FTT-1A) and Nam Tha (FTT-1). Captain Johnson understood the task of the Sayaboury team as one of local training and advisory duties, with some limited reconnaissance and intelligence-gathering activities. The split detachment at Nam Tha would deploy to the front line with GM-11 to assist and advise them during combat actions, and if possible, Johnson wanted the teams to then switch roles. If that was not possible, then individual members of both teams could rotate back and forth between the two locations. At Nam Tha, Sergeant 1st Class Cannon, the U.S. Army field artillery NCO assigned from an Army division in Korea, was attached to FTT-1 to assist with the FAR artillery batteries at Nam Tha and to also assist in calls for fire for the team. First Lieutenant Bruce Nevins, another artillery advisor, was also assigned to Nam Tha.

FTT-1 was flown to Nam Tha in early February to join with GM-11, currently defending the Nam Tha perimeter to the south and southeast of the town. The mission for the team was to train Laotian soldiers and Auto-Défense companies of GM-11. After meeting with the resident senior SF control team in Nam Tha, FTT-1 was provided with a jeep and trailer to move to GM-11's lines.

On the front line, life was rugged and austere but at least the team could use the jeep to go into Nam Tha to procure water and bring back bags of rice for GM-11. Team members lived under poncho liner shelters and dug individual fighting positions. "Too Tall" Simmons, the demolitions man on the team, remembers: "We slept in hammocks with a foxhole next to us. We were mortared most nights. Because of that, I dug a two-man foxhole to sleep in. I used an entrenching tool to make an eight-foot hole, with two sleeping areas. Miller [the team medic] told me not to use my bayonet when defending the fox-hole. Ned said, 'You'll just get it stuck; hit him with the rifle.'"[10]

An improvised team command post was constructed by folding over bamboo stalks and brush to build a small shelter for radio comms, storage of supplies, and cooking. Ammo boxes served as tables and chairs. C4 plastic explosive was used for cooking because it did not give off smoke that might alert the enemy as to the team's location. The team used a small stream to obtain drinking and cooking water, located about three quarters of a mile away. Mail was delivered via Air America drops.

The crude CP also served as a gathering place for coordination with Lao leaders and on occasion, to conduct sick call for the Laotian troops.

Other FTTs were present in the area, but were slowly being pulled out as their rotations came to an end. (There was also a transfer of teams to the Kha tribal guerrilla program down on the Bolovens, depleting SF team strength at Nam Tha.) As other SF teams departed, FTT-1 assumed overall control of the *White Star* mission in Nam Tha and moved into the Seventh Day Adventist Mission building (the nominal headquarters for the *White Star* mission and the location of the MAAG representative, a colonel). It was here the team also acquired an additional jeep.

Each member of the team used his MOS skills to train and enhance GM-11's units. As an example, SP4 Edward F. Eckerman served both as the radio operator and operations and intelligence man. He joined Special Forces when he was almost nineteen years of age. He explained his two duties on the team:

> Once I arrived to the team (I had left Luang Prabang where I was sharpening up my skills; Ned Miller met me on the airfield as my Air America C-47 flight was taking fire during landing), one of my jobs was checking other radio operators on the outposts. My job also included writing reports, working on area studies, and did the intel work for the team. I was selected as the artillery intelligence person for the team. We would look around the airfield for shell holes and do crater analysis, even when they were still firing on us. We tried to ascertain such things as the azimuths of the incoming rounds, shrapnel burst, and other factors.[11]

FTT-1 conducted reconnaissance and intelligence-gathering patrols with their counterparts to ascertain the limits of Pathet Lao positions and to provoke a firefight to expose those positions; if engaged, the patrol broke off and worked its way back to their own positions, trying to see how far the Pathet Lao would pursue. Over time, FTT-1 team members and local troops on the lines became quite adept at reacting to ambushes and operating under indirect fire.

Sayaboury—FTT-39 (FTT-1A)

The town of Sayaboury, the provincial capital of Sayaboury Province, lies to the southwest of Luang Prabang. Sayaboury Province was considered more remote from other regions of Laos, with little activity from the Pathet Lao. At most, only one FTT was deployed in the province to assist in training of the local BI and BV forces; some village militias were also trained. It was a mountainous region devoid of large towns and with little or no roads, but was important for its rice-growing capabilities and its logging industry. The indigenous populations were mostly comprised of tribal Thai groupings. The town itself was arranged in a grid pattern with wider avenues than those found in remoter regional towns. It lay on the western banks of the Nam Hung River, a tributary of the Mekong (located about six miles to the east). The town sat in a picturesque valley, surrounded by high, forested ridgelines. The airstrip was located about a mile away, slightly south of the town.[12]

First Lieutenant Robert G. Lunday commanded the split-team with Master Sergeant Frank Nolen, Jr. The team consisted of the command group, two weapons men (senior and junior), a radio operator, and a medic. Though a split from FTT-1, they took the designation FTT-39 (vice FTT-1A) from a prior SF team assigned to that location. The team arrived for duties in Sayaboury in the second week of February.

The mission for the team consisted of giving basic tactical skills training to a local Lao military unit. The team was soon at work building training ranges, creating training aids, improving the airfield and making enhancements to the team house. Classes consisted of small-arms training and small-unit tactics. Part of the training was taking out patrols in the surrounding jungle. The threat from the Pathet Lao in that area was minimal.

The Tightening Siege at Nam Tha

On February 1 NVA and Pathet Lao forces moved in 120mm mortars around Nam Tha and began shelling the airfield, soon able to range farther and fire on the town itself. This action resulted in the closure of the airfield, forcing the defenders to rely on parachute-delivered supplies.

NVA forces continued to extend siege lines and earthworks to the northeast and to the southeast. In response, as an attempt to break the siege, General Phoumi reinforced the garrison. On February 12, the 1st Batallion Parachutistes were parachuted onto a DMZ west of Nam Tha, located within four and half kilometers of enemy lines.

GMs 11 and 18 were then reinforced with GM-15 and its three battalions. (GM-15 deployed to Nam Tha over the months of February, March, and April.) The garrison was additionally provided with 105mm howitzers and 75mm mountain guns to give them a ranging capability to shell enemy forces.

The FAR conducted a limited counterattack to reduce the threat. General Sananikone noted in his post-war monograph:

> The force was placed under the MR-I commander, Colonel Sibarovong, and in mid-February attacked east out of Nam Tha to expand the perimeter and reduce the enemy fire on the airstrip. By the end of the month, all of the limited objectives had been taken and American transports could land again at Nam Tha. Among the cargo they deposited at Nam Tha were three 105mm howitzers, together with the Filipino technicians to reassemble the pieces. [The guns arrived on March 3; the Filipino technicians were from the ECCOIL.][13]

White Star Activities in MR-I, January–March 1962

In early March, Major Gordon Ripley assumed command of the BB Detachment at Luang Prabang with an eighteen-man element.

The Special Forces teams and control elements for the 7th Rotation of *White Star* deployed into Laos between January and March of 1962. In Military Region I, Captain Charles L. Johnson remained deployed at Nam Tha with his team split between there and Sayaboury (Lieutenant Robert G. Lunday was at Sayaboury). Included with Johnson's element at Nam Tha was his team sergeant, Sergeant 1st Class Guy T. Edmondson, Sergeant Ned L. Miller, the medic, two demolitions men, Sergeant Vincent O'Rourke (and later, SP4 Robert H. "Too Tall" Simmons), and SP4 Edward F. Eckerman, his radio operator. FTT-1 would be reinforced at Nam Tha in March by First Lieutenant Lynn S. Halteman's split-team FTT-43, deployed to train and advise the 34th BV. Captain Reuben Mooradian's FTT-24 conducted training for the 1st and 2nd commando platoons of GM-11 south of Luang Prabang.

Captain Gleason commanded FT-22 at Kiou Ka Cham with First Lieutenant George Marecek, Master Sergeant Harry D. "Crash" Whalen, and three other team members.

FTT-2 commanded by Captain Henry L. Ellison deployed into Laos at the same time of the new B-team assuming control, and split his team between duties at Ban Houei Sai and support to the NCO academy at Luang Prabang.

Ban Houei Sai

Ban Houei Sai is situated on the east bank of the Mekong River across from the Thai village of Chaing Khong. It was a river commerce town, economically existing off fishing in the Mekong River and the operation of ferries for trade traffic moving back and forth from Thailand to the west. There was also river commerce activity from trade originating farther north up the Mekong using Ban Houei Sai as a debarkation point. The area was notorious as a nexus for the opium trade between China, Burma, Thailand and Laos.

Although there were some modest structures in the middle of town, the notable aspect of Ban Houei Sai was the distinctive wood and thatch construction of its longhouses. The town lay on a north–south axis, along the high ground and ridges on the east bank of the Mekong. A dirt and sod airstrip was located to the immediate south of town (L-25), with a crude, hut-type shelter made of four poles and a roof, a POL refuel area, and some steel, perforated World War II airstrip planking. Route 3 connected Ban Houei Sai to Nam Tha (to its northeast) via a winding dirt jeep track. On a high hill overlooking the town sat an old French fort, Fort Carnot, now occupied by a Laotian BI. The airfield was about three kilometers south of the fort.

There was a large island in the river between Ban Houei Sai and Thailand. The next largest population center was a short trip north up the Mekong to Cheng Rei.

Captain Henry L. Ellison deployed to Laos with his 1st SFG team from Okinawa flying aboard C-130s, which landed first in Bangkok; the team transloaded aboard Air America C-47s for the ride into Luang Prabang to link up with Detachment BB. At Luang Prabang, the team split in half; Captain Ellison would take his six-man FTT to Ban Houei Sai while his XO, First Lieutenant Robert H. Ammerman, had responsibility for the NCO academy at Luang Prabang (FTT-2A). After drawing weapons from the B-team, Captain Ellison prepared for his new mission. Although there had been a 7th SFG team at Ban Houei Sai from the previous *White Star* rotation, they redeployed prior to Captain Ellison's and FTT-2's arrival; no transition was possible, thus compounding the lack of information on the area and the Laotian unit. Ellison related, "We got our brief on the mission from the B-team, but they did not know much about Ban Houei Sai. From there, we took H-34s to Ban Houei Sai."[14]

The BI-18 Royal Laotian Infantry Battalion's XO met the team as their escort and took them to a house on the Fort Carnot compound. At one end of the camp sat the fort; farther down the hill sat the officers' quarters and a house for the French officer of the province. The team settled into a cluster of buildings about 200 yards down from the fort near the Tom Dooley clinic, in fact, in Dr. Tom Dooley's former residence. Another house nearby was occupied by the Laotian battalion commander. The Tom Dooley Foundation hospital was sited in a one-story block building run by Dr. Carl M. Wiedermann and his assistant, Al Harris, who had been a corpsman in the Navy. From this high ground, the team had a commanding view of the town and the Mekong River, about a mile away.[15]

The team house included a sleeping area, radio-watch room, and cooking and dining area. An old kerosene-fueled refrigerator previously belonging to the U.S. embassy helped keep the food fresh. The team had a cook along with his wife who did the laundry. The team acquired a quarter-ton vehicle; Sergeant Russell became the team's mechanic to keep it running.

The team assisted Dr. Wiedermann with medical support as part of their civic action. Dr. Wiedermann, in a letter to Colonel Simons, praised the efforts of FTT-2 to help him establish a functioning medical center at the old Tom Dooley Foundation house, along with help in treating critical patients

FTT-2 personnel were not the only Americans in the vicinity. Bill and Gordon Young, members of a missionary family working for years in Laos, Thailand and Burma, were working up in the Cheng Mei area. Bill lived across the river in the only hotel in Chaing Khong. (Bill was a CIA operative and may have been using the Operation *Brotherhood* program as cover.) With the opium trade in the area, and the relocation of the Chinese BS-111 to just north of Ban Houei Sai (and the American effort to fly them back to Taiwan), this presumably required someone to run covert operations in the area. The Young brothers also helped FTT-2 with updated situation reports, advice, and support, particularly when the team transitioned to training the local guerrillas and militia.

Fortunately, there was no enemy threat in the Ban Houei Sai area. The Lao battalion had small arms, machine guns and 81mm mortars for the defense of the fort. FTT-2 carried M2 carbines and their personal sidearms (Captain Ellison carried a snub-nose .38, Smith & Wesson).

FTT-2 settled in and began their advisory support. Retired Colonel Ellison described their work:

> We conducted straight infantry training with them, but very little tactics. I would describe our training as being tailored to them for defending the fort. Later, we trained some men from one of the hill tribes; there were about seventy-five to eighty of them. The Agency equipped and armed them. The course lasted from around April through May. We showed the Lao how to put in ranges in a place where a valley was alongside the road which paralleled the river. We did not get many visits from the B-team; I would visit them about once a month. There was limited radio contact with them other than our normal radio checks with the B-team. There were no French trainers at our location.[16]

As the battle and siege at Nam Tha progressed, Captain Ellison knew something was wrong; up the trail on Route 3 Laotian soldiers and units began to disperse from Nam Tha and were seen in his area. He could not, however, anticipate that the whole Laotian contingent would soon be fleeing through Ban Houei Sai in early May.

The Nam Tha Siege

As part of the reinforcement of the defenders of Nam Tha, the Seno-based 55th Bataillon Parachutistes conducted an airborne operation into Nam Tha on March 27, 1962 (this reinforcement due to battalions of GM-11 being pulled back to Vientiane for a parade). Along with the battalion were three of the SF advisors from FTT- 21.[17]

Lieutenant Robin Luketina's FTT-21, a split-team, continued their assigned duties as advisors and trainers to the Laotian 55th Bataillon Parachutistes (see earlier chapter on Se Bang Fai River operations).

In mid-March 1962, the 55th BP was pulled back to Seno to prepare for a combat jump to reinforce the beleaguered forces in Nam Tha. Lieutenant Colonel Simons and Major Marr visited Nam Tha to assess the situation. Simons returned to Vientiane to provide his opinion to the embassy on the growing battle and sent a helicopter for Lieutenant Luketina to discuss the mission with him. Simons was clear in his guidance to Luketina: basically, with the team having only one more month left in country, Simons thought it would be infeasible for the team to deploy into what was now an ongoing siege, as no one could predict the time of its end. FTT-21 would have to sit out the anticipated airborne operation.

To ensure the credibility of the SF advisory effort, Luketina knew he would have to make a case for the FTT to jump into combat with the unit, or lose face as advisors to the battalion. Simons relented, but only allowed for three SF advisors to accompany the battalion.

Luketina chose his medic, Sergeant 1st Class Merland F. Francis, and radio operator, Corporal John T. Haralson as the rest of his "split, split-team."

The 55th BP refitted for the operation. Twenty-one-year-old Corporal John T. Haralson knew it was time to get down to business when he was informed of the upcoming jump. "My team sergeant had two combat drops with the 82nd in World War II and gave me some advice as I was packing. He said, 'Travel light and be ready to fight!'"[18]

The battalion loaded onto RLAF C-47s, with about forty men to each aircraft, and flew first to Wattay in Vientiane, and then on to the Luang Prabang airfield.

The 55th BP had approximately 300 troops for the combat jump. Some of the troops deserted before the operation in fear of pending combat with the Pathet Lao and NVA. For some odd reason, Haralson noted only about fifty of the paratroopers on the jump had helmets, while the rest wore bandanas around their heads. Maybe a hundred of the Laotian paratroopers had boots, but most were wearing flip-flops.

The 55th BP was carrying several 60mm mortars and .30-caliber machine guns for the operation, along with their small arms. The immediate mission of the 55th upon dropping into Nam Tha was to search west for some type of direct fire weapon harassing the airfield, and destroy or capture the gun (this was later found out to be an 85mm AAA/field gun).

The jump was executed at 400–500 feet above ground level, without a reserve parachute. The FTT had just completed one of the few combat drops of American forces since the Korean War. Along with bruises and injuries associated from any combat jump at low altitude (without reserves, which normally cushion at least some portion of the front of the body), a few Laotians were wounded by direct fires onto the DZ. Haralson recalls, "We assembled and moved to an area in which we remained for about a day, or day and a half, getting the battalion ready for the mission. I remember the terrain to the objective was rough, uphill, and very hard going." The three SF advisors moved with the 55th BP command group.[19]

During movement west, the FTT and 55th BP moved through GM-11's positions and coordinated a quick passage of lines with FTT-1 located alongside a trail. Haralson noted:

> The hills or maybe saw-tooth hills is a better description, were difficult to climb, very wet and slippery, and steep. We encountered small arms fire and incoming mortar fire. After a couple of days we occupied the high ground to the west, overlooking Nam Tha, and we dug defensive positions. During several counter-attacks, the communist forces were blowing bugles as they came toward us. Strange. I remembered Korean veterans telling about the Chinese blowing bugles during their attacks. I don't remember anyone telling us *that we were fighting the Chinese!*[20]

Once atop the heights, the battalion dug in. Five or six days into the operation, and under a mortar attack, Corporal Haralson worked by candlelight to decode a message from the control team in Vientiane. The team was queried by the control team if they wanted to extract to Luang Prabang, since their unit was scheduled to return soon to Okinawa, and, wondering if the team planned on accompanying them home. Luketina answered the question by relaying the sentiments of the team. "Of course we said yes." Control responded, "OK, an Otter aircraft will be landing at the airstrip tomorrow, about 1000; be there."[21]

Two hours after this odd communication the unit came under attack, initiated by the blowing of bugles. Portions of the 55th BP were overrun as enemy forces ran through their positions lobbing grenades. Corporal Haralson was blown out of the back of his bunker by one of these explosions. After several Laotian soldiers were killed and captured, the unit maneuvered back toward the direction of Nam Tha.[22]

Luketina led his team down from their foxholes and bunkers from atop the hill, escorted with one squad of Laotian paratroopers. To their surprise, precisely at 1000 hours, an Otter flown by an Air America pilot arrived and flew them back to Luang Prabang, all the while under mortar fire as they took off.

To replace Luketina's team, Captain George M. Buck deployed to Nam Tha from Seno with a split-team in April (part of FTT-21). They were to see heavy combat.

By April, the airfield and FAR units on the front lines, as well as the town of Nam Tha, were receiving around a hundred artillery shells a day. The 3rd Battalion of the 330th NVA Brigade arrived to reinforce the siege lines.

In that same month, Brigadier General La Pathammavong took command of the garrison with orders from General Phoumi to resume the offensive. On April 8, General Pathammavong conducted a two-GM attack (GMs 15 and 18) to break the siege. The attack initially succeeded in recovering ground from enemy forces, but due to heavy resistance from NVA and Pathet Lao, stalled. (In this operation, Sergeant 1st Class William A. Clark was awarded the Bronze Star with

"V" device for his heroism, rendering medical aid to Laotian soldiers while under hostile gunfire.)

Government troops now defending Nam Tha were approximately 5,000 at their peak, consisting of nine BI and BV battalions.

As in all campaigns in Laos, the seasonal monsoon rains would affect the tempo of operations. The North Vietnamese command, concerned about the upcoming wet period, pushed forward to conclude the Nam Tha battle while the weather was favorable. Initial ground-probing attacks on the defenses of Nam Tha began on May 2, 1962, first on the southeast perimeter, followed by attacks on outposts within two kilometers of the town. The approximate strength of the communist forces at this time was estimated at between 2,500 and 4,000 troops.

Events between May 3 and 4 would set the conditions for the looming catastrophe for the Laotian defenders. On May 3, the company-sized BV garrison at Moung Sing capitulated in the face of the 4th Battalion of the 335th NVA Brigade. The news of the loss of Moung Sing, a critical post on the line of communication to Nam Tha, rattled the Lao commanders. In response, on May 4 a battalion of Laotian paratroopers moved to reinforce Moung Sing and recapture the airstrip; their progress was slowed by the rains. On the morning of May 5, the battalion was ambushed outside the town. Paratroopers fled in disorder back to Nam Tha, pursued by the enemy. Enemy forces occupied the high ground north of Nam Tha. All along the line, government forces were attacked with artillery and machine-gun fire.[23]

On May 5, FTT-1 learned of the pending attack from a wounded paratrooper. Up to then, the team had not been kept fully apprised of the battles and skirmishes around Nam Tha. That night, when Captain Johnson queried the Lao higher command, he was told by Brigadier General La Pathammavong to ensure there were helicopters available for extraction the next morning.

On May 6, in the early hours of dawn and under the light of flares, a four-battalion NVA attack hit the northwest quarter of the defenses. The attack was supported by combined mortar barrages and Pathet Lao supporting attacks, streaming down from the heights encircling the Nam Tha position from the east, southeast, and northeast. As successive FAR positions were overrun, FAR artillery units began spiking their guns. By 7 a.m., 5,000 Laotian defenders began fleeing Nam Tha.[24]

As the front lines around Nam Tha began to collapse, Captain Johnson called for evacuation by L-20s and H-34s. PFC Eckerman departed in a team jeep with a time of forty-five minutes to find the U.S. Army artillery advisor assigned to the FAR's 75mm howitzers. Once he returned, Sergeant Ned Miller and PFC Simmons drove in the other jeep to transport the MAAG colonel and a Laotian general to the alternate airstrip for evacuation.

Seeing they had been abandoned to the enemy, Captain Johnson organized the team for an E&E to the north of town, toward the Chinese border. He knew he did not want to follow the fleeing troops as they scrambled with refugees down Route 3 to the southwest, now being closely pursued by Pathet Lao and NVA. Sergeant Miller offered, "Let's go to the alternate airstrip; there's a trail running off of it we can use." [25]

In Sayaboury, hearing of FTT-1's plight, Lieutenant Lunday prepared his split-detachment to reinforce Captain Johnson. The team loaded with parachutes and deployed to the airfield. The FTT stood down when it was clear FTT-1's situation at Nam Tha was soon overcome by events.

At Nam Tha, FTT-1 loaded aboard jeeps after destroying what equipment and sensitive items they could at the team house and drove to the alternate landing zone. They heard and saw the B-team buildings explode in the air.

Picking up a familiar trail used to conduct team medical visits, they drove up the side of a hill where a small village was located. Some fleeing Laotian police were picked up along the way. Leading out of the village was a small foot trail the team intended to use to E&E west toward Burma.

The team unloaded their gear from the jeeps and shot holes into the gas tanks. After setting their vehicles afire, the team began to head west. Fortunately, two Air America H-34 helicopters arrived on-scene; the team could see them flying up the valley. FTT-1 made contact with the pilots;

It was about 9 a.m. Ned L. Miller remembered: "We radioed them and told them the bad guys had taken the town, but if they would look out their left window, they could see the smoke from our burning jeeps. They landed and picked us up and flew back with us to Luang Prabang, where our B-team was located. Those crews did not have to buy any beer that night!"[26]

FTT-1 would never return to Nam Tha. After recovering in Luang Prabang, the six men of FTT-1 were sent to Sayaboury for link-up with the rest of their detachment and to get some well-deserved rest.

Meanwhile, the panicked and retreating hordes of Laotian military forces being pursued down Route 3 would soon arrive at FTT-2's location at Ban Houei Sai.

Action at Ban Houei Sai

In Vientiane, the débâcle of the defeat of the FAR at Nam Tha shook the government. At the U.S. embassy, fears of Pathet Lao and NVA continuing their attack to the Mekong River sparked the need for an assessment of just how far the enemy would advance. Across the river from Ban Houei Sai, two battalions of Thai infantry were quickly deployed under the command of Thai generals. Thai riverine forces began to patrol in the immediate vicinity and up the Nam Tha River.

Panicked hordes of fleeing Laotian troops, followed by refugees, soon forced the civilian evacuation of Ban Houei Sai. Captain Ellison and FTT-2 had not anticipated the confusion. Ellison observed, "The Lao were totally out of control at the river crossing. They used whatever floated to flee. The soldiers were mixed up with women and children, and closely behind them came the stragglers from the RLA."[27] Across the river Royal Thai infantry forces confiscated weapons from the Lao and moved them into refugee camps for holding.

Sergeant Don Valentine, one of the radio operators attached to assist FTT-2, described the chaos: "The nearest safe place was across the river in Thailand. The nearest place to get a boat across the Mekong River was at Ban Houei Sai so that is where our fleet-footed warriors headed."[28]

Anticipating his team's receiving an order to withdraw in the potential onslaught of the Pathet Lao, Captain Ellison sent his two communications NCOs (Valentine and Staff Sergeant Homer Rice) out of the fort and into town to monitor the situation and provide reports back to the base station in Luang Prabang. They were also prepared to cross the Mekong with the radios and the cryptologic materials. The remainder of the team prepared to evacuate equipment from the now abandoned fort. Soon, Air America helicopters began the ferrying process across the river.

Refugees and Laotian soldiers poured by the thousands down the trail into the town and on to the docks. Laotian soldiers, in panic, pushed aside refugees to get on boats and cross the river. By the end of the day, with most of the soldiers safely across the river, the villagers followed on anything which remained floating, including logs, all the while herding livestock across the river with them. Soon the banks of the Mekong were beginning to fill with the dead, bloated animals which did not survive in the crossing attempt. Hundreds of abandoned dogs roamed the streets of Ban Houei Sai.

Valentine and Rice, presuming the team had now been ferried across by helicopter (including the MAAG personnel), secured a boat and made it across the river. That night, the last of the team members to cross were Murphy and Loobey, who had remained behind to blow up abandoned gear, vehicles and ammunition in order to deny their use to the enemy.[29]

The team could not stay in Thailand. Captain Ellison ordered them to set up a defensive position on the large island out in the Mekong River. Once it became apparent the enemy was not pursing FAR elements into Ban Houei Sai, the team forayed from the island and took up positions in town and around the airfield, conducting daily security patrols.

White Star headquarters ordered the reinforcement of Ban Houei Sai. Johnson's FTT-1 in Sayaboury and Captain Ellison's other split-team (at the NCO academy in Luang Prabang) soon arrived. Total SF strength was now twenty-one men and the interpreters. The MAAG chief, Brigadier General Reuben Tucker, ordered Captain Ellison to take a patrol and go back toward Nam Tha to ascertain just how far the Pathet Lao were pursuing. He told Captain Ellison, "Don't stop until you make contact." Captain Ellison met with senior Lao military personnel at the refugee camp across the river where he gained a concession from Lao military commanders to provide about fifty Lao commandos to help conduct the patrol. They loaded aboard H-34 helicopters and established an outpost near the village of Ban Phoung. From this forward position, the small task force conducted patrols farther up Route 3, but little contact with enemy forces occurred.

Engagement at Ban Phoung—FTT-1

The cluster of wooden, thatch huts on stilts known as the village of Ban Phoung lay to the north just off of the dirt track of Route 3. The village could be reached by a trail leading from Route 3; a trail on the opposite end of the village reconnected to Route 3 heading to the northeast. Behind the village ran a swiftly flowing stream, the village's water source. It was a somewhat prosperous village, surrounded by pastures and fields of crops. Some of the better longhouses were fenced in, and enclosing well-kept yards.

Improvements were soon made to the base camp, with security outposts emplaced, dugouts for fighting positions prepared, and with a CP established in one of the houses. Each day, local security patrols from the company of commandos fanned out to check the perimeter while reconnaissance patrols operated up Route 3.[30]

After three or four days, Captain Ellison was relieved by Captain Johnson's team (a rotational schedule began), who took some Lao commandos (chosen from among the Lao army camped out across the Mekong River in Thailand) on a far-reaching patrol up Route 3, farther than Captain Ellison's team had previously accomplished. They moved at night, established surveillance, and rested during the day. After a few nights of this routine, Johnson established a camp back down the trail, after suspicious behavior and evasive answers from locals in a village. It was during the morning routine of camp activities the patrol was ambushed by Pathet Lao. The patrol fought off repeated attacks, often hand-to-hand.

As part of the camp's morning routine, SP4 Robert H. Simmons was cutting bamboo to make furniture when the enemy assault erupted:

> I was on my fifth or sixth section hanging over the overhang when my mother's son's whole world started blowing up! Talk about noise, talk about heat, talk about concussions, talk about scared, they had somehow gotten inside both of our outer security posts, surrounded our inner security, and once the signal was given, they all opened up with their rifles, pistols, automatic rifles, grenades, submachine guns. You name it, they were firing it! Bullets were cracking, ricocheting all over the place; the tracers were lighting up the shadows as they were weaving in and out through the bamboo. Their leadership was superb.[31]

Simmons quickly dispatched two attackers with his .45-caliber pistol, then grabbed his rifle.

As they lost more troops from among their commandos, Johnson ordered a fighting retreat back down the trail. The patrol fought its way back to defensible terrain, with SP4 Simmons and Sergeant Ned Miller leading the way, firing their weapons to kill enemy ambushers along the trail.

After further attacks by the Pathet Lao were fought off, the now severely under-manned patrol returned to the outpost at Ban Phoung, and was then flown back to Ban Houei Sai aboard Air America H-34s. (Simmons later found an expended enemy bullet in his trouser pocket). When Captain Ellison moved back to the village for his team's turn of duties, he soon learned the Pathet Lao occupied the far side. Ellison split his Lao commandos and team members to the east and to the west, to conduct an attack. He moved Sergeant 1st Class Murphy and Sergeant Loobey to the east to establish a roadblock, along with some commandos, who were also equipped with a .30-caliber machine gun. Soon, Ellison heard gunfire from the roadblock position. He called for Captain Johnson's team to reinforce him from Ban Houei Sai. H-34s of Air America delivered them to the LZ and the reinforced patrol continued the engagement with the Pathet Lao. As dusk approached, Ellison broke off the engagement to extract back to Ban Houei Sai. Murphy and Loobey were missing; during the attack on their roadblock, and being overrun, the two men successfully crawled and evaded through Pathet Lao lines, heading southwest. After three days of escape and evasion, they were successfully located (along with a starving dog) and returned back to Ban Houei Sai. The Special Forces teams were then assigned to defend the airfield at Ban Houei Sai, where they established security positions and conducted some light patrolling. No further action by the enemy ensued.

FTT-1 eventually returned to Luang Prabang, while FTT-2 remained at Ban Houei Sai until the withdrawal of all Special Forces teams from Laos in the fall of 1962.

Other *White Star* Activities in MR-I, 1962: FTT-22, Kiou Ka Cham

One of the major WSMTT activities in MR-I was holding the FAR defensive position at Kiou Ka Cham, south of Luang Prabang. GM-11's mission was to secure the area, provide presence, and block the Pathet Lao from any movement north toward the royal capital.

PFC James W. "Jim" Young, Jr. had served a four-year tour as a Marine on Okinawa where he first learned of the 1st SFG (A). After his discharge, he was encouraged by an NCO friend to enlist for a mission in the growing activities of U.S. advisors serving in Southeast Asia. He enlisted in the Army, but was not allowed to enlist for Special Forces. He served as an airborne-qualified paratrooper in an Honest John rocket battery, in the 101st Airborne Division. In May of 1961 he volunteered for Special Forces. He joined the 7th Special Forces Group (Airborne) and trained as a communications operator. In January of 1962, after completing all training requirements, he received his "3" designator and was assigned to SF team A-3, a brand-new team. Captain James E. Gleason was the detachment commander, First Lieutenant George Marecek the XO, and Sergeant Harry D. "Crash" Whalen the team sergeant. A few weeks later, the team received orders for deployment to Laos. Upon their arrival in-country, they were met by U.S. embassy representatives in Bangkok, but were not allowed to get off their C-124 until an Air America aircraft was alongside. After transferring team gear, they flew directly to Luang Prabang to link up with Major Ripley's B-team, where they would first learn of their mission. The team would become FTT-22, and conduct split-team operations at Kiou Ka Cham with GM-11. Captain Gleason took three men with him to operate at the command's headquarters location with Colonel Poonchan (a separate FTT) and Lieutenant Marecek formed FTT-22 to work at one of GM-11's battalion base camps, led by Lieutenant Colonel Wong.

While the bulk of the team remained at Luang Prabang preparing for the mission, Captain Gleason, Lieutenant Marecek, Sergeant Whalen, and Sergeant Clarence R. Parke flew aboard an H-34 helicopter to meet with the outgoing FTT at Kiou Ka Cham and conduct a reconnaissance of the positions. (The previous team trained with BI-25 and BI-26 of GM-16; it is not known which battalion FTT-22 was with. The outgoing teams, FTT-23 and FTT-23A were commanded by Captain David L. Wise, FTT-23, and Lieutenant William R. Beal, FTT-23A. Captain Rueben Mooradian had his team north on the road from FTT-22 at Xiang Ngeun.)

James W. Young described their first week at the B-detachment:

> The rest of us remained in Luang Prabang, because we were told were having a new team house (hootch) being built for us. Gleason and the others returned. Two days later, Gleason took his split-team and departed to their mission site, working with the GM-11 commander at the village of KKC [Kiou Ka Cham]. Our split-team hung around Luang Prabang for five or six days. Lieutenant Marecek kept us busy doing map studies—we had a relief map of the area, like a 3-D map, we used for the study. He wanted at least two of us to go out on every patrol the unit went on. We were also told that we would be "welcomed" by Pathet Lao mortar fire, something they did whenever they heard choppers landing.[32]

Lieutenant Marecek's team left Luang Prabang with what they could carry aboard an H-34 and headed to Kiou Ka Cham. The battalion location was thirteen to fourteen kilometers from Kiou Ka Cham, near the Nam Ming River crossing. (The Lao had constructed a floating, pontoon-type bridge there.) Coming from the direction of Xieng Ngeun in the north, one traveled down the road from the top of a hill toward the bridge and river. Across the bridge there was a flat area and a few huts, and then the road continued south as it climbed the next hill.

Colonel Poonchan, commander of GM-11, had a headquarters at the top of the hill; Captain Gleason collocated his small FTT with the colonel. The road continued south from this location (Route 13) and curved up and around a mountain to a knob-type ridge, where a battalion of GM-11 was located. South, across the valley in front of the battalion camp, were Pathet Lao positions. (GM-11 replaced GM-16 for the blocking and presence mission at Kiou Ka Cham.)

The battalion camp was secured with minefields and wire, some of which were still in existence from the earlier days of French occupation. The *tahans* hung cans with rocks inside to make a noise, and also hung Buddha charms to ward off the enemy. There were trenches for fighting positions along with weapons bunkers. The Lao battalion was armed with 60mm mortars and a 57mm recoilless rifle. There were exits out of the camp: the main exit was on the oxcart trail which connected to Route 13, then some tactical exits for patrols and outposts on the south-southeast side.

The battalion mission (similar to the overall GM-11 mission) was to secure Route 13 and prevent the Pathet Lao from reaching Kiou Ka Cham; it was considered as an area security mission. Patrols ran to the south down to the major road intersection with Sala Phou Khoung, where Route 7 intersected Route 13 (about twenty kilometers from the camp). The Nam Bing River flowed to the western side of Kiou Ka Cham and was also patrolled by the battalion. Young emphasized, "There was a lot of Pathet Lao activity in that area."

The team arrived at the camp and soon came under mortar fire. "We got mortared once in awhile. This seemed to be based on when a helicopter came, and that time when we first got there when they 'welcomed' us."[33] Young described other enemy activity:

> We would get probes of the camps. Some in the day, some in early evening, but it seems they usually were late afternoon, just around dusk. Our team had a reaction plan and we had our own trench. In front of our trench was an MG bunker position. We took care of our area of responsibility during these probes. Marecek would go to the battalion commander or XO's position. The team sergeant went to other leadership positions or a crew-served weapon position. I was in the trench with Ken Adams as our position. Although we were fired at, I did not fire back during these probes, due to not seeing what I would be shooting at; that's the way I was taught, don't fire unless you have something to fire at.[34]

During the night, the team took turns standing a one-hour watch, normally lasting till 0530 a.m. when everyone was wakened by whoever stood the last post. The team was assigned a houseboy, who appeared around 0600 to cook throughout the day and keep the team hootch clean. Although they could not prove it, the team suspected the "house boy" was really a battalion plant to report on the activities of the team. Lieutenant Marecek procured an immersion heater for their use and they built a shower/bath arrangement, requiring a ladder to get up into. One of the morning rituals consisted of driving a jeep with a trailer loaded with fifty-five-gallon drums (provided to the team by the battalion) down to a stream near Route 13 to fill up with water. If the jeep was unavailable, detachment members carried a Lister bag on a pack board down to the stream.

After breakfast, the day got started. SP4 Peter Zaleski, the team medic, began his day visiting the Lao battalion aid station, obtaining updates and situational awareness on medical issues and problems in the camp. PFC Young (commo) conducted his morning BTB and commo checks, transmitted any messages Marecek needed sent, and forwarded any requests for gear or chow. (There were three commo checks a day—morning, mid-noon, and early evening.) Marecek and Sergeant Whalen began their day by meeting with the battalion leadership.

During these activities, the remainder of the team conducted a "morning walk" around the defensive positions to check on the readiness of the battalion, accompanied by the team's interpreter. Young describes a common "morning walk": "We talked to the troops, asked them questions to see if they knew what they were doing, when they had serviced their weapons, etc. We checked the wire; we checked the firing pins on the crew-served weapons. Sometimes we would find the firing pins missing. This was that Buddha cultural thing where they did not like to kill others, so they took the pins out."[35]

Team training classes started first thing after breakfast, around 0800 hours. Each class was dependent on which element of the battalion was scheduled for training, and which subject needed to be taught. A class size was normally two squads of *tahans*. Young explained:

> We were responsible for training our own skill proficiencies, but we also helped and pitched in with other classes for cross-training. Some classes were just individual crews, like the 57mm recoilless guys. We kept them interested by bore-sighting the weapons at the Pathet Lao across the valley and let them look into the scope when we fired. Other range classes were conducted in the clearing at the entrance to the camp—we did not have enough open area to build ranges. We would use string with markers at 100 yard intervals to mark the distance; we put up paper targets on the trees for them to shoot at. We did hand grenade throwing.
>
> Everyday there was a morning reconnaissance patrol, out past the outposts and down into the valley. It left the camp through the minefield lanes on the southern side.
>
> We could see a Pathet Lao guy in a tree; they had OPs too, with that one guy in a tree as lookout. We never had close contact with them, we did not try to ambush them, and we just patrolled out to check things out. But, there was a lot of firing in other areas around the camp when they did probes to our position; they only ever used a few guys when they did this.[36]

About 1100 daily, activities tapered off and the Lao took their *poc* time for a couple of hours. If possible, after *poc* time, the team tried to fit in a class or two. The training had its odd moments, given the education level of the common *tahan*, as described by Young:

> Once Lieutenant Marecek was giving a map class. He was using an orange to illustrate how the earth was round. The students (who knew little beyond their village) asked him to point out where the Mekong River was located, because that was the biggest terrain feature they knew about. He showed them on a map where it was. They asked what all the other blue was on the map, and he tried to explain what the oceans were. They were incomprehensive, did not believe him, so they just got up and walked out of the class.[37]

At the end of each day, Marecek met with the battalion leadership to go over the day's activities and plan for tomorrow. The evening radio transmission was conducted, and the team serviced their weapons, sharpened their knives, and had dinner.

The "Long Patrol"

The longest patrol conducted by FTT-22 was four days in length. One day, Lieutenant Marecek went to a meeting in Luang Prabang where the situation with the Pathet Lao in GM-11's area was discussed. Upon his return, he talked over the matter with the battalion commander, suggesting they put a patrol together and go out and seek the Pathet Lao. Colonel Wong seemed to think there were fifteen to twenty Pathet Lao who were working the Nam Ming River valley; they appeared to follow the river, and go from village to village to recruit young men. The commander of GM-11 heard from his sources that if the villagers did not provide young men they were just taken by the Pathet Lao. He decided to send out an ambush patrol to stop them.

Sergeant 1st Class James D. Hunter (operations and intelligence) went out on the patrol with a platoon of *tahans* and their lieutenant. Young carried a PRC-10. Marecek decided to form an additional patrol to investigate. There would be some risk, as Young remembered: "We had no planned combat support for this mission. Major Ripley made it clear to us that we were on our own and he would not consider any requests for stuff like air support from Air America. Colonel Poonchan had some artillery, but you could never get any of that either."[38]

The patrol of twenty *tahan* passed through the town of Kiou Ka Cham and maneuvered down to the village of Nam Ming, about two kilometers north of Kiou Ka Cham. It was an old, abandoned village which appeared to have been bombed earlier in the war, but still had a few huts standing. The patrol did not experience any major problems with the Pathet Lao during this foray. Marecek positioned himself with the team sergeant and Sergeant Hunter in the front of the patrol, in order to advise the Laotian lieutenant. Zaleski took the middle, and Young walked at the rear of the patrol. At the front of the main patrol, the Lao lieutenant sent forward a vanguard element to scout the trail.

The patrol reached the river in the late afternoon, between 1500 and 1600 hours. They took the opportunity sit in the water and wash the sweat and dirt off from the day's walking (the water was chest deep), and rested. About an hour later, a Lao Theung tribesman came to meet them and invited the patrol to spend the night in his village across the river where the patrol spent the night, and the next day re-crossed the river to set up an ambush near a village (where they thought the Pathet Lao would be coming next). While in the village, sources or informants told Lieutenant Marecek the size of the Pathet Lao contingent was larger than thought; the patrol had already taken pot shots throughout the day so it was decided to leave the area.

In the middle of this ongoing operation, Marecek, the team sergeant, and Hunter went to Bou Gia on an Air America H-34 to go discuss the situation with the Hmong villagers.

Whenever the patrol was in a village, Zaleski the medic worked with the elderss to try to impart some medical knowledge about using water—how to sterilize it, where to bathe, clean, and where to defecate—in order to improve their health.

When the patrol reached a position west of Kiou Ka Cham, the mission ended. After all personnel were accounted for, there was a minor problem. Young explained: "We returned from the patrol, we were out west of KKC. We entered through their outpost area. I was in the vanguard with five *tahans*. We would then check our gear and equipment. We used those toe-popper mines, M14s. One of the *tahans* was missing one. We used the mines for ambush patrols. It bothered us one was missing, and we worried who may use it or find it."[39]

On July 23, 1962, the camp held a celebration to commemorate the signing of the neutrality declaration. As the withdrawal of *White Star* FTTs commenced, the entire FTT reformed and redeployed to Vientiane; they were counted out by the ICC and flown to Bangkok, where they were debriefed by Agency representatives prior to flying on to Hong Kong. Jim Young summed up FTT-22's mission in Laos: "I think we were prepared and accomplished the mission due to the people in the unit. They were sharp, serious, and problem solvers. No one on the team was dependent on another; we could get things done on our own, but we were good as a team working together. Marecek was a fine officer. He knew his tactics. He was a good people man, he could read people. He also stayed two steps ahead of most."[40]

Other SF Activities throughout Laos

Operation *Pincushion* continued on the Bolovens, while Operation *Momentum* at Sam Thong continued to be run by Major Faistenhammer's B-team, with three ODAs to run a major training camp for Hmong SGUs. Schools and military academies continued to run throughout each military region. In Paksane, two split A-detachments served during a quiet, ceasefire stalemate at that location. SF advisors and trainers continued their work at all of the major military training centers, and SF advisers maintained their work with Laotian BIs and BVs in Thakhek, Savannakhet, Pakse, Saravane, and Dong Hene.

The Declaration of Neutrality for Laos, July 1962

Prior to the rout of the FAR in Nam Tha, talks in Geneva became stalled over the issue of a coalition government. As a hardline response to the communist violation of the ceasefire, Kennedy took coercive diplomacy measures to break the deadlock with a display of American military might, hoping to force China, North Vietnam, but mostly the Soviet Union to reign in communist aggression in Laos and support his position of neutrality for the kingdom.

He ordered the Seventh Fleet back to the Gulf of Thailand, withdrew almost 1,000 troops participating on a SEATO exercise to move to Ubon, and began deployment of an additional 4,000 troops to Thailand. It was intended to send a signal of American resolve to prevent a communist takeover of the Laotian government, and it worked. Behind the scenes, the USSR urged communist participants to close a deal at Geneva.

With the defeat of the FAR in Nam Tha, any hope the RLG could change President Kennedy's pursuit of a neutral Laos vanished. To prevent further bloodshed, Souvanna Phouma and Boun Oum agreed to form a new coalition government with the Rightists, Neutralists, and Pathet Lao. General Nosovan was out of options. The "solution" for Laos would not come about by military power, or American intervention, and Phoumi reluctantly gave in to a political solution.

The three factions met in early June on the Plaine des Jarres and reached agreement to form a Government of National Union—the coalition government was announced on June 11, 1962. Its composition would be eleven Neutralist positions, four Rightist positions, and four positions for the Pathet Lao. On June 23, the new government was sworn into office.[41]

Talks in Geneva resumed on July 2, 1962, and three weeks later, on July 23, 1962, the Declaration on the Neutrality of Laos was signed by all participants. Dean Rusk and W. Averell Harriman signed for the United States of America.

The MAAG, *White Star*, CIA, and ECCOIL had just received notice their time in Laos was coming to an end (including the Thai PARU). The declaration also applied to the withdrawal of North Vietnamese troops operating in Laos, but would be patently ignored. Air America flights still remained legal as part of the USAID economic assistance program. The CIA-propriety airline would continue to serve as the lifeline to Vang Pao's guerrillas during this period.

On July 23, 1962, U.S. military strength in Laos was reported as:

> MAAG Laos: 363 Officers and Enlisted Men, of which 60 were assigned to the FAR Military Regions, plus 445 MTT personnel; given as: WSMTTs—80 Officers and 322 Enlisted; Artillery MTTs, 10 Officers and 33 Enlisted; plus the MAAG Detachment in Thailand, of approximately 20 Officers and Enlisted; including USAF of 15 Officers, 16 Enlisted in Laos. Total U.S. Forces in Laos counted above—828.[42]

Three SF detachments from the 7th SFG (A) were scheduled to deploy into Laos the first week of July 1962, but in light of the direction of the pending agreement in Geneva, their orders were cancelled at the last minute (detachments led by First Lieutenant David P. Williams, First Lieutenant Paul M. Roberts, and Captain John E. Bloomfield).

The protocols outlined the procedures for the withdrawal of foreign military personnel to ensure compliance with the declaration. The International Commission for Supervision and Control in Laos (the ICC) would supervise compliance. Procedures for the withdrawal, which all *White Star* and MAAG participants had to comply with, were outlined in articles 2 and 3 of the protocol. All foreign troops, regular or irregular, were to be withdrawn from Laos, within thirty days of the ICC establishing departure and inspection points.[43]

The protocols also prohibited the reintroduction of foreign regular and irregular forces into Laos (presumably aimed at the Thai government). France was required to conclude their military involvement in Laos through agreements and arrangement with the royal government. Similar to the 1954 Geneva Agreement, however, the government of Laos could continue to receive conventional military assistance "necessary for the defense of Laos." All prisoners and interned personnel were to be released within thirty days upon the entry into force of the protocol. (Sergeant Ballenger would be repatriated in August of 1962.)

The agreement was not a good one, and merely locked in the status quo of territory occupied by the opposing forces. The ICC was neutered by the declaration, in that they were not designed nor had the authority to enforce ceasefire lines or investigate violations of ceasefire in the field. In July, Ambassador Leonard Unger replaced Ambassador Brown. There were an estimated 10,000 NVA still operating in Laos.

The Americans were wary that the North Vietnamese would not abide by the agreement, since they had not been disposed to comply with any previous agreements. During a reconnaissance flight of RF-101 Voodoo jets flying over northern Laos in the first week of August, photos revealed hundreds of North Vietnamese vehicles moving in a column along Route 7 out of North Vietnam into Laos. The convoy consisted of troop trucks, tanks, armored cars, and artillery pieces. The NVA contingent headed for the Plain des Jarres and set up encampments. Later, a flight of RF-101 aircraft conducted a mission to confirm NVA positions; one of the aircraft was hit by anti-aircraft artillery on August 13, 1962. The plane limped home to Bangkok.[44]

It was not long before China and North Vietnam established their embassies in Vientiane. The appearance of Pathet Lao and NVA on the streets of the capital became a common sight.

Military Region IV, Paksong—The Stalemate

Military Region IV was under the political patronage of Prince Boun Oum. Other than the Agency *Trailwatch* activities being conducted out of Savannakhet, Pakse, and Attopeu against communist activities along the Ho Chi Minh Trail, the remainder of Military Region IV remained fairly quiet.

There were company- and battalion-sized units of Pathet Lao throughout the region, and North Vietnamese companies occupied positions near the trail. The Pathet

Lao were armed with a variety of U.S., French, and communist-make weapons, up to 57mm recoilless rifles and 60mm mortars. They wore a khaki or black uniform, soft caps, and a mix of footgear from sandals to tennis shoes and boots. Although they were deemed better than any FAR unit in the region, they rarely had contact with them, preferring to stay off the trails and move through the jungle. They lived in jungle base camps, and only visited villages for a small time, primarily to procure supplies and glean information on the FAR.

Pathet Lao sympathizers did not carry out overt or covert resistance activities and focused on supplying main force units with food and information. The Lao intelligence system was never good enough to determine which villager was in the resistance or not, since villagers switched their loyalties based on whoever was around with the most power.[45]

FTT-Paksong

Captain William J. Richardson's FTT at Paksong was typical of the period after the signing of the declaration. The missions for the SF teams again resembled the conditions of the earlier *Hotfoot* teams—service at a static site with complacent Laotians, who were not much concerned about the enemy during the relative quiet on the battlefield. Richardson would face some of this Laotian and U.S. embassy mission's malaise during his FTT's mission.

The ODA was one of the last deploying teams in a batch of three teams scheduled for deployment to Laos in late June 1962. (The other two teams were commanded by Captain Maurice G. Bostwick—FTT-20 at Thakhek, and Captain Joseph I. Zummo, with duty at the Dong Hene officer's academy). First Lieutenant Richard M. Drenzek served as the XO on Captain Richardson's team and Master Sergeant John R. Callahan as the team sergeant.

Captain Richardson was serving with the 505th, 82nd Airborne in Europe when he put in for a tour back to the United States. He had requested duty at Fort Bragg, NC, where he joined the 7th Special Forces Group. After completing his SF training, he was assigned to Company A in the Group.[46]

The team received their orders to deploy to Laos on June 28, 1962. There was not much predeployment training, but Richardson took the time to canvas suggestions and opinions from others who had served a tour in Laos, ensuring his team did not experience any previous pitfalls. They arrived in Bangkok, transferred aircraft, and flew to Savannakhet, with a further flight down to Pakse. It was at the B-detachment where he first learned of his mission—go help a battered BI from GM-18 resting and refitting at Paksong after their return from the battle at Nam Tha. He was told by the B-team leadership, "Go put them back together."

While in-processing at the B-team, Richardson sent Sergeant Callahan ahead to Paksong to reconnoiter for a place to live. The detachment drove to Paksong and prepared their quarters for the mission.

To their dismay, they were not met by anyone in Paksong representing the U.S. mission. Captain Richardson went to the Laotian army camp to formally meet with the commander and the deputy commander, and discuss the requirements for the unit's training and equipment replacement. He later learned the deputy commander was highly suspected of being a Pathet Lao plant. Richardson said, "I had made contacts with people throughout the area, as a means of having situational awareness. It was a couple of months later I was hearing from some Swede and French expats of their suspicion about this guy. I reported this to the Agency and the B-team, but I do not know if anyone ever took action against him."

Another source of information was the ten to fifteen employees of the Operation *Brotherhood* organization. It appeared to Richardson the Filipinos had been very close to the previous team, and even had lived at times in the team house (this practice soon put to an end by Richardson).

The team held a meeting to discuss the training mission and design their plan for a training schedule, but they soon found out it was difficult to get things going with the BI. Their best success was in the training conducted at the Paksong NCO academy. Even with these difficulties, the team trained the BI mainly on weapons and patrolling.

While things were slow due to the Geneva Agreement (even the local Pathet Lao never bothered anyone), the team conducted civic action with the local populace. The team set up and ran the movies in the center of town on a soccer field. This helped the team to get closer to the townspeople—who appeared to love the gesture; the townspeople also provided a good source of information on the communists in the local surroundings. The team did several MEDCAPs in the surrounding villages and held a sick call once a week at the team house for walk-ins.

The team's best work was to establish an intelligence network of sources not only in their local area, but between Paksong and Pakse. Old French army veterans and other Europeans farmed in the area; through helping them out with barter goods, Richardson was probably one of the most informed FTT commanders on the local threat. When the farmers' potato crops lessened in yield, Richardson got seed potatoes from his commissary account to give them to plant another crop.

Contacts were also cultivated in Paksong. Off the Bolovens, on the road to Pakse, the team always visited the GM's Ranger company, which they considered a good outfit; they helped the Rangers with training and some equipment needs. In turn, and sometimes after the ceremonial Lao-Lao drinking custom, they received keen insight from the Ranger unit on any threats along the highway.

In the team's final months in Laos, the calm on the battlefield even allowed for the presence of a small amount of Pathet Lao seen visiting the villages. There was never a shot fired in anger by the BI. Richardson was amazed at the different directions of the course of the war exhibited by the embassy, the Agency, the Laotians, and the chain of command. "The left hand did not seem to know what the right hand was doing. It was very disappointing."

Upon their withdrawal in September, the team flew back to Bangkok, where they sat around for several days awaiting a flight home. Each day they were told the flight was on, and then it was subsequently cancelled.

One day with little notice, they were alerted to board the aircraft for its first leg of the flight, to Hong Kong. "We got back to Pope in the middle of the night, with no one there to meet us. That summed up the attitude about Laos duty. There were times when I really did not know why we were there or what we were accomplishing."[47]

Richardson summed up the final days of the almost two and a half years of SF involvement in Laos, at least for his team:

> The training for the NCO Academy was our bright spot—they seemed to appreciate that. Training with the Lao battalion was hit or miss. I did not think the B-team was engaged or helped out the ODAs with support … I could not understand how things could ever be coordinated throughout the country. However, our team remained professional and cohesive during the tour and we took our job seriously.[48]

The Withdrawal of U.S. Military Forces

In August, the PARU advisors and ECCOIL technicians departed Laos. Admiral Felt, CINCPAC, urged the MAAG to maintain the highest possible number of U.S. military forces in Laos until the withdrawal deadline.[49] *White Star* MTTs began withdrawing from Laos during the period 21 through 28 September of 1962. (*Pincushion* had already closed out on September 14.)

Many of the *White Star* teams continued to accomplish their mission, while some were idled, and some were pulled out of their mission assignments as early as June 23. Most teams left their camp, its infrastructure, and extra weapons, fuel, and ammunition to their counterparts. At Sam Thong, the camp was stripped by refugees and soldiers as the Americans departed. Reuben Mooradian succinctly captured the status of his team at the end, "When they signed the Geneva Accords, we knew we were leaving. My team and Gleason's team withdrew to Luang Prabang. In the last month of our deployment, we sort of sat around on our asses. Upon redeployment to the States, we went back through Vientiane, then Bangkok."[50]

It was during this period teams attempted to accomplish civic action projects prior to their departure. When it neared time to depart, WSMTT personnel boxed their weapons, accounted for sensitive items, and reported to their departure airfields. Once there, they stood in line to get on aircraft. One by one, they moved to ICC tables, presented their passports, and were counted off the checklist of known U.S. military personnel serving in the kingdom. Pathet Lao lined the airfield at Wattay, laughing and jeering at the Americans.

The B-detachments departed on October 2; the field control team in Vientiane departed October 6, 1962.[51]

MAAG Laos reported the total U.S. *White Star* contingent withdrawn from Laos as 796 officers and enlisted. The MAAG was the last to go. Arthur J. Dommen in his book, *Conflict in Laos: The Politics of Neutralization*, captured the moment: "One of the last to leave, MAAG Commander Major General Reuben H. Tucker, referred to the situation in Laos as 'a can of worms.'"[52]

After October 6, 1962, only fifteen U.S. military personnel remained in Laos, now assigned as military attachés to the U.S. embassy.

The Future of Laos

Neutrality would prove impossible given the objectives of the Pathet Lao and the need for North Vietnam to operate the Ho Chi Minh Trail. As the United States switched its efforts to give primary support to South Vietnam, an inevitable clash would emerge to confront NVA forces operating in Laos (where they were required to ensure supplies, men and equipment flowed down the trail into South Vietnam).

The coalition government would not hold for long. By 1963, a renewed civil war emerged in Laos with the RLG and Neutralists in a loose alliance to fight the Pathet Lao and NVA. America would embark on a campaign of "Secret War," using direct action and covert reconnaissance teams, Thai volunteers, and Hmong guerrillas to confront the NVA.

PART IV

U.S. ARMY SPECIAL FORCES
IN LAOS 1966–1974

CHAPTER ELEVEN

Special Forces in Laos 1964–1974: Project 404

"I generally worked with the commanders. It was important to establish rapport and gain their trust. I gave military advice in the form of tactics and different procedures to try, stuff like that. I think we should think about our allies who perished along with us, not just memorialize our own who fell in Southeast Asia. Language, rapport, trust, and understanding of a culture is very important. Many of the American problems and failures were caused by our culture of impatience, trying to get things done right away."

LTC (RET.) JOHN R. "CASS" CASSADY
PROJECT 404 ASSISTANT ARMA, 1970–1971

The strategist Colin S. Gray reminds us in his work *Explorations in Strategy* that the selection and use of any form of military power—air, sea, land, space, SOF—in conflict is shaped by what capability it brings based on fulfilling the strategic task. He stated, "It is not necessarily reductionist in a pejorative sense to recognize that there are conflicts to which a geographically or functionally specific 'key force' is strategically more important."[1]

After the withdrawal of U.S. forces from Laos in 1962, the U.S. still desired to thwart communist expansion in the region as its foreign policy objective in Southeast Asia. Some form of commitment to Laos was required to reassure allies of American resolve and to ensure Laos at least remained a neutral country. Larger geopolitical issues included adhering to the spirit of the Geneva Agreement and not providing a cause for Chinese intervention, thus widening the conflict.

Given that the U.S. could still provide assistance and military aid to Laos, allowable by the Geneva Agreement for the defense of the country, any U.S. military course of action would need to be small and discrete, yet with a big payoff (and inherently an economy of force as the war in Vietnam grew).

The use of SOF (both Army SF and USAF Air Commandos) gave policy-makers a surgical tool to support the political and diplomatic goals of the ambassadors and to militarily ensure the success of the Military Assistance Program to modernize Lao forces to achieve a better effect on the outcome of the war. (The selection of the appropriate "key force" in and of itself, gives it strategic utility.) This course of action was called Project 404.

Background

After the signing of the July 23, 1962 Geneva Accords, all U.S. military personnel departed Laos, with the exception of the embassy's military attaché offices. General Reuben Tucker took the Military Advisory and Assistance Group (MAAG Laos) to Thailand, establishing his headquarters in the Capital Hotel in Bangkok located on Phahon Yothin Road, separate from the JUSMAAGTHAI on Satorn Road. To continue administration of the Military Assistance Program inside Laos, a requirements office (RO) for military assistance was created within the USAID in Vientiane and manned by retired military personnel.

For cover in Thailand, the MAAG Laos was renamed as the Deputy Chief JUSMAGTHAI. The function of the DEPCHJUSMAGTHAI (as seen by the ambassador in Laos) was providing military assistance for end use in Laos; the "advisory" function was dropped in compliance with the Geneva Agreement (thus only one "A" in the MAAG title). The deputy chief's authority ended at the Mekong River border between Thailand and Laos.

Prior to JCS implementation of Project 404, the air and army attachés in Vientiane surreptitiously augmented their staff with personnel on temporary duty assignment into the kingdom, attached to the attaché offices. The additional TDY personnel were of necessity based on the lack of sufficient personnel in the RO to administer the Military Assistance Program, countrywide.

The initial use of covert U.S. personnel augmentation began in 1964, when U.S. Army personnel were sent into various military regions to observe end-use of American-supplied equipment and to provide battlefield intelligence.

In the early operation of the program, the attaché's offices agreed any personnel augmentation required permanent manning, not in-and-out, six-month TDY personnel. On May 5, 1966, the JCS approved Project 404 as a measure to provide the needed personnel support in a permanent change of station (PCS) status to the attachés. The initial Project 404 package consisted of 117 military personnel and five civilians. Project 404 personnel were assigned to and administratively managed by the Deputy Chief JUSMAGTHAI, with OPCON to the air and army attachés in Vientiane. Funding was provided by CINCPAC.[2]

The mission of Project 404 personnel was to "observe and administer" the effectiveness of the military support being given to Laos. Later, their duties would include military advisory assistance, technical support, and intelligence gathering. The assistant attachés were required to submit status reports on the condition of U.S. equipment and the performance of the Lao military.

The U.S. embassy had been allowed to keep its military attaché office as part of the 1962 agreement. Within the military attaché's office both a senior USAF and U.S. Army attaché were assigned, along with their staffs. Upon arrival of Project 404 personnel to Vientiane, they were designated as *assistant* air attachés (AIRA) and *assistant* army attachés (ARMA) and placed under the control and direction of the appropriate senior service attaché. This gave them cover as "non-combat" personnel in Laos. U.S. Army Project 404 personnel supported the U.S. embassy with combat support and combat service support and provided military advisory teams throughout all the five military regions of Laos.

There were basically two types of U.S. Army Project 404 "observers" and "augmentees":

- Logistic, support, and administrative: these personnel came from branches such as signal, army security agency, intelligence, clerical, and other critical support skill sets and worked from the embassy to administer support. This list also included PSYOP, counterintelligence, and interrogation support.
- Assistant army attachés (ARMA): these were as little as one man or up to three- to five-man teams assigned as regional observers and advisors stationed in the military regions of Laos (MR-I through MR-V). A normal composition of a team in a military region was one lieutenant colonel or major, possibly one or two captains, and one or two enlisted men as radio operators.

The JUSMAGTHAI in Bangkok assisted in advising Laotian psychological operations staff in Vientiane to prepare various PSYOP products for delivery by Royal Laotian forces. Project 404 ARMAs were supplied with PSYOP leaflets from the U.S. embassy in Vientiane for use in the field.

U.S. Army enlisted (EM) and NCO personnel assigned to Project 404 attended the military assistance training advisor course (MATA) conducted by the U.S. Special Warfare Center at Fort Bragg, NC. Personnel assigned to Project 404 required knowledge of tactics and techniques of internal defense and development operations (IDAD) and duties of a military assistance training advisor. The MATA course was twelve weeks long.

Academic instruction consisted of background information and statistics on the country of Laos (geography, culture, history, and so forth), then military, paramilitary and interagency organization in the host country. Instruction included the administration of unconventional warfare programs, tactical subjects oriented on the tactics and techniques for combat in Laos, pacification and civic action, and the role of the U.S. advisor. Additionally, Project 404 students were oriented and trained on the types of weapons, communications, and demolitions they would be exposed to as trainers and advisors. Language training was a requisite, preferably Thai

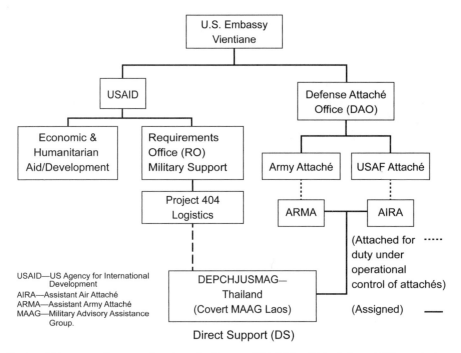

Project 404 personnel were assigned to the Deputy Chief Joint United States Military Assistance Group (DEPCHJUSMAG) in Bangkok and then further assigned in support of the U.S. embassy's defense attaché's office in Vientiane.

or Lao, but proficiency in the French language could suffice for course qualification (up to 300 hours was devoted in the course for language training).

Project 404 personnel were also required to serve as observers and to collect intelligence. Courses were taught on intelligence-collection activities, photography, and reporting. A working knowledge of political warfare and psychological warfare was essential to understand how to combat communist ideology.

Project 404 Communications

Communications to control the Project 404 personnel in the field were conducted from the attaché compound using a UNIVAC 1004 terminal, run by the Air Force. Both Air Force and Army communications personnel were responsible for the field operations of Project 404 radio operators. For Army Project 404 communications personnel, all radio operators and communications chiefs lived in House 18, located between the Palace Hotel and the Satthi. (The Palace hotel was also the preferred lodging for Air America personnel.)

To facilitate communication with Thailand, a microwave radio station was established at Udorn, run by Page engineers. A microwave station was also later constructed at Pakse, to make communications with Ubon.

In the field, KWM-2s were located at Pakse, Savannakhet, Luang Prabang, and Long Tieng. These were bulky devices; in the event of imminent evacuation from any of these sites, the radio operators were required to destroy the commo equipment in place, since the equipment could not be loaded aboard helicopters. In an effort to overcome this liability, portable SSB radios were issued to the radio operators.

In the field, the radio operator's job was to report back to Vientiane (RTT method) with their logistics, personnel, intelligence, and situation reports. At the base station in Vientiane, Project 404 radio operators transmitted information down pertaining to the deployed teams' operations. (This communications system was not used to relay any psychological warfare products or transmit any PSYOP products.)

Master Sergeant (Ret.) Fred Sebren was serving in the 77th, and then later 7th Special Forces Group at Fort Bragg, during the early 1960s. He helped support the deployed *White Star* teams, but did not deploy to Laos. Sebren was a Special Forces 05B, and then became a 312 Area Communication Chief. His next tour was with the 1st Special Forces Group on Okinawa, as the Group Communications Chief.

He received a phone call from Ms. Alexander (personnel) about duties with project 404; he was friends with others who had served with Project 404, and was familiar with and had an understanding of the assignment; he agreed to accept the tour. (Fred was assigned to the JANAF attaché office—Joint Army–Navy–Air Force—Project 404, from April 3, 1970 through March 2, 1971.)

Sebren signed into the Project 404 Headquarters in Bangkok, reporting to the six-story Capital Hotel building. He found everyone dressed in civilian clothes. He reported to the sixth floor, met by armed guards when the elevator opened. After in-processing, he was flown to Vientiane. Sebren described his initial activities upon arrival:

> Most of my Project 404 in-processing was conducted in Vientiane. I flew in the embassy shuttle—a C-47—and was met by Kurt Moyer and Sergeant Noltes. I conducted in-processing, receiving an embassy ID card, Lao driver's license, and a set of travel orders from the JANAF section which made me priority #1 for travel. Interesting though, was it was a JANAF order but it had a Navy fund cite. I was to be the Comm Chief for the JANAFs in the Attaché's office.[3]

The Air Force communications officer was Gene Rossi. Sebren said, "I worked with Duskin, Kurt Moir, Norman Nolting on the administration side. Other SF personnel I knew were Billy Phipps and Reuben Mooradian, who came on board in July 1970. My position required being responsible for the Air Force supported terminals and DCS operations support to the JANAF staff. In addition supporting the RSOs in the field, I had four SF commo operators: Hotujec, Swick, Long—all TDY from the 6th Group—and Rachfort Hayes TDY from the 1st Group."[4]

Sebren's duties as Army comms chief required him to travel to the field to coordinate with Army communicators and solve problems. He normally lodged in the ARMA compounds during his travels. He traveled using Air America assets; most of his flights were safe but there was one time on a flight to Sam Thong when the aircraft came under pot-shots from enemy forces.

His most exciting venture in Laos occurred during the evacuation of Long Tieng when the Air America ammo dump was blown up. Sebren joined sergeants Swick and Hotujec to fly with Bob Moberg, using the attaché's helicopter. At Long Tieng, the three recovered communications gear at the site. Sebren described the strange sight they made upon their return to Vientiane: "When we got back to Wattay, we commandeered a Royal Lao Army 2½-ton truck to move the commo gear through town. We must have been a strange sight—Americans in civilian clothes driving a Lao Army truck!"[5]

At the end of his one year Project 404 tour, Fred was replaced by Master Sergeant Spivey; Sebren returned to duties as communications chief with the 1st SFG (A) on Okinawa.

Army Chief Warrant Officer Raymond J. Millaway served with Project 404 from 1970 up to its phase-out in-country (as a result of the Paris peace treaty). He served as a communications and crypto officer and traveled extensively throughout Laos to provide communications advice and training. One of his duties was exchanging crypto materials with other U.S. military personnel operating in Laos. He also worked with supporting bases throughout Southeast Asia which also assisted Laos operations. He often worked alongside SOF ARMAs and AIRAs deployed out in the military regions, especially during seasonal combat operations. He described his impression of how Project 404 was handled between Vientiane and Bangkok:

> It was apparent once you processed into Deputy Chief JUSMAG-Thai that it was a "paper tiger;" it was pretty obvious the embassy in Vientiane was the power. The Ambassador, AIRA and ARMA were joined at the hip.
>
> The embassy approved everything going on in Laos. Ambassador Godley, also known by the nickname the "Field Marshal," traveled extensively throughout Laos and considered himself the equivalent of any military General Officer! Once, he personally drove a captured enemy tank partially back to Vientiane from a battle up north.
>
> No one got assigned to Project 404 without the Dep Chief knowing about it, even if you were just TDY. Project 404 message traffic was handled separately in all the strategic and tactical communication systems. Messages with "404" headers were forwarded to the ARMA and AIRA; the Dep Chief was not even CC'ed on the day-to-day in-country operational traffic. They were only like ADCON of the program. However, when they moved to Udorn, where all the classified stuff was going on with the various agencies and military headquarters there supporting directly the War in Laos, they got more involved.[6]

By the year 1969, American involvement in Southeast Asia was primarily focused on winning the Vietnam War, while Laos was relegated to a backwater, economy-of-force mission. U.S. strategic objectives in Laos consisted of preventing the communist overthrow of the Royal Laotian Government, tying down and punishing North Vietnamese forces, and interdiction of the Ho Chi Minh Trail. To circumvent the Geneva restrictions forbidding the introduction of U.S. combat forces into a neutral country, the military strategy for Laos consisted of covert support to Hmong guerrillas under General Vang Pao and secret training camps and air bases in Thailand for the training of irregulars and Lao army and air force units (using the 46th Special Forces Independent Company and the Air Commandos *Waterpump* detachment). Project 404 expanded the military attaché's office within the U.S. embassy in Vientiane by assigning U.S. Army and USAF Air Commandos as "assistant attachés" to boost the numbers of Military Assistance Program advisors throughout the five military regions and major combat airfields in Laos.

The First Special Forces Assistant ARMA

Captain Jim R. "Rod" Paschall (U.S. Army Special Forces) was one of the assistant army attachés assigned to Laos in the summer of 1964 (two years before Project 404 became official).

Captain Paschall had just returned to Fort Bragg, NC from his assignment with the 5th SFG (A) commanding an A-detachment in Darlac Province, South Vietnam. His team's mission consisted of border-surveillance duties on approximately a seventy-kilometer front. Later at Fort Bragg, in the spring of 1964, he was serving as an aide to General Yarborough when he received a call from Washington D. C. He had been selected to go to Laos and work for the army attaché. The requirements for the job included language (Paschall spoke French), combat experience in Vietnam, and preferably someone Special Forces-qualified who understood and had experience in working with local and native forces at the small unit level.[7]

He arrived in Vientiane and received his mission from the army attaché: deployment to the Plaine des Jarres to observe and "hold hands" with General Kong Le and his Neutralist forces (FAN). Paschall settled into the embassy villa reserved for military assistant attachés and prepared to begin weekly forays up to the Plaine des Jarres. (Kong Le's headquarters at this time was located at Ban Na, but the FAN would soon be in the process of moving to Moung Soui.) Paschall would work alone as the only U.S. military advisor to the FAN at this location. (There were other, permanent assistant army attachés on the PDJ—one was Lieutenant Colonel Chuck Elliot). Rejecting the surreptitiousness and secrecy surrounding the addition of more U.S. military personnel to the battlefield, Paschall wore his military uniform and carried a concealed .45-caliber pistol and his military ID card. Being captured was a concern; the military advisors working in Laos wanted to be treated as POWs under Geneva protection, if caught.

He flew back and forth to the PDJ on either a U-10 Helio Courier or in Air America's Pilatus Porters. As an advisor, he lived in a tent like the Neutralist forces

254 • THE GREEN BERETS IN THE LAND OF A MILLION ELEPHANTS

he was assigned to and shared their food. He had three duties to perform, as assigned to him by the army attaché:

> My number one job was to observe and report on Kong Le and the FAN, on a weekly basis. I would travel out to the PDJ on Monday, stay all week, and then return to the embassy on Friday. For some reason, the forces in Laos did not fight on the weekends! I typed up my report each Friday and gave it to the Military Attaché.
>
> The second task I had concerned the introduction of a Thai 105mm artillery battery onto the PDJ. My job was to coordinate to have them "sanitized" so they did not appear to be from the Thai forces. This battery was located at Korat. The intent was to outfit them, dress them, etc. to look like a Lao Army artillery battery. This mission was a total failure! The sanitization. They had distinct Thai equipment.
>
> The third thing was known as the Vientiane "Coup" patrol. Every time there was a Coup in the capital, it always seemed that the coup plotters moved tanks to surround the U.S. ambassador's residence. So, we had a job to patrol the streets at night looking for any signs of this activity. We patrolled in an embassy sedan. The tank park (which had about five tanks) was located about a mile and a half from the ambassador's house. I did this job, pulling guard, mostly on the weekends when I was back from my weekly trips to the PDJ.
>
> I had personal conversations with Kong Le, maybe an hour or longer. He was very familiar with U.S. doctrine and tactics; we had trained him in several schools, as well as him being knowledgeable of Russian military doctrine and tactics taught to him by the communist forces on the PDJ. He had five PT-76 tanks.[8]

The assistant ARMAs were also required to gather intelligence. Paschall described his role: "I got a further task from the Army Attaché, Bill Law (who had been an OSS agent and one of those who parachuted into Thailand to help them fight against the Japanese). One of my ongoing tasks during the performance of my duties was to collect intelligence on the Pathet Lao and NVA weaponry on the PDJ. This task came from the DIA. But this task also covered the entire country."[9]

The procedure was simple. "On Friday, the Attaché would meet me upon my return to Vientiane (in the afternoon) and give me a list of places where the Royal Laotian Army had recovered communist arms (like AKs, mines, etc.). I put trading material (cigarettes and booze) onto an H-34 and we flew to the location and negotiated, bartered, and so forth, with the regimental commanders to 'buy' that stuff off of them."[10]

After "cutting deals" in three or four places to procure items of intelligence usefulness, Paschall returned with his pilot to Vientiane and cross-loaded the items on an Air America C-46, which had been waiting at Vientiane, then on to Don Muang airport in Bangkok, landing at night.

To preserve secrecy, the plane taxied over near the hangars, stopping short on the runway. Alongside the runway ran a ditch, in which Civil Air Transport (CAT) maintenance technicians and loadmasters remained hidden. They took the collected items off the plane and transloaded them onto a USAF C-130, which then flew to Okinawa. After a few nights' rest in the Oriental Hotel, Paschall returned to Vientiane to continue his duties. (An additional intelligence task performed by Captain Paschall was reporting on the road the Chinese were constructing in northern Laos.)

His most difficult intelligence task was in procuring a PT-76 tank for the Department of the Army's Aberdeen Proving Grounds. The amphibious tank belonged to Kong Le, who generously gave it to the Americans, refusing to accept payment (there was $250,000 in gold available to buy the tank).

Another intelligence task for Captain Paschall was providing information on enemy forces for nomination as targets by the air attaché in Vientiane. Being an assistant ARMA also included exposure to combat. Along with the threat of occasional bombardment from NVA mortars, Paschall also participated in one of GM-11's major operations—Operation *Triangle*. He performed as a ground liaison officer to FAR combat forces involved in one of the three prongs of the attack coming south from Luang Prabang along Route 13. GM-11's mission included clearing communist forces from Route 13 and linking up with elements of the FAR maneuvering north from Vientiane. Paschall described this maneuver:

> I was involved in a major operation in July of 1964, a combat operation, but not with Kong Le's guys, but with GM-11. This was Operation *Triangle*. I was in the constant planning of this operation each time I went back to Vientiane. The mission of GM-11 was to take the strategic crossroad at the junction of Route 7 and Route 13 (south of Luang Prabang), Sala Phou Khoun. I was flown into Phou Chia (west of the intersection). The objective, the intersection, was thought to be held by a battalion of Pathet Lao, maybe 250 guys. I think D-Day was 22 July.
>
> I landed at Phou Chia; the Agency had given me an SSB radio and a small generator to communicate with. The day after I got there, an Air Commando was flown in with his radio. He accompanied me during the attack. We took off on foot the next morning with the commander of GM-11. He was a very competent and loyal officer. We went through the jungle, starting at about 10:00 a.m. We moved eastward all day, and when it got dark we bedded down. We moved out the next morning toward the objective, but the Pathet Lao had left the intersection, firing off one shot from a recoilless rifle. The embassy was delighted when I reported our activity.[11]

Colonel (Retired) Rod Paschall reflected on the influence of the ambassador over the early assistant attachés: "It was the Ambassador's war. Leonard Unger was very much involved with what was going on and making the decisions about the war." Any initiatives by the army attaché or the assistant ARMAs in the field not in consort with the ambassador's designs were quickly put to rest by the ambassador.[12]

Major Reuben L. Mooradian, Project 404 MR-III, Savannakhet

Captain Reuben L. Mooradian was a prior veteran of Laos, serving earlier during the *White Star* Rotation VII period along with his SF team, located south of Luang Prabang in 1962. In 1966, he was serving in the 10th Special Forces Group at Bad Tölz, and was nearing completion of his tour. He wanted another Special Forces assignment, but was displeased when he learned the Department of the Army was putting him on orders to be an ROTC instructor at a high school in Miami. He went to Colonel Cavanaugh, the 10th Group commander, to seek help with a different assignment. Colonel Cavanaugh told him, "We'll tell the Pentagon you volunteer for Southeast Asia." It did not work; his assignment was changed to Fort McClellan to head a department for infantry training.

Upon his return to the United States, he traveled to Washington DC to speak with the career management office, but was subsequently told to follow orders. He met General Spivey walking in the hallways (Spivey's son was one of the first West Point second lieutenants to deploy to Laos on Operation *White Star*). Spivey fixed the problem; Mooradian would get an assignment to Project 404 if he could complete prerequisite language training at the Defense Language Institute (DLI). (Mooradian attended DLI in 1956 for the Vietnamese language).[13]

He was assigned to the 6th SF Group at Fort Bragg where after one month he received orders for the DLI in Monterrey, California. He completed a twelve-month Thai language course in just six months, and then studied the Lao language: "There was no formal program at DLI for it, so they gave me materials to self-study, with an instructor once in a while to help me. (DLI taught ad-hoc Lao—the instructor was a native Thai instructor who had lived on the Lao/Thai border). We held no classes for the six months. I studied at my quarters and met with the instructor once a week."[14]

He arrived in Bangkok in 1967, newly promoted as a major, and went to the Deputy Chief JUSMAGTHAI office (the "unofficial" MAAG–Laos) for in-processing. He flew to Vientiane in an Air America C-47 and was met by members of the staff from the army attaché's office and told he would be performing his mission in Savannakhet. He asked, "What's the mission?" They said, "You will find out from the ambassador that you only report and observe—you will not do military advising and you will not get involved in fighting."

Unbeknownst to Mooradian, Project 404 officers serving in Laos required preapproval from the Central Intelligence Agency assets in-country (as a result of the misconduct of previous assistant attachés). Fortunately, the chief of station was an old friend of Mooradian's; they had served together in Vietnam. His assignment was heartily approved as well as warm hospitality afforded him by other case officers when he arrived for work in Savannakhet.

Once in Savannakhet, Mooradian met the Project 404 army assistant attaché he was replacing. (The officer was being relieved for cause, thus the earlier apprehension and control over Army assignments by the Agency in Laos.) In the small time given for their transition, Mooradian and the outgoing assistant ARMA conducted a familiarization drive around Savannakhet and then went on to the ARMA villa, a large, four-bedroom house.

The outgoing assistant ARMA briefed Mooradian off a map in the house's library (concealed with a cloth).

> He had all the positions of the Lao military forces posted on the map, but nothing to indicate the positions of the enemy. He briefed me on the names of the commanders in the Military

Region, and told me he tried to visit each one of them every month. There were about four or five Group Mobiles assigned to the region. He said about the commanders, "But none of them are good." He pointed out which ones spoke English, which ones had American training like C&GSC, airborne, "and so forth." I was next visited by a Laotian Colonel. He was the Chief of Staff for the CG (Commanding General) of MR-III. He turned out to be a good friend and helped me a lot with information I needed to perform my job.[15]

In time, Mooradian learned the disposition of friendly forces in Military Region III. There was a residual French force still at Seno—it was a small unit assigned to the Lao airborne GM at the airfield. There was a GM located at Thakhek, responsible for Route 9, which ran east all the way to Khe Sanh. There was a GM, additionally, out near the Ho Chi Minh Trail, which was known to be a very aggressive GM. (Mooradian notes, "They always got POWs; killed NVA.") The commander of the GM was considered a tough guy, and was airborne trained. Mooradian would get along well with him, as they both spoke in broken English to one another.

There were no GMs within driving distance of the villa where Mooradian lived and lack of air transportation would hamper him from doing his job in a more effective manner. Most of his attempts to at least get increased helicopter support fell flat with the embassy, even though his job required he fly out to where the GMs were located. He accomplished most of his flying by hitch-hiking rides with Agency case officers. On the ground, he was able to make it as far as Thakhek, even though it involved driving his vehicle over bad roads.

His daily activities consisted of driving to the Agency compound to get updates and information on the local situation, followed by a visit to the Lao army headquarters. He did not attend the formal update briefings held in the morning, but preferred to discuss matters with individuals on the Lao staff, and with the colonel who was the chief of staff. He had no radio to report to Vientiane, nor was he required to write weekly reports. "I had no way of sending a message to Vientiane, except by the daily Air America flight. I could talk, however, daily with the Attaché's office on my phone, but it was in the clear, so it was hard to discuss classified operations. I did not file official reports as part of my job. There were monthly meetings. I would just bring all my stuff with me at that time."[16]

Things began to heat up in Military Region III. Just before the Tet offensive in Vietnam, the NVA were highly desirous of ridding themselves of the aggressive Lao GM operating near the Ho Chi Minh Trail. Bringing in tanks and artillery, the NVA attacked and routed the GM, forcing the Lao forces east into Vietnam. Although Mooradian was scheduled to hitch a ride out to their position the day of the attack, he missed the flight and was stranded in Savannakhet. He quickly informed Vientiane of the rout, and his dilemma in trying to reach the isolated pocket of GM forces. "We had commo with SOG over in Vietnam so we could get information on this unit. The Ambassador, when he found out about the battle and the rout, was furious. He directed that we get the Lao to come back. He told me to solve it. But, he would not let me go over to Vietnam to bring them back. I told him I could not accomplish this mission if I could not go retrieve them. The SF in Vietnam (where the GM escaped to), after talking with them, decided to take care of them and started using them on their operations."[17]

It was during this period of the war in Laos that an expanded special guerrilla unit (SGU) program was employed in Military Region III, with its purpose to take the fight to the Pathet Lao and NVA forces. Most of the Agency case officers living in Savannakhet were redirected toward this effort and began to aggressively push their units to engage in combat. Mooradian was critical on the way to employ the guerrillas: "The mistake which was made was that the Agency re-organized the G's into battalions—but they were not ready to fight in this style. Things started going downhill in 1968. When new CIA guys showed up, I did not have the rapport I had earlier and I lost my freedom of maneuver with them. When I left later, the G-force was holding its own, but only if they were not committed to a large battle."[18]

Major Mooradian was among the assistant ARMAs who extended their tours for another six months. Upon completion of his own tour, he wrote his personal observations report and submitted it to the embassy. (He did not conduct a transition with the new, incoming assistant ARMA before he left.) In July of 1969, he volunteered to go back to Laos for an additional Project 404 tour and would serve in Pakse, Military Region IV (July 1969 to 1970). Sam Todaro was one of Mooradian's radio operators in Pakse.

Project 404—Staff Sergeant Sam Todaro, Pakse 1969–1971

Staff Sergeant Sam Todaro was serving in the signal command in Bangkok when he received verbal orders for a Project 404 six-month TDY tour in Pakse from 1969–1970. He was a staff sergeant, 11F4S/05C4S/26L4S. Colonel John Frye was the army attaché at the time. After in-processing in Vientiane, he reported to his assistant ARMA team leader in Pakse, Lieutenant Colonel Reuben Mooradian. There were four members of the team living together in a villa. Two other SF operators were on the team: William Hansen, an 11F (SF operations and intel) and Sergeant Jim Pendleton, a commo operator. The team was provided two CJ-5 jeeps and blanket orders to travel, all from a fund cite by PACOM. The RO at the embassy provided the team with their supplies.

After the breakfast each day, Lieutenant Colonel Mooradian plus one member of the team visited the local FAR unit and attended their headquarters' morning briefings. At times, Sam would visit the local Thai artillery battalion. (He was Thai-language trained and served as the team's interpreter.) The team used their CJ-5 jeeps for travel around the Pakse area. Lieutenant Colonel Mooradian wore his military fatigues, but the remaining members of the team mostly worked in civvies.

The Project 404 advisory duties consisted of instructing Lao counterparts in rappelling, airborne operations, the 57mm recoilless rifle, weapons training, and tactics. On occasion, the members of the team distributed PSYOP products. If needed, team members assisted Air America and others to help deliver supplies by air, serving as "kickers." Other duties included the sending of a daily sitrep and the operation of an intelligence net (Todaro and William Hansen ran the net—they were both 11Fs, operations and intelligence qualified.)

Todaro describe the threat in the Pakse area during his tour. "The threat in this area was mostly outside of Pakse. I did come under fire during a visit to Kilometer 21 (north of town) when I woke up on the front line with the Thai artillery to help them with returning fire on the enemy, using direct fire 'beehive' rounds. Interestingly enough, the Lao troops with us ran away during this engagement. (We had been told by earlier *White Star* guys about them doing this.)"[19]

There were also dangers when flying with either Air America or assisting the local Raven FACs. "On occasion, I would fly as a 'Covey' back-seater with the Raven, conducting Forward Observer duties (FO). One day we had an emergency with the aircraft. The pilot felt he could get the plane returned to the airfield, but he wanted to play a joke on the tower. When we got near, he told me to parachute out of the hatch floor while he simulated the aircraft in trouble. We were flying in a Pilatus Porter STOL aircraft. After the tower panicked, the pilot re-powered the aircraft and landed!"[20]

Lieutenant Colonel Don Wilson replaced Mooradian. The project 404 team participated in a large FAR operation. Todaro reflected on his experience:

> There was a big operation going on (this is 1971?). We loaded aboard trucks with about 500 soldiers and moved to Kilometer 21. By the time we established the camp, we were down to around 400 *tahans*; then it dropped to 350, and by the next day we only had 150 men. The operation [this may be *Maharat II*] was supported with Air Commando CH-53s and maybe some CH-3s. By the time it was ready to launch, we only had about 60 troops. We used Hmong (Meo) troops to secure and protect the launch site.[21]

While in Pakse, the team assisted the Air Commando AOC (air operations center) with transmitting their sitreps and weather reports. In April 1972, Todaro went up for a short tour at Long Tieng as a radio operator to support an Agency operation. The team was always armed when operating out in the field. Todaro also served on a short mission in Luang Prabang to assist them with commo and operations and also occasionally a short trip to Savannakhet to support that site.

While he was in Laos he met other SF assistant ARMAs: Lieutenant Colonel Charlie Brewington, John Newsome, Tommy Ennis, Fred Sebren, and Ehfel Duffield. (Later, Todaro served as a translator in Phitsanulok, Thailand, to help interpret cockpit controls for T-28 student pilots.)

Lieutenant Colonel Alan E. Rozen, Project 404 ARMA, Long Tieng (LS-20A)

After his earlier tour in Laos as a *White Star* SF detachment commander (FA-68 in 1961), Al Rozen served as the battalion/brigade S3 of the 1st Infantry Division at Fort Riley, KS. He went on to an assignment in Germany, serving in an armored battalion, and then received orders for Vietnam. He subsequently found out he was selected for Project 404 to serve as a special projects officer for the Army Attaché in Vientiane, Colonel Duskin, in 1968.

After three months into his assignment in Vientiane, he was ordered to deploy to Long Tieng and serve as a liaison officer to General Vang Pao. Vang Pao was just beginning his push to retake the PDJ and Colonel Duskin wanted his man on the spot. Rozen was provided a communications NCO and moved to Long Tieng. He had not been trained, however, as a Project 404, MATA-course qualified advisor, but his SF experience and earlier deployment in Laos provided him with the necessary skills to serve as a liaison officer and advisor to the Hmong forces.

Upon his arrival to Long Tieng, he met with the CIA representative. They both attended a dinner and held a *bacci* with Vang Pao. This socialization was important to Rozon and allowed him the venue to effectively coordinate what he required for the mission. (A key component of Special Forces technique is the establishment of good relationships with senior personnel in the mission area.) In time, Rozon found the Raven FACs in control of the U.S. military liaison function, precluding his need to act as a liaison officer to Vang Pao, so he decided to be helpful in another way and moved to help organize the defenses on Skyline Ridge and a 105mm site east of Long Tieng. Rozon remembered some key events at Long Tieng: "There were a lot of B-52 arc-light strikes on the PDJ during the operation. The PDJ looked like a bunch of pot-holes. One night two tanks tried to overrun a position and were destroyed. Out of a bunch of captured equipment, I got a Russian jeep to use, solving my transportation problem! I used the nighttime ABCCC. I could talk directly to them for air support. The radio operator was Steve Swick, who was with Lieutenant Colonel Charlie Brewington. Some of this story for those times can be found in a TIME International article, 'Lifting the Veil.'"[22]

Project 404 ARMA—Major Dennis W. Lid, Military Region V— Vang Vieng with FAN, 1967–1968

Major Dennis W. Lid served with MAAG–Vietnam from December 1962 to September 1963 (he was DLI-trained in the Vietnamese language). He returned to the States and served as an infantry company commander, followed by attendance to a State Department Laotian language course in Alexandria, Virginia. He volunteered for Special Forces and completed the Special Forces officers' course in October 1967.

He was assigned to the 1st SFG (A) on Okinawa, where he commanded B-310 in Company A. After serving only three months, he received a classified mission to deploy to Laos as a Project 404 assistant ARMA. He, along with approximately fifteen other members of the 1st Group, shipped to Vientiane. The Project 404 assistant ARMA assignment given him was advising and assisting the Neutralist headquarters at Vang Vieng (the other 1st Group members were assigned to work for the embassy during their five-month TDY). Lid recalled: "I was to be an advisor to Colonel Sompet, the leader of the Neutralist army [Forces Armée Neutraliste], the FAN. They were stationed at Vang Vieng, with some of their forces to the north and east."[23]

Although he preferred to wear his military uniform, any patches or accouterments identifying him as a Special Forces officer were not allowed (he did wear his CIB and airborne wings). He was not allowed to carry a weapon, but weapons were readily available from the FAN for personal defense. He went in light, with no other military equipment than an SUV-like panel truck with right-hand steering. The Bureau of Public Roads, colocated at the site, provided him water from a water tanker truck, initially. Local Lao workers later dug his water well with a pick and shovel (it took one month; Lid was frustrated with how long it took the embassy to honor his request for money to pay them.)

The previous assistant ARMA at the site, a lieutenant colonel, was gone before Lid could conduct a transition into his new job. There was at least a radio and antennas left for his use at the site; Dennis brought the codebooks with him.

The army attaché directed Lid to "get in tight" with the FAN S3 and his staff, go where the S3 went, do what he did, and get situational awareness of the unit. (Fortunately the FAN S3 spoke English.) Lid followed up each day's activities with a daily radio report from his house.

Traveling with the unit consisted of driving on dusty roads in a jeep, or by boat, or on foot. Lid traveled on the rivers with his counterparts using a pirogue, powered by a motor attached by a long rod. In his water travels, he made it as far as Luang Prabang using this method.

The FAN headquarters was situated on the northeast side of Vang Vieng, off the main road of Route 13. The camp had barbed-wire fencing and was about four city blocks in size. It mostly consisted of wooden buildings, but there were some cement structures. The Neutralists had jeeps, 2½-ton and ¾-ton trucks, along with some French vehicles. There was a dirt strip airfield in the middle of the town. The town had bamboo thatch buildings, tin-type roofs, and some cement structures also.

The French Military Training Mission at Vang Vieng was commanded by a colonel, who had previous combat experience fighting against the Viet Minh in Laos. There were about 150 French personnel who ran the camp and provided the support personnel.

Lid was able to use an Air America aircraft to reconnoiter the FAN front-line units:

The troops were Regular Army Neutralists (FAN). They did drill, military exercises, and had a series of outposts. This was along Route 13—they had LPs and OPs. Daily, I would get up and maybe do radio comms, then go out and check stuff and gather info. I checked up on the French contingent. They were trying to get heavy mortars to the FAN, 4.2 inch (they had 81mm). The FAN troops had small arms, MGs, .30 caliber, and M1 Garands. There were some captured AK-47s they used. The troops did military combat operations against the enemy, mostly to the northeast at the Plaine Des Jarres, or near it.

The G3, LTC Chongsaly, went on some of the operations. I went for a day or two in order to gather information; once I went for a few days operation. I was not involved in their combat.[24]

At some point, Lid found the duty with the FAN boring, particularly as combat action dwindled. It also became extremely hard to get information from front-line troops necessary to fill out his reports. "I did not do formal advisory work, just speaking or discussing events with the Colonel. I would give advice to the G3, the Security Commander, the Police Commander—how to improve commo techniques, my observations when I went out on exercises, things of interest, but not really advice on tactics. My main mission was information and intelligence gathering—to be the eyes and ears for ARMA as an assistant Army Attaché."[25]

He pursued various avenues to glean situational awareness from other agencies and departments located at Vang Vieng: Operation *Brotherhood*, the USAID, and the Bureau of Public Roads. In order to establish rapport and build personal relationships, he befriended employees of these organizations and shared meals with them, to even include the local Buddhist monks.

Since he was stationed at one of the few places where the French Military Mission had assets, the army attaché tasked him to additionally report on their activities. "The big thing with the French was for me to keep an eye on them, keep them out of Moung Soui, and get them to not bring in those heavy mortars."[26]

Lid was not replaced at the end of the tour with another assistant ARMA. He and the 1st Group contingent redeployed back to Okinawa. He summed up his tour as a Project 404 ARMA: "My biggest success was preventing the French from getting 4.2 inch mortars for the FAN! Otherwise, I collected information to collate intelligence."[27]

Project 404 ARMA—Major Jack Abraham, Military Region V, Vientiane—November 1967 to January 1969

Major Jack Abraham's story reveals the dynamic between military personnel and the other support personnel assigned to and working with Project 404. Abraham served as a Special Forces officer from 1959 to 1965 prior to his tour with Project 404. He was the commander of A-233 at Boun Mi Ga and then built and commanded the A-team camp at Boun Ea Yang, in the II Corps area of South Vietnam (1964–1965), completing two tours of service in RSVN.

While he and Reuben Mooradian were attending Thai language class in Monterrey, CA, his orders were changed from the 1st SFG (A) in Okinawa to an assignment on Project 404.

He processed through Bangkok, and then was flown on to Vientiane where he was met by unidentified people from the embassy before reporting to the army attaché's office. He was briefed on the mission of Project 404. Abraham remembers, "I was replacing Rex Bludgett at Camp Chinaimo, working with General Abhay Kouprasith. General Kouprasith was the MR-V commander and his headquarters was at the camp. Rex and I then had a three to four day overlap."[28]

Major Abraham settled into a house with George Fisher, an MI officer. Fisher often entertained a number of members of the Lao military at the house in order to elicit information on the situation in Laos. After Abraham had lived with Fisher for about three months, Fisher departed Laos. Abraham wanted something closer to the camp to shorten his daily drive, so General Kouprasith helped him to procure a house in the southern suburbs of Vientiane.

Major Abraham began his work day with attendance at the morning Lao staff briefings to try and get a feel for what was going on in last twenty-four hours and then ascertain what was coming up in terms of future Laotian military activities. If any Lao military officers planned to go out in the field, he tried to accompany them.

Colonel (Retired) Abraham described his general duties: "My mission was observing and advising and getting hands on occasionally, trying to improve the Lao with their military training. I also made observations and reports on the BVs. As a result of my travels, often I was tasked to conduct reconnaissance out in the field. I also reported to the Military Attaché's office two to three times a week. I carried a pistol, but I was never under fire in MR-V."[29]

Abraham reflected on the proper role of the military advisor, which was often not followed during Project 404: "Once there was an operation northwest of Vientiane in MR-V. Colonel Miller was the Attaché then, and told me not to spend the night out with the Lao. I did not think that was right as an advisor, so I did not come home on the last helicopter. I told the Attaché that I was awaiting the last helo, but it never came. I just did not think it was right as an advisor to abandon the unit."[30]

The Battles of Moung Soui

In response to Vang Pao's dry-season offensive northeast of the Plaine des Jarres (Operation *Pigfat*), the North Vietnamese surprised the RLG with a counteroffensive. During the beginning of the 1969 wet season, NVA forces attacked onto the heights surrounding the PDJ, pushing Vang Pao's forces back west off the Plaines. Basically, all that stood between the communists and Route 13 was a line of Neutralists, headquartered at Moung Soui, with their defensive positions pushed east about five to six kilometers along Route 7. The Neutralist positions were bolstered by Thai Special

Regiment (SR) artillery battalions deployed in firebases to support FAN maneuver. In the early morning hours of June 24, 1969, the North Vietnamese attacked the Neutralist forces at Ban Khay; the attack incorporated a regiment of infantry and PT-76 tanks, followed by a subsequent attack on Moung Soui.[31]

Moung Soui was critical for the basing of a Lao T-28 RLAF squadron. Being forward-positioned allowed for more sorties in response to calls for fire on the PDJ. L-19 aircraft were stationed at the airfield for use by the artillery forward observers. It was a lucrative target and a thorn in the side of the NVA. The position was earlier threatened by NVA Dac Cong sapper attacks, both in early 1967 and again in 1968, but these had failed to hinder FAN operations.

On the last day of December 1968, the Thai SR artillery battalion of 155mm howitzers departed their positions at Ban Khay and emplaced their guns farther eastward in order to increase their effective range on the PDJ (in response to the NVA retaking the Plaines). This action was preparatory to a large T-28 strike pro-grammed for execution after the New Year. In support of the fires attack, twelve U.S. advisors deployed to the Moung Soui airstrip to assist in bomb storage and aircraft maintenance. Along with USAF personnel, Project 404 advisors were on hand to assist and advise the FAN. If the strike was successful, it was to be followed by a FAN attack on the western-most position of the communists. This limited, combined-arms maneuver—the attack included attached 105mm howitzers—required more planning than expected, so it was delayed for one month to coordinate the various pieces. Vang Pao was designated as the overall commander of the operation, with control over Colonel Sing's FAN at Moung Soui.[32]

American advisors on site soon increased to fifteen personnel. Project 404 officers included Captain Joseph Bush along with Sergeant Daniel Smokes. One officer from the RO was present, and the rest were USAF personnel. Captain Bush was an aggressive combat officer and had earlier distinguished himself during the Thai artillery bombardment of the PDJ over the December 31, 1968–January 1, 1969 attack.

Staff Sergeant David L. Pompili was assigned initially to a Project 404 assistant ARMA billet in Savannakhet. He was looking for a more ambitious role as a Project 404 advisor, and successfully transferred to Military Region II, Moung Soui.

> I went up to Moung Soi (LS-108). I replaced Sergeant 1st Class Alexander Friedus, an SF Sergeant. He was Hawaiian, and very taciturn; he did not say too much. But he did guide me on how NCOs worked the duty position. There were no other Americans at Moung Soui. I met the ARMA, Captain Joe Bush. He gave me a cursory briefing on what was going on. We lived in a little, low building, painted green with a galvanized tin roof. It was a little above, and about 50 yards from the airstrip. (I called it "reference point 1"—a visible target for Pathet Lao and NVA shelling!) We were separated by a karst from the Neutralist Headquarters, commanded by Colonel Shankamawan Sing.[33]

The mission for Project 404 at the site was to tour each unit, collecting sitreps, intelligence, and headcounts of troops for pay purposes. Captain Bush and Sergeant

Pompili were trying to build an order of battle (OB) on each unit. An average battalion was supposed to be about 525 men. The United States was providing the pay for the troops but the Laotians juggled the figures, and getting an accurate OB was difficult.

Officially, the American advisors were not authorized to carry weapons, but on site they procured M16s, .38- and .45-caliber pistols, and AK-47s. They began their duties in civvies, but later changed into military fatigues. The two advisors both worked with and flew with the A-team and B-team T-28 pilots, performing as back-seaters in the role of artillery spotters. Pompili noted, "Captain Bush and I had a SSB radio with a 450 Watt booster; we made our antennas. For ground comms, we had the HT-1s. We also had a PRC-127 SSB. We put these radios on a jeep, a 5-quarter ton. Later, we were provided a jeep configured with all the radios—we mostly used this vehicle on the airfield. I was collocated with the Thai artillery, Special Regiment 7. I stayed with them. They put up a house for me, which I also called 'Registration Point 1.'"[34]

After some time with Captain Bush, Pompili took a break and went to work in Vientiane. He was replaced by Sergeant Danny Smokes at Moung Soui.

On the night of February 10, 1969, a company of NVA sappers infiltrated the town of Moung Soui to attack the military camp. Using B-40s to breach the wire and perimeter defenses, Dac Cong sappers attacked the installation with grenades and machine guns, almost killing Colonel Sing and his family in their quarters. The ARMA quarters was also attacked with rocket fire. Bush and Smokes raced out of their sleeping quarters, armed with M16s.

Bush killed one sapper, and then was killed by AK-47 fire. Smokes was wounded, but played dead. The RO escaped detection. In dawn's light, the toll was eleven Neutralist soldiers and one American dead; several more personnel were wounded. More depressing news followed: Nakhang (LS-36) fell to the NVA on February 28. (Captain Joseph K. Bush was posthumously awarded a Silver Star for his action.)[35]

A short time after the attack, Dave Pompili was working in the Project 404 section of the embassy when he ran into Colonel Sing. Sing saw Pompili and asked, "Why are you here?" Pompili told him about some disagreements with Captain Bush and that as a result, he was taking a break from Moung Soui for a while. Sing told Pompili he was taking him back to Moung Soui, because Bush had been killed.

Pompili returned to Moung Soui and worked with Major Russell Simonetta, a field artillery officer. The team had two O-1 Bird Dogs at their disposal for aerial spotting. Pompili, being flight-qualified, flew his own Bird Dog. When Major Simmonetta left, Pompili once again went back to Vientiane.

The Loss of Moung Soui, June 24–27, 1969

By March of 1969, the enemy was in control of Sam Neua Province, with only remnants of Hmong and FAR troops remaining in isolated outposts to oppose them.

NVA troops and equipment continued to pour into Laos, clearly with intent to capture the entire Plaine des Jarres (or at least the eastern half) in order to protect their infiltration routes along routes 6 and 7.

It was Vang Pao's rainy-season plan (beginning in June) to conduct an economy-of-force effort north and northeast of the PDJ, simultaneously conducting guerrilla attacks along enemy supply lines. He also wanted to recapture key positions in Xieng Khouang Province, particularly the recapture of Xieng Khouangville. This would be a three-pronged attack, with the FAN and Thai Special Regiment Artillery team conducting offensive actions out of Moung Soui, east along Route 7. As part of their mission, the FAN required a preliminary move to Phou Kout to hold and seize key terrain overlooking Route 7.[36]

To set the conditions, Ambassador Sullivan eased bombing restrictions on the PDJ in order to conduct a massive interdiction campaign to attrite communist forces in the remaining months of the dry season (March–April). Called Operation *Raindance*, it began on March 17, 1969, severely pounding enemy storage sites, and lasting through April 7; the destruction paid off, with the FAN able to push out from Moung Soui and occupy extended positions in the surrounding mountains. The near destruction of Xieng Khouangville from the air prepared the ground for Vang Pao's forces positioned on Phou Khe to essentially walk in and capture the town.[37]

In response, in early May Pathet Lao and NVA forces counterattacked, recapturing the town and airfield at Xieng Khouangville and pushing Vang Pao's and RLG forces back from their positions at Phou Khe. The flow of enemy forces to Xieng Khouangville attracted the attention of the USAF, which began a second interdiction campaign along routes 6 and 7. This operation began on May 22, codenamed *Stranglehold*, and destroyed additional communist supplies, equipment, and enemy troop positions over a five-day period. With promise of additional air sorties for *Barrel Roll*, Vang Pao decided to begin his wet-season offensive in the latter part of June 1969. The FAN at Moung Soui began the preliminary operation, moving east to take the Phou Kout position. To assist, six American advisors from Project 404 were assigned to Colonel Sing's FAN and the SR-8 Thai artillery battalion.[38]

It was then NVA forces changed the wet-season/dry-season dynamic which had existed in the seesaw battles on the PDJ heretofore. Instead of going on the defensive, the NVA launched Operation *Thoan Thang* (Total Victory) to spoil the FAN prong of Vang Pao's rainy-season campaign in Xieng Khouang Province.[39]

On the morning of June 24, NVA forces, supported with tanks and commandos, attacked and pushed through FAN elements at Phou Kout and were soon closing on FAN and Thai artillery positions at Ban Khay. Although artillery and airstrikes destroyed some of the NVA armor (PT-76 tanks), the garrison soon began to lose its FAN and Thai artillery pieces.

First Lieutenant Robert J. Moberg served as a Special Forces *White Star* team leader during its VI Rotation in Laos, advising and training Vang Pao guerrillas in MR-1, near the Sala Phou Khoun road junction. When he returned to the States, he became an army aviator. Now as a captain, he was one of the Project 404 assistant ARMAs working at Moung Soui the morning of June 24. (He was the senior advisor to the Neutralists; out of the five Americans in the Moung Soui area with him were Captain Bessilieu and Sergeant Pompili, his artillery advisors.)

Pompili heard a report come in from the front lines stating eight NVA battalions had attacked FAN positions at approximately 0100. One of Pompili's duties included the coordination of airstrikes as a forward air guide (his call-sign was "City Hall"). He was rated to fly the Thai L-19s positioned at the airfield at Moung Soui to spot as an observer for the Thai Special Regiment artillery batteries, along with the FAN artillery. In an emergency, he could also coordinate airstrikes if a rated FAC was not in the area.[40]

Pompili was now working for Captain Moberg: "I was down in Vientiane eating at the compound (a chocolate ice cream!), when a long-faced fellow approached me and said he was the new ARMA, and that I had a reputation for 'killing off all your Captains.' This was Bob Moberg. He had been a First Lieutenant in *White Star* earlier in Laos, then went to OCS, and became a pilot. He got two DFCs when he flew in Vietnam."[41]

In April, Moberg sat Pompili down one day and said, "The shit is fixing to hit the fan." This was in reference to the build-up of NVA and Pathet Lao around Moung Soui. Dave Pompili continued:

> The FAN had some 105mm batteries. They, along with their troops, were basically just sitting in place and not being aggressive. It was a sort of stalemate. We got the mission to get them going and do something. So, we started shifting around the 105mm positions, shelling the enemy. We went hill hopping with the 75mm pack howitzers. Drop into a site, fire a bunch of rounds, then leave. The 75mms could move with 44 rounds and a two-man crew. You could drop 20–30 rounds with that thing; it would not heat up the barrel like on a 105mm tube. It fired 500 yards shorter than a 105mm, so you had to move, hop, pop, and then get out.[42]

By June, there was increased Pathet Lao activity—estimated at 9,000 troops—against the FAN. Moberg, Captain Bessilieu and Pompili were at the Thai compound, across from the BV-25. They were told by Ambassador Sullivan to let the Neutralist families evacuate. At 1230 hours on the night of the 24th, rounds began hitting their building. They called over to the FAN BV for some help, but the unit had disappeared: they had evacuated when their families went out.

Moberg had been calling for airstrikes throughout the early hours of the 24th. He remembers the day's activities:

> When the smoke from over 200 A-1E and F-4 sorties was clearing in the valley around my headquarters with the Thais during the morning of 24 June we found the NVA in the wire

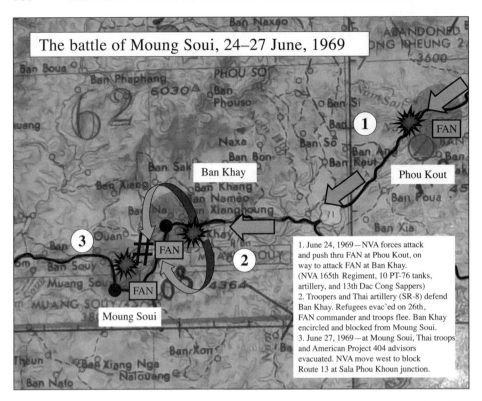

The battle of Moung Soui, 24–27 June, 1969

Ban Khay

Phou Kout

Moung Soui

1. June 24, 1969—NVA forces attack and push thru FAN at Phou Kout, on way to attack FAN at Ban Khay. (NVA 165th Regiment, 10 PT-76 tanks, artillery, and 13th Dac Cong Sappers)
2. Troopers and Thai artillery (SR-8) defend Ban Khay. Refugees evac'ed on 26th, FAN commander and troops flee. Ban Khay encircled and blocked from Moung Soui.
3. June 27, 1969—at Moung Soui, Thai troops and American Project 404 advisors evacuated. NVA move west to block Route 13 at Sala Phou Khoun junction.

Map derived from U.S. Government Joint Operation Graphic (JOG) 1:250,000; Laos series. (*Author's photo*)

and that we had lost all of our artillery. The artillery positions to the east had fought bravely with enemy PT-76 tanks in the wire, as well as numerous wounded, when an F-4 with a hung bomb flew overhead and accidentally dropped the ordnance in the middle of the 155 Howitzer position causing thirty casualties. In my compound we had sustained thirty-five wounded and five KIA. Sergeant Pompili handed me the PRC-10 and I heard, "City Hall, this is Gravel Voice! (Major Michael Werbiski, "Ski"). I'm over here at LS-108 (Moung Soui). What do you want me to do?"[43]

(Major Werbiski, hearing of the battle, hopped a ride with an Air America helicopter and was now on site at Moung Soui, becoming the senior advisor on site.) Moberg flew to Ban Khay to assess the situation.

On the night of June 24 and throughout the 25th, gunships, flare-ships, CAS, and artillery kept the base open. Pompili described the air support:

Over the next four days we took a lot of artillery shelling. Some was from the DK82mms, manned by females of the NVA. Prior to that, I used Spooky gunships to help in the defense. I was doing the ground–air calling for them. I would plot targets, translate, etc. Spectre came in. They opened up. We used two of the gunships—Albatross 67 and Albatross 68 (again, this was prior to the four days of intense shelling).

We also conducted FACing for the artillery. Captain Moberg would fly and acquire targets, shoot his 2.75-inch rockets to mark targets, and then rock his wings. We would contact Barrel Roll for fast movers. (The Artillery then was Special Regiment 8, from the 11th Infantry at

Lopburi in Thailand, the Queen's Guard.) We ran some "baby run" B-52 strikes. We FAC'ed for A1-Es, F4s, etc. We did ground and air control for H-34s, UH-1-Ds, Helios, and Porters (these were used mainly to transport logistics and ammo).[44]

On the 25th, Moberg was at Ban Khay when a Huey helicopter from the army attaché flight detachment landed amid periodic and sporadic small arms fire, carrying Major General Dhep, the 333rd Thai commander, along with the U.S. army attaché. They had both flown up to assess the situation with the Thai artillery contingent. While the senior visitors were on the ground, their helicopter was employed to backhaul wounded Thai artillerymen. Moberg had earlier planned for the eventual evacuation of the site, so the two officers met with him to discuss the details. Vang Pao responded with a fifty-man Hmong contingent to reinforce the Ban Khay garrison.

On June 26, the evacuation of FAN family members sparked a panic, and soon Colonel Sing and his FAN fled the position. The NVA encircled the outpost (now down to American advisors and SR-8) and set up blocking positions to the west, between Ban Khay and Moung Soui. Throughout the day, senior Thai and Lao military officers visited the base to assess the situation. In pride, the senior Thai army official, Major General Dhep, declared his determination to hold at all costs. It was a forlorn hope; the decision was made to evacuate the remaining Thai artillerymen and the fifty reinforcing Hmong during the afternoon of June 27.

A mix of Air America and 21st SOS helicopters at Udorn readied for the pending operation. Called Operation *Swan Lake*, the evacuation began as planned using more than sixteen helicopters, supported with A1-Es and jet aircraft overhead.

Project 404—Joseph M. Bossi (Command Sergeant Major, Ret.), Vientiane, Moung Soui, and Savannakhet

Army Special Forces Sergeant 1st Class Joseph M. Bossi was assigned to Vientiane as a Project 404 assistant ARMA in 1968. He performed his duties as a desk officer with the task to monitor the situation of Project 404 teams in each military region. His job also required taking orientation flights out to each of the locations where Project 404 personnel operated.

> I was working in Vientiane during the Captain Bush incident during the attack on Moung Soui. I was put on the plane to Ban Khay after that (being the newest guy in the section)— Bob Moberg was there when I got there (26 Jun 1969). The plane had U.S. Attaché painted on the boom, so that was not so good for OPSEC about Americans being up there! But, I wore my jacket from Vietnam with my Recondo patch on it, so they would have known I was an American. We carried weapons. Ban Khay had been already under attack when I got up there.[45]

Also assigned to serve at Moung Soui and Ban Khay were Major Werbiski and Captain Nelson. They saw the famous Laotian pilot, Ly Lue crash his T-28 in July of 1969 at Moung Soui. Afterwards, Nelson was killed along with Major Werbiski on August 19, 1969 when a Hmong soldier shot at the Air America Porter they were flying in, resulting in its crash. (Vang Pao purportedly had the soldier executed.)

Sergeant Joe Bossi and Sergeant David Pompili were assigned as Project 404 assistant ARMAs to the Thai artillery battalion, SR-8. They lived with the unit. One of their duties was flying as artillery forward observers in the backseat of T-28s, most notably, with Ly Lue, the famous Hmong T-28 pilot. Bossi flew with him one day on a bombing mission to Xieng Khouangville. He remembered the flight, "What a dive! When he pulled up everything floated to the top of the cabin of the aircraft, including my stomach!" Their duties included sending weather reports from their location and coordinating with airborne control *Moonbeam* and *Alley Cat* for the purpose of air support. Bossi described the battle:

> On 27 June, Ban Khay was overrun. Colonel Sing, the commander of the battle there, could not be trusted. When they evacuated the families, we lost our ground support—a lot of the troops pulled out to go with their families. We were angry when Sullivan made that decision. You knew the troops would not hang around if their families left. Pop Buell was real key up there taking care of refugees.
>
> During the final attack my job was to report on the radio with updates. We were getting shelled all the time. I remained at the outpost as one of the last people there, and then got evacuated to Long Tieng. I went up there to observe and report on the 155mm artillery unit of the Thais.[46]

Bossi and Pompili were the last two remaining men evacuated from the Moung Soui airfield. They had just finished trying to sabotage as much equipment at the site as they could before evacuation. Pompili described their activities: "We sabotaged the 105mms by firing them out of battery. We thermited the 155mms. During this, the USAF suppressed the enemy mortars. Two Jolly Greens came in, but one blew an engine. We had a big field by the compound. Joe told me he would be the last guy to leave! We evac'ed to Long Tieng, 20A."[47]

As the two CH-3s approached, one landed on a fence post, impaling the belly of the helicopter and rendering it unusable. The crew fired a protective burst of machine-gun fire into the surrounding rice paddies and then made their way for extraction onto an Air America H-34. Bossi added:

> I saw the 21st SOS bird that landed on a stake. It was across the strip from me; Pompili was down at the other end of the strip. We went around putting thermite grenades on the breeches of the 155mm. We also thermited the USAF jeep and radio. We tried to bend the barrels of any weapons left. The CH-3s came in as a SAR. We were going to E&E to Long Tieng before that, we did not want to be captured by the NVA. I gave the Jolly Green crew an AK-47 for rescuing us. I met the pilot of the bird that had rescued us later in civilian life—Bill Warren."[48]

After the battle, Sergeant Bossi returned to Vientiane and deployed to Savannakhet, MR-III, working with Lieutenant Colonel Otie Biggs. He arrived at Savannakhet during Operation *Junction City* (conducted July through March 1969). He was issued a blue and white ID card from USAID, stating he was working for their rice program, as part of his cover. Bossi worked with the Lao BP-103, constantly trying to get them the newer MAP equipment such as PRC-25 radios and M16s.[49]

Operation *Off Balance* was designed to retake Moung Soui. After the FAR cleared the Sala Phou Khoung road junction, the FAN at Xieng Dat (1,000 men) stalled in their attack against Moung Soui. A parachute battalion was able to get within a few miles of the Moung Soui airstrip, but were attacked and cut off by the NVA. Operation *Off Balance* was a failure, and ended on July 14. It would not be until later in the year when Auto-Défense du Choc units retook the position.[50]

Pompili returned to Vientiane. He was offered a mission in Thailand, but preferred to remain with the Project 404 mission in Laos. He would later deploy with a Project 404 assistant ARMA team back out to the field, linking up with the FAN located at Ba Nan Phit, between Moung Soui and Luang Prabang.

Project 404—Major Herman Adams, Communications Chief, Vientiane, October 1969–October 1970

Captain Herman Adams was a signal officer (SIGO) serving with the 1st SF Group on Okinawa as the communications officer. His assignment officer wanted to send him back to Vietnam for a third tour. His wife was seven months pregnant at the time, so Adams stated to him that he did not want to leave on a tour until the baby was born.

Adams started in Special Forces as a radio operator, 05B/O5C, and serving initially at Fort Bragg with the 5th SFG. He conducted a tour in Vietnam with the 5th SFG when he was an NCO. (Adams also later served in the 3rd SFG.) He had wanted to go to infantry OCS, but the waiting list to get in was long; a slot opened up at the signal OCS and Adams took the slot.

One day the assignment officer called again: "I got you a job, but I can't say what it is." The assignment officer relayed to him that it was "Project 404." Adams had no clue what that job entailed. He talked around with some enlisted personnel, friends, and one of his close friends, Shane Saldado, who had served on Project 404. Saldado told him, "Take the job! You will like it." One of the requirements for the job was the need for a SIGO with a "3" designator. Adams went back to Bragg, prepared for the job, and headed to Bangkok in October of 1969.

He arrived in Vientiane after spending two weeks in Bangkok. He was posted to serve as the JANAF comms chief.

The Army communication center worked out of the old USAID compound, where the air and army attachés worked; it was about a half mile from the embassy. On the compound was the Embassy Club, the commissary, housing, and other embassy functions. It was near the Arc de Triomphe monument in Vientiane.

Adams brought over four E-4 SF Army communicators for the assignment. Steve Swick, who is now deceased, was one of them. Along with them was Ratchford Haynes, an E7. Swick and Jeff Hotujec were sent by Adams to work at 20A (Long Tieng), along with Ratchford and a PRC-47 radio. They supported Vang Pao at this site.

The command and control at this time for the Army comms chief was working directly for the army attaché in the senior office of the JANAF, Lieutenant Colonel Duskin.

The section worked five and a half days a week, about ten hours a day. The Army personnel on the compound consisted of about fifteen to twenty people. The comms section ran a twenty-four-hour center plus the HF radios to the field for 24/7 operations. They were also responsible for the secure phones, rekeying them every day. Some civilian techs supported the comms center. The section also kept the microwave system going—this was the backbone of the SEA system. On the weekends, they were responsible for the embassy traffic. Herman described the variety of tasks performed:

> Every day, we would catch up on whatever traffic there was. I also used to visit field sites. My predecessor did not do that, or ever visit his folks in the field. Once, I went to Bangkok to solve our immediate commo needs in Vientiane. We did not have commo with our folks once they left the compound. I procured some police-type walkie-talkies from the Motorola store.
>
> As to command: I don't think the Ambassador gave any micro-management to the 404 teams and advisors in the field. The assistant ARMAs ran their show under the broad guidance they were given.
>
> I traveled to several sites during my tour, Pakse, Savannakhet, Luang Prabang, and Site 20A at Long Tieng. I went to Savannakhet to ascertain the problems with our tropo-scatter system. General Reinzi flew there, and after seeing the problem, got us a new system. There were several features of the old system which were working fine, but with the new system, we had problems for about a month till we worked the bugs out.
>
> The threat: One time Bob Moberg flew me to the PDJ. As soon as we landed, 122mm rockets hit the site after we landed and shut down. I also helped in the evacuation of Sam Thong. On our flight was one of the wives of Vang Pao. We had gone up there to evacuate the comms gear during the threat of the Pathet Lao against Sam Thong.[51]

(Herman Adams was released from the Army as a major, reservist, but went back to work at Fort Bragg as the comms chief for a special mission unit.)

MR-V Project 404 ARMA—Major John R. "Cass" Cassady, Camp Chinaimo and Vang Vieng (FAN) 1970–1971

Major John R. "Cass" Cassady was Ranger-qualified and joined Special Forces out of the 82nd Airborne Division in 1964. His first assignment after the SF officer's course was to the 10th SFG (A) in Bad Tölz, Germany. From there, he served as an SF camp commander in Vietnam with the 5th SFG (A), under Colonel "Splash"

Kelly, in 1966. He further served in Company E (Provisional) of MACV–SOG, and then as the S3 of FB-2 in Kontum.

When he returned to the States, he was chosen as a Project 404 officer (he was Special Forces-qualified, combat-qualified in Vietnam, and spoke French). He reported in to the Deputy Chief JUSMAGTHAI in Bangkok, processed-in, and flew to Vientiane to report to the military attaché section in the American embassy. He worked for Colonel Ed Duskin, the army attaché, in October 1970, under Ambassador McMurtrie Godley.

He was assigned to work with Lieutenant Colonel G. Moravick at Camp Chinaimo, Military Region V. His 404 mission was to advise and assist in MR-V. The assistant ARMA team worked with General Kouprasith and his staff. General Kouprasith's nephew, Tonkham Abhay, a staff officer, became Cassady's best Lao friend. Major Cassady reported to Camp Chinaimo on a daily basis. For transport he drove a ¼-ton, M-151 jeep. He also availed himself of Lao RLAF, Air America and attaché aircraft to accompany the Lao leadership and visit the troops in the field, and occasionally accompany them on combat operations. While in flight, Cassady conducted aerial reconnaissance and air communication relay for the troops on the ground. He wore his military uniform—some Project 404 personnel only wore civilian clothes—and carried a radio, maps, and his M16.[52]

His reporting requirements consisted of verbal reports, intelligence reports, and communications. One of the information requirements for his team was acquiring intelligence and information on any POWs in Laos. As a combat advisor, Cassady occasionally maneuvered with the troops during their operations in MR-V:

> I went on a combat operation with regular Lao troops in MR-V, south of Vang Vieng. We were going out to find a communist headquarters. We had very light contact and the enemy troops bugged out. We got into their headquarters area and I found, in one of their buildings, a Russian Calendar, a silk print of Mao Tse Tung, and secured an NVA map (which I still have). I frequently experienced getting shot at while out flying with Air America. The head of the International Control Commission, a Canadian Colonel, Archambeau, gave me an ICC armband in jest, as a talisman against getting shot at because I kept coming back in planes with bullet holes in them.[53]

Cassady received a new mission: assist and advise the Neutralist FAN troops at Vang Vieng. He remembers starting his tour:

> The mission was later expanded to work with the Neutralist troops (FAN) at Vang Vieng. I considered many of them to be mercenary cutthroats and I was always concerned about being alone with them. Apparently the ARMA previous to us did not work out. They disliked him and put a contract out on him! They got along OK with me due to my speaking French and establishing rapport.
> The day I was assigned to them, I first flew up there in a small Air America aircraft. The FAN met us at the airstrip, and we moved to a small hootch they had set up on the side of the runway. Outside the hootch was a flagpole, flying the Royal Laotian flag. The pole was set in a concrete base, shaped like a star. It was painted with white-wash. The monsoon rains began,

and as we were talking you could see the white paint melting off; underneath was red paint (representing the communist star)! The battalion commander of the FAN was a very good tactical commander—he had been trained by the North Vietnamese.[54]

He flew out weekly to their camp, and lived and ate with them. His "quarters" was a small hootch. Occasionally he got a resupply of food from the embassy commissary, but normally ate military rations and local food. Throughout his tour he remained uncomfortable being around the FAN due to their reputation for treachery.

The FAN conducted security patrols in their area to disrupt the Pathet Lao. It was light combat; searching for enemy equipment and arms caches, and so on. There was not any serious contact and most engagements were with snipers or a few shots fired by unknown perpetrators.

Sergeant Richard J. "Jeff" Hotujec

One of the interesting Project 404 ARMA SF deployments, and also the longest serving assistant ARMA in Laos (1970–1974), was Richard J. "Jeff" Hotujec's time in Laos. Sergeant Hotujec began his ARMA tour in 1970, and would extend, and conduct multiple tours, eventually remaining in-country up to 1974, being the last assistant ARMA to exit the country.[55] Jeff described his introduction to Project 404:

> I was in the 6th SF Group at Fort Bragg, NC in March of 1970. I was unmarried. I was a Sergeant E5 O5B/C radio operator. There was a requirement for four radio operators for Laos. I volunteered. I did not attend any specialized training after notification of assignment for a Project 404 tour; I processed out of the 6th SF Group and headed straight to Southeast Asia.
>
> We turned in all of our military gear, and military IDs, and were given $250 to go downtown, K-mart, and get civilian clothes. Someone went to Washington DC and got us official passports. We got somewhere around five or seven days notification to deploy. There was no preparation or pre-deployment training.
>
> We flew commercial to Bangkok, got a hotel, and spent three or four days resting up to get some sleep and get over jet lag. We lodged in the Windsor Hotel. One day, an E7 came into our room and told us we were all going "upcountry." We processed for that and went out to the airport to board a C-47 or C-46. I don't remember who was flying that airline. We flew to Vientiane and were put up in the AIRA house on the compound there. The next day we did more in-processing. We got three sets of sterile jungle fatigues, jungle boots, and an M16. After that, we reported to the Army Attaché in our civilian clothes. During my tours with Project 404 we wore civvies sometimes and other times wore military clothing. For instance, we wore military clothing when we had to do our parachute drops.
>
> There were four of us; two remained in Vientiane, and two were assigned to work out in the Military Region sites. I went to Long Tieng, Site 20A. Sam Thong, LS-20, was just lost two days prior to me going up there, and I was advised to "keep your head down."[56]

The project 404 team in Military Region II consisted of a lieutenant colonel, an E7, and Sergeant Hotujec. The team flew to Long Tieng, Site 20A, daily, utilizing the UH-1s from the UTT (helicopter utility flight) out of Udorn. The team lived in the American Community Association (ACA) compound which also held the USAID, the RO personnel, and the AIRAs and ARMAs. There was also a JANAF. Hotujec continued:

> Our three-man team of advisors/observers would go out to Long Tieng or Sam Thong (after it was recaptured) to observe, gain situational awareness, and we also helped to teach the Hmong. I helped to teach commo. We would put our daily activities and situational awareness into a daily SITREP. I carried an AK-47 during these excursions. When I was at Long Tieng, we experienced enemy 122mm and 130mm indirect fire. I had a lot of "bunker" time.
>
> In September of 1970 (I think?) I put in for an extension. I did not hear anything, and one day was packed and ready to end my tour on a Sunday, but then I was told I had got extended. Most people on Project 404 tours spent one year in country. There were maybe 25–30 ARMAs each year in Project 404 (estimate).
>
> Other SF guys I knew in Project 404 were: Don Bailey, Dick Whipple, and Syd Jensen. Syd served at the PKK Training Center—Phou Khao Khoui.[57]

Hotujec's second tour on Project 404 was in MR-III, Savannakhet. The team leader was Colonel Otie Biggs, along with SF Sergeant Jimmie Moore serving as the operations NCO. Hotujec served as the assistant operations NCO; one USAF radio operator covered the communications. The mission for the Savannakhet Project 404 team was to serve as advisors and observers for the Royal Lao Army and gather data on the units. H-34 helicopters from Air America assisted the team in getting to field sites. They had one interpreter for their use, a *tahan* sergeant named Van Souk. Fortunately, there was no combat at this location.

Subsequent to his tour in Savannakhet, Hotujec went to Luang Prabang to serve on a three-man Project 404 team. During the battles of Skyline Ridge, Jeff fortunately was on a well-deserved leave in Wisconsin, watching the news of the battles on television with his family. He remembered seeing the house he lived in at Long Tieng being bombed.

After two six-month tours, Jeff volunteered to return to Laos for a one-year tour. During this period, he conducted a short stint mission once again at Long Tieng.

> After Luang Prabang, I went back to Long Tieng. It was a short stint. Vang Pao and the Agency and all of us were run out and we went south to LS-272, Ban Xhong. We did not stay there during the nights. Our job again, was to advise. During that time the Army Attaché was an SF guy, Colonel Jack Frye. On July 25, 1972 Ban Xhong [Ban Son] flooded. I had to go up there to clean up some of the mess from the flood, the commo wire, equipment, etc. This was the day Leigh's dad dropped me off before his crash. Then I went to Moung Kassy [Vang Vieng].[58]

(While earlier in Laos, Jeff married Leigh, the daughter of an Air America pilot. Leigh worked at the U.S. embassy in the JANAF section.) Hotujec would also serve alongside five other assistant ARMAs assigned to TF-*Broomhilda* during the *Maharat II* operation in January of 1973, designed to clear Route 13 and reopen the Sala Phou Khoun road junction.

Sergeant 1st Class Billy Phipps—Project 404 ARMA, Luang Prabang, Military Region I, 1970

Sergeant Billy Phipps served in Vietnam with the 5th SFG (A), assigned to the CCC of SOG. After his Southeast Asia tour he was assigned into the 6th SFG (A). In 1970, the personnel section offered him language school and an assignment to Laos. He took the forty-seven-week Laotian language course at DLI in Alexandria, VA, and traveled commercially with five members of his class to Laos, meeting up with another Project 404 member in San Francisco, who was from one of the Project 404 flight detachments. When they arrived in Bangkok and were awaiting transport to Laos in a few days, it was the flight detachment member who showed them around the city. They got their orders from the Deputy Chief JUSMAGTHAI for Vientiane.[59]

Upon arrival in Vientiane, the army attaché provided them a briefing on the situation throughout all the military regions, followed by security briefings and other administrative briefings. Phipps was asked to serve in Military Region I, Luang Prabang, to replace Sergeant Jimmy Stewart. He was flown there aboard an Air America Porter STOL aircraft. "We had contract housing at Luang Prabang. Our team consisted of an officer and me as the operations sergeant, and a commo sergeant. Occasionally the team would be augmented with an artillery E-7. There was a USAF AIRA Project 404 officer there also. We were not authorized to carry weapons when we got into Laos, but we got some off of the Laotians."[60]

Lieutenant Colonel Headricks was the team leader in Luang Prabang; he was replaced by Major Merle Pugh. The Project 404 team's mission was to assist and advise the Laotian army headquarters in Luang Prabang on their military operations. The team also gave military classes, consisting of river-crossing techniques, rappelling, and other small-unit tactics. Like all Project 404 teams, they had responsibilities for intelligence-gathering. All information gathered was put into a daily sitrep, encrypted, and then sent to the embassy using the military radio in their house.

To do this, they attended morning briefings with the Laotians at their camp. Because they had been trained in the Lao language, they were not assigned interpreters. Phipps remarked on how they handled the language barrier. "Between our language skills and those of them who could speak English we figured it out. We took the data from their G2 briefings, then modified them and updated them with what we knew. Laotian briefings were way too lengthy—they would include everything including who was getting married that week, so we just cut them down to what was militarily relevant."[61]

The team was issued two civilian-type jeeps. They were forbidden by the embassy to go out on field operations with the Lao, but they did go out on field exercises and training events. The team did not go out on combat operations during their tour.

There was no perceived threat around Luang Prabang because it was the royal capital. The Pathet Lao avoided attacking the city and the FAR did not seek to engage them in that location. It was almost a truce condition; the team would often observe Pathet Lao shopping for groceries and vegetables in the town! The Pathet Lao also attended the king's annual harvest festival. The NVA, however, were never seen by the team.

The threat between Luang Prabang and Vientiane along Route 13 was not known, however, so the team avoided driving to Vientiane. They used Air America assets to fly back and forth from Vientiane or when visiting other assistant ARMAs in Sayaboury. On occasion, they flew with the helicopter UTT flight detachment stationed in Thailand. On these few times they enjoyed access to the helicopters, the team performed visual reconnaissance to augment their intelligence-gathering. The assistant ARMAs also flew with the assistant AIRA FACs in Luang Prabang, performing as their back-seaters.

Luang Prabang was a quiet combat assignment and life was good. Phipps' team took advantage of that:

> We ordered supplies from the U.S. embassy in Vientiane; supplies of a military nature we ordered from the Attaché's office. Our cook shopped downtown for food. Once in awhile we would send someone down to Thailand to scrounge around for stuff we needed. There were some French military forces in Luang Prabang and we got our wine from them in 5-gallon buckets!
>
> We were required to still make our admin parachute drops while in Laos. Jimmy Stewart may have been one of those who went to Thailand to scrounge parachutes; we did not get them from Vientiane. We did our admin jumps from Air America aircraft or from the helicopter from Thailand.
>
> We had no contact with USAID. There was a Swiss medical team in Luang Prabang, of the MEDCAP type. There was one doctor and two or three nurses. I broke my leg on a jump (a fracture) and I used these folks to get a plaster of Paris cast on my leg. It was not that great of a job, because it kept falling apart.[62]

While serving on Project 404, the team received combat pay and all were credited with a Vietnam combat tour to cloak their existence in Laos. Sergeant Phipps enjoyed Project 404; he tried to extend for an additional tour, but was refused.

Lieutenant Colonel Charlie W. Brewington, MR-II Advisor, Long Tieng, 1970–1971

Lieutenant Colonel Charlie W. Brewington served as a Project 404 assistant ARMA with General Vang Pao at Long Tieng from early 1971 to early 1972. He replaced Major Al Rozon. (Both Brewington and Rozon had served earlier in Laos during *White Star*.) His team consisted of Sergeant Jeff Hotujec as the radio operator and an artillery NCO advisor, Walter Plitz.

He was on assignment as an operations officer in Worms, Germany when he was picked for Project 404. He was informed in a letter from the attaché in Vientiane that he was being chosen for a secret assignment in Southeast Asia, but no other information was forthcoming. He would be fully briefed when he arrived in Bangkok. (Brewington already had language training, one of the prerequisites).

> I had two SF radio operators. Jeff Hotujec was with me. I was a LTC at the time and was the advisor for General Vang Pao in MR-II. I reported to the Army Attaché. I was in combat on the ground and also shot at while riding around with Air America. Air America was going to one of our furthest outposts. We were going over the mountains when something started hitting the aircraft which sounded like hail. We lost radio contact. We landed, then reestablished radio contact, and flew back to Long Tieng.[63]

Brewington's main task was to forward daily situation reports to the army attaché in Vientiane concerning enemy activity and friendly forces' operations. (Project 404 cadre could also share rides with CIA operatives visiting field sites.) He worked alongside a well-staffed Agency section with several paramilitary case officers.

The army attaché's office provided two helicopters for the assistant ARMA Project 404 teams out in the military regions. With most of the major combat activity at this time in MR-II, the Project 404 team at Long Tieng normally had priority for the daily use of the helicopters. Brewington used the helicopters to fly out to the locations of the para-military officers, a way to get first-hand information on operations. Meanwhile, the artillery NCO on the team visited artillery units in the region.

After attending the senior Agency officer's meeting each night, Brewington then consolidated all the information from his team into a daily sitrep and forwarded it on. Whenever Brewington was away, Sergeant Hotujec remained at the Project 404 team house in Long Tieng to transmit and receive radio reports.

During Brewington's tour, Vang Pao's units were on the PDJ. Brewington recalls reports of enemy armor from the Hmong field units:

> When the NVA took the Plaine des Jarres the last time, friendly troops reported hearing tanks moving northeast of the Plaine at night. The tanks were used to assault positions on the Plaine. The friendly artillery positions farther to the north used one of the 105mm guns to destroy one of the tanks. Some of the troops captured by the NVA escaped because the NVA would fall asleep along the evacuation route. Some of these troops made it back to friendly lines. General Vang Pao was not allowed to operate north and east of the Plaine, so he tried to defend the area with troops on the Plaine and west of it.[64]

Brewington was at Sam Thong when the NVA attacked with mortars. He requested an extraction. After Captain Moberg left Moung Soui, he was sent to Sam Thong to replace the senior advisor who had been killed with Major Werbiski. Following that assignment, Moberg was asked to form a UTT flight detachment at Udorn, with three UH-1H Hueys. He would once again fly to Sam Thong, but this time to rescue Charlie Brewington during the mortar attack:

Colonel Charley Brewington had replaced me at Sam Thong and the NVA had now got into position to put rocket and mortar fire around Sam Thong and 20A. Ted [Theodore Untalan] and I flew up to 20A to support Colonel Brewington who had got caught under heavy mortar fire at a site just north of Sam Thong.

I advised Charley that we would be on the ground approximately 10 seconds and to get his ass in the chopper if he wanted to have dinner with us that night. We landed. He did. During takeoff a round exploded under the tail boom causing enough damage for us to return to Vientiane. Ted calmly turned around to me after takeoff and said, "You took 11 seconds!" We made Charley pay for the steaks in Vientiane that night and took the aircraft back to Udorn for tail boom replacement the next day.[65]

Brewington and his team lived at Long Tieng (Site 20A) until the NVA began its attacks on Skyline Ridge. Due to this threat, Project 404 advisors were required to return to Vientiane each night.

Operation *Broomhilda*

On December 12, 1972, four battalions of Pathet Lao—the 13th, 46th, 701st and 705th—attacked westward along Route 7 to engage the 1st FAR Division defending in the area of Sala Phou Khoun. The 1st Division troops fled in panic, leaving behind most of their equipment, fleeing south down Route 13. The highway was effectively cut between Vientiane and Luang Prabang. In response, the RLG planned Operation *Maharat II* (codenamed *Broomhilda* by the Americans) to retake the road junction at Sala Phou Khoun, reminiscent of Operation *Triangle* conducted in 1964. Again, the concept consisted of a three-pronged attack. One column of FAR, about five battalions, along with 1,000 Thai volunteer soldiers, was planned to attack north from Moung Kassy. The force was designated as the southern column, commanded by General Paitoon.

The smaller northern column prepared to attack south from Luang Prabang, with a third column made up of local guerrilla forces and a reinforcing BP from MR-III (totaling about 3,000 men) attacking from the air. The air assault column was scheduled to conduct a combined helicopter and parachute assault on the Sala Phou Khoun junction as the northern and southern ground columns converged on the intersection. The paratrooper and guerrilla forces were prepositioned at Vang Vieng, after being transported from Pakse by USAF C-130s.

The 56th SOW provided seven CH-53s from the 21st SOS and Air America provided two Chinooks for the aerial assault portion of the operation. The air contingent could carry about 1,000 men in each wave of the assault.[66] Mike Ingham, codenamed as the operative "Hard Nose," was the assigned Agency case officer for Task Force *Broomhilda*.

I was the agency "commander" of BROOMHILDA. I had officially finished my tour in Laos and had been replaced as the head of the Thai program by LUMBERJACK and was asked by Landry to run this little shoot up. The operation wasn't much, but a couple of things stand

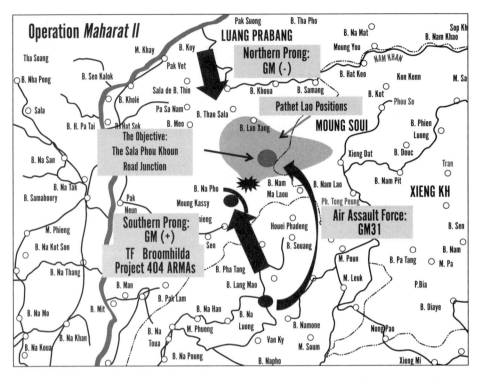

Derived from French topographical map of Laos, Indochine Series, Graphique du Laos, 1950s. (*Courtesy of John F. McCallum collection*)

out. One was the incredible power of the Chinooks which were new to AAM [Air America] and to me, as I had been a Marine and the Chinook was an Army chopper. The other was that this little operation was the occasion of the only tank battle that I know of in Laos. The FAR were involved and they had some old American tanks. One day, the Pathet Lao or NVA came down the road in a PT-76 right toward one of the FAR tanks. A few rounds were exchanged with no damage done. The FAR crew skedaddled and the fight was over.[67]

At the start of the operation, the northern prong of *Maharat II*, moving south from Luang Prabang, made very little progress. By January 6, 1972, the southern prong had advanced north of Vang Vieng, reaching a position about twelve kilometers south of the Sala Phou Khoung junction. It was at that location when the BV-53 commander was killed in action. This precipitated a withdrawal of forces back to the vicinity of Moung Kassy, on January 8, 1972. To reinforce the new defensive position, four Thai Unity battalions serving with Vang Pao were sent the next day to buttress the lines along Route 13, just north of Moung Kassy.[68]

Major John Sullivan, Project 404 Assistant ARMA

USSF Army Major John Sullivan (an artilleryman) was one of the Project 404 assistant ARMAs supporting TF *Broomhilda*. After attending the defense attaché's course and then language school, followed by a SERE course, he received orders to report to the Deputy Chief JUSMAGTHAI. He arrived in Bangkok, spent the night, then flew aboard a USAF C-47 to Udorn Royal Thai AFB and reported in. After in-processing at Udorn, he was flown to Vientiane by a Royal Thai Air Force C-47, where he was met and escorted to the army assistant attaché compound. Sullivan remembers the peculiar nature of being introduced to Project 404, of which he was still lacking any knowledge about its operation:

> I was questioned about my Artillery experience, ability to work with foreign troops, my Lao language level. Neither of them spoke Lao so I had to speak with a Lao receptionist who then told them in English how I did—I passed. The meeting lasted less than one hour and I was then told to get into fatigues, pack a bag with no civilian clothes, draw a weapon from supply and get to the airport from where I was to be flown by Air America Huey to Moung Kassy FOB and be met by a five person group of Americans. I arrived at the FOB [forward operating base] just about 13 hours after being in-processed at Udorn. I never went through in-processing in Vientiane either at the embassy or the attaché's office. I did have to surrender my Diplomatic Passport; my only means of ID were my dog tags! (After coming out of the jungle when TF Broomhilda was disbanded, I was issued a U.S. embassy ID card.) I had yet to be briefed on Project 404. That briefing took place on the FOB and I was basically told I would work with the Artillery and, on occasion, with the maneuver forces. I was dual slotted as an Artillery and Infantry "Liaison" Officer.[69]

The army attaché assigned Sullivan to a five-man team working at Moung Kassy. The FOB at Moung Kassy was located about eighty miles north of Vientiane beyond Vang Vieng. The assistant ARMA team was called Task Force *Broomhilda,* headed by an Army lieutenant colonel (infantry branch) and also consisted of two majors (one MI and the other FA), an MI captain, and a radio operator (Special Forces Sergeant Jeff Hotujec). Sullivan continued:

> I knew little to nothing about Project 404 until I arrived at the FOB. The 05 briefed me about the mission to "liaison" with the indigenous forces. Since I was FA, I worked with a four-howitzer battery of M114, Towed 155mm unit. The other FA Major had not been working with them because he could not speak Lao and English-speaking Lao officers were in short supply. The Lao colonel who commanded the troops could speak some English as did his Lieutenant Colonel Intelligence Officer. I had attended the Foreign Service Language School, in Rosslyn, VA for eleven months before departing for Laos. As a result, I spent much of my time translating/interpreting for my compatriots while trying to "liaison" with the Lao Artillery.[70]

The six men assigned as TF *Broomhilda* were designated to liaison with the Lao forces, now assembled into a *groupe mobile.* The GM had a name, but to get all the force commanders to agree on the name caused it to go through a myriad of changes depending on the language used—Thai, Lao or Hmong. Sullivan said, "The Case Officers, when they were there, did not help the effort because it didn't matter to them and they didn't attempt to get their counterparts to accept any name." He described the mission of his counterpart unit:

> The Mission of this polygot organization was to act as a blocking force on the only north/south road in the country. The enemy forces were north of us on the Plaines de Jarres and wanted

to use that "highway" to attack south through us and eventually end up in Vientiane. Our forces had a combat strength on line of around 1,000 soldiers—give or take on any given day. Explanation: Some days, members of the Thai and/or Lao would simply take a day or two to return home for a visit. Headcounts were not part of their daily process. We were not allowed to stay at the FOB during the night so we helo'd each evening to the Neutralist Capital, Vang Vieng, south of Moung Kassy and returned each morning.

Equipment for the mission included a radio for contact with the attaché's commo center (Major Sullivan's call-sign was "Boxer"). For personal weapons, members of the team had either M16s, AK-47s, and/or sidearms. (Sullivan carried an issue M16 and a 12-gauge sawed-off shotgun he had procured at the FOB, along with a .357-caliber sidearm loaned to him by the Air America pilot who flew him up to the site.)

The team wore jungle fatigues, some with "Name, Rank and U.S. Army" sew-ons. When and where they had to perform their duties along the lines dictated what they chose to wear: web harnesses, butt packs, bandoliers of M16 ammunition, claymore mines, hand grenades, hand-held flares, signal mirrors and a canteen. They had access through the attaché's office to LRRP (long range reconnaissance patrol) rations which they carried for lunch. Breakfast and dinner were eaten at the laager in Vang Vieng.

They had no flak jackets and either wore boonie caps or went without headgear. Sullivan related, "I think you now have the picture that this was not an 'A' team as organized or recognized by SF."[71] Every day, each one of the team had his task to accomplish—either training Lao or going out with the FAR units.

For transport, they had one jeep painted white with water buffalo horns on the hood. This was supplied out of the attaché's motor pool and transported to the FOB by Air America. Sullivan related, "The horns were our idea. We didn't have to drive far because everything was within walking distance and the jeep did not do well traveling over rice paddies. Medical aid was scarce; the team only had a corpsman bag. If anyone was seriously injured, they were flown to an Operation *Brotherhood* field hospital located thirty miles south of the FOB, near the Mekong River. The Laotian units had field medics with them for any minor injuries."[72]

Because the battle was all around, there were very few villagers in the vicinity; most had already moved south. Those who did remain were farmers, and, if treated right by the friendly forces, provided information and intelligence on enemy activities near the position. Sullivan continued:

There was no previous team from which to receive a mission. We were six soldiers trying to do our best. The other five had only been at the FOB for a very short time. The two MI officers communicated directly with the OPS/Intel sections at the Attaché Office reference any intel they could glean from the local military staffs or find themselves. The other FA officer worked with me until he returned to Vientiane. The radioman monitored our communications system. We were a group of soldiers hastily formed to provide assistance to an also hastily formed Group Mobile unit. Only our LTC, myself and the radio operator were designated Project 404—the others were considered assistant Army Attaches. The six of us sat down my second day and developed an operational procedure for us to work at our jobs and interface/assist each other every day. Short meetings were held several times each day to share information and to respond to our "liaison" requirements. If something occurred requiring immediate response, we all knew what to do … I spent much time each day interpreting/translating for our guys and the non-English speaking Lao and Thai.[73]

Major Sullivan spent most of his time with the artillery battery except when taking time to train the FOs assigned to the combat units. The FOs were known as "FAAGs"—forward air and artillery guides. They were trained in Thailand and were quite effective. Sullivan did not find the same quality in the artillery gunners:

Unfortunately, the folks back on the guns were not. When I saw their first fire mission after arrival, I shut them down until I could train them. Their idea of a fire mission was to have someone stand behind each tube, point in the general direction they wanted the projectile to go, load the tube and pull the lanyard. They had no idea of the importance of laying the battery, deflection, quadrant elevation and sometimes what charge to use. The result was that the infantry seldom used the artillery's capabilities. The projectiles would explode somewhere out in front, kill a lot of foliage and monkeys! Don't know where it went but it left here with a hell of a roar.[74]

He described the defensive layout at their position:

The Lao conducted their patrols daily and reported findings to their intel folks. We got it second hand. We had several rings of razor wire surrounding our hillock FOB. We also had claymores set up and primarily facing north. The Lao had one tank, an M24, for protection from enemy armor, PT-76s. It was probably not going to be much help if the enemy decided to attack south with armor along the road which came through a narrow defile in the mountains. The Lao plan was to knock out the lead armored vehicle in that defile thereby blocking the road for others. I had the artillery position, with one 155mm howitzer daily for direct fire on the same road defile. The mountains were so steep and composed of limestone that the enemy tanks were road-bound.

The infantry were spread in depth across the front, pointed north. They covered about 2,000 meters across the valley with the major focus on enemy troops coming down the road or through the mountain trails. We also had small anti-tank shoulder-fired equipped weapons squads with the infantry closest to the road. There were rumors that, before I and the team arrived, anti-tank mines had been planted on the road to our north—this was not confirmed. This defile was very narrow and then opened up onto the Vientiane Plains. No enemy vehicle could go off the road after reaching the Plain because of flooded rice paddies and no overhead cover. The infantry, following the tanks, would also be at the same disadvantage. Airstrikes and artillery would ruin their day.[75]

But one day the tanks came. On January 11, troops in contact with Pathet Lao forces near Moung Kassy reported the sounds of armor.[76] Raven FAC Chuck Hines was flying to the PDJ that day and landed en route at the Moung Kassy airstrip. Hearing of the plight of the Laotian forces, he conducted an aerial reconnaissance up Route 13 and detected two tanks headed toward Moung Kassy. After confirming to Task Force *Broomhilda* that the enemy in fact had tanks, he flew back over the enemy tanks and fired the only ordnance he had at them—white phosphorus marking rockets. They had little effect.[77]

Army Special Forces Sergeant Jeff Hotujec was one of the six team members located there. He described his time through this battle:[78]

> After my tour in MR-II with Vang Pao, I went to Moung Kassy [Vang Vieng]. The team was led by John Sullivan (who had been with Syd earlier at PKK to conduct artillery training—he was an Army FA Major). Another member of the team was Russ Simonetta. This was during Operation "Broomhilda." We were under the command and control of LTC Ray Mullins. We were advising and observing a Laotian battalion at Moung Kassy. We had a USAF jeep with KWKT crypto and crystals. We used the radio to send intelligence reports and SITREPS. There was a red clay airfield there; we had to fly out each end of day.
>
> Lieutenant Colonel Mullins was getting enemy situation reports from the Lao. One day he had a report of 40–70 ground troops with tanks coming from the direction of Luang Prabang. We made calls for an extraction from any Air America aircraft in the region. My call-sign was "Silvertooth." [Jeff had a silver-plated tooth in his front teeth.] The aircraft in the region, as well as us, could not see anything due to being socked in with weather. I heard an Air America aircraft going over our position, then the rat-a-tat-tat of gunfire. I got a call from the pilot, "Silvertooth, they are closer than you think!"
>
> When the news of the enemy having tanks got around, and the noise of enemy tanks was heard, the Laotians went and got an old tank they had as a display on a berm outside of the battalion area. They got it running and drove it down the hill from our position, and a little farther down the road toward Moung Kassy. The enemy tank appeared in what was going to be one of the rare tank-vs.-tank battles in Laos. It may have been a T-34 or T-54. [The tanks would turn out to be PT-76s.]
>
> The enemy tank fired first and missed. The Laos returned fire, and that round went up in the air. Right after that, the old tank lost power. However, the enemy tank retreated. Friendly troops later destroyed two tanks in the village. After that, I went back to Savannakhet, and Thakhek.[79]

Ken Conboy, in his book *Shadow War*, described the tank "duel." The first Pathet Lao PT-76 routed Unity battalion BC618A and continued down the road, hosing down suspected positions with its machine gun. Upon nearing Moung Kassy, the "tank-vs.-tank" duel began between the Laotian M-24 and the Pathet Lao PT-76. During the duel, elements from other Unity battalions engaged the second PT-76 with LAW rockets, scoring a direct hit and killing the crew. The first tank reversed back up Route 13, but was also engaged and destroyed.[80]

Although the Pathet Lao assault was repulsed, the southern FAR forces refused to move any further. In the north, the Luang Prabang forces continued to stall. The CIA's Savannakhet unit was ordered to resume operations against the road junction, using GM-31 as the assault force. They were transported by air up to the Vang Vieng airstrip in preparation. After sending in pathfinders to identify drop zones, on January 19, the FAR opened the next phase on January 20, 1973 with an artillery and mortar bombardment on the Sala Phou Khoung junction. Air Commando CH-53s (the *Knives*) and Air America Chinooks began the insertion into the objective, transporting about a third of the force; four of the insertion helicopters were hit by enemy fire as they transported GM-31 into battle.[81] Almost predictably, there was little help in the assault from the southern and northern ground columns, but after four days of intense fighting by the regiment, the junction was secured. During the fighting, RLG forces were resupplied by Air America and CASI aircraft. The Pathet Lao disappeared.[82]

With the enemy gone, the southern and northern task forces cleared Route 13 up to Sala Phou Khoun, ending the operation in early February. Vang Pao ordered GM-203 (BCs 618A, 619A, and 626) to garrison the route junction. GM-31 returned to MR-III and a Thai Unity artillery unit established a firebase at Sala Phou Khoun in support: Fire Support Base *Goldfinger*.[83]

John Sullivan and the other members of TF *Broomhilda* were recalled to Vientiane upon the conclusion of *Maharat II* and resumed other duties. In Vientiane, Sullivan awaited additional instructions for the rest of his tour.

While in MR-V, he took the opportunity to visit with the Lao artillery regimental commander, Colonel Sakhoun Sananikhone, who asked him (Sullivan) to accompany him on inspections of artillery units throughout the other military regions. Sullivan spent the rest of his Project 404 tour advising and assisting Lao artillery units, teaching them skills to improve their performance.

He also served as the attaché's liaison to the Joint Casualty Resolution Center (JCRC) headquartered at Nakhon Phanom RTAB (NKP), and was utilized by the JCRC as a cultural expert and foreign area specialist, particularly for the development of PSYOP products used in support of finding U.S. servicemen lost in Laos and North Vietnam.

In his last five months as a Project 404 officer, Major Sullivan was assigned to the National Training Center at Phou Khao Khoui north of Vientiane. (The JCRC moved to Laos and established an office for rescue and recovery operations in the attaché's office in Vientiane, headed by a colonel, precluding the need for Sullivan's presence in Nakhon Phanom.)

Staff Sergeant Sydney N. "Syd" Jensen, Project 404, MR-V, PKK— Phou Khao Khoui 1972

Phou Khao Khoui (PKK–LS-51) was a large training camp known as the National Commando Training Center with training designed to upgrade and improve the FAR. It was staffed with Laotian officers who had attended courses in the United States. The purpose of the course was to improve FAR battalions for COIN operations—light infantry "commando" instruction. PKK was located north of Vientiane, up the plains, and over the first ridgeline at the beginning of the mountains. There were two Project 404 NCOs and one officer at that location.

In June of 1970, Staff Sergeant Sydney N. "Syd" Jensen (a Special Forces 05B/11B) was informed by a friend of his working in the Special Warfare Center about a good mission his friend could put him on, but Jensen would first have to take the DLAT (defense language aptitude test), and if passed, would require language training before deployment. Jensen had just returned from his assignment with the 5th SFG (A) in Vietnam (his third tour) and was currently assigned as a training group instructor.

He attended a year-long course at the Defense Language Institute at Fort Myer, Virginia. Attending the course were five other Special Forces NCOs: Sergeant 1st Class Lonnie Wilhight, Sergeant 1st Class Jerry O'Daniel, Sergeant 1st Class Neal Sumner, Sergeant 1st Class John Newsom, and Staff Sergeant Keefer. Six months into the course, they were all pulled out and given orders to go to Laos to replace other Project 404 personnel in-country. They returned to Fort Bragg, processed with the PERSCOM, and were assigned to the Deputy Chief JUSMAGTHAI for duty on Project 404. Each man was given a clothing fund to go downtown and buy civilian clothes.[84]

They all traveled separately to Bangkok on commercial airlines. Upon Jensen's arrival, he went to the Air America terminal and paired back up with Neal Sumner for a flight to Udorn, aboard a Volpar aircraft. They were met by a JUSMAG representative, in-processed for Project 404, and taken across the river to Vientiane. Their records remained in Udorn.

In Vientiane, the six sergeants were once again all together during in-processing. They were not given their missions until they reported to the ARMA compound, where they received their assignments out to the military regions. Jensen recalls: "My assignment was the Laotian Training Center at Phou Khao Khoui—LS-51. [The main Laotian training camp was at Camp Chinaimo near Vientiane, also the location of the Lao military academy.] The officer for the team was Major Williams. After a month, the team rotated and Major Simmonetta replaced Major Williams. After a short time, he departed to work in the same location as Jeff Hotujec."[85]

(Jensen would be replacing other Special Forces NCOs at the camp: George Davis and Mike Buchanan.)

The camp sat in a bowl surrounded by ridges. A dirt road led into the camp from over the mountain. North of the road were ranges for small arms, 3.5-inch rocket and M-72 LAW training. There were barracks for the troops, a headquarters building, a kitchen, and a dispensary; Jensen's team had separate hootches for billeting. There was a place for Lao civilians and dependents, like a small village. The engineers occupied a portion of the camp; another section of the camp was used for indirect fire and artillery instruction (4.2-inch mortars). The runway (LS-51) was outside the main area of the camp.

The camp was commanded by a Lao army lieutenant colonel or major. Although part of Military Region V, the camp came under the command and control of army headquarters in Camp Chinaimo. There were seven captains and lieutenants who had all been trained in the U.S. in leadership schools, some in the SF qualification course, and all had attended airborne school. The camp was designated as one of the FAR national training centers, but it was treated like a red-headed stepchild in getting assets.

The FAR picked one battalion of troops at a time from one of the military regions and sent them to the center for standardized military training, which lasted six to seven weeks. The core training schedule consisted of subjects from U.S. military doctrine.

The assistant ARMA team pulled advisory and training duties during the work week; on the weekends they returned to Vientiane. The camp was rustic; there was no running water and generators provided electricity. The 404 team lived in their hootch at the camp during the training week. Jensen described their training days:

> Our job was to liaise with the Laotian training cadre, coordinate logistics such as uniforms, and help them with other stuff with respect to their logistics system. We got our supplies from the Agency, the embassy in Vientiane, and from the JUSMAG in Thailand. We also taught the Lao officers on various subjects.
>
> We wore jungle fatigues and a patrol cap. We wore our rank, but no other patches. We could carry .45 caliber pistols for self-protection, which we kept in a small bag. If we did local patrols with the students, we carried CAR-15s. I had a Motorola radio with a repeater to make commo with the ARMA directly.
>
> We had no translators, just using our Lao language training and using the Laotians who spoke some English. I ended up by myself the last four or five months when everyone rotated out or were reassigned somewhere else. I got through this by making some good friends with the Laotians. One of them was like a brother to me.[86]

The team helped train three Royal Lao Army battalions during their tenure. They were alternatively assigned one Hmong battalion from Vang Pao's SGUs, but the Hmong only trained a short time before they were sent back into combat. Unfortunately, some died at the camp when they had a UXO (unexploded ordnance) accident. For graduations, the Laotians always held a parade, and handed out certificates. Jensen helped type the graduation certificates and sometimes helped with other administrative paperwork.

The French military trainers used the camp once to bring in military academy cadets from Vientiane. During this two-week period, Project 404 personnel were removed from the camp and returned to Vientiane until the course completion, when the French departed. (Sometime in 1972, a split-team from the Thailand-based 46th Independent Special Forces arrived to help with anti-tank training.)

The enemy threat in this region was Pathet Lao. The camp did not have a lot of security, but it was surrounded by barbed wire and weapons bunkers. There were positions for .30-caliber machine guns and 60mm mortars. The Laotian NCOs made up the security company while the troops of their battalions participated in training only. One night the Pathet Lao breached the wire and ran shooting through the camp, for about thirty minutes; they also burned down two hootches.

Richard "Dick" Whipple served as a logistician (76Z MOS) at PKK a year previous to Syd Jensen, and remembered some of the threat to the camp (1971–1972). He was working at Camp Mackall on Fort Bragg when he was contacted to serve in Project 404. Upon arriving in Laos, he was assigned as a "civilian" for administrative duties. He served with Major Kenneth Crabtree.

Dick described one of the attacks by the Pathet Lao, "The threat in that area was from the Pathet Lao. Once, they blew up the ammo dump/demo site/gas station. I think two advisors were killed, but I'm not sure they were U.S., or Agency, or some other country."[87] (There are no records of Americans killed at PKK; this may have been advisors from the French Military Training Mission contingent.)

In anticipation of further incursions by the Pathet Lao, Jensen incorporated local villagers as part of the intelligence and early warning system: "We had a sort of early warning system. There were two Hmong villages about a forty-five-minute walk from the camp. I got some medical supplies and did some MEDCAPs at the villages. I helped to establish a small school. We hired a dependent wife as one of the school teachers. We got materials from Vientiane for these projects. In this way, the villages became part of our force protection and would warn us if the enemy was around."[88]

Other techniques to avoid the Pathet Lao included staying off the roads, but that was not always possible: "To get around we used Air America's PC-6 Pilatus Porters. We had a Willys jeep for our use, but we never had much gas for it. We also had a Dodge power wagon ¾-ton. We used that to drive to Vientiane, and would often take it loaded with Hmongs to go to the market there during the dry season. The route was a dirt road. This was frowned upon by Colonel Chamberlain. We were never ambushed, however."[89]

The Last SF Project 404 ARMA in Laos—Jeff Hotujec

Sergeant Jeff Hotujec is recorded as the last Army Special Forces Project 404 member to be serving in Laos. Jeff Hotujec recalls, "In May of 1974, we were told that all Project 404 personnel were told to be out of country. I went to Brigadier General Trefry, JUSMAGTHAI commander, and requested permission to stay. I had some things in Vientiane to attend to. I spent another couple of weeks there. I was the last guy out of country!" His wife, Leigh, remembers mention of Jeff's nickname as the longest serving Project 404 advisor: "We heard that the Pathet Lao around Vientiane were looking for *Silvertooth* at that time"![90]

Project 404 Administration—the 1970s

To effect better coordination between the deputy chief and Vientiane, DEPCHJUSMAGTHAI moved its headquarters to Udorn in December of 1971.

In February of 1972, control of all advisors in Project 404 was transferred from the U.S. embassy in Vientiane to the Deputy Chief JUSMAGTHAI, Brigadier General John W. Vessey, Jr. It was an attempt to regain theater military control and direction over Project 404 personnel heretofore directed solely by the ambassador and his senior military attachés. Budgetary constraints from Congress also forced the program to be administered by the deputy chief as the single fiscal manager in October of 1971.

In October 1972, DEPCHJUSMAGTHAI once again became MAAG–Laos. In February of 1973, during the ceasefire in Laos pursuant to the peace accords, the new deputy chief, Brigadier General Richard Trefry, took back control of Project 404 personnel upon becoming the Chief MAAG for the U.S. embassy (albeit still forced to keep his headquarters in Thailand). It became his job to manage the downsizing of the American military effort in Laos while simultaneously attempting to improve Laotian military forces. He quickly assumed control of the RO in April, combining their efforts with Project 404 activities.

Project 404 was slowly phased out as the U.S. involvement in Laos virtually ceased after the Vietnam peace accords. On February 21, 1973, the warring factions in Laos signed the Agreement on the Restoration of Peace and Reconciliation in Laos. Article Four of the Agreement dictated the removal of foreign military forces from Laos: "Within a period no longer than 60 days, counting from the date of the establishment of the Provisional Government of National Union … the withdrawal of foreign military personnel, regular and irregular, from Laos, and the dismantling of foreign military and paramilitary organizations must be totally completed." [91]

The Project 404 Raven FACs departed in June of 1973. On September 5, 1973, General Trefry moved from Udorn with a small staff and became the defense attaché office in Vientiane (DAO).

After the establishment of the Provisional Government of National Unity (PGNU) in Laos in 1974, Project 404 disbanded in accordance with the sixty-day timetable for withdrawal of all foreign military forces (just prior to June of 1974). The last Army Project 404 advisor, Jeff Hotujec, left Laos in 1974. Portions of remaining U.S. military equipment in Laos were transferred to the RLAF and the Laotian army. Under the direction of the DAO Vientiane, USAF Project 404 personnel then worked to develop suitable tables of organization and equipment (TO&Es) for the "new" Laotian Air Force.

The Contribution of Project 404 ARMAs

All Project 404 assistant ARMAs, particularly those Special Forces qualified, provided a solution to the ambassador's need to augment the RO with eyes and ears out on the ground. During their duties they assisted and advised their Laotian counterparts and contributed to the making of sound tactical decisions by local commanders. Assistant ARMAs conducted their work in small teams, with a low silhouette, allowing U.S. military forces to skirt around the restrictions of the Geneva agreements. Retired Sergeant Major David Pompili summed up the rewards of a Project 404 tour:

In Project 404, my job was to be an observer, monitor the situation, gather intelligence, be a ground air guide, an artillery FO and to do target acquisition. People there told me I could not do all that, you had to be a Field Grade officer to conduct those activities. However, I did all that and called my own stuff. It was a very unique job.

You don't need several layers of bureaucracy between the guy on the ground in combat trying to get his job done—just give him all the tools he needs. Let people do their job so they can throw a jab back at the enemy.[92]

In December of 1975, the DEPCHJUSMAGTHAI disbanded. It was the end of almost fourteen years of U.S. military assistance to Laos.

CHAPTER TWELVE

Special Forces in Laos 1966–1974:
The Enabler: The 46th Special Forces Company (Independent)

> "All of these programs were under the command and control of the CIA. No one else was allowed in the camp, they were closed to visitors. I wrote my reports and messages which were handed to the Agency; they would screen these to leave only non-attributable information for release to the commander of the 46th. All of our administrative and logistics requirements were handled by the Agency or by the Ambassador in Vientiane, Ambassador G. McMurtrie Godley."
>
> FRANK JAKS, COMMANDER B-461

One covert course of action in unconventional warfare is the training of guerrilla forces or other allied indigenous forces off-site; that is, to establish military training camps outside of the conflict in a friendly, allied country. There are several advantages to this method, first among these, an ability to conduct the action away from the scrutiny of the press or other international inspection commissions.

Special Forces strategic utility in this role is to operate with plausible deniability (covert operations) and give diplomats room to maneuver, wage war economically, prolong the conflict for the enemy, and deny the enemy a military or political victory. The role of the Special Forces in Thailand also helped to reassure America's main ally in the region.[1]

Such was one of the roles of the 46th Special Forces Company (Independent) in enabling the RLG, the Royal Thai government, and the United States to train Hmong guerrillas, the Royal Laotian Army forces, and Thai regular and volunteer units for combat.

The Origin of the 46th

Company D (Augmented), 1st Special Forces Group was established at Fort Bragg, NC on April 15, 1966, under General Order #34, CONARC. The initial authorized strength for the unit was 369 personnel, who deployed and were operational in Thailand by October of 1966. On April 10, 1967, it was redesignated as the 46th Special Forces Company by USARPAC. It was authorized a headquarters and three B-detachments: B410, B420, and B430 (consisting of four SF-Alpha teams each).

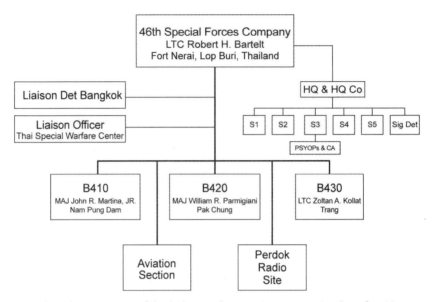

The task organization of the 46th Special Forces Company in October of 1966.

The unit established its headquarters at Fort Nerai, in Lopburi, the headquarters of the Royal Thai Army Special Forces (RTASF). The 46th Special Forces Company was under the operational command of the Military Assistance Command Thailand (MACTHAI), PACOM. The 46th SF Company was initially assigned a classified mission to support the Studies and Observation Group (SOG) activities in Laos, launched from bases within Thailand. Due to diplomatic concerns about Thai unwillingness to support an out-of-country mission, the unit began its deployment with its originally assigned overt mission: support to counterinsurgency efforts of the Thai government. The three B-detachments spread out to establish their operations, one in each of Thailand's geographical regions.

For some time prior to the arrival of the 46th, DEPCHJUSMAG–Thailand was responsible for the American portion of training Lao FAR battalions in Thailand; the CIA took responsibility of training Hmong guerrilla units. In this role, Laotian units were rotated into camps in Thailand for retraining and reequipping, along with receiving specialized courses in counterinsurgency tactics and long-range reconnaissance. Soon, A-detachments and B-detachments of the 46th became involved in training these forces, under a veil of extreme secrecy.[2]

Prior to the establishment of the 46th Special Forces Company in Thailand, the CIA, Royal Thai Army, Royal Thai Special Forces, and the Thai Border Police shared duties to train Laotian forces in select combat operations. Two initiatives in Laos sparked the demand for training off-site: the first was the growth in the Laotian irregular forces and the establishment of guerrilla zones throughout Laos, now in addition to the massive special guerrilla unit program expansion for Vang Pao in MR-II. The increase in irregular forces exceeded the capacity of Agency and RLG resources.

The second factor was the need for intelligence-gathering, reconnaissance, airborne insertion, and patrolling skills required for "probing" field teams and the *Roadwatch* teams (for duty along the Ho Chi Minh Trail). Additionally, train-the-trainers and team leader courses were required. The bulk of these training courses were conducted at Phitsanulok.[3]

The largest expansion of guerrilla forces occurred in MR-III in Laos. These forces were commanded by conventional FAR officers, who would require leadership instruction in guerrilla warfare and irregular operations. In March of 1966, the first contingent of forty officers from MR-III was sent to Phitsanulok camp (called "Phitscamp" by Americans operating in Thailand) for leadership instruction on these methods.[4]

B410, 46th SF, opened a training camp at Nam Pung Dam in October and November of 1966, with its four A-teams: A-411, A-412, A-413, and A-414. This camp would later be used to train Lao from the SGUs and to conduct select heavy-weapons training to Lao forces. B420 (later designated B4620) established their camp at Nong Takoo, with A-421 and A-424.

From March to July of 1967, the leadership cadre of the 1st SGU Battalion in MR-III was sent to Phitscamp for training. This unit was advised by George McGrath, who had served as a Special Forces member in Vietnam prior to his work in Laos.[5]

Other units sent for training included the 1st BP (September 1967), which conducted refresher training prior to their use in the battle of Nam Bac. In June of 1968, BG227 (BG: *bataillon guerrier*) deployed as a whole battalion to Phitscamp to receive guerrilla warfare training, under a program named Project 007; in August of 1968, BC208 (BC: *bataillon commando*) began their training, graduating in October of 1968 and returning to the fight in MR-II. In late 1968, the commando raiders from MR-II and MR-III, forty men in each contingent, conducted training at Phitscamp.[6]

46th SF Company Activities in 1969

In early 1969, Captain Willie Card was selected to lead a seventeen-man Army Special Forces team from Lopburi to Phitsanulok and establish a three-month training program for Laotian units, which also included airborne training. This began the covert support by the 46th Special Forces Company to the war effort in Laos. Captain Card's contingent became B-464 (later named B461), with two A-teams: A-44 and A-45 (eventually replaced with A-32 and A-33). The course consisted of small unit tactics, weapons proficiency, and demolitions. The SF cadre split the trainees into ten-man teams, and assigned one Special Forces team member to each contingent. The augmented SF detachment trained another sixty-man Laotian contingent in the fall.[7]

Project 007, the training of the FAR, shifted from Lopburi to the camp at Pranburi, and was renamed Project 009. Four battalions were retrained at the camp in 1970. Due to crowded conditions, three 100-man companies of the FAR were subsequently trained back at Lopburi. There was a small-scale effort at Lopburi to conduct M-60 machine-gun training during this period. In February, BC205, formerly the 11th BP, conducted training at Pranburi for a period of three months.[8]

From the spring of 1970 to late summer 1970, fifty trainees from the Pakse unit commando raiders trained at Phitsanulok. Seeing the advantage of the training, the Luang Prabang unit (Agency operatives) also sent their Raider company to Phitscamp for training.

Thailand increased their commitment and support to Laos by raising Thai volunteer battalions for use in combat inside Laos. These were often mislabeled as "Thai mercenary" battalions. Named Project *Unity*, this initiative was initially designed to prepare up to ten battalions for combat. From March through December 1970, one SF B-team (with ODAs A-10, A-11, A-16) from the 46th, under the command of Major Gene Earlywine, conducted training for the Thai volunteer battalions at Kanchanaburi. This mission was later transferred to Phitscamp, with the A-teams redesignated as SFT-31 and FTT-2. The 46th SF detachments were part of a team effort with trainers from the RTA and the Thai Border Police. The initial Thai contingent consisted of BC601 and BC602; upon graduation, the two units were sent to operate in the Bolovens Plateau region.[9]

From February 1970 to May 1970, BC205 from MR-II trained at Pranburi. In March, the 2nd SGU Battalion, followed by the 3rd SGU battalion, graduated after beginning training in the fall of 1969.[10]

Initially, the participating SF detachments were sequestered from the 46th SF Company to run three secret camps, controlled by the CIA. Major Frank Jaks joined the 46th SF Company following his tour with CCC in Vietnam. After an interview with the commander of the 46th, Lieutenant Colonel Paul Combs, he was offered three choices of duty within the 46th. Jaks chose to work with the CIA at Udorn in the classified training program for the Laotians.[11] On July 4, 1970, Jaks became the commander of B-461, responsible for all classified training of Laotians in Thailand. He described his role: "I became the commander of B461, the company who trained the Laotians. I went to Camp Surat Sena, 29 kilometers east of Phitsanulok. The camp was overseen by the Thai SF and Thai paratroopers. The special battalion for the Thai Prime Minister came from these units. I initially ran three camps (these were all closed camps; no one could get in without agency authorization.) These troops were being trained by individual unit packets for General Vang Pao."[12]

Project 007 was designed to retrain three GMs for Vang Pao. Upon Major Jaks' arrival, BG205 of GM-23 was already in attendance at the course in Phitscamp. Soon, BG209 was sent for retraining. The course was designed to retrain one battalion at a time, with 300 men to a battalion. Due to lack of space and facilities, Jaks opened up a camp at Nong Takoo, where two battalions of the GM-21 were trained and graduated; the camp was closed at the completion of that mission. Another camp was opened at Nam Pung Dam in June of 1970, and began the training of BG206.[13]

Sergeant Major (Retired, U.S.A., Special Forces) John R. Martin completed three tours to Thailand. He was a member of the original formation of the 46th Company—D Co., 1st SFGA (Provisional)—formed in the spring of 1966 at Fort Bragg. He deployed on his first tour to Thailand in October of 1966, serving eighteen months, with one of his missions at Pung Dam. He subsequently served tours in Vietnam and Okinawa. He went on to serve two more tours of twelve months each with the 46th Special Forces Company.

> I helped train Laotian troops; it was my second tour to 46th in January of 1970. I was an individual replacement in the 46th Special Forces Independent Company. I came from Vietnam—I was in a recon company, III Corps Mike Force. Because of my experience with recon, I was assigned to the Thai Infantry Center at Pran Buri, about 200 miles south of Bangkok. When I got to the camp, the Lao training was already set up. They were formed into company-sized units. Our team designation was A-11, or A-12/A-14. This was not based on SF ODA designations, the 46th assigned these designations.
>
> It was a real hush, hush operation. I had heard about Project 404. Colonel Millett, the MOH recipient for his famous bayonet charge in Korea, showed up at the camp. He was the DEPCHJUSMAGTHAI (which was the organization for MAAG–Laos). It was vague as to who was running the Lao training program, whether the DEPCHJUSMAGTHAI or the MAAG–Laos.
>
> We were training Lao (Yao tribesmen) reconnaissance companies. Sometimes the troops came with their Thai advisors. We ran a quick Ranger course—it was eight weeks, culminating in a practical, field exercise. There were six of us SF initially for the training program. A Captain led the team; as we grew in strength to fourteen EMs, a team leader eventually arrived (Captain Dan Edwards).
>
> We did not have any interface with our other in-country people. We were definitely told that *we would not go across the border!* This was a TS project and we were not to talk to anyone else about it.[14]

46th SF Company Activities in 1971

Four officers from the Laotian 324th Heavy Weapons Battalion in MR-III were trained in January.

The Cambodian government provided forces as commando raiders for service in Laos, under Project *Copper*. One battalion of Cambodian commando raiders trained in Thailand, and deployed to southern Laos.[15]

In February of 1971, Thai Unity battalions BC603 and BC604 completed training at Pranchinburi, followed in March by the graduation of BC605 and BC606. Again, the camp soon became crowded, so the team moved to open a camp at Kanchanaburi, the site of the River Kwai. Three USSF teams, totaling forty-four men, opened a twelve-week basic training course for the battalions. Additionally, they conducted a three-week training course for the battalion cadre.

In April, BC608 and BC609 graduated, followed by BC610 during the June–July time frame. This unit was sent to the PDJ for operations. In July, BC613 and BC614 were prepared for operations. Captain Card, one of the SF detachment team leaders, was killed when the camp at Pranchinburi was being closed out. Seeing a box floating in the river, he went to investigate. The box had explosives in it, which blew up, killing him and wounding CIA operative Tony Poe (resulting in Poe's missing fingers).[16]

Michael Ingham transitioned from being an infantry/recon Marine in Vietnam to serve as one of the OGA paramilitary operatives in Laos, where he spent two-plus years (1971–1973) advising Thai troops trained by the 46th Special Forces in Thailand. Ingham eventually ended up as the senior Thai advisor in MR-II, working from Long Tieng. He replaced retired Special Forces NCO Doug Swanson. He visited the training camps to pick up Thai units trained by the 46th SF cadre:

> When the Hmong were getting their ass kicked, the U.S. asked Thailand for help. In late 1967 and early 1970s, a deal was struck for Thailand to help with the Thai volunteer battalions.
>
> We would spend three to five days in Thailand, then pick up the unit. The structure of the Thai battalions was: 550 troops; infantry battalion of 350 troops, and 105mm and 155mm towed howitzers. The Agency cast around in Thailand for SF troops to train them. The first units were in a training camp in Thailand in 1970. My experience directly with these training camps was limited. I was the CIA case officer for the Thai. CIA case officers did not work at the company level like SF, we were at the couple of battalions' level as case officers. Our mission was to assist and sustain them, and if needed give advice at the higher level.[17]

Due to the increase of Unity battalions training at Phitscamp, Major Jaks left the overcrowded base and shifted the B-461 headquarters to Nam Phong in October 1971.

In 1971, SGUs from Nam Yu were trained in Thailand. In the fall of 1971, BC616, BC617, and BC618 were trained at Kanchanuburi. The BC619 training had to be moved back to Phitscamp when Thai units returning from Vietnam reoccupied the camp. A unit comprised of Thai Royal Marines, graduated on December 20. Returning UNITY battalions from Laos were sent to Nam Pung Dam (three Thai battalions were at the camp in December 1971, being trained by three 46th A-teams; one battalion was being retrained at Ban Nong Saeng.) These units had previously been mauled at the battle of Skyline Ridge in Long Tieng and required reorganization and retraining.[18] In late April, GM-22 was sent to Thailand for a two-month retraining cycle.[19]

46th SF Company Activities in 1972

At the end of 1971, and the beginning of 1972, the NVA opened Campaign Z, designed to retake the PDJ and capture Long Tieng. In January of 1972, eight Unity battalions ultimately became involved in Laos for this operation, including the dramatic battle of Skyline Ridge (which almost resulted in the NVA and Pathet Lao driving Vang Pao's forces from Long Tieng), and were sent back to Thailand for rearming, refitting, and retraining. The course was short in order to get them back into the fight. Based on the condition of the battalion, the training lasted from as little as a week to ten days. By January 24, Unity battalions 603A, 604A, 606A, 607A, 608A and 610A were in Thailand. They were all part of Task Force Vang Pao (Unity battalions combined with Thai artillery units). They were soon followed by 605A and 609A.[20]

U.S. Army Special Forces officer Scott Crerar served as the UW staff officer in the J-3 MAC–Thai, from 1969 to 1972. His role was to coordinate SF/PSYOP-related matters with AMEMB Bangkok (POL/MIL, Attachés, Minister Counselor for CI, CIA) and sometimes with the U.S. embassy Phnom Penh, MACV and CINCPAC. He was also a MAC–Thai member of the embassy Counter-Insurgency Group and PSYOP Coordination Group. He worked close with Lieutenant Colonel Paul Combs, commander of the 46th SF Company, during the compartmented training. He relates: "Part of the program was to train Lao irregulars (about 300 people a class) and Thai irregulars (about 600 or so). We had beside us a Thai cadre. In the beginning they were well-qualified Army and Marines, but later they began to incorporate police and others and it was not as effective. We had to do this training because the training the Lao got was very basic—how to load and shoot a weapon, maybe. It was pretty sad the level of skill they gave these guys before putting them into combat."[21]

He added, "Before 1965, the Thai had one or two batteries of artillery in Laos. The advisors for Thai artillery units were U.S. field artillery officers sent out of the 25th Division in Hawaii. There were really some atrocious practices amongst these units—no sights, no understanding of laying in the guns, and other fire employment problems. Up near the PDJ, the fire bases were set too far apart so they had no ability to reinforce each other with fires."[22]

In May of 1972, GM-26, with their four battalions BG211, BG222, BG232 and BG235 deployed to Thailand for a three-month training course at Nam Pung Dam.[23]

On April 1, 1972, the 46th Special Forces Company was renamed as the U.S. Army Special Forces Thailand (USASFT). In accordance with existing TO&E for Army Special Forces companies, B-461 was re-designated as Company A, USASFT.

Don Munson replaced Major Hubbard, the S3 operations officer of the 46th SF Company during this period. Munson explained the rationale for the redesignation:

> The re-designation occurred because the Army had changed the Tables of Organization & Equipment from the former version to the latest iteration of organization of SF units. Technically, the change caused the 46th SF Company to be designated as the 3rd Battalion of 1st SF Group in Okinawa, however, the Thai government objected to the concept. As it was explained to me, the Thai government insisted that the unit headquartered in Lop Buri must continue to be an "independent" organization. The designation 3rd Battalion, 1st Special Forces Group was therefore "classified" even though the newly formed detachments were numbered from 31 through 45. [Detachments 1 through 30 comprised the other two battalions of the 1st SF Group.][24]

On June 12, two Unity battalions were sent to Nam Phong for refit. GM-5 from MR-I sent three Nam Yu irregular battalions to Phitsanulok for training.[25]

As part of the effort by the DEPCHJUSMAGTHAI to improve the military proficiency of the FAR prior to the pending withdrawal of all U.S. military assistance in Laos, the commander, SF Thailand, Lieutenant Colonel Radtke, designated Major Walter Nelms and his FTT to command three ODAs for training missions in Laos on June 15, 1972. One team was led by Captain Udo Walther, and the second by Captain Jim Bruton. The teams were fully formed with twelve men, but Bruton's team was split to form another training element (ODA-1). This mission was conducted at the training centers of Phou Khao Khoui, one in Seno and another at Wat Phu. Bruton designated his split-team ODA-2, and deployed to Wat Phu, the PS-46 (Pakse Site) training camp, on June 25; this camp was located south of the provincial capital of Champassac.[26]

Initially, the teams were restricted to the conduct of training during the day, with return to Thailand by evening. This problem was eventually worked out by Brigadier General Vessey, the DEPCHJUSMAGTHAI, so the teams could remain in Laos during the training week. The then Captain James K. "Jim" Bruton described his mission at Wat Phu:

> I was assigned as an assistant S3, or one of several captains working as S3 action officers under Major Hubbard, upon my arrival to the 46th in January 1972. A requirement for training Lao regular forces came down one day in May, with a levy for a control team run by a Major and two ODAs. Udo Walther became the over-all control, with his intact team. The team I was on was ad hoc. I was not the original commander, he was relieved and I took over. We were based out of Udorn, and Air America would fly us in each day to do the training, and then return us to Thailand before evening. On mid- to late-June, we got permission to stay overnight in Laos. The team I commanded then split, with Lieutenant O'Malley taking the training requirement as ODA-1 at Phou Khao Khouai CATC [Combined Arms Training Center]; I was ODA-2 at Wat Phu, PS-46. Walther was at Seno with ODA-3. The whole thing was under the command and control of FTT-1 in Udorn, commanded by Major Walter Nelms.[27]

Once the team had authorization to remain in Laos for the training week, they procured an old French house within the training compound, lived off the economy, and began supervising the training cadres of GM-4004. (GM-4004 consisted of the Neutralists—BI-16, BC207, and 104 BP). The team worked in close association with the Project 404 team from Pakse, headed by Major "Mac" McGuinness. (McGuinness had been to FSI language school and spoke some Lao.) A program of instruction already existed for the training, developed by the junior Lao officers who had attended military schools in the United States, and who were very enthusiastic about the program. At times inattentive leadership from "old guard" senior officers and occasional cadre absence plagued the mission, with ODA-2 stepping in on several occasions to give the classes themselves (using their minimal knowledge of the Thai language). Bruton noted, "We spoke and instructed using an elementary mix of Thai and Lao; hands-on training, like with the mortars, made it easier to gesture and demonstrate."[28]

It was a simple camp, consisting of wooden barracks, a dining facility, and weapons ranges. Nearby was a C-123 capable airfield, with another, smaller landing strip inside the camp where Air America PC-6 Porters could land.

As a requisite to graduation, the GM performed a four-day field exercise. The 46th SF were under restrictions to not maneuver with their units into a combat situation. Bruton's split-team, wearing sterile fatigues and carrying M16s, soon found themselves in a "live fire" field training exercise (FTX). He described the action:

> My most memorable moment before graduation was our live fire FTX! This was in August 1972. The 57mm RR [recoilless rifle] was carried close to the point element of the lead battalion. The 57mm RR element was very good at springing ambushes set up by the Pathet Lao. Our whole split-team went out on the exercise and several men got close to the firefight. Some Pathet Lao were reportedly killed and two captured. We (our Lao forces) took no casualties. I think two of the SF on the team received CIBs at a ceremony in Lopburi later in '73.[29]

Activities of the 46th SF Company in Laos

Sergeant Sydney Jensen was a Project 404 ARMA in MR-V, assigned for duties at Phou Khao Khoui (PKK) National Commando Training Center (CATC) in 1972, and remembers ODA-1's involvement. PKK's focus was training designed to upgrade and improve the FAR. It was staffed with Laotian officers who had previously trained and graduated from military courses in the United States. The purpose of the course was to improve FAR battalions for COIN—light infantry "commando" instruction. Jensen described his time at the camp:

> I was assigned to DEPCHIEF JUSMAGTHAI with duty on Project 404. My assignment was the Laotian Training Center at Phou Khao Khoui—LS-51. (The main Laotian training camp was at Camp Chinaimo near Vientiane—it was also the location of the Lao Military Academy.) I was a Staff Sergeant, 05B/11B.
>
> Sometime in 1972, a split-team from the 46th Independent Special Forces in Thailand came to help with anti-tank training. They usually flew up in the morning, then flew back to Udorn, Thailand in the evening, due to restrictions of having U.S. military personnel in the country. This procedure was very wasteful of training time. The 46th split-team would use the "Elephant Run," a C-46 route flight which traveled from Vientiane, to Udorn, and then return. [The team was ODA-1, deployed on this mission in June of 1972 through December 20, 1972.][30]

ODA-3, a full-up twelve-man SF team, led by Captain Udo H. Walther (one of the raiders on the Son Tay prison camp operation), deployed to Seno in June to help retrain the 2nd Strike Division, beginning with the 21st Brigade. This mission, all six battalions, was completed around December and the ODA returned to its bases in Thailand.[31]

Also in the summer of 1972, GM-21 was sent for a two-month refit and retraining at Phitscamp.[32] From the summer of 1972 to October 1972, all of MR-IV's GM irregulars were sent to Phitscamp. These units were from GM-41 and GM-42.[33]

In September, Bruton's ODA began training with GM-4001. In October, BV-44 and BI-7 were pulled out of Wat Phu training to reinforce Khong Sedone, though BV-47 remained in training.

In mid-October, the teams received an Agency request to provide anti-armor training to select forces; elements of FTT-1, ODA-2, and some from ODA-3 provided a two-week course of instruction at a site north of Pakse. The Lao force receiving anti-tank training was GM-33, commanded by Colonel Khao Insixiengmay. GM-33 had just helped defeat a PAVN regiment at Khong Sedone in September of 1972. Bruton met with Colonel Khao to coordinate the anti-tank training.

As soon as the threat around Khong Sedone calmed, the two battalions of GM-4001 returned to Wat Phu to complete their training cycle. Their FTX occurred in early December of 1972. A week later, Bruton's mission concluded and his ODA returned to Lopburi.

A rotation of five teams from the 1st SFG deployed for their 179-day tour in Thailand in October of 1972.[34]

The increase in forces to train at Nam Pung Dam required more training space. Soon, two satellite training camps were established, one at Phu Keng jungle camp to the northeast of Nam Pung Dam and the other at Camp Inthanin, southwest of Nam Pung Dam.

In November 1972, BC623, BC624, BC625, and BC626 graduated and were sent to Long Tieng.

Sergeant Major (Retired, U.S.A., SF) Martin spent his third tour with the 46th working four to six weeks at Nam Pung Dam before he was transferred as part of a split A-team to the Agency site at Ban Nong Seang, east of Ubon on the Thai–Lao border:

> My second experience with training Lao/Hmong was at Nam Pung Dam. We were training and equipping Lao in a built-up area outside of the camp. The training was for one company at a time, of about 200–250 men. We only helped out. We moved the project to Ban Nong Seang, about ninety km from Ubon, four kilometers from the Thai-Lao border. Our mission was to train-up heavy weapons battalions from the Long Tieng area. It was a four- to six-week POI. We had to do a pretty fast turn-around. We incorporated FDC [fire direction control] training into the curriculum. The Yaos (ethnic Laos from the northwest) could not read or write and they did not know numbers. Our medic, Cecil Keaton, tried to teach them math.
>
> The project was run by a case officer, and that is where we got our C2 from. Other case officers came in with the troops. Upon their arrival, we would brief them on training to date, pertinent information on the troops, etc. We would get feedback from them on the situation in Laos—for example, how the troops fought, what combat conditions were like. Then we would adjust the training to take this into account. A case officer showed us how the Lao kept an ammo can filled with grenades, with the pins pulled (the old M2 pineapple grenade), and with a 3.5 inch rocket motor attached to it. When they were in their trenches, they would ignite the motor and fire it out in front of them like a cluster bomb. Very adaptive. The troops were basically equipped with World War II equipment. Again, we were very concerned about safety. We had no major incidents.
>
> The units arriving were a diverse bunch. We would await them on the airstrip to see what came off. We used the Army Infantry School POI for 11B/11Cs, and then adjusted the POI to what the case officers needed. We always had plenty of arms and demolitions, ordnance.[35]

In preparation for the withdrawal of American military forces from Laos, the CIA arranged for fifty Thai covert operatives to be trained for stay-behind operations to support future irregular force programs in Laos. Although not prepared for teaching tradecraft and spying, the USSF team at Nam Phong did their best to prepare the designated stay-behind agents for their role.

46th SF Company Activities in 1973

The ceasefire in the spring of 1973 began the road to downsizing of classified missions for the USASFT; Major Jaks began this process in the fall of 1972 with the withdrawal of one SF team at Nam Pung Dam. In January of 1973, the team at Ban Nong Saeng was withdrawn followed by the six teams of the 1st Special Forces Group, who were sent back early to Okinawa in February of 1973. (One of their last missions would be the training of the headquarters staff of the Unity GM in November of 1972.)

The USASFT headquarters was closed out at Nam Phong in early 1973 and shifted to Lopburi. This left two camps, one at Phitsanulok and the team left at Nam Phong (shut down in the fall of 1973), eventually followed by the closure of the mission at Phitsanulok.[36]

SFT-31 Phitsanulok, 1973–1974

Sergeant William F. Rouleau volunteered for Special Forces and was trained as a medic. While in Company B, 7th SFG (A), he received orders for the 46th SF Company in Thailand. He had tried to go to Vietnam, where he thought the action was. He said, "Surprisingly, I had never heard about the 46th SF."[37]

Upon arrival to Bangkok, he checked into the Opera Hotel, where he was told he would be picked up. He was informed he would be going to Site 603, in Phitsanoluk. He remained in Bangkok for a week, and then got instructions to ride the train 600 kilometers to Lopburi, where he was picked up by another Special Forces medic (Staff Sergeant Cecil Keaton) and driven out to the military camp, twenty to thirty kilometers outside of town.

The next day at breakfast his team members (SFT-31) told him they were training Hmong special guerrilla units for use in MR-II in Laos (Vang Pao's units). SFT-31 consisted of twelve men, commanded initially by Captain F. B. "Bev" Garrett, and then by Captain James J. Morrison. First Lieutenant Farris C. Thomas was the detachment XO and Master Sergeant Robert G. Hughes was the team sergeant.

The SGU trainees numbered about 300 to 400 men in a unit. Sergeant Rouleau was tasked to give the medical portion of the training to the SGUs. "I was ordered to conduct my portion of the training, which was Basic Medical Training, for each of the two SGUs we trained; my course was one week for each SGU … I taught the critical med skills I thought they needed based on how they operated in Laos: bandaging wounds, how to treat puncture wounds, blast wounds, and application of tourniquets."[38]

Site 603 was the most sensitive operational security site in Thailand. Training occurred inside the camp, away from the eyes of the populace. The camp was divided by a river; the upper camp held the Thai. The SGUs were refitted at the camp with new weapons and uniforms. The uniforms were Tiger camouflage fatigues and some ODs. They were also issued new underwear and boots. Rouleau recalls, "Many of them had been fighting in sandals. The rifle was the M16. The SGU troops were ragged and in bad shape. There was what looked like to be a lot of teenagers with their Dads—not much in-between. One guy we had was forty-five years old—very beat up. He was a survivor of years of war. He smoked an Opium pipe in the evening to relieve his pain."[39]

SFT-31 team taught weapons maintenance, assembly and disassembly, weapons cleaning, and then conducted live fires. The team also taught patrolling techniques, but very simple and basic subjects. It was a two-month curriculum.

SFT-31 ran day and night operations, focusing on getting the SGU to improve their tactical movement techniques. Rouleau relates, "We taught them files, flank/rear security, and other skills. We could not get them to pass basic patrolling so we could go to a more advanced stage of training. We had to work hard to keep them in their formations; they liked to bunch up and talk to each other. They had very bad movement discipline."[40]

The SFT schedule of training ran seven days a week. The two SGUs rotated out and two more SGUs came in. Said Rouleau,

> The pressure was on to get these guys trained. The Case Officers checked in with us to ascertain the status of training. Their emphasis was for us to keep things moving. "What do you need? Etc." Things only slowed down when it started raining—due to floods and equipment, men being wet.
>
> We then did an FTX live fire. It was a night attack against a bunker. The attack was initiated with a M72 LAW. The scenario was them in a night defensive position, and then requiring a limited attack. We used mortars, illumination rounds, and then FFE with the mortars. We had them fire light AT weapons, then attack the bunker. It was very basic; the SGU on line, with their M16s. We only had one guy get shot from behind in the calf/thigh during these maneuvers. I will say though, the SGU guys were very serious about this training (knowing they were going right back to the fight in Laos)."[41]

The End of the 46th Special Forces Company (Independent)

USASFT was inactivated and closed out by its last commander, George Marecek, and redesignated as the 3rd Battalion of the 1st SFG on Okinawa (although this was kept a close secret).

Epilogue: Legacy and Lessons Learned

> "The linkage of local and regional conflicts into a global conflict is not necessarily wrong in itself; there is a requirement to explain how conflicts, disputes and insurrections in different parts of the world affect one another. However, the consequence has been, and will continue to be, that liberal powers are pressured to take sides and invest military credibility in conflicts that may have no clear military solution within the terms of war as traditionally understood."
>
> EMILE SIMPSON, *WAR FROM THE GROUND UP* (OXFORD UNIVERSITY PRESS, 2012)

On February 21, 1973 the RLG, Neutralists and Pathet Lao signed The Restoration of Peace and Reconciliation in Laos.[1] An immediate ceasefire went into effect, but as in previous ceasefires, the communists continued their attacks on government forces to seize more ground. One of the last acts in this drama occurred on April 16. When NVA forces pressured the FAR near the front lines at Ta Vieng (southern PDJ), the U.S. agreed to B-52 strikes as punishment for violating the ceasefire. A two-man USAF CCT from the Air Commandos emplaced an offset bombing beacon to facilitate the strike. At the end of the B-52 sorties, the two Air Commandos extracted the beacon and returned to their base.

In April 1974, Ambassador Godley departed and was replaced by Ambassador Whitehouse.

As Thai Unity battalions withdrew from Laos, the 46th Special Forces Company (now USASFT, United States Army Special Forces Thailand) commensurately downsized their clandestine training support, eventually ending this effort in the fall of 1973.

The protocols to ceasefire were signed by the three factions on September 14. On October 12, 1973, two Pathet Lao security battalions appeared, one in Wattay and one in Luang Prabang, to observe and monitor the implementation of the peace accords and the ceasefire.

Instructions from the State Department were cryptic and totally out of synch with the situation on the ground. The ambassador was urged to take all measures to keep the Royal Laotian security forces "operational."

In April of 1974 a Lao coalition government formed as the Provisional Government of National Union (PGNU). One of the PGNU's stipulations was the removal of all foreign forces within sixty days (by June of 1974).

Project 404 ARMAs became involved in standardizing the TOEs of the FAR and transferring U.S. military gear from the SGUs and Thai battalions to the RLG armed forces.

On May 22 the last of the Thai Unity battalions departed Laos; on July 1, U.S. military aid to the RLG was transferred to control by the State Department, and dramatically cut. In September, the 4802nd JLD disbanded, ending Agency-led overt support to the Laotians.

Over the next year the FAR suffered defeat after defeat, now without U.S. advisory "stiffeners" and military funding. In constant decline, and with low morale, the FAR was for all intents and purposes non-effective. Vang Pao and his Hmong fled for refugee camps in Thailand. In December 1975, the king abdicated his throne and the Pathet Lao took over the government, now named the People's Democratic Republic of Laos (PDRL). As was the case with all communist governments, the country continually fell behind over the following years due to the effects of a state-run economy.

In the 1980s, resistance movements began operating against the PDRL, both from Lao and Hmong groups supported by Thailand. Vang Pao settled in America and continued to run the "resistance" until his death. To date, none of the resistance movements has been effective. A *New York Times* article reported on the sad plight of Hmong resistance fighters inside Laos as late as 2007.[2] Bitterness and recrimination among those who fought and served in Laos remain to this day with respect to the abandonment of not only Laos, but the Hmong.

Strategic Use, Utility, and Application

The secret war in Laos provided a laboratory to discover the strategic potential of special operations—converting tactical actions into successful policy and political objectives. This formula for the use of force and utility of the force was absent throughout the 1950s, when special operations assets were used more as worldwide trainers and instructors. Early special operations doctrine focused on "fighting the last war," with their application and use defined by guerrilla warfare, support to resistance movements through operations in the enemy's rear. Notwithstanding these conditions would not be present in modern warfare, the opportunities to use special operations in this manner virtually disappeared as the U.S. military focused on fast and violent warfare conducted by overwhelming military force.

As the notion of conducting war on the scale of World War II diminished, the rise of revolutionary warfare as the new "way of war" gave an opportunity to shift the use of military force and the rise of counterinsurgency and limited war doctrine began to emerge. These conditions were precisely the venue for why Special Forces evolved and became relevant again.

The objectives of insurgency and counterinsurgency are ultimately political, not military. Many of the successful counterinsurgencies conducted in the latter half of the twentieth century were ultimately concluded as political solutions, using the military to achieve them. If there were any outliers to this formula, it was due to brute force and repression on the part of the counterinsurgent.

Laos differed from the war in Vietnam. In Laos, American objectives were political: prevent the communists from taking over the government and ensure Laos remained at least neutral toward the West. In Vietnam, a military war was fought to defeat the insurgents and the NVA.

In Laos, the involvement of American military forces was used as an economy of force to allow room for diplomacy. This strategy relied on at least a minimal effort on the part of the RLG to shoulder the burden of the military aspect of the internal defense and development program. Even with the poor performance of Lao armed forces, government corruption, and lack of mobilization of the Lao populace, the use of special operations forces by the ambassadors to Laos were successful in keeping the government in power for at least about fourteen years. In Laos, the ambassadors and the Department of State ran the U.S. effort; in Vietnam, the Military Assistance Command–Vietnam (MACV) ran the war, a war of attrition.

Another measure contributing to the success of policy objectives in Laos was in the "way" American forces were used: conducting Special Warfare and Special Air Warfare. Larger military intervention in Laos came in the latter stages of the secret war when conventional airpower was used to punish the NVA and interdict the flow of communist forces and supplies transiting the Ho Chi Minh Trail. The bulk of this air campaign was in support of military operations in South Vietnam.

Laos also provided the opportunity to expand the role of special operations into the interagency word of clandestine and covert activities. Using U.S. Army Green Berets provided an option for the ambassadors to bolster and reassure allies in the region and assure policy-makers and decision-makers in Washington DC their use would not widen the war in Southeast Asia (plausible denial feature). In Vietnam, special operations were ultimately used to support U.S. conventional force maneuver. A clear contribution to the growing maturity of how special operations could be used evolved in the use of operational and strategic reconnaissance (along the Ho Chi Minh Trail) and the conduct of raids, such as the Son Tay prison raid which helped to raise the morale of the American public and gave hope to the families of POWs.

In Laos, the Green Berets exhibited the fungibility of special operations forces. In 1959, Special Forces trainers were secretly used to improve the capability of the Laotian army through Operation *Hotfoot*. It was a foreign policy objective of the U.S. to ensure the Laotian security forces could hold their own and not concede further territory to communist forces. The Military Assistance Program (Security Assistance) was designed to at least prevent the military defeat of RLG forces and keep the Royal Laotian government in power. Denying the communists more control over the country also denied the Pathet Lao any power to negotiate for a coalition government.

As communist military activity increased, President Kennedy increased the overt involvement of U.S. military forces. It did not require the deployment of conventional forces to Laos; the use of Special Forces serving as combat advisors fit the bill. In April of 1961, the new role for the Green Berets was known as Operation *White Star*, which lasted until October 1962 when foreign military forces were withdrawn from Laos with the signing of the Geneva Agreement in July 1962. *White Star* combat advisors maneuvered with all the major Laotian army units, and also helped to support the guerrilla warfare campaign being conducted by General Vang Pao on the Plaine des Jarres—with a commensurate unconventional warfare campaign on the Bolovens Plateau. All of these activities helped to bolster Laotian forces by challenging communist attempts to "fight while negotiating," giving time for diplomacy to work during the ceasefire and ongoing negotiations in Geneva.

From 1966 to 1974, Special Forces advisors returned to Laos under Project 404 to serve as the eyes and ears of the ambassador, gathering intelligence and monitoring the implementation of continued, and more modern military aid. In Thailand, the 46th Special Forces Company (Independent) supported U.S. government covert activities to train, equip, and professionalize Lao, Hmong, and the Thai volunteer forces for duty in Laos. These activities were conducted out of six secret camps throughout Thailand, and gave the U.S. plausible deniability on their increased involvement in the secret war.

The political, and policy objective in Laos was maintaining a pro-Western, neutral government. The selective use of special operations forces, in a sociopolitical-based counterinsurgency, allowed America to achieve its goals and objectives until the political objective was no longer worth the cost. The outcome for the SOF community was in a growing understanding of the strategic utility of special operations, vice being doomed to a force for tactical employment.

The Legacy and Lessons of Army Special Forces in Laos

The use of Special Forces in Laos was a good example of "limited" war use of SOF and avoided the need to insert conventional forces into the kingdom. Initially, Ambassador Winthrop G. Brown augmented his PEO with Special Forces trainers in a manner to not upend the delicate balance of diplomacy framed by the requirements of the 1954 Geneva Agreement (Operation *Hotfoot* in 1959). Army SOF are an excellent tool in coercive diplomacy, going where conventional forces are not desired, and can be cost effective and help accomplish low key foreign policy objectives, giving room and time for diplomacy to work. U.S. Army Special Forces were chosen to operate as discrete, small teams (without a large logistical overhead) to conduct foreign internal defense and confirm American military aid was not only getting into the hands of the FAR, but to also ensure the FAR received the correct training on the use of weapons and equipment supplied. In this application, Special Forces teams assisted in building partner nation capability.

President Kennedy also used the Army Special Forces presence to "signal" American intentions to keep Laos neutral when he converted the *Hotfoot* mission to Operation *White Star*, an overt advisory effort under a formal MAAG. This accomplished two major objectives: it averted a superpower clash in Southeast Asia between the United States and the USSR, and prevented a communist takeover of the Royal Laotian Government during his administration.

The use of unconventional warfare, along with other covert means, helped to contest NVA and Pathet Lao encroachment on the Plaine des Jarres in Military Region II, while in the south, Operation *Pincushion* and the Kha guerrilla tribal program facilitated the retaking of much of the Boloven's Plateau; this effort stymied any aggressive military maneuver of the Pathet Lao in that region.

More could have been done, however, if the ambassadors expanded operations and used this capability to its fullest extent. The lack of military PSYOP teams operating with the Army Special Forces teams handed the psychological warfare initiative in rural areas to the communists. Not deploying civil affairs teams—although in this period they were not part of the SOF community—and no integration of major USAID civic action projects into areas where the teams operated weakened government legitimacy.

It was in the area of strategic and operational intelligence—in SOF terms, special reconnaissance, or SR—where the SF could have made a large difference to keep the ambassadors informed of the ground situation. There was a constant need to identify locations and intentions of the enemy, as well as to identify and monitor NVA operations along Route 7, the mountain passes between Laos and North Vietnam, and activities along the Ho Chi Minh Trail. The *Trailwatch* program alone was not sufficient to fill this gap. Additionally, Special Forces operations could have been used to augment the CIA in identifying the Pathet Lao resistance organization and design operations to decimate their local political structure (counter-organization measures).

The ambassadors also failed to use the direct action (DA) capabilities inherent in special operations. SF teams, leading well-trained, host nation commandos could have been employed to penetrate and raid behind enemy lines. The refusal to conduct a POW raid to free Captain Moon, Sergeant Ballenger, and the other allied prisoners, known as the "perilous option" role of SOF, resulted in the POWs languishing through starvation and sometimes torture, for no good purpose. Lieutenant Colonel "Bull" Simons dedicated three operational detachments for such a raid, but was consistently turned down by Ambassador Brown. The lack of organic and dedicated SOF air power hampered such activities, although everyone had high praise for Air

America, Continental Air Services and Bird & Son pilots who supported the Green Berets in transport, resupply, and high-risk extraction operations.

But in counterinsurgency all military maneuver ultimately supports political objectives and *Hotfoot* and *White Star* successfully accomplished all the missions assigned to them by the ambassadors. After the August 9, 1960 coup d'état by Kong Le, the MAAG's use of the Laotian Training Advisory Group (LTAG), consisting of MAAG advisors and *White Star* advisory teams, became the entire training and advisory effort for the FAR (particularly after the French withdrawal from the combined training program). During this period, with the exception of losing Nam Tha in the north, the FAR held its ground along the ceasefire lines and no major towns or cities along the Mekong River valley were threatened by Pathet Lao expansion. CINCPAC summed up this achievement on February 21, 1963 in a memo to the Joint Chiefs of Staff, identifying the lessons learned of the MAAG and Special Forces Activities in Laos:

> The mission of MAAG Laos up to the time of the withdrawal was to advise and assist the FAR in the accomplishment of its mission to maintain internal security against Communist-inspired subversion and insurgency and provide maximum initial resistance to aggression by external forces. In providing assistance to FAR, MAAG performed functions of (1) planning, programming, and training and equipping Lao military and Auto-Défense Forces (2) requisitioning, receiving, and issuing military supplies and equipment and (3) monitoring the end-use of MAP supplies and equipment. MAAG advisors and advisory teams carried out advisory and training functions through FAR General Staff divisions, Military Region and Zone headquarters, logistics organizations, depots, and schools. WSMTTs served as the MAAG training element for FAR ground force combat units or irregular forces.[3]

The mission performed in Laos by SF confirmed the doctrinal approach and procedures used to conduct unconventional warfare, through the strategic application of Special Warfare. Laos was a testing ground for the organizational and operational concepts for guerrilla warfare outlined in DA FM 31–21 and FM 31–21A (Secret), and were found to be sound; in the words of the MAAG, the doctrine was "satisfactory for field operations with irregular forces."[4] Much of what was learned would be incorporated into the Special Warfare Center's future versions of doctrinal manuals as well as be applied by Special Forces teams conducting unconventional warfare in the Vietnam conflict. For example, in one area, the use of special funds to pay irregular troops and to purchase supplies, the collaboration with controlled American assets, and the use of third-country trainers and interpreters were solid concepts incorporated into future UW operations.[5]

There was some thought given to a more strategic use for Special Forces. Training of the FAR could have been accomplished by a conventional U.S. cadre of trainers, allowing Special Forces to focus on strategic and operational units like the commandos, Rangers, and paratroopers. These forces were quick reaction assets (in the context of Laos), highly mobile, and considered elite. They often provided the "stiffener" needed for engagements with the Pathet Lao, similar to what NVA advisors and units performed with the Pathet Lao. SF advisors were not used to accompany these forces on raids behind enemy lines or upon the Pathet Lao and NVA lines of communication.

Overall, Army Special Forces conducted the tasks they were given to perform in a credible manner. They were certainly successful in their two guerrilla warfare endeavors, Operation *Momentum* with the Hmongs and Operation *Pincushion* with the Kha, the bedrock of the Green Berets' *raison d'être*. As said by Retired Special Forces Colonel Charles M. Simpson in his book *Inside the Green Berets*: "Operation White Star is a classic example of a successful operation run on a shoestring. The multiplier effect has never been plainer. A small number of dedicated professionals produced thousands of effective guerrillas who operated in their native environment, using tactics suitable to the terrain and the enemy disposition."[6]

Admiral H. D. Felt, CINCPAC commander provided his overall conclusion on the efficacy of these operations in the MAAG after action report on *White Star* in Laos:

> The various lessons learned and operational and administrative techniques developed in Laos have been applied to U.S. military assistance activities throughout PACOM and have served to improve our efforts in the field. These lessons may be applied to many other countries of the world faced with insurgency or subversion and susceptible to U.S. military assistance. The basic conclusion which can be drawn from the U.S. military assistance venture in Laos is that it is not possible to obtain short term results in training an unskilled military force which at the same time is faced with a major insurgency problem. Additionally, it is extremely difficult to develop fighting ability among a people whose national character and characteristics are basically un-warlike. It is to be concluded that a minimum of 10 years is needed to transform a nascent military establishment into an effective fighting organization. Less time would be necessary for an irregular force assuming it is adequately led.[7]

This was sound advice, which would certainly ring true over and over again for future American military involvement in guerrilla warfare, political warfare, and in insurgency and counterinsurgency environments.

The Geopolitical Results

America ceded winning the war in Laos to focus on stopping communist expansion in South Vietnam. As a backwater effort, the U.S. Military Assistance Program to Laos continued through a new organization designed to replace the MAAG in Vientiane, the Requirement Office, placed within the embassy's USAID structure. A Deputy Chief JUSMAG formed in Thailand to serve as a titular MAAG Laos, funneling its operations and equipment through the RO. Laos would not be the Southeast Asia country where America preferred to fight a larger conflict. The "eye on the prize" for future military action in Laos would be focused against "non-attributable" NVA activities and their operations to support the Ho Chi Minh Trail network, while

America maintained the deception of respecting neutrality for Laos with regard to its foreign policy position.[8]

America would begin its own "non-attribution" activities using a combination of Thailand as a support base and the conduct of covert operations inside Laos, in hopes of preventing the inevitable communist victory in Laos. This posture was successful until the American withdrawal from Southeast Asia. Upon U.S. withdrawal, the communists inevitably won.

The Lessons of Laos

There were two major lessons to take away from the American involvement in Laos. The first was a mismatch of strategy, that is, the ways, means and ends were totally out of balance. The war was fought politically, to achieve foreign policy goals back in the United States, not being fought to achieve strategic military objectives in the theater. The war was molded by what could be achieved around a delicate balancing act to at least give the impression America was abiding by the several Geneva accords and agreements. The *ends*, as envisioned by U.S. foreign policy, were the guaranteed neutrality of Laos and the expulsion of North Vietnamese from the country. The *means* were military assistance and foreign internal defense, using SOF, as well as covert activities. The *ways* were totally out of synch: each ambassador to Laos saw a different path to support the RLG. If the policy was not working, then change the policy. There was no clear way the use of SOF alone could have helped the Laotians achieve a military victory.

SOF conducted their mission in this atmosphere: buy time for diplomacy and exhaust and attrite the enemy. It is remarkable the communists were prevented from taking over the Laotian government for almost fourteen years while SOF operators performed their mission.

The second lesson was militarily strategic: failure to effectively interdict the Ho Chi Minh Trail ultimately spelled the doom of South Vietnam. The failure to orient SOF assets, working in conjunction with Laotian security forces, to effectively address the NVA's major supply route was a complete underutilization of what could have been achieved. Although SOF alone would not have stopped all movement along the trail, any decision to employ them with larger conventional forces might have produced a different outcome.

It is likely counterinsurgency and small wars will persist as a form of warfare and embody basic principles and characteristics which make them attractive to an adversary—the study of these methodologies is still relevant. There are other lessons from the Army SOF experience in Laos which could ultimately be incorporated into the application of *Special Warfare* to confront these contingencies.

One cannot "Americanize" another country's army and build it into the image of the U.S. Army. If the country does not have enough national fervor to fight a war, assumes it is working for legitimacy with its populace, but is not, and does not have the technological savvy and culture to accept modernization (including development of effective landpower), then the endeavor will fail, or be predictably slowed down. Sometimes "good enough for Laos," with easily maintained equipment, might have had a better payoff.

Host nations must have both offensive and defensive airpower in this environment. A large utility of airpower in irregular wars and counterinsurgency is in supporting ground maneuver. However, lacking strategic targets owned by the enemy, airpower is essential for battlefield air interdiction and in support of troops in contact. Enemy forces should not feel protected in their base camps or in sanctuary, either.

There is a definite line when the mission shifts from Special Warfare to conventional ground operations (normally with the introduction of conventional American landpower). It will be important to understand the roles and missions of both special operators and conventional forces, and recognize where the line crosses as to whom does what missions. If not, special operations missions and forces are subject to improper use and a waste of resources.

Special Warfare application requires flexibility, adaptiveness, and to some extent independent-ness of operations. Irregular warfare environments will require the ability to adjust to local conditions; rarely will the character of the conflict remain constant. Operations must also be integrated, not only with the host nation, but also with other governmental agencies, given the social-psychological nature of the conflict.

Other forms of landpower which are not military may be quite useful in executing the campaign. In some countries, paramilitary police and village militia can be harnessed (mobilized) in support of the war.

Force protection is essential when regeneration of combat power is difficult. Landpower assets in small nations need to be husbanded and protected. Also important, the professionalization of a host nation's army to perform base defense, protect infrastructure, maintain their equipment, perform OPSEC procedures, and maintain a credible medical capability (along with medevac) will preserve combat power. Host nation assets are not easily made up or replaced if lost to the enemy. Along these lines, mentoring of senior leaders and soldiers in relevant tactics, techniques and procedures which keep them alive in combat is also important—many will serve in their country until they win, lose, or die.

The Use of SOF: An Essential Capability

The United States maintains a special operations capability to give senior leaders and decision-makers an array of strategic options to choose from when implementing national security policies. If those options must be limited, discrete, precise, scalable and non-traditional when they achieve a strategic effect for the nation, then special operations can serve as a viable choice out of proportion to its size and cost. It is in the nature of special operations to be distinct or *different* in application of power, thus requiring specialization. They are *specialized* in order to achieve the ability to mitigate or overcome risk, achieve relative superiority with small numbers, and to approach problem-solving on the battlefield (and in peacetime) with unorthodox and indirect approaches to increase their strategic utility.

Army Special Operation Forces were created and tasked to conduct activities interdependent with national security policies for collective security arrangements, regional stability, and provide strategic options and situational awareness for policy makers. Army special operators in Laos provided low-visibility, light footprint, and discrete, precise, and scalable (modular) forces expert in the use of *Special Warfare*. ARSOF were used by the ambassadors to engage and reassure Thai and Lao partners, build strategic relationships, and operate in a politically sensitive environment.

Much of *Special Warfare* is conducted with foreign forces. The direct application of military power is replaced with the ability to leverage and influence others (force multipliers; economy of force) and to enhance and enable conventional force maneuver to achieve campaign *military* objectives. The effects achieved by the conduct of *Special Warfare* are generally exhaustive, erosive, and attritional against the enemy (with the art of applying these simultaneously to create a fog and friction on the competitor). In this sense, *Special Warfare* is not based on large combat formations as key to war. The Army special operators are not designed, nor rarely used, to participate in direct confrontations of strength with opposing military forces. In irregular warfare, *Special Warfare* is focused on the *political-societal-psychological* vulnerabilities of the competitor, not their military forces.

The expeditionary deployment of ARSOF to Laos served as a symbol of American commitment to allies and partners and used persistence as leverage in the Laotian security assistance and foreign internal defense missions to enable solutions to ambiguous and complex threats.

ARSOF helped to extend U.S. foreign policy through participation in the U.S. embassy country team's and ambassadors' goals to prevent outbreaks of wider conflict and mitigation of military crisis during major communist thrusts. These measures were conducted through various security assistance programs, coalition-building endeavors, foreign internal defense assistance, and if needed, direct combat.

The utility of ARSOF for the ambassadors during the war was to help RLG security forces hold their own and prevent any potential conventional clash of war with the Chinese or Soviet Union. All out U.S. intervention in Laos was not a practical option. In this type of security climate, ARSOF achieved a low-cost means to achieve foreign policy objectives.

ARSOF were successful in accomplishing their assigned missions. The work of the "Ambassadors' SOF" was instrumental in shaping events and gaining time and space in Laos to allow diplomacy to work. The story of ARSOF in Laos is little recorded in military history. In light of the irregular style of wars in the 21st century, the lessons of the Army SOF operators in its early days and how they were used will be an important one to the current and future generations of Army Special Operations Forces and ARSOF strategists pondering solutions to irregular warfare environments.

Army SOF historian, Shelby L. Stanton, summed up the contribution of the Army SOF community in his work, *Green Berets at War*:

> The Special Forces had completed its first Asian combat assignment under difficult conditions, aggravated by the lack of French cooperation and shifting directions caused by internal changes within the Laotian government. The Special Forces advisory effort during the Laotian emergency had rapidly expanded past initial Pentagon expectations. The Special Forces had arrived in Laos as technical advisors, but became full-fledged operational military advisors on a conventional battlefield. The most important result was the new role Special Forces had assumed as an instrument of national policy. By virtue of President Kennedy's belief in its individual and collective excellence, the Special Forces became the principal counterinsurgency force of the United States.[9]

Per President Eisenhower's wishes, Army Special Operations Forces kept "the cork in the bottle" for almost fourteen years. The choice of SOF provided decision-makers with a means to conduct a limited war, as an effective response to Pathet Lao and NVA aggression. Their combined efforts with the RLG bought what American diplomats needed most to achieve U.S. foreign policy objectives—time. SOF substituted where U.S. conventional forces could not go.

The use of SOF, combined with the paramilitary capabilities of the interagency, provided a successful template which would later be used in the beginning of the war in Afghanistan.

When it was no longer feasible or within reach to achieve any further pol-mil objectives, the United States departed Laos rather than remain bogged down because of American prestige. As Guy Morechand clarified in his article "The Many Languages and Cultures of Laos," one cannot nation-build in a country of ethnic diversity and complexity unless the populace unites against an agreed-upon enemy.[10]

Endnotes

Foreword

1   Conboy, Kenneth (with James Morrison). *Shadow War: The CIA's Secret War in Laos.* Boulder, CO: Paladin Press, 1995.

Introduction

1   Briscoe, Charles H. (PhD) "The Good 'Ole' Days of Special Forces: Marginalized Before JFK." Fort Bragg, NC: USASOC History Office, *Veritas*—The Journal of Army Special Operations History, Vol. 13, No. 1, 2017, pp. 21–28.

2   Eisenhower, Dwight D. *Waging Peace, 1956–1961: The White House.* New York, NY: Doubleday, 1965, p. 609.

3   The design of the Special Forces SSI is attributed to Captain John W. Frye, who served in the 10th Special Forces Group. It was officially approved in the mid-1950s and in the shape of a teal-blue arrowhead, to symbolize the unorthodox way of fighting used by the American Indians. (The 1st Special Services Force in World War II wore an SSI with a red arrowhead.) The symbol of the commando knife and three lightning bolts, each to signify the three methods of infiltration—air, land, and water—were added onto the teal-blue arrowhead.

4   The Organization of the Field "A" Team: The basic structure of the Field A-team was based on the skills necessary to train and operate with a 1,500-man guerrilla battalion. Most often the case, a Special Forces team consisted of twelve men, each trained in one of these necessary skill sets, with the ability to split the team if needed. The composition and structure of the team consisted of:

      1 Captain as the Detachment Commanding Officer
      1 Lieutenant as the Detachment Executive Officer (XO)
      1 E-8 Team Sergeant
      1 E-7 Operations and Intelligence Sergeant
      1 E-7 Heavy Weapons Sergeant
      1 E-7 Light Weapons Sergeant
      1 E-7 Senior Medic
      1 E-6 Junior Medical Specialist
      1 E-7 Senior Demolitions (and engineer) Sergeant
      1 E-5 Junior Demolitions Sergeant
      1 E-7 Senior Radio Operator Supervisor
      1 E-5 Junior Radio Operator

(Very rarely did an SF team achieve these ranks among the enlisted skill sets. In Laos, many radio operators, medics, and demolitions men were PFCs, SP4s, and buck sergeants—E-5s.)

5   Discussion with LTC (U.S.A., SF, Retired) Eugene G. Piasecki in Fayetteville March 14, 2015. For an excellent explanation of the organizational structure and changes of a Special Forces Group over the years, see his article in the *Veritas* magazine, published by the USASOC Command Historian, Vol. 5, No. 4, pp. 1–4.

6   Barker, Geoffrey T. *A Concise History of U.S. Army Special Operations Forces.* Tampa, FL: Anglo-American Publishing Company, 1993, p. 179.

7   Prados, John. *Safe for Democracy: The Secret Wars of the CIA.* Chicago, IL: Ivan R. Dee, 2006, pp. 282–284.

8   The Senator Gravel edition of "The Pentagon Papers: The Defense Department History of the United States Decisionmaking on Vietnam." Volume II. Boston, MA: Beacon Press, 800. This excerpt of Kennedy's speech can be found in the Public Papers of the President's, Kennedy, 1961, p. 229.

9   Ibid, pp. 286–289. This initiative is also covered in Richard J. Walton's *Cold War and Counterrevolution.* New York: Viking, 1972, p. 169.

10 Gray, Colin S. *Explorations in Strategy.* Westport, CT: Praeger, 1998: p. 141.

11 Smith, Rupert (General). *The Utility of Force: The Art of War in the Modern World,* NY: Alfred E. Knopf, 2007, pp. 14–20.

12 Ibid, pp. 5–7.

13 Ibid, p. 8.

14 Ibid, pp. 14–15.

15 Ibid, pp. 25–26.

16 Ibid, p. 184.

17 Ibid, pp. 323–324.

18 Art, Robert J. and Kenneth N. Waltz. *The Use of Force: Military Power and International Politics* (Seventh edition). NY: Rowman & Littlefield, 2009, pp. 3–6.

19 Gray, Colin S. "Tactical Operations for Strategic Effect: The Challenge of Currency Conversion." MacDill Air Force Base: The JSOU Press, Special Report November 2015.

20 Draft telegram concerning Laos, 5 February 1961, held in the National Security Files, boxes 131–139, Laos (Boston, MA: John F. Kennedy Library). Found in an article written by David K. Hall.

21 Castle, Timothy N. *At War in the Shadow of Vietnam: U.S. Military Aid to the Royal Lao Government 1955–1975,* New York: Columbia University Press, 1993, pp. 77–97.

22 Prados, pp. 278–279.

23 Kenneth Conboy and James Morrison. *Shadow War,* p. 159.

24 Kenneth Conboy, *The War in Laos 1954–1975,* Vietnam Studies Group Series No. 6063 (Carrollton, TX: Squadron/Signal Publications, 1994), pp. 43–50.

Chapter 1

1   Conboy, Kenneth and James Morrison. *Shadow War: The CIA's Secret War in Laos.* Boulder, CO: Paladin Press, 1995, pp. vii–ix.

2   Conboy, Kenneth. *The War in Laos 1960–75.* London, UK: Osprey Men-at-Arms Series No. 217, Osprey Publishing, 1989, pp. 12–15.

3   Ibid, pp. 37–38.

4   Prados, John, *President's Secret Wars: CIA and Pentagon Covert Operations Since World War II.* New York, NY: William Morrow and Co., 1986, p. 265.

5   Cummings, Joe. *Laos, A Lonely Planet Travel Survival Kit.* Australia: Lonely Planet, Hawthorn, Vic 3122, 1966, p. 41.

6   Ibid, pp. 41–42.

7   Ibid, pp. 42–43.

8   Fall, Bernard B. *Anatomy of a Crisis: The Story of the Laotian Crisis of 1960–1961*. Garden City, NY: Doubleday & Company, 1969, p. 24.

9   Oral interview between the author and Tom Humphus conducted Tuesday April 29, 2014, at his residence.

10 COL (Retired) Vladimir Sobichevsky interview with the author conducted June 29, 2014.

11 Conversation between author and Steve Schofield, October 20–21, 2014 in Maitland, FL.

12 Personal interview by the author with Robert G. Willis in Augusta GA, July 12, 2014.

13 Sananikone, Oudone (MG, RLA). "The Royal Lao Army and U.S. Army Advice and Support." Indochina Refugee Authored Monograph Program, OAD-CR-155, Washington D. C.: Department of the Army, Office of Chief of Military History, Contract performed by General Research Corporation, McClean, VA, 7 November 1978, p. 14.

14 Ibid, p.18.

15 Ibid, p. 26.

16 Castle, Timothy N. *At War in the Shadow of Vietnam: U.S. Military Aid to the Royal Lao Government1955–1975*. New York, NY: Columbia University Press, 1993, p. 30.

17 Zasloff, Joseph J. *The Pathet Lao: Leadership and Organiza*tion. Lexington, MA: Lexington Books, 1971, pp. 76–77.

18 Langer, Paul F. and Joseph J. Zasloff. *North Vietnam and the Pathet Lao: Partners in the Struggle for Laos*. Cambridge, MA: Harvard University Press, 1970, p. 114.

19 Dommen, Arthur J. *Conflict in Laos: The Politics of Neutralization*, New York: Praeger, 1971, p. 310.

20 Ibid, pp. 63–64.

21 Ibid; this assessment came from prisoner and detainee interviews, p. 124.

22 Ibid, p. 111.

23 McDonnell, Wayne. *The NVA in Laos: 1951–1973*. The border battalions consisted of the 922nd, 923rd, 925th, and 927th battalions. Fort Leavenworth, KS: Student Monograph, U.S. Army Staff College, 1977. (www.dtic.mil, ADC011408.pdf), pp. 22–23.

24 Langer and Zasloff, pp. 151.

25 "Suitability and Effectiveness of Weapons and Equipment Used in U.S.-Supported Operations with the Royal Laos Army (U)." Arlington, VA: Research Analysis Corporation, Staff Paper RAC-SP-1 (SEA), September 1962, Prepared for DARPA, pp. 5–6.

Chapter 2

1   Gray, Colin S. *Explorations in Strategy*. Westport, CT: Praeger Publishers, pp. 168–173.

2   FOREIGN RELATIONS OF THE U.S.—EISENHOWER –MFS XV/XVI (1958–60) 524. Excerpt of memorandum for record of discussions among Houghton, Quarles, and Guillaumat, January 13, 1959. "Current situation in Laos." Secret. I p. WNRC, RG 330, OSD/ISA Files: FRC 63 A 1672, 353 Laos. [0602]

3   Conboy, Kenneth (with James Morrison). *Shadow War: The CIA's Secret War in Laos*. Boulder, CO: Paladin Press, 1995, p. 28.

4   Guardia, Mike. *Shadow Commander: The Epic Story of Donald D. Blackburn—Guerrilla Leader and Special Forces Hero*. New York, NY: Casemate, 2011, pp. 155–156.

5   Ibid, p. 156.

6   Stanton, Shelby L. *Green Berets at War*. New York, NY: Ivy Books, 1985, pp. 20–21.

7   Conboy with James Morrison, p. 24.

8   Ibid, pp. 16–19.

9   Personal interview by the author with Kenneth H. Hain conducted in Fayetteville Friday, July 11, 2014.

10   Descriptions of the FC-3 team house and living conditions provided by Dr. (MD) Samuel J. Skemp during July 17, 2014 telephonic interview; follow-up visit by the author to his residence in Wisconsin.

11   Conboy with James Morrison, p. 24.

12   Telephonic interview conducted by the author with MG (Ret.) Bernardo "Burn" Loeffke March 18, 2015. (Later in his career General Loeffke served in Vietnam and afterwards was the Commanding General of Army South. He is a recipient of the Purple Heart for his wounds in combat. He was also assigned as the Chief of Military Mission in Communist China, was an Army Attaché in Moscow, and served as a Staff Officer in the White House. After retiring in 1992, he completed medical studies to become a Physician's Attendant and worked as a medical humanitarian with Samaritan Purse in Africa. His story is told in his book, *From Warrior to Healer* [The Pacific Institute: 1998].)

13   Conversation between the author and a member on the FTT in Pakse, May 5, 2014. (Veteran desired to remain anonymous, known only as RK.)

14   The story of FA-3 is taken from Master Sergeant James C. Williams' (MSG, U.S.A.) self-published autobiography, "A Green Beret's Journey," published in Kanchanaburi, Thailand in 2014. James provided a personal copy to the author for the purpose of the SOF in Laos history project.

15   Ibid, p. 51.

16   Ibid.

17   Ibid, p. 58.

18   Personal interview by the author with Kenneth H. Hain conducted in Fayetteville Friday, July 11, 2014.

19   Telephonic interview conducted by the author with CWO4 (Ret.) John Meadows March 28, 2015.

20   Ibid.

21   Ibid.

22   Telephonic interview between the author and Ken R. Bates conducted May 1, 2014.

23   Ibid.

24   Ibid.

25   Ibid.

26   Ibid.

27   Ibid.

28   Ibid.

29   The description of FA-5/60's experiences as an FTT in Luang Prabang were provided by Thomas O. Humphus via telephone interview initially, then a follow-on oral interview by the author conducted April 29, 2014, at his residence.

30   Ibid.

31   Ibid.

32   Ibid.

33   Telephonic interview conducted by the author with George W. Sevits February 20, 2015, followed by two personal interviews conducted in Fayetteville, NC.

34   Ibid.

35   Tom Humphus interview.

36   A description of Savannakhet experiences, titled "Legends of Laos," was provided by Retired Colonel Bruce Simnacher in his recollections provided to his family and friends May 2, 2013, via email. Copy personally provided to author of this work to assist with the Laos book project August 30, 2014.

37   Personal interview by the author with Charlie W. Brewington conducted March 12, 2015.

38   Ibid.

39   Rust, William J. *Before the Quagmire: American Intervention in Laos 1954–1961*. Lexington, KY: The University Press of Kentucky, 2012, pp. 168–169.

40   Ibid, pp. 170–174.

41   Castle, Timothy N. *At War in the Shadow of Vietnam: U.S. Military Aid to the Royal Lao Government 1955–1975*. New York, NY: Columbia University Press, 1993, pp. 18–25.

42   Conboy with James Morrison, p. 32.

43   Details of Team *Derby* provided by Reuben "Ben" L. Densley in personal interview conducted by the author in Maitland, FL, October 21, 2014

44   Ibid.

45   Ibid.

46   Ibid.

47   Ibid.

48   Ibid.

49   Ibid.

50   Conboy with James Morrison, p. 32.

51   Ibid, pp. 35–36.

52   Conboy, Kenneth with James Morrison, p. 34.

53   Gruenther, Richard L. and David W. Parmley. "The Crusade of a Green Beret: Eleazar Parmley IV in Southeast Asia." Fort Bragg, NC: Special Warfare, USAJFK Center and School, Vol. 5, No. 1, pp. 43–44. Gruenther and David W. Parmley incorporated MAJ Eleazar's dairy notes from his experiences during the Rightist drive to retake Vientiane from rebel Captain Kong Le.

54   Telephonic interview by the author with Ned L. Miller conducted early March; questionnaire follow-up March 7, 2014.

55   Richard L. Gruenther and David W Parmley, pp. 43–44.

56   Conboy, p. 37.

57   Conboy with James Morrison, 36. Conboy relates the tale based on the personal diary of Captain Ipsen.

58   Ibid, p. 37.

59   Stanton, Shelby L. *Green Berets at War*. New York: Ivy Books, p. 24.

60   Ibid, pp. 40–41.

61   Brown, Mervyn. *War in Shangri-La: A Memoir of Civil War in Laos*. London, UK: The Radcliffe Press, 2001, pp. 63–64.

Chapter 3

1   Gray, Colin S. *Explorations in Strategy*. Westport, CT: Praeger 1998, pp. 168–174.

2   Rust, William J. *Before the Quagmire: American Intervention in Laos, 1954–1961*. Lexington, KY: University Press of Kentucky, 2012, pp. 237–238. He cites CINCPAC to JCS, November 23, 1960, in U.S. Department of Defense, "Chronological Summary," p. 45; Sterling Cottrell to Parsons, December 1, 1960, FRUS, XVI, MFS.

3   Sananikone, Oudone (MG, RLA). "The Royal Lao Army and U.S. Army Advice and Support." Indochina Refugee Authored Monograph Program, OAD-CR-155, Department of the Army, Office of Chief of Military History, Washington DC. Contract performed by General Research Corporation, McClean, VA, November 7, 1978, pp. 74–75.

4   Conboy, Kenneth (with James Morrison). *Shadow War: The CIA's Secret War in Laos*. Boulder, CO: Paladin Press, 1995, pp. 42–44.

5   Telephonic interview conducted by the author with Charles H. McLendon February 25, 2015; additional remarks annotated in March 2015 via mail.

6   Ibid.

7   Ibid.

8   Conboy with James Morrison, pp. 43–44.

9   Charles McLendon interview and email.

10   Conboy with James Morrison, pp. 43–44.

11   Ibid, pp. 43–45

12   Charles McLendon interview and email.

13   Gruenther, Richard L. and David W. Parmley. "The Crusade of a Green Beret: Eleazar Parmley IV in Southeast Asia." Fort Bragg, NC: Special Warfare, USAJFK Center and School, Vol. 5, No. 1, pp. 43–44. Gruenther and David W. Parmley incorporated MAJ Eleazar's dairy notes from his experiences during the Rightist drive to retake Vientiane from rebel Captain Kong Le.

14   Ibid, pp. 43–44.

15   Sananikone, pp. 76.

16   Dommen, Arthur J. *Conflict in Laos: The Politics of Neutralization*. New York, NY: Praeger, 1971, p. 185.

17   Telephonic interview conducted between Ray Ambrozak and the author November 5, 2015.

18   Ibid.

19   Ibid.

20   Ibid.

21   Ibid.

22   Ibid.

23   Ibid.

24   Ibid.

25   Ibid.

26   Conboy, p. 51.

27   Sananikone, p. 77.

28   From speeches in the files of the John F. Kennedy Presidential Library.

29   Sananikone, p. 52.

30   After initial telephone contact by the author, Richard L. Largen's story sent by email March 27, 2015.

31   COL (Ret.) Alfred H. Paddock provided the author detailed notes from his deployment to Laos on *White Star* Rotation IV, via emails April 21, 2015 and April 27, 2015. He also published a story of FA-65 in the *Small Wars Journal* blog post, titled "Personal Memories of Operation White Star in Laos, 1961." The author is grateful for his extensive help and telephone conversations in preparing the story of FA-65.

32   Ibid.

33   Paddock's field note entry.

34   Ibid.

35   Ibid.

36   Initial telephonic contact with John W. "Ranger" Roy March 24, 2015; follow-up telephonic interview by the author conducted April 8, 2015.

37   Ibid.

38   Ibid.

39   Email correspondence from Irving Hoffman March 30, 2015.

40   Ibid.

41   Ibid.

42   McLendon interview.

43   Ibid.

44 Telephonic Interview conducted by the author with Robert F. Mulcahy Jun 23, 2014.
45 Ibid.
46 Ibid.
47 Ibid.

Chapter 4

1   Warner, Roger. *Shooting At The Moon: The Story of America's Clandestine War in Laos*. South Royalton, VT: Steerforth Press, 1996, pp. 14–18.
2   Ibid, p. 32.
3   Ibid, p. 34.
4   Al Paddock email to the author, April 21, 2015.
5   Ibid, April 27, 2015, titled "Organization of GM-15, Formation of Meo Company, Future Operations for Meos."
6   Ibid.
7   Ibid.
8   Paddock notes from emails.
9   Telephonic interview between the author and John Retterer conducted February 5, 2015.
10 Ibid.
11 Ibid.
12 Ibid.
13 Ibid.
14 Telephonic interview by the author with Kenneth R. Bates conducted May 1, 2014.
15 Ibid.
16 Quincy, Keith. *Harvesting Pa Chay's Wheat: The Hmong and America's Secret War in Laos*. Spokane, WA: Eastern Washington University Press, 2000, p. 200.
17 Conboy, p. 65.
18 Warner, pp. 53–57.
19 Personal interview between the author and George F. Stewart at Augusta, GA July 12, 2014; follow-up interview, August 9, 2014, at his residence.
20 Ibid.
21 Personal interview by the author with Ralph G. King June 13, 2014, SF Convention Columbia, SC.
22 Ibid.
23 Ibid.
24 Stewart interview.
25 Ibid.
26 Ibid.
27 Ibid.
28 Ibid.
29 Ibid.
30 Ahern, Thomas L., Jr. *Undercover Armies: CIA and Surrogate Warfare in Laos*. Washington, D. C.: The Center for the Study of Intelligence, CIA, 2006, pp. 105–106.
31 Ibid, p. 107.
32 Conboy, p. 89.
33 Personal interview by the author with Ludwig Faistenhammer at his residence, April 29, 2015.
34 Ibid.
35 Ibid.

36 Stanton, Shelby L. *Special Forces at War: An Illustrated History, Southeast Asia 1957–1975.* Charlottesville, VA: Howell Press, 1990, p. 371.

37 Ahern, pp. 127–129.

38 Personal interview by the author with COL (Ret.) Henry L. Ellison in Calhoun Falls SC, August 16, 2014. During the interview, COL (Ret.) Ellison presented some of the rarest photos known of the Yao guerrilla initiative, his men training the Yao.

Chapter 5

1 MG Oudone Sananikone provided an overview summary of RLG military operations in each military region, basically from after the ceasefire in May down into the late fall of 1961. See "The Royal Lao Army and U.S. Army Advice and Support." Indochina Refugee Authored Monograph Program, OAD-CR-155, Department of the Army, Office of Chief of Military History, Washington, D. C. Contract performed by General Research Corporation, McClean, VA, 7 November 1978, pp. 101–102.

2 Ken Cox's letters to his wife were recovered by nursing staff after his death and forwarded to the U.S. Army JFK Special Warfare Museum, when it was apparent they could not find surviving members of his family. The letters were graciously provided by Ms. Roxanne Merritt, the museum curator, to the author for research purposes. The original letters are back in the museum.

3 Ibid, letter from Ken Cox to his wife July 25, 1961.

4 Letter from Ken Cox to his wife July 30, 1961.

5 August letter from Ken Cox to his wife (Ken Cox collection, USAJFK Special Warfare Museum).

6 Ibid.

7 Personal interview by the author with Charles B. "Chuck" Darnell May 3, 2014.

8 Ibid.

9 Ibid.

10 Ibid.

11 Ibid.

12 Citation for the award provided to the author by Chuck Darnell.

Chapter 6

1 Personal interview between the author and Alfred H. "Al" Buckelew, Dahlonega, GA, January 31, 2015.

2 Ibid.

3 Ibid.

4 Sananikone, Oudone (MG, RLA). "The Royal Lao Army and U.S. Army Advice and Support." Indochina Refugee Authored Monograph Program, OAD-CR-155, Department of the Army, Office of Chief of Military History, Washington DC. Contract performed by General Research Corporation, McClean, VA, 7 November 1978, 102–103.

5 Conboy, Kenneth (with James Morrison). *Shadow War: The CIA's Secret War in Laos.* Boulder, CO: Paladin Press, 1995, p. 69.

6 Ibid, p. 69.

7 Telephonic interview by the author conducted with Richard D. "Dick" Ellmers October 13, 2015.

8 Ibid.

9 Ibid.

10 Ibid.

11 Ibid.

12 Mail correspondence to author from Ned L. Miller, September 13, 2014.

13 Ibid.

14 The story of SF teams and conditions at Phou Tinpét come from retired CSM Joe R. Garner, who wrote about his team experiences during their deployment to Laos, in his work *Code Name: COPPERHEAD, My True Life Exploits as a Special Forces Soldier.* (Simon & Schuster, New York, NY: 1994.) See full story in Chapter 5, "Anything, Anytime," pp. 57–93. This is one of the few, if only, accountings of Special Forces *White Star* at this location.

15 Ibid, 72.

16 Cummings, Joe. *Laos, A Lonely Planet Travel Survival Kit.* Australia, Lonely Planet, Hawthorn, Vic 3122, 1966, pp. 256–258.

17 Ibid.

18 Ibid.

19 Telephonic Interview conducted between the author and COL (Retired) James W. "Jim" Krause April 22, 2014.

20 Ibid.

Chapter 7

1   Ahern, Thomas L., Jr. *Undercover Armies: CIA and Surrogate Warfare in Laos.* Washington D. C.: The Center for the Study of Intelligence, CIA, 2006, pp. 129–131.

2   Cummings, Joe. *Laos, A Lonely Planet Travel Survival Kit.* Australia: Lonely Planet, Hawthorn, Vic 3122, 1966, p. 298.

3   Conboy, p. 85.

4   Ibid, p. 85.

5   Phone interview May 20, 2014 by the author with COL (Ret.) Elliott P. "Bud" Sydnor.

6   Ibid.

7   Conboy, Kenneth (with James Morrison). *Shadow War: The CIA's Secret War in Laos.* Boulder, CO: Paladin Press, 1995, p. 86.

8   Ibid, p. 86.

9   Sydnor interview.

10 Ibid.

11 Telephonic interview between the author and William E. Kellenberger July 22, 2014.

12 Phone interview by the author with Ernest K. "Ernie" Tabata in late June 2014 and handwritten letter received in the last week of June.

13 Conboy, p. 86.

14 Gene Gavigan has been one of the best sources for the Kha tribal guerrilla program by providing extensive documents, pictures, video and personal experiences. This began between him and the author with mail correspondence beginning in June through August 27, 2014; again July 12, 2014. A handwritten letter was provided in July 2014. These were followed by telephonic contact August 28, 2014 and a lengthy personal interview by telephonic means September 26, 2014.

15 Ibid.

16 Interview by the author with James Everett May 24, 2014.

17 Ibid.

18 Conboy, p. 86.

19 Garner, Joe R. (CSM, Ret., U.S.A.). *Code Name: COPPERHEAD, My True Life Exploits as a Special Forces Soldier.* New York, NY: Simon & Schuster, 1994, p. 91.

20 Personal interview by the author with Robert G. "Bob" Willis in Augusta GA, July 12, 2014.

21 Conboy, Kenneth (with James Morrison). *Shadow War*, p. 7.

22 Telephonic interview between the author and Richard A. Iori conducted June 11, 2015.

23 Ibid.

24 Initial phone contact with Michael B. Donohue August 6, 2014. Telephonic interview August 8, 2014.

25 Initial phone interview by the author with John A. Hixson October 6, 2014 and from notes on follow-up questionnaire

26 Donohue interview.

27 Ibid.

28 Initial phone contact by the author with Ivan E. Larson January 8, 2015; telephonic interview January 9, 2015.

29 Ibid.

30 Conboy, p. 86.

31 Initial phone discussion between the author and James H. Anson September 22, 2014; telephonic interview conducted October 7, 2014.

32 Hixson interview.

33 Initial ermail from Tom Bayha to author April 23 & 25, 2015; Telephonic interview conducted Tuesday, May 12, 2015.

34 Ibid.

35 Ibid.

36 Bayha interview.

37 Anson interview.

38 Donohue interview.

39 Bayha interview.

40 Conboy, p. 87.

Chapter 8

1 Personal interview by the author with Othar J. "Shali" Shalikashvili in Hochston, GA August 22, 2014.

2 Interview with George W. Sevits by the author conducted in Fayetteville, NC April 11, 2015.

3 Ibid.

4 The author and Shalikashvili interview August 22, 2014.

5 Ibid.

6 Ibid.

7 Telephonic interview by the author with Charles H. McLendon February 25, 2015.

8 Ibid.

9 Telephonic interview with Thomas O. Humphus conducted April 6, 2014; Oral interview conducted Tuesday, April 29, 2014.

10 Ibid.

11 McLendon interview.

12 Ibid.

13 Ibid.

14 Tom Humphus interview.

15 Telephonic interview by the author with Robin Luketina conducted April 30, 2014.

16 Ibid.

17 Ibid.

18 Ibid.

19 Telephonic interview by the author with John T. Haralson conducted April 12, 2014; mail correspondence week of April 21, 2014.

20 Ibid.

21 Telephonic interview conducted by author with Robin M. Luketina April 30, 2014, early evening, then follow-up by mail.

22 Haralson interview April 12, 2014.

23 Personal interview with Richard O. Sutton in Boerne, TX February 8, 2015. The details of the FTT-19 story are adopted from his book (with permission), *Operation White Star*, Daring Publishing Group, Canton, Ohio: 1990.

24 Contact via email by the author with John "Johnny" McCallum in March 2014; follow-up project questionnaire sent via email April 5, 2014.

25 Ibid.

26 Sutton interview.

27 Ibid.

28 Ibid.

29 Initial phone discussion by the author with Vladimir "Sobie" Sobichevsky June 4, 2014; telephonic interview June 29, 2014.

30 Ibid.

31 MSG (U.S.A., Ret) James C. Williams provided the author a copy of his personal book, *A Green Beret's Journey*, written in 2014 at Kanchanaburi, Thailand, which extensively documented both his *Hotfoot I* rotation and *White Star VII* rotation at Thakhek. It is from his section on the *White Star* rotation in 1962 some of the story of First Lieutenant Shelton's FTT is drawn.

32 Ibid.

33 Sobichevsky interview.

34 Ibid.

35 Williams. *A Green Beret's Journey*, pp. 88–89.

36 Telephonic interview by the author with Clarence W. "Mac" McCormick conducted November 17, 2014.

37 Ibid.

Chapter 9

1 Conboy, Kenneth (with James Morrison). *Shadow War: The CIA's Secret War in Laos*. Boulder, CO: Paladin Press, 1995, p. 24.

2 Telephonic interview conducted by the author with COL (Retired) James W. "Jim" Krause April 22, 014.

3 Ibid.

4 Ibid.

5 Sananikone, Oudone (MG, RLA). "The Royal Lao Army and U.S. Army Advice and Support." Indochina Refugee Authored Monograph Program, OAD-CR-155, Department of the Army, Office of Chief of Military History, Washington DC. Contract performed by General Research Corporation, McClean, VA, November 7, 1978, p. 104.

6 Ibid, p. 105.

7 Ibid.

8 Author's personal interview with Robert G. Willis in Augusta GA, July 12, 2014.

9 Ibid.

10 Interviews by the author with Reuben L. Mooradian between September 16 & 27, 2014.

11 Ibid.

12 Ibid.

13 Personal interview at breakfast between the author and Thomas E. Holladay, and with other Laos veterans in Maitland, Florida, October 21, 2014.

14 Ibid.

15 Phone interview by the author in late June with Ernie Tabata followed by a handwritten letter received in the last week of June, 2014.

Chapter 10

1 Conboy, Kenneth (with James Morrison). *Shadow War: The CIA's Secret War in Laos.* Boulder, CO: Paladin Press, 1995, p. 70.

2 As noted in Steve Sherman's "Who's Who from *Hotfoot* and *White Star*," Houston, TX: RADIX Press, pp. 20–32.

3 DA Msg 41142, AGPA-O DTG 022226Z January, with report date of January 10, 1962; DA Msg 42367, AGPA-O DTG 082229Z January, with report date of January 10, 1962.

4 Sananikone, Oudone (MG, RLA). "The Royal Lao Army and U.S. Army Advice and Support." Indochina Refugee Authored Monograph Program, OAD-CR-155, Washington, DC: Department of the Army, Office of Chief of Military History, Contract performed by General Research Corporation, McClean, VA, November 7, 1978, pp. 103.

5 Dommen, Arthur J. *Conflict in Laos: The Politics of Neutralization.* New York, NY: Praeger, 1971, pp. 213–214.

6 Sananikone, Oudone (MG, RLA). "The Royal Lao Army and U.S. Army Advice and Support, p. 107.

7 Conboy, p. 71.

8 Ibid, pp. 71–73.

9 Dommen, p. 214.

10 Handwritten testimony by Robert H. "Too Tall" Simmons from questionnaire, received via mail week of April 4, 2014, followed by numerous telephone conversations and a personal visit by the author to his home in Texas.

11 Telephonic interview conducted by the author with Ed Eckerman May 6, 2014.

12 Cummings, Joe. *Laos, A Lonely Planet Travel Survival Kit.* Hawthorn, Australia: Lonely Planet Publications, 1996, pp. 218–219.

13 Sananikone, p. 107.

14 Interview between Henry L. Ellison and the author in Calhoun Falls, SC August 16, 2014.

15 Valentine, Donald E. "Strap Hanger." From chapter 6 found at Don Valentine's personal website, www.don-valentine.com/gruntp. Portions of this chapter are being used with permission of Don Valentine, along with pictures provided to the author.

16 Henry Ellison interview.

17 Telephonic interview by the author with Robin Luketina April 30, 2014. Telephonic interview with John T. Haralson April 12, 2014, followed up email and surface mail correspondence and personal materials and photos provided by Haralson.

18 The story of the day of the airborne operation, and FTT-21's time with the 55th BP at Nam Tha provided in an interview with John T. Haralson 1April 12, 2014. In following weeks, Haralson provided additional documents, orders, and pictures.

19 Ibid.

20 Ibid.

21 Ibid.

22 Ibid, p. 20.

23 D. E. Close's article, "The Battle of Nam Tha," in the *Marine Corps Gazette*, February 1965.
24 Dommen, p. 217.
25 Interview by the author with Ned L. Miller, conducted April 29, 2014.
26 Interview by the author with Ned L. Miller, FTT-1 Team Medic, 2 March 2014, followed up with questionnaire March 7, 2014.
27 Interview with Henry L. Ellison conducted August 16, 2014, in Calhoun Falls, SC.
28 Valentine website story.
29 Ibid.
30 The details on FTT-1's engagement east of Ban Phoung are derived from Robert H. "Too Tall" Simmons personal written account of the battle, titled "Flashbacks of a Green Beret in Combat," written in 1985 under the pen name "Tex Too-Tall." A copy of this story was provided to the author for use in this publication.
31 Simmons, p. 14.
32 Interview by the author with James W. Young, conducted December 18, 2014.
33 Ibid.
34 Ibid.
35 Ibid.
36 Ibid.
37 Ibid.
38 Ibid.
39 Ibid.
40 Ibid.
41 Stuart-Fox, Martin. *A History of Laos*. Cambridge, UK: Cambridge University Press, 1997, pp. 122–123.
42 Pentagon Memorandum to "Romanus," Subject: Strengths in Laos, April 19, 1961–October 6, 1962. From Center for Military History archives, Washington D. C.
43 Fall, pp. 257–258.
44 Dommen, p. 238.
45 MAAG Laos, Vientiane, Intelligence Report, August 31, 1962. (U.S. Army War College Library, Reference 1229311, Report No. ID: 22/2758.)
46 Telephonic interview by the author with COL (Ret.) Bill Richardson August 20, 2015.
47 Ibid.
48 Ibid.
49 Castle, Timothy N. *At War in the Shadow of Vietnam: U.S. Military Aid to the Royal Lao Government 1955–1975*. New York, NY: Columbia University Press, 1993, pp. 49–50.
50 Reuben Mooradian interview.
51 Conboy & Morrison, *Shadow War*, p. 87.
52 Dommen, p. 39.

Chapter 11

1 Gray, Colin S. *Explorations in Strategy*. Westport, CT: Praeger, 1998, p. 7.
2 Conboy, Kenneth (with James Morrison). *Shadow War: The CIA's Secret War in Laos*. Boulder, CO: Paladin Press, 1995, p. 159.
3 Fred Sebren's initial email to the author, followed by an interview by the author with Fred Sebren conducted July 22, 2016.
4 Ibid.
5 Ibid.

6 Telephonic interview by author with Ray Millaway May 28, 2015.

7 Telephonic interview by the author conducted with COL (Retired) Jim R. "Rod" Paschall October 30, 2014.

8 Ibid.

9 Ibid.

10 Ibid.

11 Ibid.

12 Ibid.

13 Phone interview between LTC (Ret.) Reuben L. Mooradian and the author September 27, 2014.

14 Ibid.

15 Ibid.

16 Ibid.

17 Ibid.

18 Ibid.

19 Personal interview between the author and Sam Todaro conducted June 18, 2017 in Fayetteville, NC.

20 Ibid.

21 Ibid.

22 Interview by the author with Al Rozon conducted November 25, 2015.

23 Telephonic interview conducted between the author and Dennis Lid October 16, 2014.

24 Ibid.

25 Ibid.

26 Ibid.

27 Ibid.

28 Ibid.

29 Ibid.

30 Ibid.

31 Ahern, Thomas L., Jr. *Undercover Armies: CIA and Surrogate Warfare in Laos.* Washington, D. C.: The Center for the Study of Intelligence, CIA, 2006, p. 17.

32 Conboy & Morrison, pp. 207–208.

33 Telephonic interview by the author with SGM (Ret.) David L. Pompili conducted March 4, 2015.

34 Ibid.

35 Conboy, pp. 208–209.

36 Ibid, pp. 208–210.

37 Ibid, p. 210.

38 Ibid, p. 210–211.

39 Ibid, p. 212.

40 Robert J. Moberg related his experiences at the battle of Moung Soui in a testimonial to deceased Theodore Untalan, another pilot from the 281st AHC in 1968 through 1969, who flew the senior Thai commander and the Army Attaché into the site during the battle. His full accounting, along with other exploits with Theodore Untalan, can be found on www.281stahc.org/moberg/html.

41 Dave Pompili interview.

42 Ibid.

43 Moberg's testimony.

44 Dave Pompili interview.

45 Telephonic interview conducted by the author with Joe Bossi January 26, 2015.

46 Ibid.

47 Dave Pompili interview.
48 Joe Bossi interview.
49 Ibid.
50 Ahern, pp. 319–320.
51 Telephonic interview between author and MAJ (Ret.) Herman Adams conducted November 12, 2016.
52 Telephonic interview between John Cassady and the author conducted November 4, 2014.
53 Ibid.
54 Ibid.
55 Personal interview with Jeff and Leigh Hotujec by the author June 12, 2014.
56 Ibid.
57 The Hotujecs' interview.
58 Ibid.
59 Personal interview conducted by the author with Billy Phipps at SF Convention, Columbia SC, June 14, 2014.
60 Ibid.
61 Ibid.
62 Ibid.
63 Personal interview by the author with Charlie Brewington conducted March 12, 2015.
64 Charlie Brewinton interview.
65 Moberg, p. 5. www.281stahc.org/moberg/html
66 Personal interview between the author and Michael Ingham followed by email correspondence August 30, 2014. See also University of Texas at Dallas, Michael Ingham collection. (www.utdallas.edu/library/…/hac/…aam75)
67 Ibid, Michael Ingham Interview and collection.
68 Conboy, p. 389.
69 The details of Task Force *Broomhilda* were supplied from John Sullivan's questionnaire and recurring emails throughout the months of March and April, 2014. These notes serve as one of the most detailed recordings and accounts of a Project 404 ARMA team involved in a major battle in Laos
70 Ibid.
71 Ibid.
72 Ibid.
73 Ibid.
74 Ibid.
75 Ibid.
76 Conboy, p. 389.
77 Ibid, p. 389. (Chuck Hines interviewed by Ken Conboy.)
78 The Hotujec's interview.
79 Ibid.
80 Conboy, p. 389.
81 Whitcomb, Darrel D. *On a Steel Horse I Ride: A History of the MH-53 Pave Low Helicopters in War and Peace.* Maxwell AFB, AL: Air University Press, September 2012, p. 68.
82 Conboy, p. 390.
83 Ibid, p. 390.
84 Interview by the author conducted with Syd Jensen at the SF Convention, Columbia SC, June 13, 2014.
85 Ibid.
86 Ibid.

87 Telephonic interview between the author and Richard Whipple conducted June 22, 2017.

88 Ibid.

89 Ibid.

90 The Hotujec's interview.

91 Castle, Timothy N. *At War in the Shadow of Vietnam: U.S. Military Aid to the Royal Lao Government 1955–1975*. New York, NY: Columbia University Press, 1993, p. 118.

92 Dave Pompili interview.

Chapter 12

1 Gray, Colin S. *Explorations in Strategy*. Westport, CT: Praeger, 1998, pp. 170–171.

2 Scott Crerar's personal notes on the role of the 46th Special Forces Company in Thailand, provided to the author.

3 Conboy, Kenneth (with James Morrison). *Shadow War: The CIA's Secret War in Laos*. Boulder, CO: Paladin Press, 1995, pp. 164–165.

4 Ibid, p. 175.

5 Ibid, p. 177.

6 Ibid, pp. 183–214.

7 Ibid, p. 238.

8 Ibid, pp. 366–368.

9 Ibid, p. 285.

10 Ibid, p. 267.

11 Telephonic interview by the author with Frank Jaks conducted May 8, 2014.

12 Ibid.

13 Ibid, p. 238.

14 Initial email from John R. Martin August 11, 2014, followed by telephonic interview conducted by the author September 5, 2014. SGM (Retired, U.S.A.) Martin's story about establishing the site at Nam Pung Dam can be found in his article, "The 46th Special Forces Company: Part I." *The Southern California Sentinel*, Special Forces chapter 78, Newsletter Vol. 5, Issue 9, September 2014, p. 5.

15 Conboy, p. 283.

16 Ibid, p. 304–317.

17 Email correspondence with between Michael Ingham and author August 30, 2014; telephonic interview September 13, 2014.

18 Conboy, p. 317.

19 Ibid, p. 343.

20 Ibid, p. 301.

21 Telephonic interview by the author with retired Colonel Scott Crerar conducted May 8, 2014; follow-up with subsequent phone calls.

22 Ibid.

23 Conboy, p. 347.

24 Email correspondence to the author from Don Munson January 26, 2015.

25 Conboy, p. 348.

26 Ibid, pp. 372–373.

27 Telephonic interview by the author with Jim Bruton May 29, 2015.

28 Ibid.

29 Ibid.

30 Interview between Syd Jensen and the author conducted at SF Convention, Columbia SC, June 13, 2014.
31 Conboy, p. 373.
32 Ibid, p. 347.
33 Ibid, p. 352.
34 Ibid, p. 408.
35 See John Martin interview.
36 Conboy, p. 406.
37 Telephonic interview by the author conducted with William F. "Bill" Rouleau October 3, 2015.
38 Ibid.
39 Ibid.
40 Ibid.
41 Ibid.

Epilogue

1 Webb, Billy G. *Secret War*. United States: Xlibris Corporation (www.xlibris.com), 2010, pp. 421–425.
2 "Old U.S. Allies, Still Hiding Deep in Laos." Written by Thomas Fuller. New York, NY: *The New York Times*, December 17, 2007, A-1 and A-12.
3 Headquarters, Commander-in-Chief Pacific Memorandum. Subject: Lessons Learned, MAAG and Special Forces Activities in Laos (U). Signed H. D. Felt, San Francisco, CA, 21 February 21, 1963: pp. 3–4.
4 Ibid, p. 4.
5 Ibid, p. 9.
6 Simpson, Charles M., III. *Inside the Green Berets: The Story of the U.S. Army Special Forces*. New York, NY: Berkley Books, 1983, p. 96.
7 Headquarters, Commander-in-Chief Pacific Memorandum. Subject: Lessons Learned, MAAG and Special Forces Activities in Laos (U). Signed H. D. Felt, San Francisco, CA, 21 February 1963, 18–19.
8 Castle, Timothy N. *At War in the Shadow of Vietnam: U.S. Military Aid to the Royal Lao Government* 1955–1975. New York, NY: Columbia University Press, 1993, pp. 130–131.
9 Stanton, Shelby L. *Green Berets at War: U.S. Army Special Forces in Southeast Asia, 1956–1975*. New York, NY: Ivy Books, NY, 1985, pp. 34.
10 Morechand, Guy. "The Many Languages and Cultures of Laos." Found in the publication, *Laos: War & Revolution*. Editors Nina S. Adams and Alfred N. McCoy. New York: Harper Colophon Books, 1970, p. 33.

Glossary

AA	anti-aircraft
AAA	anti-aircraft artillery
AAM	Air America, the CIA-contracted airline which flew in Laos in support of USAID, the CIA, and support to U.S. and Lao forces. Aircraft consisted of helicopters, fixed-wing, propeller, cargo aircraft, and STOL-configured aircraft
ADC	Auto-Défense du Choc (Hmong guerrilla unit; village and regional militia)
AIRA	Air Attaché—USAF advisors or USAF personnel assigned for duty in Laos were attached to the U.S. embassy, Vientiane Attaché office in order to circumvent restriction of U.S. forces being assigned in Laos
The "Alamo"	Landing Site 36, used to preposition search-and-rescue aircraft and site of intense battle between Vang Pao's forces and the NVA
ALO	Air Liaison Officer
AMEMBV	American Embassy Vientiane
AOC	Air Operations Center
BA	Laotian Bataillon Artillerie
basha	a term for the construction of an individual living and sleeping position out in the jungle. A small platform was erected to sleep on, raised up from the ground, and then a poncho or jungle materials were used to construct a rainproof overhead.
Barrel Roll	area of north Laos designated for air interdiction and strike by the USAF, primarily in Military Region II
BC	Laotian Commando Battalion
BG	Laotian Guerrilla Battalion
BI	Laotian Bataillon d'Infanterie (also BIL)
BP	Laotian Bataillon de Parachutistes
BV	Laotian Bataillon Voluntaire
CASI	Continental Air Services, Inc., another airline which flew in Laos to support U.S. agencies
CAT	Civil Air Transport—the original CIA-contracted airline operating in the Southeast Asia Region, later named Air America
CCT	Combat Control Team; normally USAF ground personnel who coordinate aircraft for combat
CDNI	Committee for the Defense of National Interests (Rightest political party; anti-communist and pro-Western)

CHECO	Contemporary Historical Examination of Current Operations. These were a series of classified reports written by the USAF to examine ongoing operations of the air war in Vietnam and Laos
CIA	Central Intelligence Agency
CISO	Counterinsurgency Support Office, a logistics base established in Okinawa to support special operations and unconventional warfare initiatives in southeast Asia.
COIN	counterinsurgency
customer	a term used by contracted pilots in Laos to refer to operatives from the CIA
DZ	drop zone
E&E	escape and evasion
FA	Field Advisory team
FAC	Forward Air Controller
FAG	Forward Air Guide
FAR	Forces Armées Royales (Royal Laotian Armed Forces)
The Fence	term for the Mekong River boundary between Laos and Thailand; anyone in SOF who crossed the Mekong into Thailand was "crossing the fence"
FID	Foreign Internal Defense, a Special Operations Forces mission to train foreign and indigenous troops
FTT	Field Training Team; usually followed by a number to indicate the unit designation of Special Forces Advisory teams—FTT-21 as an example
GM	*groupe mobile*, a unit of military organization for Laotian forces, designed after the French version; about a regiment in size
hard rice	a euphemism used by contracted pilots who flew in Laos to mean their cargo was arms and ammunition, vice actual bags of rice (soft rice)
HALO	high altitude low opening (parachute descent)
Hmong	the northern, hill tribes in Laos; most of the guerrilla fighters operating on the side of the Royal Laotian Government were from this tribe.
HCMT	Ho Chi Minh Trail, the series of trails and road networks running through eastern Laos and on into South Vietnam used by the North Vietnamese as their logistics line of communication to infiltrate men and supplies into their war effort in South Vietnam; this trail was the focus of USAF and SOG interdiction efforts in Laos.
hootch	a hut in the jungle constructed from bamboo and tied with rattan strips; foliage or palm fronds are placed on top to serve as a roof; often, SF teams used discarded parachute material for roofing.
Hotfoot	operational codename for the first U.S. Army Green Berets (Special Forces) teams who deployed in 1959 to help the French training effort to improve Laotian security forces (initially twelve eight-man teams with control elements)
ICC	International Control Commission, the body chosen by the UN to monitor ceasefires and the stipulations of Geneva conventions
Irregular Forces	government-sponsored, armed indigenous forces usually controlled, supplied and led by agency sources or by Special Forces advisors, either uniformed or not

Jolly Green Giant	term for USAF HH-3E search-and-rescue helicopters
Jungle Jim Project	a program to create a counterinsurgency capability within the USAF and impetus for the creation of the Air Commandos
LZ	landing zone
Lima Site	the numbered airstrips and landing sites throughout Laos; for instance, LS-36, the location for prepositioned search-and-rescue helicopters
Long Tieng	General Vang Paos' headquarters and the site of the CIA base built there to support the war; also called LS-20A, or the "Alternate"
LPF	Lao Patriotic Front
LPRP	Lao People's Revolutionary Party
LPLA	Lao People's Liberation Army
LTAG	Liaison Training Advisory Group
Luang Prabang	the royal capital where Laotian kings reside, north of Vientiane, the administrative, government center
MAAG	Military Assistance and Advisory Group, the military portion of the embassy team, normally placed to provide support to various Security Assistance and Military Assistance Programs—thus, MAAG-Laos
MAP	Military Assistance Program
Monkhood	The code name for the addition of nine more Army Special Forces teams in early 1961 to reinforce the twelve SF teams already in Laos. The Laotian Army was authorized to grow an additional nine infantry battalions, thus requiring the extra advisors.
MR	Military Region; Laos was divided into five military regions
MTT	Military Training Team
NLHS	Neo Lao Hak Sat (Lao Patriotic Front)
NVA	North Vietnamese Army
Oogie Boogie Land	term used by 7th SF Group personnel around Smoke Bomb Hill at Fort Bragg to refer to the country of Laos; it was prohibited by OPSEC to say the word Laos
OSO	The Pentagon's Office of Special Operations where SOF and CIA coordinate activities in clandestine and covert operations
PARU	Police Aerial Reinforcement Units, highly trained Thai COIN units used during the war to help train the Hmongs
PDJ	the northern, mountain plateau in Laos, the Plaine des Jarres, named for the many, large stone pots believed to be ancient burial urns, which cover the area; the PDJ was a highly contested battleground between the RLG and General Vang Paos' Hmong fighters battling the Pathet Lao and NVA forces for its control.
PEO	Programs Evaluation Office

PL	Pathet Lao, the communist revolutionary movement in Laos; the term means *Land of the Lao*
PRC	Portable Radio Communications (PRC-41, and so forth)
Project 404	program to assign assistant military attachés to the U.S. embassy in Vientiane, to further provide military advisory assistance to Laotian forces, in order to get around the restrictions of open military involvement by the U.S.; this program predominantly was comprised of USAF personnel (known as AIRAs—assistant air attachés), but also included ground Army personnel, who were assigned as ARMAs—assistant army attachés
PSP	pierced, interlocking, steel planking; used to build airstrips
Ravens	call-sign for USAF FACs operating under Project 404
RLA	Royal Laotian Army (1950s–1960s nomenclature)
RLAF	Royal Laotian Air Force
RLG	Royal Lao Government
RO	Requirements Office, established in U.S. embassy at Vientiane under the guise of the USAID to control the Thailand-based clandestine military assistance programs for Laos
ROE	rules of engagement
R&R	rest and relaxation (tour); Bangkok was the place of choice for many of the Laos veterans
SACSA	Office of the Special Assistant for COIN & Special Activities
SAR	search and rescue
SEATO	Southeast Asian Treaty Organization
SF	U.S. Army Special Forces, or Green Berets
SGU	Hmong Special Guerrilla Units employed by General Vang Pao in Military Region II
Sky	The Hmong nick-name for CIA operatives, since they arrived on many sites "from the sky"
SOF	Special Operations Forces (Army, Navy, Marines, Air Force)
SOG	Studies and Observation Group—a codename for elite special operations forces trained to operate behind enemy lines; during the Laotian war, these forces operated out of South Vietnam under MACV-SOG, primarily to conduct reconnaissance and raids along the Ho Chi Minh trail, also a term for the CIA Special Operations Group case officers.
STOL	short take off and landing capability
TIC	troops in contact
USAID	United States Agency for International Development (part of the Department of State which delivers economic, developmental, and humanitarian goods)
USOM	United States Operations Mission
Waterpump	operation codename for program to train Laotian pilots on the T-28 aircraft; this program was conducted by Air Commandos from Det 6, 1st Air Commando Wing in Thailand at the Udorn Royal Thai Air Force Base, beginning in 1964
White Star	the reinforcing effort to the original *Hotfoot* mission of U.S. Army Green Berets to train Laotian security forces, which ran from April 1961 to October 1962.

Selected Bibliography

History and General Reference

Adams, Nina S. and Alfred W. McCoy (Editors). *Laos: War and Revolution*. New York, NY: Harper Colophon Books, 1970.

Blaufarb, Douglas. "Organizing and Managing Unconventional War in Laos, 1962 – 1970." Santa Monica, CA: Rand Corporation, January 1972.

Castle, Timothy N. *At War in the Shadow of Vietnam: U.S. Military Aid to the Royal Lao Government 1955–1975*. New York, NY: Columbia University Press, 1993.

Conboy, Kenneth. *The War in Laos 1954–1975*. Carrollton, TX: Squadron/Signal Publications, Vietnam Studies Group Issue 6063, 1994.

Conboy, Kenneth. *The War in Laos 1960–75*. London, UK: Osprey Men-at-Arms Series No. 217, Osprey Publishing, 1989.

Conboy, Kenneth (with James Morrison). *Shadow War: The CIA's Secret War in Laos*. Boulder, CO: Paladin Press, 1995.

Cummings, Joe. *Laos, A Lonely Planet Travel Survival Kit*. Australia: Lonely Planet, Hawthorn, Vic 3122: 1966.

Dommen, Arthur J. *Conflict in Laos: The Politics of Neutralization*. Praeger, NY: 1971.

_____. *The Indochinese Experience of the French and the Americans: Nationalism and Communism in Cambodia, Laos, and Vietnam*. Bloomington, IN: Indiana University Press, 2001.

Fall, Bernard B. *Anatomy of a Crisis: The Story of the Laotian Crisis of 1960–1961*. Garden City, NY: Doubleday & Company, 1969.

_____. *Hell in a Very Small Place: The Siege of Dien Bien Phu*. New York, NY: J. P. Lippincott Company, 1966.

Hamilton-Merritt, Jane. *Tragic Mountains: The Hmong, the Americans, and the Secret Wars for Laos, 1942–1992*. Bloomington, IN: Indiana University Press, 1993.

Hannah, Norman B. *The Key to Failure: Laos & the Vietnam War*. New York, NY: Madison Books, 1987.

Langer, Paul F. and Joseph J. Zasloff. *North Vietnam and the Pathet Lao: Partners in the Struggle for Laos*. Cambridge, MA: Harvard University Press, 1970.

Minh, Quang. *Au Pays du Million d'Éléphants*. Hanoi: Sur Les Presses de l'Impriemerie, June 1961.

Nolan, Keith William. *Into Laos: The Story of Dewey Canyon II/Lam Song 719*. Presidio, CA: Presidio Press, 1986.

Quincy, Keith. *Harvesting Pa Chay's Wheat: The Hmong and America's Secret War in Laos*. Spokane, WA: Eastern Washington University Press, 2000.

Robbins, Christopher. *Air America*. New York, NY: G. P. Putnam's Sons, 1979.

Rust, William J. *Before the Quagmire: American Intervention in Laos, 1954–1961*. Lexington, KY: University Press of Kentucky, 2012.

Secord, Richard (with Jay Wurts). *Honored and Betrayed: Irangate, Covert Affairs, and the Secret War in Laos*. New York, NY: John Wiley & Sons, 1992.

Shackley, Theodore. *The Third Option: An American View of Counterinsurgency Operations.* New York, NY: Dell, 1981.

Stuart-Fox, Martin. *A History of Laos.* Cambridge, UK: Cambridge University Press, 1997.

Zasloff, Joseph J. *The Pathet Lao: Leadership and Organization.* Lexington, MA: Lexington Books, 1971.

CIA Special Operations Activities in Laos

Ahern, Thomas L., Jr. *Undercover Armies: CIA and Surrogate Warfare in Laos.* Washington, D. C.: The Center for the Study of Intelligence, CIA, 2006.

Briggs, Thomas L. *Cash on Delivery: CIA Special Operations During the Secret War in Laos.* Rockville, MD: Rosebank Press, 2009.

Burke, Terrence M. *Stories from the Secret War: CIA Special Ops in Laos.* Durango, CA: La Plata Books, 2012.

Davis, Charles O. *Across the Mekong: The True Story of an Air America Helicopter Pilot.* Charlottesville, VA: Hildesigns Press, 1996.

Leeker, Joe F. (PhD). "Air America in Laos." (Online series from Air America Archives.) Dallas, TX: University of Texas, published August 11, 2008 and last updated March 4, 2013.

Love, Terry. *Wings of Air America.* Atglen, PA: Schiffer Military, 1998.

Nichols, Stephen I. *Air America in Laos: The Flight Mechanic's Story.* Ledyard, CT: Nichols/Martin, 2013.

Parker, James E., Jr. *Codename Mule: Fighting the Secret War in Laos for the CIA.* Annapolis, MD: Naval Institute Press, 1995.

Prados, John. *Safe for Democracy: The Secret Wars of the CIA.* Chicago, IL: Ivan R. Dee, 2006.

Warner, Roger. *Shooting at the Moon: The Story of America's Clandestine War in Laos.* South Royalton, VT: Steerforth Press, 1996.

Air War and USAF SOF Operations

Corum, James S. and Wray R. Johnson. *Airpower in Small Wars: Fighting Insurgents and Terrorists.* Lawrence, KS: University Press of Kansas, 2003.

Curry, Robert. *Whispering Death: Our Journey with the Hmong in the Secret War for Laos.* Lincoln, NE: Universe, 2004.

Dean, David J. (LTC, USAF). "The USAF in Low-Intensity Conflict. The Special Air Warfare Center." Maxwell AFB, Montgomery, AL: The Air University Press, October 1986.

Futrell, Robert F. (PhD). *The Advisory Years to 1965.* Washington, D. C.: Office of Air Force History, USAF in Southeast Asia series, USAF, 1981.

Hofmann, George R. Jr. (COL, Ret., USMC). *Operation MILLPOND: U.S. Marines in Thailand, 1961.* Quantico, VA: History Division, USMC, 2009.

Littauer, Raphael and Norman Uphoff (Editors). *The Air War in Indochina.* Boston, MA: Beacon Press, 1972.

U.S. SOF Ground Operations

Archer, Chalmers, Jr. *Green Berets in the Vanguard: Inside Special Forces, 1953–1963.* Annapolis, MD: Naval Institute Press, 2001.

Barker, Geoffrey T. *A Concise History of U.S. Army Special Operations Forces* (Vol 1, 2nd Ed). Tampa, FL: Anglo-American Publishing Company, 1988.

Blessing, Leonard D. Jr. *Warrior Healers: The Untold Story of the Special Forces Medic.* Lincoln, NE: iUniverse Inc., 2006.

Craig, William T. *Lifer! From Infantry to Special Forces.* New York, NY: Ivy Books, 1994.

Garner, Joe R. (CSM, Ret., U.S.A.). *Code Name: COPPERHEAD, My True Life Exploits as a Special Forces Soldier.* New York, NY: Simon & Schuster, 1994.

Gillespie, Robert M. *Black Ops Vietnam: The Operational History of MACVSOG.* Annapolis, MD: Naval Institute Press, 2011.

Guardia, Mike. *American Guerrilla: The Forgotten Heroics of Russell W. Volckmann.* Haverton, PA: Casemate, 2010.

Guardia, Mike. *Shadow Commander: The Epic Story of Donald D. Blackburn, Guerrilla Leader and Special Forces Hero.* Haverton, PA: Casemate, 2011.

Hoe, Allen. *The Quiet Professional: Major Richard J. Meadows of the U.S. Army Special Forces.* Lexington, KY: University Press of Kentucky, 2011.

Kelly, Francis J. *U.S. Army Special Forces 1961–1971.* Washington. D. C.: Vietnam Studies, HQDA, 1973.

Paddock, Alfred H., Jr. *U.S. Army Special Warfare: Its Origins.* Lawrence, KS: University Press of Kansas, 2002.

Pinn, Lionel F., Sr. *Hear the Bugles Calling: My Three Wars as a Combat Infantrymen.* Montgomery, AL: New South Books, 2007.

Plaster, John L. *SOG: The Secret Wars of America's Commandos in Vietnam.* Caliber, NY: NAL 1997.

Rottman, Gordon L. *U.S. MACV-SOG Reconnaissance Team in Vietnam.* Osprey Warrior Series No. 159. Oxford, UK: Osprey, 2011.

Sherman, Steve. *Who's Who from Hotfoot/White Star.* Houston, TX: RADIX Press, 1994.

_____. *Who's Who from Special Forces in Thailand.* Houston, TX: RADIX Press, 1996.

Simpson, Charles M., III. *Inside the Green Berets: The Story of the U.S. Army Special Forces.* New York, NY: Berkley Books, 1983.

Stanton, Shelby L. *Special Forces at War: An Illustrated History, Southeast Asia 1957–1975.* Charlottesville, VA: Howell Press, 1990.

_____. *Green Berets at War: U.S. Army Special Forces in Southeast Asia, 1956–1975.* New York, NY: Ivy Books, 1985.

Sutton, Richard O. *Operation White Star.* Canton, Ohio: Daring Publishing Group, 1990.

Walker, Greg. *At the Hurricane's Eye: U.S. Special Operations Forces from Vietnam to Desert Storm.* New York, NY: Ivy Books, 1994.

Waller, Douglas C. *Commandos: The Inside Story of America's Secret Soldiers.* New York, NY: Dell, 1994.

Williams, James C. (MSG, Ret., U.S.A.). *A Green Beret's Journey.* Kanchanaburi, Thailand: James C. Williams self-published, 2014.

Wolfkill, Grant and Jerry A. Rose. *Reported To Be Alive.* New York, NY: Simon & Schuster, 1965.

Papers

Baldwin, Ben R. "Case Study of U.S. Counterinsurgency Operations in Laos, 1955–1962." McLean VA: Research Analysis Corporation, 1964.

Breaux, Jarred James. "The Laotian Civil War: The Intransigence of General Phoumi Nosovan and American Intervention in the Fall of 1960." Thesis, Lafayette, LA: University of Louisiana, 2008.

Dean, David J. (LTC, USAF). "The USAF in Low-Intensity Conflict: The Special Air Warfare Center." *Air University Review,* January–February 1985.

McDonnell, Wayne. *The NVA in Laos: 1951–1973*. Fort Leavenworth, KS: Student monograph, U.S. Army Staff College, 1977. (www.dtic.mil, ADC011408.pdf)

St. Jean, Frederick J. (LTC), MAJ Terrance W. McClain, and MAJ Ronald C. Hartwig. "Twenty three Years of Military Assistance to Laos." Maxwell AFB, AL: Corona Harvest Professional Study No. 5689. Air War College, Air University, USAF, March 1975.

The Vietnam Archive Oral History Project Interview with David Harrington, conducted by Stephen Maxner, October 3 & 5, 2003. Texas Tech University, Lubbock, TX. (Transcribed by Laura Darden)

Internet Sites

www.preservingourhistory.com/Laos
www.air-america.net
www.specialoperations.net
www.psywarrior.com

Documents

_____. HQDA Pam No. 550–58, *Area Handbook for Laos*. Wash D. C.: Department of the Army, June 1967.

_____. HQDA Memorandum, Subject: Situation Report Nr. 30–61 Laos. February 4–5, 1961. Washington, D. C.: Office of the Deputy Chief of Staff for Military Operations (SECRET).

_____. Headquarters, Commander-in-Chief Pacific Memorandum. Subject: Lessons Learned, MAAG and Special Forces Activities in Laos (U). Signed H. D. Felt, San Francisco, CA, February 21, 1963.

_____. Department of the Army Field Manual FM 31–21, "Guerrilla Warfare and Special Forces Operations." Washington DC: HQDA, September 29, 1961.

Zasloff, Joseph J. "The Pathet Lao: Leadership and Organization." WN 7248-ARPA. The RAND Corporation, March 1971.

_____. "A Brief History of the Hmong & the Secret War in Laos." (DVD narrated by Steve Schofield (Hmong and American Veteran's Memorial Fund – www.secretwarinloas.com).

_____. "Laos: The Not So Secret War, 1970." DVD, National Archives, ARC 657070 (Amazon. com product), www.archives.gov.

_____. "The Situation in Laos." Department of State, September 1959.

_____. "Meo Handbook." Bangkok, Thailand: Joint Thai–U.S. Military Research and Development Center, Report Number 69–006, OSD/ARPA R&D Center Thailand, October 1969.

_____. United States Army Special Warfare School, Fort Bragg, NC. "Program of Instruction for Project 404," Fort Bragg, NC: On file at USAJFK Special Warfare Museum, dtd March 1969.

U.S. Senate Hearing, "Aid Activities in Laos." Subcommittee on U.S. Security Agreements and Commitments Abroad of the Committee on Foreign Relations, Tuesday, April 13, 1972, by Chairman Senator Stuart J. Symington.

Geu, Vang. "Unforgettable Laos." www.unforgettable-laos.com, accessed and downloaded July 16, 2014.

Halpern, A. M. and H. B. Fredman. "Communist Strategy in Laos." Santa Monica, CA: U.S. Air Force Project RAND Research Memorandum, RM-2561, June 14, 1960.

Liebchen, Peter A. W. (CAPT, USAF). "MAP Aid to Laos 1959–1972." HQ PACAF, Directorate of Operations Analysis, Checo/Corona Harvest Division, SAMI–7302278: June 25, 1973.

Pratt, John C. (MAJ, USAF) "The Royal Laotian Air Force 1954–1970." HQ PACAF Directorate Tactical Evaluation, Checo Division (undated).

Sananikone, Oudone (MG, RLA). "The Royal Lao Army and U.S. Army Advice and Support." Indochina Refugee Authored Monograph Program, OAD-CR-155, Washington, D. C.: Department of the Army, Office of Chief of Military History Contract performed by General Research Corporation, McClean, VA: November 7, 1978.

Stevens, Eldon L. (LTC, USAF). "Psychological Operations: Air Support in Southeast Asia June 1968–May 1971." Checo/Corona Harvest Division, 7th AF, SAMI—7200009: November 1, 1971.

Schweitzer, P. J. "Description of the Ho Chi Minh Trail." Fort Belvoir, VA: Institute for Defense Analyses, Weapons Systems Evaluation Division, WSEG Staff Study 125, Log No. 114588, prepared for DTIC contract, August 1966.

The Senator Gravel Edition, The Pentagon Papers: The Defense Department History of United States Decisionmaking on Vietnam, Vol. II, Boston, MA: Beacon Press, End of Tour Report, Major General Richard G. Trefry, DEPCHIEF JUSMAG Udorn, Defense Attaché, Vientiane, Laos, February 5, 1973 to December 11, 1974. Prepared by the Defense Attaché Office, Vientiane, Laos, December 12, 1974.

Vongsavanh, Soutchay (BG, RLA). "RLG Military Operations and Activities in the Laotian Panhandle." Washington DC: U.S. Army Center of Military History, Indochina Monographs, 1981.

Index